Philosophy of Love, Sex, and Marriage

How is love different from lust or infatuation? Do love and marriage really go together "like a horse and carriage"? Does sex have any necessary connection to either? And how important are love, sex, and marriage to a well-lived life? In this lively, lucid, and comprehensive textbook, Raja Halwani pursues the philosophical questions inherent in these three important aspects of human relationships, exploring the nature, uses, and ethics of romantic love, sexuality, and marriage.

The book is structured in three sections:

Love begins by examining how romantic love differs from other types of love, such as friendship and parental love. It asks which properties of love are essential, whether people have a choice in whom they love, and whether lovers have moral obligations to one another that differ from those they owe to others.

Sex demonstrates the difficulty in defining sex and the sexual, and examines what constitutes good and bad sex in terms of pleasure, "naturalness," and moral permissibility. It offers theoretical and applied ethical approaches to a wide range of sexual phenomena.

Marriage traces the history of the institution, and describes the various forms in which marriage exists and the reasons why people marry. It also surveys accounts of why people should or should not marry, and introduces the main arguments for and against gay marriage.

Features include:

- suggestions for further reading
- online eResource site with downloadable discussion questions
- a clear, jargon-free writing style.

Raja Halwani is Professor of Philosophy at the School of the Art Institute of Chicago. He is the author of *Virtuous Liaisons: Care, Love, Sex, and Virtue Ethics*, the editor of *Sex and Ethics: Essays on Sexuality, Virtue, and the Good Life*, and the co-author (with Tomis Kapitan) of *The Israeli-Palestinian Conflict: Philosophical Essays on Self-Determination, Terrorism, and the One-State Solution*.

Philosophy of Love, Sex, and Marriage

An Introduction

Raja Halwani

Routledge
Taylor & Francis Group

NEW YORK AND LONDON

First published 2010
by Routledge
711 Third Avenue, New York, NY 10017 US

Simultaneously published in the UK
by Routledge
2 Park Square, Milton Park, Abingdon, Oxon OX14 4RN

Routledge is an imprint of the Taylor & Francis Group, an informa business

© 2010 Taylor & Francis

Typeset in Baskerville by Glyph International Ltd
Printed and bound in the United States of America on acid-free
paper by Edwards Brothers, Inc.

Library of Congress Cataloging in Publication Data

Halwani, Raja.
Philosophy of love, sex, and marriage: an introduction / Raja Halwani.
p. cm.
Includes bibliographical references and index.
1. Love–Philosophy. 2. Sex–Philosophy. 3. Marriage. I. Title.
BD436.H257 2010
128′.46–dc22   2009036402

ISBN 10: 0-415-99350-4 (hbk)
ISBN 10: 0-415-99351-2 (pbk)
ISBN 10: 0-203-85636-8 (ebk)

ISBN 13: 978-0-415-99350-0 (hbk)
ISBN 13: 978-0-415-99351-7 (pbk)
ISBN 13: 978-0-203-85636-9 (ebk)

Please visit the book's companion website for discussion questions:
http://www.routledge.com/eresources/9780415993517

Contents

Acknowledgments

I wish to thank the previous philosophy editor at Routledge, Kate Ahl, for asking me to write this book and for her encouragement and support, and the current philosophy editor, Andrew Beck, for his help, patience, and support. My thanks also go to two anonymous referees for their extensive and insightful comments on an earlier draft. Thanks to Alan Soble for virtually creating the field of the philosophy of love, sex, and marriage and making it respectable. My intellectual debt to him is enormous. I thank all my students at the School of the Art Institute of Chicago who took my philosophy of sex and love course over the years and helped me become a better philosopher. I thank all my friends and colleagues from whom I have benefited immensely over the years in discussing with me the topics of this book, especially Barbara DeGenevieve and Steven Jones. Special thanks to Steven also for comments on some chapters and for designing the book cover. My debt to him is immense.

Introduction

Philosophy is a reflective, higher level field: it seeks to answer questions about other fields and human practices. Moral philosophy, for example, raises questions about ethical human conduct, seeking to find out what are right and wrong actions, good and bad characters, and good and bad policies and institutions. Philosophy of art raises questions about the practice, evaluation, and definition of art. The same is true of the philosophy of love, sex, and marriage.

The value of philosophy, however, does not lie only in the answers to the questions it raises. Indeed, because most philosophical questions are still unanswered, philosophy's value lies mostly in its method. Philosophical thinking is rigorous, analytical, and systematic (at least ideally!). On our way to answering the "big" questions, we philosophers often answer smaller ones and clarify our thinking about the issues involved. People who practice and study philosophy often become clearer thinkers, seeing distinctions and problems that others do not.

Like other fields in philosophy, the issues involved in philosophizing about love, sex, and marriage fall into two groups: conceptual and evaluative. The first are concerned with defining and clarifying concepts, the second with assessing whether particular actions and practices are good or bad, in the moral sense, but also in other senses (e.g., aesthetic). Some of the main conceptual issues found in the philosophy of love, sex, and marriage are the following. (1) What is the nature of love and romantic love specifically? Does romantic love differ in important ways from other types of love, such as love between parent and child and love between friends or siblings? Is romantic love an emotion similar to others, like hate, compassion, envy, and anger, or is it something else altogether, like a desire or attitude? Does romantic love have some properties essential to it – is it exclusive or constant by its nature? Does it involve concern for the beloved, and is the concern ultimately selfish, rebounding to the benefit of the lover? Is romantic love based on reasons or is it – like Christian love – based on no reasons? And would a romantic love based on reasons make it more constant, more exclusive, or, generally, a better kind of love than if it were not based on reasons? (2) Can we define sex and sexual activity? Why is the same behavior in one context sexual but in another context non-sexual? Can we define other, more specific sexual practices and actions, such as adultery, casual sex, prostitution, cyber-sex, and promiscuity?

Is there such a thing as perverted sex or sexual perversion? How do we define them? (3) Can we define marriage? Is it true, as some say, that it is confined to one man and one woman, or could it be defined to include more than one spouse or spouses of the same gender or sex? Does marriage have a purpose (or a few purposes) that is universal, not bound to culture and time? Is marriage a completely social institution or is it part of our human "nature"?

Some of the main evaluative issues found in the philosophy of love, sex, and marriage are the following. (1) Is romantic love immune from moral evaluation and criticism, or are lovers bound by the dictates of morality in their relationship to each other and to other people? Do people have a moral responsibility to fall in love responsibly? Should people love others for particular reasons but not others, and are some cases of romantic love better than others because of the reasons on which they are based? What do the main moral theories, such as Kantian ethics, consequentialism, and virtue ethics, have to say about romantic love? Is romantic love necessary or needed for someone to lead a good, flourishing life? If romantic love brings lovers not only happiness but also pain and suffering, is it prudent to fall in love? (2) What is good sex and what is bad sex? What are the different criteria (morality, naturalness, and pleasure) we can use to evaluate sex? What do the main moral theories have to say about sexual acts and particular sexual practices, such as adultery, casual sex, and prostitution? What role do the virtues and vices play in the evaluation of sexual acts and sexual desires? What does sexual fantasy tell us about people's moral characters? What is sexual objectification? Does sexual desire by its very nature objectify people? Does it objectify women more than men? Is leading a life revolving around sex compatible with human dignity? How much importance should people give sex in their lives? (3) Should marriage be confined to only two spouses? Is there anything wrong with polygamous or polyamorous marriages, and are they even better than marriages between only two people? Should marriage involve only spouses of the opposite sex or may it also involve same-sex ones? Why should same-sex couples not be allowed to marry? Why should they be allowed to marry? How important is marriage to our lives? Is it even a bad institution we should abolish?

These are the main issues addressed in this book. My hope is that reflecting on them not only clarifies our thinking, but also affects our values, orienting us to make changes in our actions and lives, so that we treat others more justly, think of them more openly, and place the proper values on love, sex, and marriage.

This book is written in what I hope is an accessible style, helpful to undergraduate students and those new to philosophy. I have attempted to cover most of the topics in the areas of love, sex, and marriage, but have left some out, opting for a more detailed treatment of the topics I do discuss. In the "Questions for Discussion" sections that accompany each chapter (found on Routledge's website), I raise questions about the topics I do not cover.

My approach is twofold. First, I offer arguments and conclusions for those issues on which I have more or less firm opinions, leaving it, of course, to the reader to decide whether the arguments are convincing. Second, I discuss the main arguments for and against those issues about which I have no firm views of my own, leaving it, again, to the reader to decide. Both approaches delve into the issues in some detail so that the reader can form a fuller picture of the ideas, arguments, and positions involved. Sometimes I involve other fields in philosophy, such as ethics, philosophy of art, and metaphysics – an unavoidable task because they are connected to the philosophical issues in love, sex, and marriage. Besides, these different fields provide the reader with additional areas to stimulate his or her thinking.

Because this is an introductory book, the reader ought to consult the books (including anthologies) and essays that have been published in this area for a more detailed study of the topics. At the end of each chapter I provide a "Further Reading" section (except for references worth emphasizing, I do not re-list works cited either in the body of the book or the endnotes).

I use the following abbreviations in the bibliography for frequently cited books:

EAP: *Eros, Agape, and Philia: Readings in the Philosophy of Love*, ed. A. Soble. NewYork: Paragon House, 1989.
PEL: *The Philosophy of (Erotic) Love*, ed. R. Solomon and K. Higgins. Lawrence, Kans.: University Press of Kansas, 1991.
POS2: *The Philosophy of Sex: Contemporary Readings*, 2nd ed., ed. A. Soble. Savage, Md.: Rowman & Littlefield, 1981.
POS3: *The Philosophy of Sex: Contemporary Readings*, 3rd ed., ed. A. Soble. Lanham, Md.: Rowman & Littlefield, 1997.
POS4: *The Philosophy of Sex: Contemporary Readings*, 4th ed., ed. A. Soble. Lanham, Md.: Rowman & Littlefield, 2003.
POS5: *The Philosophy of Sex: Contemporary Readings*, 5th ed., ed. A. Soble and N. Power. Lanham, Md.: Rowman & Littlefield, 2008.
PS2: *Philosophy and Sex*, 2nd ed., ed. R. Baker and F. Elliston. Buffalo, N.Y.: Prometheus Books, 1984.
PS3: *Philosophy and Sex*, 3rd ed., ed. R. Baker, K. Wininger, and F. Elliston. Buffalo, N.Y.: Prometheus Books, 1998.
SE: *Sex and Ethics: Essays on Sexuality, Virtue, and the Good Life*, ed. R. Halwani. Basingstoke: Palgrave Macmillan, 2007.
SPP1: *Sex from Plato to Paglia: A Philosophical Encyclopedia*, vol. 1, ed. A. Soble. Westport, Conn.: Greenwood Press, 2006.
SPP2: *Sex from Plato to Paglia: A Philosophical Encyclopedia*, vol. 2, ed. A. Soble. Westport, Conn.: Greenwood Press, 2006.
SS: *Same Sex: Debating the Ethics, Science, and Culture of Homosexuality*, ed. J. Corvino. Lanham, Md.: Rowman & Littlefield, 1997.
SSM: *Same-Sex Marriage, Pro and Con: A Reader*, ed. A. Sullivan. New York: Vintage Books, 1997.

Part I

Love

1   What Is Love?

The things we love are diverse. We love *inanimate objects*: comic books, books, art, astronomy, mathematics, human bodies, wine, beer, fried chicken, fine food, our (and other) countries, national anthems, songs, wisdom, virtue, philosophy, architecture, and nature. We love *activities*: reading books, contemplating and making art, watching the stars, solving geometry problems, having sex, drinking alcohol, eating, serving our countries, singing, doing philosophy, designing buildings, and hiking, camping, and mountain climbing. We love *animate* things: cats, dogs, horses, cedar trees, beluga whales, daffodils, God, the gods, and, of course, people, whom we love in different ways, forming different types of love: we love some romantically; others we love as friends or as brothers and sisters; yet others we love as our children, and some claim to love the entire human race. We call all these "love." But we also form feelings for and attitudes toward other people that resemble love but are not the same (and sometimes people confuse them for the "real thing"): we respect some people, we admire others; we have crushes on some, and we are infatuated with others. Sometimes we just sexually desire others. When the confusion sets in, we also call them "love."

Do all these types of love have something in common so that we call them all "love"? If there is no common thing, why *do* we call them all "love"? One philosopher argues that they all involve valuation; if we love something, no matter what it is (human, animal, object), we must value it in some way (Brentlinger 1989). Another claims that what is common is that "your own well-being is tied up with that of someone (or something) you love" (Nozick 1991, 417). Other philosophers are not hopeful of finding love's common denominator, because even if it exists, it should explain to us "why a case or type of love *is* love" (Soble 1998, 115). If this common denominator exists at all, it might prove easier to find if we focus only on love and relationships between people.

Three Types of Love

Philosophers classify love between people into three types, sometimes using the Greek terms *eros*, *philia*, and *agape* to refer to them. *Eros* refers to sexual love; we can also call it "erotic love," "passionate love," or "romantic love."

Philia usually refers to friendship love, which includes friendships *and* any friendship-like love, such as that between siblings, colleagues and co-workers, parents and children, and even husband and wife (depending on the type of marriage they have and at which stage it is). *Agape* (*caritas* in Latin) is different because it is not based on the qualities of the beloved. Whereas in *eros* or *philia* we (supposedly) love others because of who they are or what qualities they have (e.g., "he is my son," "she has a beautiful mind"), with *agape* we love others gratuitously; it is a love that "does not depend on our own attraction" (Lewis 1960, 182), the kind, for example, that the Christian God is said to have for His children.

Do these types of love have something in common? Concern for the beloved immediately comes to mind. Whether we love romantically, in a friendship-like way, or *agapically*, surely the lover is concerned for the happiness, well-being, or flourishing of the beloved ("happiness" for short)? But as plausible as this suggestion sounds, it faces difficulties. First, consider the love that very young children have for their parents. To claim that toddlers are concerned for the happiness of their parents is implausible. Prior to a certain age, children do not have the maturity for such a concern and act primarily to satisfy their own needs. To deny that what these young children feel for their parents is love might not be so outrageous. We might plausibly say that to love another, a minimum level of maturity is required (but then do none of our pets love us?), and that what young children experience is not really love. Perhaps they only possess intense desires to fulfill their needs, and they focus on their parents as they associate them with need-satisfaction.

But even if it is convincing to exclude young children, another difficulty faces the suggestion that concern is an element common to all types of human love. To understand it, we need to ask two questions. First, is the concern for the beloved's happiness ultimately for the sake of the beloved or the lover? Second, does this concern reflect the beloved's happiness as he or she sees it or as the lover sees it? However we answer these questions raises doubts about the above suggestion. One might argue that when it comes to romantic love, the concern for the beloved's happiness is ultimately selfish: the lover wants his beloved to be happy because if she were not, then *he* won't be. This selfish element, the argument continues, need not be found in some or even all forms of *philia* (e.g., parents' love for their children), and, as we will see with Aristotle below, it does not characterize friendship at all. Certainly it is not a feature of *agape*: it would be incoherent to say that God loves us selfishly, since He is, according to monotheistic conceptions, morally perfect, and insofar as we emulate God's love for us and love each other *agapically*, our love for each other is not selfish either. If this argument is successful, the concern found in these three types of love is not of the same kind, so what we identified as a common element is not so, due, perhaps, to vagueness in our use of the word "concern."

Similar issues occur in response to the second question (I set *agape* aside as its treatment here raises issues beyond our scope). Sometimes lovers and friends act paternalistically; parents almost always do so. When this happens, lovers seek the happiness of their beloveds *not* as their beloveds see it or conceive of it, but as the lovers do. Yet this need not always happen. Sometimes friends and lovers (and even parents) do not act paternalistically toward their beloveds; in these instances, they seek the happiness of their beloveds as their beloveds see it. If this is all true, we again do not have the same conception of concern running through the three types of love. Depending on the case, the concern might or might not be paternalistic. So what we thought was a common element to these types of love turns out to be a mistake. Keep in mind that we are not seeking what all *good* or the *best* types of love have in common (if this is our quest, perhaps the answer is easy: lovers should not love paternalistically or selfishly). Our task is conceptual: *Do* these types of love actually have a common element?

Our topic is really romantic love, not the other types. Like many topics, it seems simple to study, but it actually raises fascinating and complex questions and puzzles when subjected to some philosophical questioning.

Characterizing Romantic Love

What is the nature of romantic love? One way to answer this question is to try to define "romantic love," because when we define something, X, we try to find those features that X and only X has. This way, we can differentiate X from all the things that are not X, putting ourselves on the path to figure out the nature of X. So, for example, if we define "human beings" as "rational animals," we attribute to them two features that human beings and only human beings have, setting them apart from, say, other animals and gods: having the ability to use reason (animals, supposedly, don't have this) and being an animal (the gods don't have this). So for something to be a human being, it is sufficient to have these, and only these, two features, and no additional information is needed. Each feature is also necessary, because no object can be a human being unless it has each feature.[1] Can we, then, define "romantic love"?

Let us begin with a crude definition. Because we can love all sorts of things, we need to define "romantic love" in such a way to set it apart from all these other types of love. Roughly speaking, romantic love can be characterized as usually having particular features that *tend to* distinguish it from other types of love. Here is a tentative list:

1   It is the type of love that people have for each other (unlike, say, the love that people have for comic books).
2   If reciprocated, it usually exists between two, not more, people (unlike, say, the reciprocal love between three or more friends).
3   It usually has, or at least begins with, a sexual dimension (unlike, say, the love between parents and children).
4   It usually involves very strong emotions and desires between the lovers, such as care and concern for the welfare and happiness of each other (much stronger emotions than those that people feel, say, for their pets).

5   It, at least nowadays and mainly for heterosexuals, eventuates in marriage
    and procreation.
6   It generates certain social and moral expectations that other relationships
    do not. For example, lovers are expected to spend the bulk of their time
    with each other and to often prioritize each other when it comes to the
    amount of attention they give to others.

Note two points. First, although the six features characterize romantic love,
they do so only in a *general* way. There can be, and are, cases of romantic love
that do not have many of these features. For example, there are cases of unrequited love, cases in which one person romantically loves more than one other
person, cases of love that don't result in either marriage or children or that do
not generate social or moral expectations (those that are secretive or those that
are despised by the surrounding people, who expect the lovers to not spend
time with each other at all, say).

Things get complicated with the other features, however. It is hard to
imagine a person romantically loving a non-person, such as his pet or iPod.
There are many cases involving human beings having sex with animals, but
whether any of them amount to romantic love is the issue. Moreover, can one
love another if one does not care about the other's happiness or well-being? In
the novel *Lolita* by Vladimir Nabokov, the main character Humbert Humbert
kidnaps Lolita, a young girl, because he claims he is in love with her. But this
is doubtful *precisely* because Humbert Humbert is utterly indifferent to her well-
being (perhaps if *he* believes that what he did to her was for her own good, then
that is enough to make his case one of love; I will return to this issue later).
Finally, can there be cases of romantic love with no sexual dimension at all?
Although it is easy to think of long-time couples who no longer have sex with
each other or sexually desire each other (the "death of desire"), it is harder to
think of cases of love that have no sexual dimension *at any point in the relationship*.
Some claim that courtly love (found in parts of Europe in the twelfth century)
was non-sexual, but the lovers had sexual *desires*, although these desires were
never consummated (Singer 2001a, 81–82). So although some of the above
features (the first, third, and fourth) *might* be essential to romantic love, the
other three are not.

Let us dwell briefly on the first, third, and fourth features. Suppose that Andy
and his dog, Maybelline, exhibit all the signs of romantic love: Andy elevates
her above all the rest, he spends most of his time with her, cannot imagine life
without her, and has sex with her! Maybelline loves him back in her own way
(as dogs often do). Although most of us are inclined to reject this relationship as
one of romantic love, it is hard to do so with *certainty*. Even though Maybelline
does not love Andy back "as much as" he loves her (being a dog and all), not all
lovers reciprocate their love equally. And although Maybelline does not have
the cognitive and emotional capacities often associated with adult human love,
sometimes love between human adults doesn't have them either (imagine cases
in which x is in love with y, who is in a coma, or cases in which two severely

mentally challenged people are in love). So it is difficult to be certain that romantic love always occurs between humans, though it usually does.

Now imagine the love between Noah and Nora (both adult human beings, for a change); they, too, exhibit all the usual signs of romantic love but with one difference: they never had, they do not now, and they never will have sexual desires for and activity with each other. Is what Noah and Nora have between them romantic love? Some might deny this and say that what they have is "mere" friendship. But on what grounds can we be certain? Although some "mere" friendships can be emotionally very intense, we shouldn't rush to the conclusion that Noah and Nora's relationship is best described this way, because perhaps such emotionally intense friendships are really romantic love. Indeed, that Noah and Nora don't have sex with each other should not also automatically classify their relationship as friendship, because sexual desire and activity do not rigidly distinguish romantic love from friendship (many friends have sex with each other). The point, again, is that although most romantic loves include a sexual dimension, not all do, and these will not command immediate agreement that they are not romantic love.

Concern is different. The reason why it is hard to think of cases of romantic love that don't include concern by the lover for the well-being of the beloved is that the concept of love seems to by definition include concern. In the above two examples we did not quibble with whether Andy loves Maybelline or with whether Noah loves Nora, but with whether their love is romantic. But there is no quibbling with the claim that for any type of emotion or relationship, whether romantic or not, to be love, it must include concern. It is impossible to understand how x loves y (romantically or non-romantically) if x is indifferent – or, worse, hostile – to y's happiness. X's concern for y's well-being might ultimately be selfish, x might conceive of it not as y does, but as x does, and so on. The truth of these claims might make x's love for y bad or immoral; but it need not raise doubt about the existence of the love. The lover's concern for the happiness of the beloved is a necessary feature of romantic love because it is a necessary feature of any love.

The second thing to note about the above features of romantic love is that each tends to distinguish it from other types of love. For example, romantic love's existence between people distinguishes it from types of love between people and animals or objects. The sexual dimension in romantic love, romantic love's often resulting in marriage and children, and its confinement to two and only two people, tend to distinguish it from virtually every other type of love. However, while the intensity of the care and concern in romantic love distinguishes it from that found in friendships and perhaps even between siblings, it doesn't when it comes to parent–child love. Here, the concern is at least equal to, if not stronger than, that found in romantic love. Finally, there are no social expectations that, say, friends prioritize each other when it comes to attention (things are more complicated in parent–child relationships).

Once again, however, we need to be careful. The above features can easily be found in other types of love. Some friends have sex with each other, if not on a regular basis, at least experimentally or temporarily. Some friends have a very intense amount of concern or care for each other (as we will see with Aristotle, this is what characterizes the best form of friendship). Some paired friends are quite exclusive, disallowing any third parties to be part of the friendship.[2] Some friends marry each other for all sorts of reasons (e.g., allowing one to obtain the Green Card), and many cohabit with each other. Finally, depending on when and where one lives, the social expectations can vary widely. Apparently, certain cultures consider romantic love to be some sort of neurosis on the part of the lovers, albeit an amusing and entertaining one (Solomon 2006, 48–54), with, obviously, none of the social expectations we have. Other cultures (e.g., the ancient Greeks) have social expectations similar to ours but with respect to friendships, not love.

Our first lesson is this: although it seems that the first, third, and fourth features might be *necessary* features of romantic love, none of the six features seems to be sufficient. Indeed, we may argue that it is possible for two friends to exemplify all six features together. We have failed to define "romantic love" using the above list of features, but we have not exhausted all the possible features that might be essential to romantic love. As this chapter proceeds, we examine a few more.

But we have not emerged empty-handed. First, we do have a rough but good idea of what romantic love is. Second, we know the difficulties that lie ahead in defining "romantic love"; this should prompt us to look for other ways to understand the nature of romantic love if the project of defining it fails. Third, we can agree that concern for the beloved is at least one element that is necessary for romantic love, even though it is not sufficient. For now, let us look at a few more definitions given by some philosophers and see whether they fare any better.

Romantic Love as an Emotion

It is common sense that romantic love is an emotion. However, some philosophers wonder whether this is true because emotions have important features that romantic love seems to lack.[3] One crucial feature is that emotions are often caused by or made out of beliefs (the differences between "caused" and "made out of" don't matter for our purposes). For example, if I am angry with John for insulting me, I must believe that John has insulted me. If I am sad that my grandmother has died, I must believe that she has died. Even if I am angry with John, period (without further specification), it is natural to ask me for my reasons. And the reasons I offer should explain, if not even justify, my anger. Moreover, as soon as the underlying belief changes or is no longer held, we usually expect the emotion to change or disappear. If I find out that I was wrong to think that John insulted me, my anger will go away, sometimes even immediately. Philosophers call this feature of emotions "intentionality."

How is romantic love different? A lover might claim that she loves her beloved but doesn't have any beliefs as to why she loves him (Green 1997, 211). If love is an emotion, the problem is how this can be when in some cases love lacks intentionality. Furthermore, it is common that the reasons for which we often love another person change without our love changing. For example, Cleo may have fallen in love with Mark because she believed he was a go-getter, good looking, and dizzyingly witty. Over the years, Mark grew fat and became a couch potato and a dullard. Yet Cleo still loved him. If romantic love is an emotion, and if like other emotions we expect it to change once the beliefs on which it is based change, why has Cleo not stopped loving Mark? Or does she still believe, contrary to what her eyes and ears tell her, that Mark is a go-getter, handsome, and witty? In short, if we think romantic love is an emotion, we cannot explain its *constancy* (Green 1997, 211).

If romantic love is not an emotion, what is it? One suggestion is that it is a set of *desires*. Now desires are often *parts* of emotions – being angry with John, I want him to apologize – but they are not identical with emotions – desiring that John apologize does not exhaust my anger. So to define "romantic love" as a set of desires is not to define it as an emotion. If Marlow loves Harlow, perhaps love is the desire to be with Harlow as much as possible, to have sex with Harlow, to want to maintain and increase Harlow's happiness, to want Harlow to reciprocate the love, and so on. The list of these desires is up for grabs, although the four just mentioned would likely appear on any list. But is attempting to define "romantic love" as a set of desires promising? Is it even necessary?

First, it does not seem very promising. It is hard to see how the desires can be sufficient. All could be present in a case of friendship, albeit one that includes a sexual component. Worse, all could be present in a case involving a primarily sexual relationship between two people so long as they desire, to some extent, each other's non-sexual company.

The desires might also not be necessary. Do all lovers want to constantly be with each other? Just ask a couple who have lived with each other for years and years; chances are that each could use some time alone. The third feature is also doubtful because of cases like Humbert Humbert and Lolita, and cases in which the lover is so insecure that he does not desire the happiness or well-being of the beloved, fearing that if the beloved is faring well, he or she might leave him. Finally, the fourth feature is also not necessary. Consider a case in which *A* sincerely thinks of himself as unworthy of *B*'s love and so genuinely desires that *B not* reciprocate his love.

Second, defining "romantic love" in terms of desires is unnecessary, because the idea that romantic love is an emotion can withstand the difficulties thrown at it. Consider first the problem of constancy, which, recall, is that if love were an emotion, it would be based on the lover's beliefs about the beloved. If the features on which these beliefs are based change, we expect the beliefs to change and therefore the emotion. Since love does not behave in this way (it is constant), it is not an emotion.

But other emotions are, like romantic love, constant – long-term emotions that survive their original beliefs. Three immediately come to mind: bitterness, resentment, and grief. Consider a case paralleling Cleo's constant love for Mark. Suppose that Susie feels bitter because she believes that her friend, Jana, has tried in the past to emotionally exploit her. Suppose that Susie's belief is true. Jana, however, has changed and become a better person and friend, and Susie knows this. It is nonetheless possible that Susie continues to feel bitter; she may even spend her entire adult life feeling bitter (she may be wrong to continue to feel bitter, but this is not the issue). Similar cases can be constructed about resentment. What about grief? Suppose that Omar's younger sibling, Marwan, dies. Suppose that Omar loved him to the point where he believed that Marwan gave his life meaning and purpose. After Marwan's death, Omar's grief is immense and continues to be so, despite Omar's belief that Marwan is no longer the center of his life (how could he be? He's dead!). Unless grief, resentment, and bitterness are not emotions, we cannot deny that romantic love is an emotion on the basis that it survives the lover's beliefs.

Yet how are we to explain love's constancy in the absence of the original beliefs? I suggest the model of crowd surfing. You throw yourself into the crowd at a concert, and no single pair of hands carries you all the way. You are moved from one pair to another until you reach the back of the arena. Like other types of love, romantic love is usually sustained in the context of a relationship. So even though the original beliefs on which it was based may no longer be held by the lovers, they may come to hold different, successive beliefs that keep the love going strong (and it is probably more than just beliefs that do this; more on this and on constancy in Chapter 2).

Most importantly, we should not assume that all emotions are based on beliefs. Suppose that Rachel is terrified of snakes, even to the point where they become such an obsession with her that she studies them: how many species there are and what they are, which are poisonous, which are constrictors, and so on. Despite this knowledge, she is still terrified even in the presence of a snake she knows to be harmless. How are we to explain her fear given that she has the belief that this snake slithering in front of her is harmless?

Although it is plausible that emotions have *some* cognitive element, it need not be beliefs but something else, such as thoughts or images. Consider Steve who, after eating one night at a particular restaurant and then spending the rest of the night being sick because the food did not "sit well" with him, simply cannot bring himself to eat at that restaurant again. He continues to feel revulsion at the mere *thought* of eating there, even though he *believes* that the food is sanitary, that the restaurant has a new chef, and so on. What is the difference between beliefs and thoughts? The philosopher Noel Carroll offers the plausible answer that

> to have a belief is to entertain a proposition assertively; to have a thought is to entertain it nonassertively. Both beliefs and thoughts have propositional content. But with thoughts the content is merely entertained without commitment to its being the case; to have a belief is to be committed to the truth of the proposition.
>
> (Carroll 1990, 80)

Steve need not assert or believe that the food at that particular restaurant is poisonous; he merely needs to hold the idea in his mind to feel revulsion. Perhaps, then, any cases of romantic love that are not based on beliefs are not empty of cognition, but involve thoughts or images. If romantic love, then, like some other emotions, could lack beliefs but not thoughts, we have not yet ruled it out as an emotion.

We have no good reason, then, to reject the idea that romantic love is an emotion, so defining it as a set of desires is unnecessary.

This discussion makes it clear that emotions are intentional; they are about something. To that extent they involve beliefs or thoughts. But emotions are not only beliefs (otherwise we would not distinguish between the two). In addition to *desires*, they also involve a felt quality to them or a *feeling*, since otherwise we should really not call them "emotions." When we are angry, sad, or bitter, we not only have beliefs, thoughts, and desires, we also *feel* a certain way. This idea raises a problem for the view that romantic love is an emotion. Given that romantic love is not always felt, we cannot define it as an emotion if emotions involve feelings.[4]

 What does it mean that romantic love is not always felt? Unless someone's love is an obsession, he is not going to feel it every minute of his life. Dan can be in love with Leo, yet not feel the love all the time – when he is, say, absorbed at work, with friends, or engaged in his hobby. During these times, two things seem to be true about Dan: he is in love with Leo but he is also not thinking about Leo or *feeling* his love for him. If emotions are felt, then romantic love cannot be an emotion.

In evaluating this view, we can reject the idea that sometimes lovers do not feel their love for each other, insisting that they always do, or we can reject the idea that for something to be an emotion it must be always felt. The first option fails because it goes against the obvious fact that lovers do not always feel their love for each other. Indeed, when they have fights or go through difficult times, some feel so angry or bitter that they cannot detect in themselves any presence of love for their beloveds. The second option is more promising. Consider hate. Someone can hate another for long stretches of time. Unless the hate is obsessive, the hater need not feel his hate the whole time. All other long-term emotions – resentment, grief, and sorrow, for example – are similar. Of course, not all emotions are long term, and those that *usually* are need not be. Grief and resentment, two examples of long-term emotions, can be short-lived, and some emotions are long or short term depending on the individual case. Anger is like this: depending on its causes, on the individual nature of the person having the emotion, and on whether and how it is rectified, anger might be short or long term. Another example is fear: sometimes it is short-lived (e.g., as long as the horror movie lasts), sometimes it is long term (as long as the person who is afraid believes that she has reason to be afraid). So if romantic love were an emotion, it would not be unusual in this respect. We still have no good reason, then, to abandon the idea that it is an emotion.

But perhaps romantic love is a virtue instead of an emotion (Solomon 1991). Is this a plausible idea?

If we adopt a rough Aristotelian view of the virtues, then, generally speaking, a virtue is a dispositional state of character that allows its person to exhibit, in a particular situation, both the proper judgment and emotions, and to thereby act morally correctly. Consider generosity. If virtues dispose their possessors to act correctly, a generous person is not someone who squanders her money.[5] She spends it, as Aristotle says, "at the right times, about the right things, toward the right people, for the right end, and in the right way" (Aristotle 1999, 1106b20). Moreover, if virtues exhibit not only proper judgment but also proper emotions (not all the virtues need do so), and if pleasure or joy is the emotion connected with generosity, the generous person feels just the right amount of pleasure or joy when and in acting generously. The virtues are moral *excellences*; they are not just any state of character, but states of character allowing the person to feel and do the *right* thing. Indeed, this is the whole point behind them and why they contrast with *vices*, which are not so good (to put it mildly) states of character.

Given that virtues are moral excellences, the implausibility of the suggestion that romantic love is a virtue becomes obvious. Without having to be extreme about it and claim that love and morality are *always* in tension (Ehman 1989), romantic love, *as such*, is neither moral nor immoral. Depending on a host of factors (such as whether the lover is himself moral or immoral), it can be either. With all due respect to the popular view that love makes people better, this is not guaranteed. Indeed, insofar as love, at least in its initial euphoric stages, tends to make the lovers absorbed in each other and oblivious to the world around them, they tend to neglect the moral demands or claims that others (friends and strangers) have upon them. Put simply, romantic love is not in itself a moral excellence. This fact is sufficient to rule it out as a virtue on the grounds that virtues are, by definition, moral excellences. In this respect, romantic love is like all other emotions, none of which is in itself good (though some, like envy, might be inherently bad). Whether an emotion is good or bad depends on the justifiability of its beliefs and desires, its object, and how it is conducted. Even good emotions, such as sympathy and compassion, can be bad if not directed at the right objects and conducted in the right ways – a major and reasonable worry that many philosophers, including Plato, Aristotle, and Immanuel Kant had about emotions. Love is similar: *A* can love a thoroughly bad person (and *A* himself can be bad). And even if *A* loves a good person, *A* can exhibit her love in all sorts of immoral ways (e.g., selfishly, neglecting the rightful claims of others).

So romantic love is not (and cannot be) a virtue.[6] It is also not a set of desires. The commonsense view that it is an emotion, then, seems to be true. Moreover, it is one such that (1) its intentionality need not always be characterized by beliefs, but could be characterized by mere thoughts or images; (2) it might outlast its originating beliefs about the beloved; (3) it is a long-term emotion that need not be *felt* all the time; (4) it seems to include the desire on the part of the lover to be with his or her beloved, and the desire to have sex with the beloved (a desire that might not remain throughout a long-lasting love relationship); and (5) it is neither inherently morally good nor bad. Interestingly, none of these features is unique to romantic love as an emotion; many other emotions can also have one or more of them.

We are not yet completely out of the woods. Romantic love admits of two main stages. If it is an emotion, we must understand how these stages square with this fact. The first stage is falling in love; it includes those early stages of romantic love when the lovers are absorbed in each other, virtually think of no one else, tend to neglect their friends, family, and work, and their sexual desires for each other are at their highest, most exciting, most demanding, and most exclusive (the lovers tend not to sexually desire other people during that stage). The other main stage occurs when the passion calms down and the love becomes stable and steady. We describe both stages as love and couples in both stages as being in love. Indeed, for couples who have been together for a long time, their love for each other can be as deep as (if not deeper than) the love of a new couple. In Raymond Carver's short story, "What We Talk About When We Talk About Love," one of the characters, Mel (a doctor), recounts treating a couple in their seventies who were in a car accident, who were badly hurt, and who spent weeks in the hospital recovering. Mel says:

> I dropped in to see each of them every day, sometimes twice a day if I was up doing other calls anyway. Casts and bandages, head to foot, the both of them. You know, you've seen it in the movies. That's just the way they looked, just like in the movies. Little eye-holes and nose-holes and mouth-holes. And she had to have her legs slung up on top of it. Well, the husband was very depressed for the longest while. Even after he found out that his wife was going to pull through, he was still very depressed. Not about the accident, though. I mean, the accident was one thing, but it wasn't everything. I'd get up to his mouth-hole, you know, and he'd say no, it wasn't the accident exactly but it was because he couldn't see her through his eye-holes. He said that was what was making him feel so bad. Can you imagine? I'm telling you, the man's heart was breaking because he couldn't turn his goddamn head and *see* his goddamn wife.
>
> (Carver 1989, 151)

It's not that the man needed to see his wife because he wanted proof that she was next to him or even that she was alive. He wanted to look at her because he loved her; she was the center of his world, and without her he is bereft.

Given these two main stages of love (and all the gradations between them), are we really speaking here of one or two emotions? Perhaps we should not be too confident that there is only one emotion. But the option that there is more than one emotion fails to convince. What is this other emotion, if not romantic love? And if it is romantic love, *why* have two emotions of romantic love in successive stages? Consider again some other long-lasting emotions.

Anger, hate, sorrow, and grief can start in a very passionate, intense way, only to simmer down and become stable over time, without, however, necessarily losing their intensity or depth. Paul's hatred for Andy can passionately develop in a few days. Over time, with his desires to inflict pain on Andy frustrated, Paul's hatred becomes calmer, yet as deep. It is the same emotion – Paul's hatred for Andy. There is no good reason to think that romantic love is different.

So, to the above list of features we can now add a sixth: romantic love is an emotion such that (1) its intentionality need not always be characterized by beliefs, but could be characterized by mere thoughts or images; (2) it might outlast its originating beliefs, thoughts or images about the beloved; (3) it is a long-term emotion, one that is possessed by the lover for a long period and as such need not be *felt* all the time; (4) it seems to include the desire on the part of the lover to be with ("associate with") his or her beloved, and the desire to have sex with the beloved (a desire that may not remain throughout a long-lasting love relationship); (5) it is neither inherently morally good nor bad; and (6) it typically (though not invariably) starts passionately, only to calm down as time goes by, without, however, necessarily becoming any less deep or intense; indeed, it may, and probably does, deepen as the years go by.

Generally Necessary Features of Romantic Love

Despite our progress, if we go back to one of our original questions, namely how to distinguish romantic love from related phenomena such as friendship and parental love, it remains true that all these six features may be present in a non-romantic friendship (whether they could also all be present in other types is more debatable). Is it hopeless, then, to distinguish romantic love from other, similar emotions?

One philosopher, W. Newton-Smith, does argue that no requirement for something to be romantic love provides a precise way to distinguish romantic love from similar relationships – not even sexuality: "For we might wish to allow some feelings of a sexual sort to enter into a case of basically maternal love. And we might allow some aspects of homosexual love in the close relationship between the officer and men of a marine platoon without the relationship ceasing to be basically a fraternal one" (1989, 203). He suggests that because romantic love does not *always* or *necessarily* contain, for example, a sexual dimension (at least as a way of distinguishing it from similar relationships), we should instead use the concept of g-necessity: romantic love g-necessarily has a sexual dimension because romantic love *generally* (hence the "g"), but not always, has a sexual dimension. This idea captures two crucial intuitions about romantic love. First, we think that it has some important connections to certain features, such as sexual desire for the beloved. Second, we think that it might not always do *and* that other relationships can have such a feature. As a corollary, if a case of romantic love lacks this generally required feature, it would need special explanation (Newton-Smith 1989, 201).

Newton-Smith gives the following list, containing four clusters, of generally necessary features of a love relationship: If A loves B, then "(1) A knows B (or at least knows something of B); (2) A cares (is concerned) about B; A likes B; (3) A respects B; A is attracted to B; A feels affection for B; (4) A is committed to B; A wishes to see B's welfare promoted" (1989, 204). He claims that in paradigm features of romantic love, all these features are present to a high degree. In other cases, some features may not be present to a high degree, and others may not be present at all: "Thus we have a g-necessary truth that love involves the satisfaction of [these features] to an as yet unspecified degree" (1989, 204). These features really characterize a love *relationship* between A and B, not A's *love* for B, period (otherwise, the list should include a generally necessary feature about A's desires for B to reciprocate particular desires or attitudes).

However, with the single exception of "A is attracted to B" (the sexual feature), *all* the other features are also generally necessary of *friendship*. That is, in paradigm cases of friendship, all these features (except for the attraction bit) are present to a high degree, and if one or more were not present, we would also require a special explanation – the same reasoning that Newton-Smith applies to romantic love. (It is controversial whether this claim is true of parent–child relationships: in addition to attraction, many parents do not know their children very well, and some do not respect them; however, if, like Newton-Smith, we do not insist on the features being present to a high degree, it is probable that all the features – minus the attraction – are also generally necessary of parent–child relationships.) Let us elaborate using Aristotle's views of friendship.

In the *Nicomachean Ethics*, Aristotle divides friendship into three types. The first is based on use and the second on pleasure. In the first, *A* and *B* are friends because they find each other useful; in the second, *C* and *D* are friends because they find each other entertaining. One feature common to both is that the friendship is likely to end once the use or the pleasure ends: "these sorts of friendships are easily dissolved, when the friends do not remain similar [to what they were]; for if someone is no longer pleasant or useful, the other stops loving him" (Aristotle 1999, 1156a20). These two types of friendship are inferior to what Aristotle thinks is the best type: friendship between people of similar, virtuous characters. This is the best type of friendship because (1) the friends are similar in character; (2) they have good characters; (3) thus, they wish each other good things; and (4) they wish them for the friend's sake, not for selfish reasons (1156b6). But even the best of friendships might dissolve if one of the friend's characters changes from good to vicious and there is little hope that he would change back (1165b13).

If we now return to Newton-Smith's generally necessary features, with the exception of attraction (and even here Aristotle often says something to the effect that attraction can be the start or part of a good friendship; 1999, 1164a8), all are present in Aristotle's view of good friendships. The friends must know each other; they care about each other, they like and respect each other (they are in concord, as Aristotle states; 1167b5–15), they feel affection for each other, and, most obviously, wish each other good things.[7] Note that Aristotle's conception of the best type of friendship is not far from ours. We agree with him that use and pleasure friendships are not good (or even genuine) types of friendships, and that true friends wish each other good things for each other's sake (though we may not agree with him that they have to have good characters).

If all the features except for attraction are also generally necessary in other types of love, perhaps it is *only* the sexual feature that serves to distinguish romantic love from other types of love in a generally necessary way. In other words, even though the sexual dimension cannot serve as a *precise* or *necessary* feature distinguishing romantic love from other types of love, romantic love differs from other types of love in that it *generally* has, at some point in the relationship, a sexual component.

I think this is correct as far as *Newton-Smith's* list of generally necessary features is concerned, because the sexual feature is the only one playing this distinguishing role. However, if we consider features not on Newton-Smith's list, other plausible features can delimit or distinguish romantic love from other types of love between people in a generally necessary way. At this stage, then, we can turn to a discussion of these features and compare romantic love to two other types of crucial, similar relationships: friendships and parent–child relationships. I conduct this discussion in terms of relationships, not emotions, but translate below the results into features that romantic love as an emotion has, to finalize their list.

Seven more features, all of which are good candidates for being generally necessary features of romantic love, require further discussion (and some of which will be discussed even further in later chapters): voluntariness, exclusivity, intensity and dependence, marriage, social expectations, union, and jealousy. They are all popular beliefs about romantic love and are found in the philosophical literature on it.

Involuntariness. Romantic love is commonly thought to not involve choice. The metaphor of "falling in love" seems to attest to this, giving the impression that we succumb to romantic love instead of consciously choosing it. This is different from beliefs about friendship and parent–child relationships. We may believe, along with Aristotle, that we choose our friends, and it sounds right that couples choose whether to have children. Lack of choice may then be another generally necessary feature of love that distinguishes it from friendship and parenthood.

However, this view is too simple. Although some philosophers claim that romantic love does involve choice because we choose our emotions (Solomon 1990, esp. ch. 17), it is debatable whether emotions are chosen (at least directly), and there is a better way to settle the issue of choice. If choice refers to the very having of the emotion in question, we generally have no choice about whether we acquire the emotion of romantic love, but the same is true of the emotions found in friendship and parenting. Much as we feel washed over by the emotion of romantic love when we meet and spend time with a potential beloved, we feel washed over by emotions of love when we meet a potential friend (though the emotions may not feel the same or be as intense), or when we first encounter our new-born children. So there is no necessary difference here. If choice refers to the decision to cultivate a particular relationship – to pursue a potential beloved, to pursue a potential friendship, and to have children – then we have an array of specific choices in all these areas. Even if emotions of romantic love wash over us, we can choose to act on them, much as we can choose to cultivate a friendship and to become parents. So depending on what "choice" means, all three types of relationship lack choice or all have it. Voluntariness, then, is not a generally necessary feature of romantic love.

Exclusivity. This concept usually means that love is exclusive to one and only one person – the love relationship is confined to two and only two people. If this is what "exclusivity" means, it would be a generally necessary feature of romantic love, because parents usually love all their children (though not necessarily equally), and, despite the occasional exclusive pairs of friends, intimate, close friendships often cluster in three, four, and perhaps higher number of friends (the higher the number, the more the friendships might be diluted, so the less intimate and close they are). Even though some philosophers have argued that one can romantically love more than one person at the same time (McMurty 1984, Wasserstrom 1998), romantic love is usually exclusive. Thus exclusivity is another generally necessary feature of romantic love.

Intensity and dependence. "Intensity" refers to the strength and depth of the emotion of love, in both its early, passionate stages, and in any successful, long-term love relationship. It is also rare that friendships manifest a degree of intensity of emotions equaling that found in love. Moreover, even if some love relationships do not start with intense passion (some say that most do not; see Gregory 1984), almost *all* successful love relationships are emotionally intense. Just think of the tremendous amount of grief, sadness, loneliness, and so on the lover experiences when her beloved dies, suffers a tragic accident, or is inflicted with a fatal disease or sickness. Although friends seriously grieve when these things happen to their friends, it is rare that they go through the same amount, depth, and duration of sadness and grief. Moreover, friends are not emotionally and in other ways as dependent on their friends as lovers are on each other.

In parent–child relationships, parents are stricken with the same amount, intensity, and duration of grief or sadness when their children die or become seriously ill as when a lover's beloved dies or becomes seriously ill (though probably the same cannot be said about children with respect to their parents). Thus perhaps intensity and dependence do not set romantic love relationships apart from parent–child relationships. However, there may be crucial differences. First, unless the children die or suffer serious illnesses when they are still under their parents' care, parents are not left with a deep feeling of loneliness and lack of purpose when this happens. By the time their children mature, reach adulthood, and become independent, parents go on to lead their own lives. So if adult children suffer serious misfortunes, chances are that they have their own spouses or lovers (or even their own children) to take care of them. Their parents won't usually suffer a lack of purpose and loneliness (though their grief would still be immeasurable). Second, unless the children are still under their care, parents are not usually emotionally dependent on them. When they lose them, they do not suffer a deep sense of being bereft of support, whereas lovers do.

Despite my misgivings about the above line of reasoning (it is glib when it comes to what parents and children feel when death or misfortune strikes), it sounds plausible. Moreover, if we set aside the fact that in certain subcultures (especially in the past) friendships seem to have deeper ties than marriages and what we consider today to be love relationships, the reasoning is quite forceful. Thus romantic love's emotional intensity and dependence seem to provide another generally necessary feature of romantic love.

Marriage. I understand marriage not only as a legal arrangement under which two people are recognized as spouses, but also any substantive, cohabitating arrangement by which two people are married in all the usual senses except legally (think of long-term gay or heterosexual couples who live together). The philosopher Richard Mohr defines it as "the development and maintenance of intimacy through the medium of everyday life, the day-to-day … [it] is the fused intersection of love's sanctity and necessity's demand" (2005, 61). Therefore two people can be married in a substantive but not legal sense.

If this is what we mean by "marriage," we can uncover another generally necessary feature of romantic love. Parent–child relationships do not end in marriage (nor should they!), and even though some friends legally marry each other for many reasons, this is rare. Moreover, those friends who live together often do so more as roommates than as married couples; they do not "maintain their intimacy through the medium of everyday life." If we also set aside past notions of marriage, according to which marriage was more about political alliances, money, social cohesion, and other socially and politically pragmatic reasons, it is true today and in almost all parts of the world that romantic love does tend to successfully push the couple toward marriage, if not legally, at least substantively. We have, then, another generally necessary feature of love.

Social expectations. If we set aside past notions and practices of friendship, today and in almost all parts of the world there are relatively common social expectations of lovers. Briefly put, once we allow for lovers' duties to their work, friends, family, and children (if any), lovers are expected to be the primary and main receivers of each other's time, energy, affection, and attention (sex included). If, without special explanation, one lover is focusing his affection on someone other than his beloved (including his friends), we think something is amiss, and sexual attention toward someone other than the spouse is considered adultery, with its usual negative associations.

Whether these social expectations are justified, they exist and, seemingly, only with respect to lovers, not with respect to friends (although friendships generate their own social expectations). They do exist with respect to parent–child relationships but only up to a point, after which children are expected to lead their lives independently. Therefore the social expectation that the lovers are the primary recipients of each other's time, attention, energy, and affection is another generally necessary feature of romantic love.

Union. The idea that lovers seek union with each other has a long history in philosophy, starting with the speech by Aristophanes in Plato's *Symposium* (see Chapter 2). "Union" has different meanings, some strong (so implausible), some weak (more plausible). In the next chapter, I discuss the strong versions of the view. Because we want to find those features of romantic love that are genuinely generally necessary, we should discuss the concept of union in its weak and so more convincing forms.

Under a weak concept of union, the lovers form, or desire to form, some sort of single entity. While some philosophers call this "shared identity" (Solomon 2006, ch. 4), others, like Robert Nozick, call it a "we." To Nozick, the desire to form a "we" is not accidental to love, but is intrinsic to its nature (1991, 418). One feature of the "we" is that the well-being of each lover is tied up with the well-being of the other (Nozick 1991, 419). If something bad (or good) happens to one, something bad (or good) happens to the other. A second feature of the "we" is that it requires lovers to make some decisions jointly, thereby limiting each other's autonomy (1991, 419). A third feature is that the formation of a "we" alters each lover's identity: "to love someone might be, in part, to devote alertness to their well-being and to your connection with them" (1991, 419–420; cf. Conlon 1995, 297–298). The idea is that each lover becomes psychologically part of the other: they think and worry about each other all the time, and one lover even has imaginary dialogues with the other when the latter is not around (1991, 420).

The first feature – the lovers' well-being tied to each other's – is not promising as a generally necessary feature of romantic love. By Nozick's own account, this feature is common to all forms of love (1991, 417). Unless we require a certain degree of intensity and dependence in the case of romantic love but not in the other types of love, we are not going to get very far. The second feature is more promising, because, barring special cases, romantic love does limit lovers' autonomy and decision making in ways and to degrees that friendships do not. Friends typically make decisions independently of each other. They may take their friends' advice and even interests into account when they make these decisions, but they don't make them jointly. And although parents and children, by the very nature of their relationship, curtail each other's autonomy, this happens only until the children become independent (unlike lovers, who curtail each other's autonomy for at least as long as the relationship endures).

The third feature, the alteration of identity, is controversial. Aristotle, for example, would not think that alteration of identity is typical only of lovers, and he requires of friends what Nozick thinks is true of lovers:

> Whatever someone [regards as] his being, or the end for which he chooses to be alive, that is the activity he wishes to pursue in his friend's company

… They spend their days together on whichever pursuit in life they like most; for since they want to live with their friends, they share the actions in which they find their common life.

(1999, 1172a2)

By "living together" Aristotle means that friends share "conversation and thought, not sharing the same pasture, as in the case of grazing animals" (1999, 1170b13). Aristotle's view of friendship opposes Nozick's, because Aristotle thinks that friends are also psychologically part of each other. If Aristotle's view is plausible, Nozick's is more controversial than it appears. So the third feature of the "we" is probably not a generally necessary feature of romantic love.

This means that only the second feature of the "we" – that romantic love tends to limit the autonomy of the lovers – is a plausible, generally necessary feature of love.

Jealousy. Friends sometimes feel threatened and thus jealous by the interference or entanglement of other people into their friendships, but this does not usually characterize friendship. Parents tend not to be jealous of their children, and children tend not to be jealous of their parents. However, with lovers, jealousy is quite common, and although some philosophers portray it as a bad emotion (G. Taylor 1979, R. Taylor 1982), others argue plausibly that it need not be (Farrell 1989); if properly exhibited, it shows a healthy regard for one's love relationship.

Still, jealousy may not be a generally necessary feature of romantic love. Siblings often feel jealous of each other, so jealousy may be a mark of another type of love relationship (sibling ones). However, the jealousy exhibited by siblings is different from that of lovers. Usually, a boy, say, feels jealous of his brother because he wants to share or to also have what his brother has (e.g., his mother's attention, a bicycle, a new video game). But a man who feels jealous at the sight of his wife or girlfriend flirting with another man does not (usually!) want to have what she is having (though he may demand that he, too, be allowed to flirt with other people). Instead, he wants the man with whom his wife is flirting left out of the picture. The jealousy of lovers tends to be protective of the love, excluding from the relationship what is deemed to threaten it, whereas jealousy among siblings tends to be inclusive: the siblings want to have what the other also has. Because jealousy in romantic love is different from that among siblings, and because it is rarely found among friends and parents and children, it seems to be a generally necessary feature of romantic love.

Romantic Love and Infatuation

Can we distinguish romantic love from infatuation and crushes, two phenomena that resemble it but that tend to be of short duration? Not much has been written on this issue in the philosophical literature, and almost all of it is on infatuation. I focus on infatuation because if we can find a way to plausibly distinguish it from romantic love, I suspect we can then do so with respect to crushes.

There are two general approaches to distinguishing between infatuation and romantic love. The first is to consider them as different in kind, the second as different in duration. The second approach views infatuation as unrequited or unfulfilled love. If correct, it explains the short duration we tend to associate with infatuation. Thus, Mark Vernon writes, "unrequited love produces eros' most exquisite passion – infatuation" (2005, 34) and Nozick states, "However and whenever infatuation begins, if given the opportunity it transforms itself into continuing romantic love or else it disappears" (1991, 418). Strictly speaking, Vernon does not *identify* unrequited love with infatuation, but claims that it *produces* infatuation. However, identification is more plausible, because it is not obvious why unrequited love causes infatuation instead of, say, bitterness, some other emotion, or no emotion at all. In any case, the suggestion that infatuation is unrequited love is intriguing and plausible. For it is tempting to think along the following lines: the emotion Bill is going through is clearly infatuation; if only Chris were to reciprocate, it would blossom into full-fledged love! Philosophers call this reasoning "counter-factual": *had* Bill's emotion been returned, it would have been love. Tempting as it is, we should not identify infatuation with unrequited love, because then any instance of infatuation would be love had it only been returned. But this is false: it is entirely possible that some cases of requited infatuations never blossom into love (some end in disaster). There is another reason why infatuation is not unrequited love: the word "infatuation" (and "crush") has particular linguistic associations – infatuation is short-lived, whimsical, immature, not serious, not rooted in anything potentially enduring. Taken seriously, these associations go against the idea that infatuation is unrequited love, because they imply that even if the emotion is reciprocated, it is not going to "work" (more on this below).

Susan Mendus suggests that we should distinguish between love and infatuation as follows: "in the case of infatuation the lover's error lies in wrongly evaluating the qualities of the beloved" (1989, 240). Mendus is not suggesting that the lover's mistake lies in thinking that his beloved has qualities she does not actually have, but in his having mistaken beliefs *about* these qualities. For example, if John "loves" Martha because he thinks she is a chess player whereas in fact she is not, then what John feels for Martha is not infatuation, but, according to Mendus, an "irrationally-based love" (1989, 240). However, if John "loves" Martha because he thinks she is the greatest chess player whereas, in fact, she is at best mediocre, he wrongly evaluates her properties, so what he feels for her is infatuation.

This suggestion won't do. It is difficult to maintain the distinction between mistakenly believing that the beloved has a particular quality and having a mistaken belief about a quality that the beloved has. Consider the second chess example: we might as well say that John mistakenly believes that Martha has the quality of being the best chess player in the world; any mistaken belief or evaluation about a quality that the beloved has can be translated into a mistaken belief about a quality that the beloved does *not* have. So Mendus's suggestion must boil down to the idea that infatuation is not true love because it is based on false beliefs about the beloved's qualities. But because there are many cases of infatuation involving no false beliefs about the beloved, this way fails to distinguish romantic love from infatuation; it is certainly a tall order that every case of infatuation *must* involve false beliefs. Indeed, there are some theories of (true) love that *require* that the lover have idealized (so false) beliefs about the beloved (Stendhal 1975, Book I). Moreover, as we have seen, there is no good reason to think that romantic love cannot survive changes in the lover's beliefs about the beloved, including the discovery that what one thought about one's beloved is actually not true (Newton-Smith believes that true love must survive such changes; 1989, 214–215). If some loves survive such false beliefs, infatuation cannot be simply identified with being based on these beliefs.

Alan Soble suggests understanding infatuation in terms of the content of the desires that the infatuated person has: while the lover primarily has the desire to benefit her beloved, the infatuated primarily has the desire to simply be with her beloved or to have sex with him (1989a, 197, n. 1). But we can imagine cases in which the infatuated person does have primary desires to benefit the person with whom he is infatuated. Imagine a college freshman infatuated with his teacher and who would do anything to benefit her, such as helping her grade exams, mowing her lawn, and walking her home late at night. Of course, although the notions of "primary" and "primarily" are tricky, they are not exclusive, and a person can have many desires (among many others) all of which are equally primary. So the college freshman may have a primary desire to have sex with his teacher, without denying that he has another primary desire to benefit her. If this is correct, we cannot use Soble's suggestion to distinguish between love and infatuation.

One last suggestion is worth exploring. John Armstrong, relying on the novel *Spring Torrents* by the Russian writer Ivan Turgenev, thinks that infatuation is having mistaken beliefs about the *fit* between the qualities of the beloved and one's own: "The fantasy [the infatuated person] elaborates is attractive, the problem is that it does not correspond with the reality of his personality and needs" (2003, 78). Infatuation is "attraction to what we want, not to what we need" (2003, 79). Infatuated people mistakenly think that the life they imagine with their beloved is suitable for them, whereas in fact it is not. If Armstrong's view were correct, it would explain our intuitions that infatuation is silly, whimsical, and short in duration (could this be what Mendus is really claiming?).

Armstrong's view is the most plausible. One thought in its support is that insofar as we think infatuation to be foolish, temporary, and so on, we do so because we often think that the love is *unattainable* or will not work. We chide the poverty-stricken girl for falling in love with the prince, the high school student for falling in love with his teacher, the wife for falling in love with her gym trainer, and the Hindu girl for falling in love with a Muslim (as in Vikram Seth's novel *A Suitable Boy*). Yet unattainability due to lack of fit may not be all that there is to infatuation, and it might be wise to not simply identify the two, because, again, we can come up with counter-examples (there are moderately successful cases of love between people who are in many ways mismatched for each other). But Armstrong's suggestion is interesting because it captures something crucial and common about our thoughts regarding infatuation, whereas the other accounts do not.

So infatuation might be a type of unfulfilled love after all, not because the emotion is unreciprocated, but because, even if reciprocated, the relationship would (probably) not work. Note what the claim is: infatuation is a type of love such that if it were to be translated into a relationship, that *relationship* won't succeed. The issue is not that the lover has mistaken beliefs about the qualities of the beloved; indeed, his beliefs are true: the prince *is* charming, the boy *is* Muslim, the gym trainer *is* hunky, and the teacher *is* beautiful and smart. The issue is that the lover has mistaken beliefs about whether he can be with his beloved.

Summary

There are sixteen crucial features of romantic love, one of which is necessary (feature 16, found in *all* cases of romantic love), eight of which are generally necessary (features 8 through 15), and seven of which are not necessary (features 1 through 7, only sometimes found in romantic love). So, romantic love is an emotion such that:

1 It occurs between adult human beings.
2 Its intentionality need not always be characterized by beliefs, but could be characterized by mere thoughts or images.
3 It might outlast its originating beliefs about the beloved.
4 It is a long-term emotion, one that is possessed by the lover for a long period and as such need not be constantly felt (especially when reciprocated).
5 It seems to include the desire on the part of the lover to be with the beloved.
6 Like many other emotions, it is inherently neither morally good nor bad.
7 It typically starts passionately, only to calm down as time goes by, without, however, necessarily becoming any less deep or intense; indeed, it may, and probably does, deepen as the years go by (especially when reciprocated).
8 It has the desire to have sex with the beloved (a desire that might not remain throughout a long-lasting love relationship).
9 It is exclusive.
10 When reciprocated, it exists between only two people.
11 When reciprocated, it pushes the lovers toward marriage (legal or substantive).
12 When reciprocated over a long period, its emotional intensity and dependence are more intense and thorough than what we find among friends and different in kind than what we find between parents and children.
13 There are social expectations that the lovers are the primary recipients of each other's time, attention, energy, and affection.

14   When reciprocated, it limits the autonomy of the lovers.
15   It has jealousy as one of its main accompanying emotions.
16   It always has concern on the part of the lover for the well-being of the beloved.

Because all the features on this list can be found in other types of love, it does not constitute a definition of romantic love.

In the next chapter, we take a deeper look into some of the features (both g-necessary and not g-necessary) believed to characterize romantic love, not in order to see whether they distinguish romantic love from other types of love, but to discuss them in their own right, to understand what it means for romantic love to have them, and whether some are incompatible with each other.

Notes

1 Strictly speaking, we define concepts, not things – the concepts "human being" and "tiger" – because we are asking what features something must have in order to be correctly subsumed under its concept.
2 Michel de Montaigne's description of his friendship with Etienne de La Boetie sounds very much like a description of romantic love (see de Montaigne 1987, 205–219).
3 In this discussion, I use the views of O. H. Green (1997) as my inspiration.
4 This underlies Mike Martin's (1996) discussion of love as an attitude. See also Dilman 1998, 18–19, Vannoy 1980, 154–155.
5 One can be generous with things other than money (e.g., time), but let us stick with money for simplicity's sake.
6 This conclusion does not show on its own that love is not an emotion. Solomon (1991), for example, argues that it is an emotion but that some emotions are virtues. This idea, however, is implausible (see Halwani 2003, 128–132).
7 For Aristotle's view of friendship, see Aristotle 1999 books VIII and IX. For a good discussion of Aristotle's view, see Price 1997, Sihvola 2002.

Further Reading

A number of good books expand on the issues discussed in this chapter. Badhwar (1993) contains influential essays on friendship in general and on the moral and political issues it raises. Graham and LaFollette (1989) contains good essays on all types of intimate relationships. Kierkegaard (1962) is one of the most influential treatments of Christian love. O'Neill and Ruddick (1979) has excellent essays on children's and parents' rights, obligations, and interests. Pakaluk (1991) has essential readings from past important philosophers on friendship. Plato's *Lysis* is one of the oldest works devoted to a discussion of friendship. Soble (1989b) contains classical sources, commentaries on these sources, and contemporary essays on the three types of love. Vannoy (1980, Part II, ch. 2) discusses whether love can be defined and how it differs from infatuation and friendship. White (2001) has an interesting discussion on love, friendship, and children. Williams (1995) has good essays on the three types of love, including excerpts from non-philosophers (e.g., singers, poets).

2 Romantic Love

Aristophanes on Union

In the *Symposium*, one of the most famous works by Plato, a number of people (including Socrates, usually Plato's mouthpiece) are eating, drinking, and enjoying themselves. They decide to give speeches praising love. One of the speeches – by the playwright Aristophanes – offers the mythic, yet interesting, view that the main feature of romantic love is the lovers' desire for some sort of union with each other.

According to Aristophanes, "in the beginning" humans were:

> completely round, with back and side in a circle; they had four hands each, as many legs as hands, and two faces, exactly alike, on a rounded neck. Between the two faces, which were on opposite sides, was one head with four ears. There were two sets of sexual organs ... They walked upright, as we do now, whatever direction they wanted. And whenever they set out to run fast, they thrust out all their eight limbs, the ones they had then, and spun rapidly, the way gymnasts do cartwheels, by bringing their legs around straight.
>
> (Plato 1997g, 190a)

Moreover, each creature had one of three types of genital organs: male–male, female–female, and male–female (189e).

These "original" human beings were powerful and ambitious. "They made an attempt on the gods," which prompted Zeus to diminish their power by cutting each in half (190c). He then asked Apollo to clean up his surgical mess. Apollo turned their faces around to face the wound and he stretched their skins and tied them in a knot to form the navel. He shaped the breasts and smoothed the wrinkles (but some were left as a reminder of their fate; 190e–191a). With this major transformation, each new creature now longed for his or her other half. They hugged each other, but because their genitals were on their backs, they couldn't do much. So Zeus felt sorry for them and moved their genitals to the front: "The purpose of this was so that, when a man embraced a woman, he would cast his seed and they would have children; but when male embraced male, they would at least have the satisfaction of intercourse, after which they could stop embracing, return to their jobs, and look after their other needs in life" (191c; Aristophanes is silent on sexual activity between two women halves).

To Aristophanes, this story or myth explains the origin of love: "This, then, is the source of our desire to love each other. Love is born into every human being; it calls back the halves of our original nature together; it tries to make one out of two and heal the wound of human nature" (191d). Indeed, if Hephaestus, the god of craftsmanship, saw any two lovers (not just these original creatures, but any two human beings) lying together and asked them whether they want to be physically welded together, they would readily accept. Because we used to be whole in bygone days, "now 'Love' is the name for our pursuit of wholeness, for our desire to be complete" (192d–193e).

Aristophanes's speech raises interesting issues. *If* we assume that the original split is carried down later generations, the idea that we are always searching for our halves seems to explain a few things. First, it explains why people accept the popular view that for each person there is a special someone "out there." Second, it explains how love between two people can be (sometimes) successful: the two are a "perfect" match for each other. Third, it explains why love makes people happy: when the two halves reunite, they are happy because they are whole again. Fourth, it explains why we feel elated when we see our beloveds – we are bound to feel this way upon encountering our other half (Soble 1990, 89).[1]

However, we cannot assume that Aristophanes's split carries through down the ages. Aristophanes spoke of what happened to the *original* human beings; after the split, future human beings had to be born through regular sexual intercourse between males and females. But these newly born human beings are like us – they walk on two legs, have their genitals on their front sides, and so on. *They* have no lost halves. If the original human beings desired union because *they* were split in half, *we* are not split. Do we then have no desire for union? If we do, how are we to explain it?

Referring to the original human beings, Aristophanes says, "Whenever one of the halves died and one was left, the one that was left still sought another and wove itself together with that" (191b). Aristophanes does *not* claim that if one half died the other wallowed by itself in loneliness until *it* died; it instead sought another half (another widow or widower?). This is puzzling, because we would expect that if each half were *the* match for the other, once one died, the other would not seek another entity. Perhaps Aristophanes is not after the idea that one half can *only* love its other half, but that one half loves another half that somehow completes it. So even among the original human beings, there was no such thing as one perfect match for another *such that* their union is necessary for love. Thus, even if the original split carries through down the ages, this would not mean that for each person there is one and only one special person "out there."

If seeking one's other half is not necessary for the desire for union, what is? This question is especially pressing in light of the possibility that Aristophanes's view is internally contradictory. If one half can seek any other half (not specifically the split one), why does Aristophanes insist that, "Love ... calls back the halves of our original nature together" (191d)? Indeed, he thinks that his view explains why some men seek women (and vice versa), why some men seek each other (male homosexuality), and why some women seek each other (female homosexuality). In each case, the explanation lies in our origins: if a man's "forefathers" were fully male, then he seeks men; if they were male–female, he seeks women, and so on (191c).[2] The only convincing explanation is the following: for the original generation, the impulse to seek one's other half is primary, but if one's half is not available, one seeks another, somehow suitable, half. The impulse is not for one's other half as such, but for what the other half can *provide* or what another suitable half can provide but perhaps only in a weaker (though still good enough) way. Aristophanes does not discuss the content of this impulse, but a plausible answer is that the original human beings were not only powerful and ambitious, but happy. When split, they lost much of their power and happiness. The impulse for union is the impulse to return to a powerful and happy state. For this to happen, it would be necessary to reunite with *someone*, even if that someone is not one's split half.

What about future generations? Aristophanes says,

> I am speaking about everyone, men and women alike, and I say there's just one way for the human race to flourish: we must bring love to its perfect conclusion, and each of us must win the favors of his very own young man, so that he can recover his original nature. If that is the ideal, then, of course, the nearest approach to it is best in present circumstances, and that is to win the favor of young men who are naturally sympathetic to us.
>
> (193c)

There are three crucial points about this passage. First, Aristophanes discusses male–male love, as was the custom in parts of ancient Greece (see Dover 1989). However, as part of that custom, the men who formed couples were not of (roughly) the same age, like contemporary homosexuality in the Western world. The male couples consisted of an older man and a younger one (with barely any facial hair). So Aristophanes is claiming that we, today, seek our halves, because to do so we have to seek someone of the same age as ourselves, whereas Aristophanes knew perfectly well how homosexual relationships were structured during his time. Second, he claims that recovering our original nature is the "ideal," but that, since we cannot attain it, we need to do the second best thing and seek someone who is "naturally sympathetic to us," meaning someone who is somehow suitable to us. Third, and although he speaks of the human race, Aristophanes seems to think that if we are to flourish, we must love properly – seek union with someone "naturally sympathetic" to us.

These remarks confirm that, first, the impulse to flourish and be happy is the impulse behind our desire for union, the impulse that seems to be transmitted from the original human beings down the ages ("Love ... *calls back* the halves of our original nature together"). Second, we cannot seek our other halves, since we have none. Since this was not necessary even for the original human beings, then, third, we seek those who are suitable for us to satisfy the transmitted impulse for union.

Two controversial and interesting points emerge. First, love is necessary for happiness or living well (flourishing). This claim is discussed in Chapter 4. Second, although *we* have no other halves, we still desire union. In the case of the original human beings, they desired actual welding with each other. Does this mean that when we desire union we desire an actual physical merger with each other? If not, what else could it be?

Nozick, Soble, and Solomon on Union

Desire for union cannot be desire for *physical* union. It is not clear what "physical union" means. It cannot mean becoming something like Aristophanes's original human beings, because not only is it physically impossible given our current technology, it is not desired by romantic lovers. First, such a desire defeats the very point of love. If x loves y, x loves y as a *separate* entity, so if x and y were to merge, there would no longer be a y that is the object of x's love, which defeats the very point of love. Indeed, *both* x and y would be obliterated in the process, with a new entity, z, made up of x and y, emerging. However, love is strange; might it not have paradoxical and self-defeating desires? I am skeptical of this thinking, because even though lovers desire to be with each other, to share their experiences, to cling to each other in the process of sexual activity, they do not desire to literally fuse into one physical entity. The idea of union must then be one of mental, emotional, or spiritual union. But what does this amount to?

Let us delve a little more into Robert Nozick's *we*. Nozick not only considers union to be crucial to romantic love, but he also defines love in its terms: "Love, romantic love, is *wanting* to form a *we* with that particular person, feeling, or perhaps wanting, that particular person to be the right one for you to form a *we* with, and also wanting the other to feel the same way about you" (1991, 418; emphases in original). Desiring to form a *we* with y (and with no one but y, as Nozick later says on page 427) is a necessary condition for romantic love. This means what?

Nozick does not flesh out the content of this desire, only the notion of the *we* itself. It has two main characteristics (three actually, but the third – shared identity – is very much common to all types of intimate relationships, so I will set it aside). First, in a *we* the well-being of each lover is tied up with that of the other: if something bad (or good) happens to y, then something bad (or good) also happens to x (1991, 419), though the bad thing that happens to the beloved need not be the same bad thing that happens to the lover (1991, 417). This is unlike friendship, whereby if something bad happens to a friend, we *feel* bad for our friend but the bad thing does not also happen to us (1991, 417). For example, suppose that Sally and Toni are lovers. If, say, Toni fails her bar exams, something bad happens to Toni. But something bad also happens to Sally, though, being a dentist, it is not failing the bar exam. Nozick is elusive on what the bad thing could be, though he would probably say that it is Sally's feeling hurt or sad (1991, 417). If Tom and John are friends, and if Tom fails the bar exam, John feels sad *for* Tom. In the case of Sally and Toni, Sally feels sad, period (could John feel sad, period? We will return to this point later).

The second feature of the *we* is limited autonomy: "people who form a *we* … limit or curtail their own decision-making power and rights; some decisions can no longer be made alone" (1991, 419). Examples of such decisions are where to live, "whether to have children and how many, where to travel, whether to go to the movies that night and what to see" (1991, 419). Nozick is not clear on *how* these decisions are jointly made, simply stating that they "somehow" are (1991, 419). He is also unclear on *which* decisions are jointly made. Given his list of examples, they seem to be about things that include both individuals in a *we*: from the serious decision about whether they should have children to the mundane one about whether to go to the movies on a particular night. As we will shortly see, and contrary to Nozick's narrow understanding of how the *we* limits individual autonomy, the *we* limits the individuals' autonomy *pervasively*.

Three crucial issues surface in Nozick's *we*. First, is the *we* a plausible idea? Second, what is the connection between the *desire* to form a *we*, on the one hand, and the *features* of the *we*, on the other? Third, is the *we* incompatible with another basic feature of romantic love, the genuine concern that lovers have for each other?

The plausibility of Nozick's we. There is some truth in the idea that the well-being of each lover is tied up with that of the other, since lovers suffer when their beloveds suffer, and are happy when they are happy. Having said this, the trouble with the first feature of the *we* is that it is either uninteresting or false.

Consider Nozick's claim that the bad (or good) thing that happens to *y need not be the same* bad (or good) thing that happens to *x*. This claim is true, for otherwise it would be utterly implausible. Failing the bar exam is the bad thing that happens to Toni, but it clearly is not the bad thing that happens to Sally. Even if Sally also took the bar exam and failed it, this is a bad thing that happens to her, but not *because* Toni failed the bar exam. So although Nozick is right that the bad thing that happens to one in a *we* is not usually the same bad thing that happens to the other, we end up – as does Nozick – with the uninteresting point that when one bad (or good) thing happens to *y*, *x* feels bad or sad. As Nozick acknowledges, this is a feature common to all types of love (1991, 417): if I love my collection of Danielle Steel novels, then if something bad happens to it (it gets stolen), something bad happens to me (I feel miserable). We could say that the sadness or happiness that occurs to *x* in a *we* is deeper than what happens in other cases. But this would be false, because some negative or positive effects to *y*'s well-being, though causing sadness or happiness in *x*, are too trivial (not coming home in time to watch *Survivor* or coming home in time to watch *Survivor*) to make the sadness or happiness deep. So the first feature of a *we* does not capture something interesting in a union.

The *we*'s second feature is the limitation on autonomy. Nozick discusses this idea in terms of limits on individual decision making. It is true, as Nozick claims, that *some* decisions will need to be made jointly, and, I suppose, the idea here is that two lovers need to sit down and discuss whether, say, they should move to another city and arrive at a decision by consensus (here we need to pay careful attention to power dynamics in a relationship, whereby one person, by virtue of his or her personality, intellectual abilities, moral attributes, or gender, usually has the upper hand; see Soble 1997, 74–77, Nozick 1991, 421). Even though Nozick does not say *which* decisions need to be jointly made and which do not, the idea is that some individual autonomy nonetheless remains in a *we*, evidenced by those decisions that do *not* need to be, or that are not, jointly made.

However, much depends on what we mean by "autonomy." If, as Nozick understands it, it means a decision arrived at by an individual alone, not by consensus or agreement, perhaps the *we* limits autonomy only when it comes to important decisions. But making a decision alone is not the same as making it independently, so another sense of "autonomy" that the *we* more thoroughly limits is the ability to make decisions without having to take into account the needs and desires of one's beloved. Granted, and unless one is a hermit, this type of autonomy is almost always limited in our lives: we have to make decisions taking into account the needs of our friends, colleagues, neighbors, and even strangers, at least in the minimal sense that whatever we decide does not (seriously?) harm them, break our promises to them, and so on. But when we enter a *we*, things become much hairier. For example, x's decision to have pizza for dinner while y is out of town is not autonomous, in that, at minimum, x needs to ensure that y would not disapprove of this decision (unless x does not care about what y thinks, a fact that might raise doubts about x's being part of a *we* with y). Whether x goes to the movies tomorrow night, whether x buys a new cell phone, whether x takes up yoga lessons, whether x goes away on a weekend by himself, and whether x starts a subscription to *US Weekly* are normally not serious, momentous, or life-affecting decisions. Yet x, as part of a *we*, cannot make these decisions on his own; he needs to ensure y's approval or, at least, non-disapproval. Outside a *we*, x has much more autonomy: he need not worry that his friends approve or disapprove of such decisions. The limits on autonomy in a *we*, then, are much more thoroughgoing than Nozick seems to believe (they increase if we bring in other considerations, such as emotional ones). They create trouble for the very idea of union and the desire for union, as we will shortly see.

So far, we may conclude that the feature of the *we* that is both interesting and plausible is limited autonomy. But it faces severe difficulties. We see this in the next two issues connected with Nozick's account.

The desire to form a we *and features of the* we. Consider a simple example which has nothing to do with the *we* or love. Suppose that I desire to have a good swim. Unfortunately, I don't know that the water is full of jellyfish, sea beasts to which I have a particular abhorrence. As I'm about to jump in, my friend alerts me to their presence. I would then probably no longer desire to jump into the water. I might still find the water alluring but would not retain the desire to jump in right then and there. Many similar cases can be generated (e.g., desiring a frosty glass of water only to be told that it is full of poison; desiring to enter a secret chamber in a castle only to be told that I will be hacked to pieces by a contraption meant to keep intruders away).

Nozick's view might face a similar conundrum. Presumably, all (or most) of us want to be in love. But if to be in love is to desire to form a *we*, would we still want to be in love given the two features of this *we*? Consider the following (this is going to get a bit complicated): if Nozick is correct, to want to be in love is to want to want to form a *we*. Philosophers call wanting to want something a "higher-order desire," a type of desire whose target is another desire. Normally, our desires target regular objects (swimming, brownies, and Matt Damon), but higher-order desires target other desires. Suppose that John doesn't like chocolate, but he feels very weird about this, seeing that everyone else likes it. So he wishes he could desire or want chocolate. John has the higher-order desire to have a desire for chocolate. Ordinarily (and back to Nozick), we do not want to limit or tie our well-being in strong and direct ways to somebody else's, perhaps because we value our independence too much (or is this a mere cultural product of societies that emphasize individualism?). The problem, then, with Nozick's view is that although most people desire love, they do not desire to have their autonomy limited or their well-being held hostage to another's in strong ways. If Nozick is right, limiting their autonomy and strongly tying up their well-being with another's are two things that people *do* desire, given that they desire love. However, as Alan Soble puts it, "Why would we want to 'pool' that hard-gained autonomy with the autonomy of someone else, thereby effectively abandoning our prize?" (1997, 91).

We have three options. The first is to argue that much like my ignorance of the jellyfish, people are ignorant of these two features of love, which means that when they desire love, they do not desire the two features; they end up being saddled with them because they didn't know about them. But people are not usually ignorant of the fact that when they are in love they lose much of their autonomy, or of the fact that in loving someone (or something) they have to brace themselves for possible sadness and loss (though they might not *dwell* on them). So the first option is a non-starter.

The second option is to accept that people do actually desire these two features, but relegate this phenomenon to human strangeness or irrationality. People often do things they know to be dangerous, to come with a heavy price, to be painful, including desiring intimate relationships, which come with their own risks, even guaranteed pain and suffering (no parent, for example, will tell you that raising her children went without a hitch). Romantic love is not unique in these respects. We desire it just as we desire having friendships and children. So either most people are irrational or strange, or something is wrong with this second option. It is the latter, because friendships, parenting, and romantic love give life purpose and meaning. They make life worth living, which explains the fact that people desire these things while being fully aware of the price tag.

This brings us to the third option – my favorite. It offers a more sophisticated account than the first two of what goes on when we desire love. Although people desire to be in love, they do not *desire* these two conflicting features, but accept them as a price worth paying. How is this possible? Suppose that I do jump into the blue water knowing that the jellyfish remain. This would *not* mean that I am no longer averse to them or that I like them, but that I decided to bite the bullet and go for a swim. One can desire something without desiring every property or aspect of that thing. Setting aside cases of self-destructive behavior, examples are many. They include the desire for ice cream but not its fattening aspects, the desire for sex but not its diseases, and the desire to travel to faraway places but not the headache of air travel. Applied to Nozick's account, people desire romantic love but not its curtailment of autonomy and the tying up of well-being. It then follows that when people desire to be in love, they do not desire to form a *we*.

Union and concern. Suppose that romantic love is characterized by the lovers' robust concern for each other. Alan Soble defines robust concern as follows: x having robust concern for y means that "x desires for y that which is good for y, x desires this for y's own sake, and x pursues y's good for y's benefit and not for x's (a corollary: sometimes at possible loss to x)" (1997, 68).[3] The concern is *robust* because x directs it at y's benefit, not x's; it is not selfish or even self-interested on the part of x. This view of concern – found in Aristotle's view of friendship – is in deep tension with the idea of union, so love cannot be *both* characterized by union and by robust concern. One has to go.

If the well-being of two lovers is intimately tied up with each other's, it is hard to see how they can have robust concern for each other. For if every time x's well-being goes up when y's does, and x's well-being goes down when y's does, it is not possible that when x does something to benefit y, x is also not benefiting himself (Soble 1997, 82). The idea is *not* that when x does something to benefit y, x is thinking, "I do this because it will also benefit me" (x might or might not think this). The idea is that Nozick's view cannot account for robust concern: where, in all this tying up of x's and y's well-being, is there "logical room" for robust concern? *Any* account of union that strongly ties together the lovers' interests, well-being, desires, and so on is going to have a difficult time accounting for robust concern, because to have it, x and y must be separate entities; only then x can view y (and y view x) as y's own person, with y's own needs and desires.[4]

Should we give up union or robust concern as a characteristic of love? We should give up union, because there are difficulties with it independent of its being in tension with robust concern, and because the idea of robust concern better explains what happens to the lover when the beloved's well-being goes up (or down). Suppose we accept that x and y have robust concern for each other. Then, when *y* fares badly, *x* feels bad or sad *because x* is concerned for *y*. In other words, the going up or down of lovers' well-being occurs not because they are tied to each other's well-being, but because *x* and *y* are robustly concerned for each other. On Nozick's view, the *reason* why *x*'s well-being goes up (or down) is that it is logically connected to *y*'s well-being going up (or down); because *x* and *y* are a *we*. On the alternative view, the reason why *x*'s well-being goes up is due to *x*'s concern for *y*'s well-being: because *x* is concerned for *y*, when *y* does well, *x* feels happy. It is telling that Nozick claims that the good and bad things that happen to *x* and *y* are not the same. This is what we would expect if *x* and *y* had concern for each other; we would also expect that *x*'s sadness or happiness varies depending on how important is the type of good or bad thing that happens to *y*.

To clarify, consider a simple example. Suppose that Henry has a lousy job. It does not pay very well, does not befit his abilities, and does not make proper use of his talents. But Henry likes it and does not want to quit, even though Catherine, Henry's *we*-mate, abhors it and wishes Henry would quit. She hates it not because it is low-paying (they are independently wealthy), but because she thinks it is undignified for Henry to occupy it. Suddenly, because of budget cuts, Henry gets fired. He is miserable to the point where his well-being is affected (he is seriously unhappy, lost). Catherine, however, though she feels a bit sad for him (she does love him, after all), is secretly happy.

If Nozick were right, Catherine's reaction would be puzzling, because her well-being should go down with Henry's. But it doesn't; it actually goes up (she is now happy all the time, whistles show-tunes, and is quite productive in her own work). To explain Catherine's reaction, we need to rely on concern: being concerned for Henry, knowing that his job was a dead-end, and knowing that he will eventually find another that will make him happy, Catherine is happy he lost the job; this event is good for Henry, even if Henry does not see it her way (is Catherine presumptuous to think that she knows what's good for Henry? We will touch on such issues when we discuss concern).

The example of Henry and Catherine is instructive. It shows that Nozick is wrong to think that a lover's well-being always goes up (or down) when the beloved's well-being goes up (or down), and it illustrates how robust concern better explains why a lover feels the way she does when the beloved's well-being is positively or negatively affected. Moreover, if it is merely the idea that when two people are in love each of their well-being is *affected* by what happens to the other's, this would be a true claim, but it should not be considered a union view of love (note how far we have come from Aristophanes's rich view), unless we are content that this is all that we mean by a "union" view of love.

One such philosopher is Robert Solomon. He rejects the union view of love that involves the "synthesis of a single identity out of two atomistic and autonomous human beings," and chooses instead "shared identity" and "shared selfhood," by which he means "self-identity conceived through identification with another person, group, or institution" (1990, 151). Solomon gives the example of someone who "identifies with a dozen or so others *as* a member of such-and-such a team" (1990, 151; emphasis in original). If I identify with my soccer team, then, when playing soccer every Saturday, my qualities (or properties) that move to the forefront are those pertaining to my soccer-playing abilities, such as how fast I run, how well I pass the ball to other team members, and how I perform as a member of a team. My other properties (that I am a philosopher, that I have a cat, that I have brown eyes) are downplayed but not eroded: I still have them, but they are not prominent or relevant to that particular identification.

To Solomon, "Romantic love ... must be understood ... as shared determination of self" (1990, 155). The individual selves of the lover and the beloved are (partly) determined in and through their relationship: "not just what I think of myself but what *you* think of me, and what I think of the way you think of me, and what you think of the way I think of you, and so on" (1990, 155). Suppose that I think of myself as an honest individual who does not like to mince his words. In a relationship, I need to also take into account what my beloved thinks of this; perhaps he thinks that it is not honesty but meanness. But I also need to take into account what I think of his thought: he's really wrong; it's not meanness, after all, but honesty. Thus, what I think of who I am and how I conceive of myself depend on my direct thoughts about myself, on others' thoughts about me (in this case, my beloved's), *and* on my thoughts about these.

Is this a view of determining a self? It is not clear what this idea really means. If it means something along the lines of defining who I am, figuring out what is my "core," then merely taking into account what my beloved thinks of my so-called honesty and of me in general is not enough to determine who I am. After all, if I only entertain these thoughts or mull them over, this will do nothing to define me. Something stronger is needed, such as accepting or rejecting these thoughts, because then I am able to define who I am (an honest person or a mean person). This means that the process of self-determination involves at least two steps. First, I take into account what I think of myself (I'm honest) and what my beloved thinks of me (I'm mean) and of my thoughts about his thoughts about myself (it's not honesty but meanness). Second, I endorse or reject these beliefs (he's wrong to think I am mean; I am, really, honest). In this way, and through my relationship with my beloved, I determine what my self is.[5]

However, romantic love is not special in this respect, because we take into account and then reject or accept not only what our beloveds think of us, but also many others: friends, family members, colleagues, neighbors, and even strangers. Solomon does not deny that selves are determined in such various ways, including by society and culture at large, but he believes that "much of the determination of self ... is to be located in our specific interpersonal relationships" (1990, 155). Although romantic love is not the only interpersonal relationship people have, it is primary because only our beloveds usually come to know us thoroughly and intimately, given that lovers tend to live with each other and spend most of their private time together. They know each other in deeper and more pervasive ways than, say, friends come to know each other. Perhaps this is why romantic love plays a primary role in the determination of the self.

Even if true, Solomon's would not be a view of union that "has bite." First, because the determination of the self can and does occur through different interpersonal relationships, it is difficult to see how in romantic love it is a form of union, even if romantic love is the primary way of determining the self. Second, on my interpretation of Solomon's view, in determining my self by accepting or rejecting my beloved's thoughts about me, it is necessary that I retain my individuality and autonomy (Solomon does not deny this), because without *some* autonomy on my part – some ability to make independent decisions about, among other things, myself – I am not in a position to accept or reject these thoughts of my beloved. This means that no union is going on – at least no thoroughgoing, interesting, or Nozickian union. If it exists, the union is innocuous, one in which lovers merely come to understand who they are in light of how they understand each other. (To call it "innocuous" is not to be glib; in societies where women or minorities are made to view themselves as having lesser value, members of these groups who are in love relationships with members of the dominant groups might come to think of themselves almost completely in terms of how their lovers think of them. Here, determination of self is malignant.) The fact that some degree of autonomy is necessary for such self-determination is crucial: it prevents a complete merging of selves, allowing lovers to feel concern for each other.

Moreover, any view of union that is a form of shared selves would have to be carefully articulated. If "shared selves" means that the lovers share their desires, beliefs, views, emotions, tastes, or experiences (it is not clear what else it could mean), three points must be made. First, the sharing cannot be literal. My belief that the sun is rising is *my* belief; it cannot, literally also be my beloved's (ditto for tastes, experiences, and so on). So "sharing" here must mean something like "both Raja and his beloved have the same *type* of belief, that the sun is rising"; we both have *two individual instances* of the same type of belief. Second, not all the beliefs, desires, and so on *can* be shared even in this sense. For example, my belief that I am in love with y, where y is my beloved, cannot be had by y, because "I" refers to me, not to her. Basically, any belief of mine that has the "I" as a part would be one that y cannot share. Third, not all beliefs and desires will be shared. In all likelihood, I will have desires and beliefs (and tastes and experiences) that my beloved does not. I might like cheeseless pizza, whereas she likes cheese-smothered pizza. I might believe that Jack is nosy and decrepit, whereas she might not have *any* beliefs about him. This is to say nothing about when she and I fight and disagree about all sorts of issues when it is likely that we do not share the majority of our desires and beliefs. So, once again, another possible way of understanding union – the idea of sharing selves – does not (and cannot) amount to any interesting form of union.

We now turn to concern.

Romantic Love and Robust Concern

If x claims to love y, but x shows no concern for y's well-being, happiness, welfare, and comfort, it is virtually impossible to defend the claim that x really loves *y*. If *x* is actively hostile toward *y*, acting in ways to destroy, or at least chip away at, *y*'s well-being, it is even more certain that *x* does not love *y*. We can, then, agree that if *x* loves *y*, *x* must have some minimal concern for *y*'s well-being. We can even agree that *x* must show quite a bit of concern for *y*'s well-being, given that this is typical of lovers.

But the agreement ends when we consider three further issues: first, whether this concern is *robust*; second, whether the well-being should be as seen by the beloved or as seen by the lover; and third, whether, supposing *x*'s conception of *y*'s welfare is utterly warped, we can still claim that *x* loves *y*. Let us start with the first issue.

Is the concern in romantic love robust? To recapitulate, *x* has robust concern for *y* means that "*x* desires for *y* that which is good for *y*, *x* desires this for *y*'s own sake, and *x* pursues *y*'s good for *y*'s benefit and not for *x*'s (a corollary: sometimes at possible loss to *x*)" (Soble 1997, 68). The concern is robust because *x*'s desiring *y*'s good is for *y*'s sake, not, ultimately, for *x*'s sake. Consider a simple example: suppose that each of Peter and Paul discovers a drowning child. Peter saves him because it is a child who is drowning, because it is a human life, period. Paul saves him because this will make Paul look good in the eyes of his community. While Peter seeks the child's good only for the child's sake, Paul seeks it as a means to his (Paul's) own good. Peter's concern is robust; Paul's is not. The issue is whether the concern in romantic love can be robust.

Some philosophers believe that the concern in romantic love is selfish or self-interested (selfishness and self-interestedness are not the same; I ignore this for the moment). One argument is that because human beings are selfish, and they always act selfishly, love is no exception. So any concern *x* shows for *y* is, appearances notwithstanding, ultimately selfish. However, the view that human beings always act selfishly is false because they sometimes do good things for others with no positive repercussions to their own well-being, sometimes even with negative repercussions (Shoemaker 2006, 21–24). So it is not true that we always act selfishly. And if it is not true that we always act selfishly, it needs to be shown why in romantic love we do.

Let us suppose that people do always act selfishly. Although it would then follow that lovers' concern for their beloveds is ultimately selfish, this would have nothing to do with love as such, but with the fact that this is how people always behave. But then the idea that the concern in romantic love is not robust becomes uninteresting, because there is nothing special about romantic love in this respect.

Philosophers who argue that romantic love is selfish usually do so because of their beliefs about the nature of romantic love. The Danish philosopher Soren Kierkegaard argues that both erotic love and friendship are morally dubious because they involve preferences:

> That passionate preference is another form of self-love will now be shown ... just as self-love centres exclusively about this *self* – whereby it is

self-love, just so does erotic love's passionate preference centre around the one and only beloved … The beloved [is] therefore called … the *other-self*, the *other-I* … But wherein lies self-love? It lies in the I, in the self.

(Kierkegaard 1962, 66)

X romantically loves y because *y*, somehow, suits x's needs and desires. X prefers *y* over others because, in short, *y* makes x happy. If this is the reason why x loves *y*, then x's love for *y* is ultimately selfish or self-interested.[6] The contemporary philosopher Russell Vannoy puts the point this way: "The erotic lover is ordinarily quite selective, choosing for a mate one who has attractive qualities that stir the emotions and gratify the lover's own needs and self-interest" (1980, 132). The idea is not that romantic love is selfish because the lover elevates one person over all others, thus treating that one person preferentially. *This* claim might be morally problematic, but it need not involve selfishness. Instead, the claim is that the lover treats the beloved preferentially not because he is ultimately motivated by the well-being of the beloved, but by his own. This is the first reason given why romantic love is selfish.

The selfishness, however, also consists in the fact that people *want* to be preferred in this way. Unlike *agapic* love (see Chapter 3), which requires us to love people as people, as equally God's children, we want to be loved for who we are as individuals. Vannoy again puts the point nicely:

> the loved one would ordinarily be distressed to think her lover would give his love to just anybody. Nor would she ordinarily accept a love given out of purely altruistic considerations, that is, someone who gives his love to whomever he sees as needing love, regardless of other qualities.
>
> (Vannoy 1980, 133)

Not only do we prefer and select who is to receive our love, we prefer to be the recipients of such selections. We do not want to be "charity cases" – this does not sit well with our pride.

There is a third reason why romantic love is selfish. Suppose that by donating $50.00 to a charitable organization I could greatly improve the life of a poor child. I jump at the opportunity, only to realize that someone else has donated the money and beat me to it. Unless I am psychologically ill this would not bother me. I could always donate the money to make another child happy. But suppose that someone else "beats me" to making my beloved happy by doing all the things I could have done to make her happy. Typically, a lover's reactions would be anger and jealousy, not "Oh, pouring your heart out to Brett and having sex with him makes you happy? Just go ahead and do so, honey. Whatever makes you happy." This reaction indicates that the lover's motives are selfish: *he* wants to be the one to provide the beloved with happiness, not someone else.

But exactly how does selfishness enter the picture? And how is it connected with concern? According to the first reason, x selects from among many the one person who most suits *x* and who makes *x happy*. According to the third, *x* strives to make the relationship with *y* a success and to make *y* happy because if *y* is unhappy *x* would be unhappy (one common answer to the question, "Why do you love me?" is "Because you make me happy"). According to the second reason, being selected and loved for who we are individually makes us feel wanted, desired, and needed. This makes us happy. In all this, "happy" does not only mean *feeling* good, but that our lives have meaning, we are useful, we have companionship, we are not lonely, we are important to someone, we are (somewhat) more financially and emotionally secure, and, if we're gay, we double our wardrobes. "Happiness" does not refer only to a feeling but to well-being in general. Romantic love is selfish because it contributes positively to the well-being of each lover.

Are these arguments for the selfishness of romantic love convincing? Suppose that I claim I want or need oxygen in order to breathe, some financial assets to be able to live a somewhat decent life, some political freedom to be able to do the things I want, and physical health so that I can maneuver around this world (at least get from one room to another). These things are all necessary, basic goods that anyone would want to have to lead a minimally decent life. They are not superfluous goods that only some human beings need to live luxuri-ously. In desiring them we are not being selfish; we are merely asking for what is necessary for our lives to even take off. And if wanting them were selfish, then "being selfish" would no longer have bad connotations or be immoral.

If happiness and well-being are also basic, necessary goods, then when people seek or want them, they seek or want what is expected of them to seek or want. We all have an interest in being happy; without it we would be, well, unhappy. When someone offers happiness as a reason why she chose a career or a country of residence, we don't balk and exclaim, "How selfish of her!" (unless in doing so she is neglecting important obligations which she has to others). If romantic love makes people happy or is a major source of happiness, seeking it would be morally acceptable self-interest, not selfishness. There is no agreed-upon philosophical definition of selfishness, but we can plausibly char-acterize the selfish person as someone who constantly seeks her own good, often superfluous goods, without paying heed to the needs of others, and some-times at the expense of others. She always puts her needs and desires first, whether for the short term or the long term. Seeking romantic love is not like that. To desire love is not, as such, to do so at the expense of others. So the fact that people seek romantic love and do so by selecting one person from among many is not a matter of selfishness, but of desiring happiness, which is one form of morally acceptable self-interest.

Similar considerations apply to people wanting to feel good about themselves. Normally, wanting to feel good about myself is not a matter of selfishness (it is so only under special circumstances, as when I feel good about myself by humiliating others). It would be morally undesirable were people to live either feeling nothing particularly good or feeling bad about themselves. So people wanting to feel good about themselves is not morally impermissible.

Thus, happiness and feeling good about ourselves are not normally selfish reasons for wanting romantic love (cf. Soble 1990, 258–260).

We may still worry, however, that if people seek love to be happy, every time x shows concern for y, x is thinking that this makes x happy ("I'll bake the best cake ever for y because y likes cakes, and if y is happy then I'm happy!"). Isn't this the height of selfishness? Not quite, because we should not confuse the reasons for why we fall in love with how we *behave* when in love. The first is about the *basis* of love; the second is about the *mode* of loving (cf. Soble 1990, 261).

An analogy with morality is illuminating. Some philosophers (e.g., Aristotle) believe that in order for people to be happy and to lead well-lived lives, they should be virtuous. They need to inculcate in themselves character traits such as courage, justice, temperance, and generosity. But once such traits are part of a person's character, they go on "automatic pilot": they don't function by asking the question, "If I now act bravely (or justly or generously or temperately), will my action make me happy?" Indeed, if they operate this way they would not be virtuous at all, because being just or courageous is not (ironically!) about the happiness of the person who has the virtues, but about being just, generous, brave toward *others*. The idea is that in order to be happy we should be virtuous, but once we are virtuous we don't act from motives of happiness, but from motives specific to each virtue (some of which may sometimes lead to our death or serious injury, as when we get maimed or killed for being brave). Thus we have two claims occupying two different levels of discussion (cf. Hursthouse 1986).

Something similar happens with romantic love. Our general reasons for wanting to be in love may very well be personal happiness. But once we are in love we are "hooked," and we don't relate to our beloveds by asking "What's in it for me?" When I buy a present for my beloved on his birthday or tend to him when he is sick, I do not do so *because* this will make him happy or feel better and *therefore make me happy*; I do so only out of the first two considerations (his happiness and his feeling better), with my happiness trailing along as a side-effect. This does not mean that lovers should never raise questions about their happiness. If a woman's husband constantly cheats on her, then, even if she deeply loves him, at some point she will ask herself, "What about me? What about *my* happiness? Can I just go on neglecting myself and what's good for me?" Although issues about happiness function at the base of love, they can also function at the day-to-day level of how lovers relate to each other only under special circumstances, not all or most of the time.

Only the third reason remains for thinking that romantic love is selfish: lovers wanting to be the source of their beloveds' happiness, not being content to have others as this source. Suppose that Nadia and Hassan are in love, but Nadia is always upset and jealous whenever Hassan spends time with his friends, he is getting along with his co-workers and happy at work, and, in general, she perceives that he is happy and doing well *because of others*. Without a special background story, not only would Nadia strike us as being somewhat deranged, she would also not seem to be concerned with Hassan's happiness and well-being, because we should not expect Hassan's well-being to be maintained and promoted only by her. Well-being and happiness have multiple sources and require different ways to be sustained and promoted. No single person – not even a lover – can do so by herself. If Nadia thinks she can, she is massively deluded; if she doesn't think she can but is nonetheless upset that others tend to Hassan's well-being, then she doesn't really care for it.

So if a lover is to show proper concern for the well-being of her beloved, she must allow him access to the multiple sources and ways that sustain and promote his happiness and welfare. Fortunately, this accords with how most lovers actually act; they are happy to see their beloveds spending time with their friends, engaged in hobbies, doing well at work, and experiencing the range of human emotions in reaction to all sorts of events, not just to what the lovers say and do. So the third reason for why romantic love is selfish should be restricted to some, not all, types of sources that maintain the happiness and well-being of the beloved.

Consider parenting. It may be important for a child's well-being that the child's parents, not just anybody, attend to it. The care, sense of security, and sense of being loved are three crucial ways (among others) for parents to engage in when seeing to a child's welfare. Strangers may not be up to the task (Soble 1990, 265). Moreover, the parents' tending to the child's well-being is important for the relationship between the child and her parents. Love and other intimate relationships are similar: there are areas where it is crucial for the lovers to be the ones who tend to the well-being of their beloveds, both for the sake of the beloved and for the relationship itself. The main example of such areas – intimacy – covers a wide range of activities: sexual activities, disclosures of deep personal matters, and the day-to-day living together (which itself includes even further varieties). These involve trust, vulnerability, a sense of security, comfort, and emotional stability (among others). To a large extent, both parties' well-being hinges on the successful maintenance and promotion of these elements. If the beloved secures these elements through people other than his lover, doubts can be raised about the success of the relationship. Conversely, when the lover insists on being the one to maintain and promote these elements of her beloved's well-being, she has a morally legitimate self-interest in wanting to be the one to do so. For if she is not the one, the relationship would in all likelihood deteriorate, putting her own happiness and well-being at stake (remember that seeking and maintaining one's own happiness is a morally acceptable form of self-interest). Therefore, lovers who insist on being the ones to engage in such maintenance and promotion of their beloveds' well-being are not thereby being selfish (Halwani 2003, 100–101). The third reason, then, is not convincing.

Thus we have good reasons to conclude that romantic love is not selfish and that the concern that lovers show each other is robust.

Concern, well-being, and autonomy. Granted that the concern in romantic love is robust, another issue immediately arises: Should the happiness or well-being of the beloved be seen through the lover's or the beloved's eyes? That is, should we think of the well-being of the beloved in terms of how the lover thinks of it or how the beloved does? Consider the following examples: (1) Pedro smokes; he knows that smoking is dangerous to his health, but he downplays its importance; Julio, his lover, begs to differ. (2) Pedro thinks that his friend, Emily, is good and trustworthy; Julio thinks she is a bad influence. (3) Pedro thinks that his job is fantastic, affording him plenty of opportunity to climb to the top; Julio thinks it's a dead-end job and that Pedro is misreading the situation at work. (4) Pedro loves to eat fried and fatty foods, thinking that their effects on his health are minimal; Julio disagrees and wants Pedro to eat more healthily. (5) Pedro is an atheist and doesn't give a damn about religion; Julio is a Christian and believes that, if Pedro doesn't mend his ways, he will rot in hell. In all these cases, there's a wide gap between how Julio conceives of Pedro's well-being and how Pedro conceives of it. If Julio is concerned for Pedro's well-being, how is he to think of it?

A deceptive answer is that Julio should act on his beliefs; after all, if this is how he perceives the situation, he should act according to his judgment. But this won't do. First, he could be wrong; if he is and acts on his mistaken views, he would act in ways contrary to Pedro's well-being, thus defeating his own (Julio's) professed goals of promoting it. Second, even if he is not wrong, in acting on his beliefs, especially all or most of the time, he is likely to drive Pedro away by not heeding his desires regarding these matters, thus undermining the very relationship he values with him (and if Julio doesn't act on his beliefs all the time, how should he decide when to do so and when to act on Pedro's beliefs?). Third, and most important, Pedro's views are part of his autonomy and independence, and autonomy is part of Pedro's well-being. If Julio has robust concern for Pedro's well-being, he must respect his autonomy, which means that he should – at least sometimes – respect Pedro's wishes, even if he disagrees with them.

So if Julio loves Pedro and is robustly concerned for his well-being, should he promote it as he sees it or as Pedro does? Without minimizing the seriousness of this issue, and granting that it is likely to be a problem in many love relationships, it does not really affect the idea that in love the lovers have robust concern for each other's happiness and well-being. To see this, suppose that Julio finds out that Pedro's metabolism is such that his habit of eating fatty foods will not endanger his health. Julio would then not object to Pedro's eating fatty foods. The real issue is that the robust concern that lovers have for each other is, ultimately, objective, not how Julio and Pedro see it. How they see it is a sign that they don't agree on what their well-being really is. But in principle, there is no conflict; if both Julio and Pedro can have access to what each of their well-being objectively consists of, they would have no disagreement about what and (possibly) how it should be promoted (Soble 1990, 268–270).

For two reasons, we are not quite out of the woods yet. First, we may be doubtful that all such disagreements between Pedro and Julio can be resolved even in principle, because some may be indeterminate – having no objective answer. Any example here is bound to be controversial, so I won't offer any. But we should keep the possibility of non-objective answers to these disagreements open.

Second, even if all disagreements over Pedro's well-being have objective answers, the *extent* to which Julio should act to promote Pedro's well-being remains an issue. Consider an extreme case. Suppose that Josephine is a womanizer, a gambler, drinks excessively, cannot keep a steady job, and is abusive toward Mary, her long-time beloved. Mary is a good woman who has stood by Josephine through thick and thin and has never seriously considered dumping her. Josephine, despite all her faults, knows that Mary has tied herself to a sinking ship: as long as she is with her, Mary's well-being and happiness are in dire jeopardy. If Josephine is at all concerned for Mary, she should leave her, despite Mary's predictable protestations. Josephine is correct: objectively speaking, Mary should be set free for her own good.

So even if we set aside questions about the objectivity as to how lovers see their well-being, and even if we assume that they agree on what each other's well-being consists of, sometimes concern for the well-being of *y* requires *x* to make sacrifices. In Josephine and Mary's case the sacrifice is ultimate, requiring Josephine to break up with Mary for Mary's own good. Not all cases are extreme, but they require *x* to sacrifice something for *y*'s good. Here is a not-so-unusual example: Rachel and Muna are another lesbian couple who are very much in love. All is going well until Muna finds out she has a debilitating sickness that requires her to stay at home. Muna's good and well-being, needless to say, consist of her receiving care, rest, and proper attention. Even if Rachel and Muna can afford a nurse, Rachel will still have to devote time, energy, and attention to Muna. She must make this sacrifice, with no issues here about whether they disagree on Muna's good or whether there is an objective answer about what that good is.

But sacrifice has its limits: Martha has recently changed: she is unable to keep a steady job, she has sex with lots of men, she's addicted to reality TV, and she drinks excessively. Her slow deterioration has occurred owing to a series of bad choices and misfortunes in her life. Her long-time beloved, Joseph, has stood by her and tried to get her back on track. Although he loves her, he is beginning to wonder whether she will ever become the Martha he once knew. He begins to wonder whether all the sacrifices he is making are worth it and whether he will ever be happy again.

These examples show that, first, even if lovers agree on what each of their good is, they will in all likelihood need to make sacrifices for each other. Conceptually speaking, if lovers agree on what their well-being is, it does not follow that no sacrifices have to be made for each other's well-being (so much for Nozick's tying together the well-being of each!). Second, in extreme cases, the sacrifices can be so high that they require the demise of the very relationship of the lovers. Conceptually speaking, *x*'s sacrificing his being in a relationship with *y* for *y*'s sake shows how sacrifice can be logically at odds with the very point of being in a relationship, namely *x*'s happiness. Third, there are cases in which it is not clear whether and to what extent *x* should go on sacrificing for *y*. Conceptually speaking, we know that *x* shows robust concern for *y*, but it is not clear whether this concern should stop and, if it should stop, at which point.

X's warped conception of y's *good*. We know that in romantic love, *x*'s concern for *y* can be robust, that in many cases it is indeed robust, that *x* sometimes needs to make sacrifices for *y*, and that *x* and *y* need not always agree on the nature of *y*'s welfare. Underlining all this is the idea that romantic love, like all types of love, necessarily involves concern for the beloved's well-being. However, if *x*'s view of *y*'s well-being is warped, can we still defend this claim? Yes, but *x*'s love will be deeply flawed.

We should not characterize any false view by *x* of *y*'s well-being as warped. Being false is necessary, but not sufficient, for *x*'s view to be warped. Being based on improper knowledge of *y* is also not sufficient (probably not even necessary). The view must be detrimental to *y*'s well-being were *x* to act on it. Consider two examples.

First, suppose that Jacob, a Humbert Humbert-like person (the main character from Nabokov's *Lolita*) thinks that Maggie, a 13-year old, is better off being with a man his age (48 years old, say). For some reason, Jacob thinks that Maggie's good consists of having a romantic relationship (which includes sex) with him. Suppose also that Joshua, a gay man in his forties, wants to revive the good old times of classical Greece. He thinks the good of 12-year-old boys consists of him falling in love with them (or boys around that age), having sex with them, and educating them by imparting his wisdom to them (as the Greeks did). Joshua meets, seduces, and falls in love with Bruce, a 13-year-old boy. In both of these cases, were the two older men to fall in love with their respective girl and boy and to act on their view of what the girl and boy's well-being consists of, chances are that such relationships would ruin the young people's well-being.

As a second example, one reflecting perhaps a more common case, consider Jarvis, who is married to and in love with Telulah. Jarvis firmly believes that a woman's place is at home, tending to her husband and children. He refuses to allow Telulah any work outside the home, to have an enriching social life, or to develop any of her talents. While of course raising children and being a good spouse are not usually a waste of someone's time and talents, they need not be done at the expense of other things. Thus, by denying Telulah the ability to develop her talents and pursue projects that she finds interesting, Jarvis is acting in a way that is quite detrimental to her welfare.

We can make one of two claims about the above cases: (1) *x* loves *y* but *x*'s love for *y* is deeply flawed on moral (and other) grounds, or (2) *x* does not love *y*. The main reason to accept (2) is that "real" love cannot be so destructive to the beloved; "real" love must be, if not beneficial to the beloved, at least not detrimental to her. But as a *general* reason for genuine, as opposed to fake, love, this idea won't do, because as we know all too well, there are many cases of love that are destructive of the beloved (and the lover), including cases of lovers who physically or emotionally abuse their beloveds. Human psychology in all its complexity often interferes to render destructive many cases of genuine love. Those who say that "real" love is not destructive of the beloved or her well-being have in mind a *normative* notion of "real" or "genuine" love, one opposed to "bad" or "immoral" love. If this is true, we should accept (1), that cases of love in which *x* has a warped view of *y*'s well-being are real, but immoral or bad.

Are there are any reasons for accepting (1) other than that (2) is not convincing? The main reason is that the lovers in these cases not only *say* that they love *y*, but they also believe and feel it. They are genuinely concerned with the well-being of their beloveds but have a wrong view of it, one that would actually be destructive to the beloved were they to act on it. But having false beliefs is not enough to show that their love is not genuine. Consider by analogy those who have zeal and fervor for their country and religion, but who think that the best or only way to preserve and enhance their country or religion is by subduing other countries or killing members of other religions. We don't usually claim that their love for their country or religion is fake; if anything, it is all too real. Instead, they are fanatics: they are utterly misguided in their love and how to secure its object. Now although we don't call lovers such as Jacob, Joshua, and Jarvis "fanatics," we have no good reason to doubt their love; only that they don't love properly.

We may then conclude that a lover's warped views about his beloved's well-being need not make the love any less real. It's "messed up" love, but love nonetheless.

Sex and the Durability of Romantic Love

We saw in Chapter 1 that one of the generally necessary features of love is the lover's sexual desire for the beloved, a desire that might not remain throughout the love relationship. As a generally necessary feature, sexual desire *characterizes* romantic love, but not every case of romantic love need have it. (I phrase this feature in terms of *desire* instead of *activity* because sexual desire is not always consummated. If we put the feature in terms of sexual activity, many cases of romantic love would implausibly lack a sexual dimension simply because the lovers did not have sex.)

However, lovers' sexual desire for each other need not – and often does not – continue for as long as the love lasts. The phenomenon of the "death of desire" eventually sets in, and the lovers – having become used to and familiar with each other's bodies – no longer find each other sexually exciting (having grown older, flabbier, and more wrinkly doesn't help, either). This does not necessarily mean that they stop having sex with each other (though some do), but that they lose the sexual excitement and thrill of wanting each other's bodies. They no longer lust after each other (which is not the same as finding each other repulsive).

Why are sexual desire and activity so important to understanding romantic love? First, in many cases, romantic love is generated, at least partly, by sexual desire. When x and y are sexually attracted to each other, the sexual attraction, even if not consummated, plays a crucial role in getting them to be with each other, to want to be with each other, and to know each other. The longer the sexual desire is active and alive, the longer x and y spend time with each other and enjoy each other's company. The time spent together, along with x and y's desires to touch, delight in, and enjoy each another, create a strong intimacy, which is the causal basis of their love. It allows the love to exist and flower.

Second, sexual desire and activity help cement the love, including those cases in which they do not generate it. For example, Richard and Ken met in graduate school but were not initially sexually attracted to each other. They became friends and occasionally spent time with each other. After a while, they increasingly desired to be with each other because they enjoyed their conversations, made each other laugh, and so on. As their friendship progressed, they began to find each other sexually attractive. Eventually, they decided or realized that they had "more" than just friendship; they had love. They had sex, and it helped their love to grow. Sexual desire and activity cemented the love between them.

Sexual desire and activity are crucial vehicles for understanding romantic love. Sex not only explains how love is generated, it also explains how an already existing young love is cemented. It does this by creating shared and deeply intimate pleasurable experiences, and by allowing the lovers to express their love for each other through sex (these two are different: casual sexual encounters tend to be deep and intimate, yet they do not express love, though they might express other emotions). Because expressing love is important for sustaining love, it bears more discussion.

Some philosophers doubt that sexual activity can express love. Russell Vannoy denies it and asks rhetorically, "Indeed, just how does a penis that is vigorously thrusting up and down in a vagina express anything at all, with the possible exception of dominance (which is hardly the same thing as love)? If one moves the penis slowly, is this an expression of love? The absurdity of this line of thinking is evident" (1980, 11). But the absurdity may be evident only because Vannoy latches on to the *manner* in which sex is engaged, and it may be that whether sex expresses love has nothing or little to do with *how* two lovers have sex. Two lovers, that is, can express their love for each other by having sex vigorously or tenderly, even painfully, as when x puts nipple-clamps on y during their lovemaking to please and express her love for y.

Vannoy may be right that it is not clear how having sex can express love. He argues that if sexual behavior usually considered to be an expression of love, such as gentle kissing and caressing, can also occur between strangers, how can the first be an expression of love while the second is not? (1997, 248). The context – that the two people are in love – is not a sufficient explanation, because there are many other things that lovers do (e.g., taking out the garbage) that don't express love (1997, 249). The intention to express love through sex won't do, either, since "some rapists have the odd notion that they are expressing love for their victims" (1997, 251).

Vannoy's argument is interesting, but it proves too much. Think of the many ways in which we express love for others: cooking them dinner, taking them out to their favorite museums or amusement parks, buying them presents. As Vannoy would claim, it is hard to see how each of these activities expresses love; after all, I can go through the same motions of cooking dinner for my boss, but this doesn't mean that I am expressing my love for him. I might also cook dinner for my beloved but without expressing love for her. Instead of rejecting all cases of sex as capable of expressing love, we need to explain or analyze exactly how some do. I do not pursue such an analysis, but I suspect that context is essential, one that includes the specific history of the couple, and the moods and the setting preceding and during the sex act (a sex act starts by expressing love and shifts to expressing anger owing to changes in the prevailing mood). So sex can somehow express love, cementing, as it does so, that love.

There are two important questions at this point. First, if sexual desire for the beloved can die, what is it that sustains the love? I begin to address this issue below and conclude in Chapter 3. Second, why is it that x and y's sexual desire for each other is expected to wane and die, but not their love? I address this question next.

The exclusivity of romantic love. One straightforward answer is deceptively simple: sexual desire is by its very nature *not* exclusive, whereas romantic love is. If correct, this answer explains why sexual desire and love eventually part company. Part of this answer seems true: almost everyone finds more than one person sexually desirable at one time and over time. Perhaps the only time during which sexual desire tends to be exclusive is in the early, passionate stages of love when the lovers are absorbed in each other. Once this stage is passed the lovers' eyes begin to rove, finding other people sexually desirable. Sexual desire is not by its "nature" exclusive to one person (the beloved) at one time, let alone to one person (the beloved) for the duration of the lover's lifetime. However, some believe that romantic love is by its nature exclusive to one person; that, somehow, if x loves both y and z at the same time, then x's love (for y? for z? for both?) is not really love.

The exclusivity of romantic love could mean one of two things. It could mean, first, that *at one time* x can only love one person, or, second, that x can love only one person for x's entire lifetime (that is, if x loves y, then whatever emotion x feels for z, at any point in x's life, it is not love) (Soble 1990, 169–70). Because it is obvious that x can serially love more than one person during x's lifetime, I set aside the second meaning of "exclusivity." The issue, then, is whether one can romantically love more than one person simultaneously.

Two considerations indicate that romantic love is not exclusive. First, other types of love are not exclusive: to give two examples, parents love their children simultaneously, and friends love their many friends simultaneously. Why should romantic love be different in this respect? Second, every other emotion can be directed simultaneously at more than one object, without raising any philosophical eyebrows: one can hate, be jealous of, envy, feel sad for, pity, and be angry at many people at the same time. If love is an emotion, why would it be any different?

One argument for love's exclusivity is that love requires things that entail its exclusivity. What things? When x and y are in a love relationship, they need to devote time, attention, energy, and commitment to each other. These are time-consuming (especially if x and y work or have other things to attend to). So to have more than one love at a time seems impossible.

This argument, however, seems to be about practical considerations surrounding love, not the "nature" of love (Soble 1990, 172). In addition, practical considerations or not, friends often face the same requirements, yet friendship is non-exclusive. Perhaps love, by its very nature, demands more time and energy on the part of the lovers to attend to each other than friendship does. But we have to be careful that the picture of love we rely on to defend this point is not culturally contingent. That is, the idea that love is more demanding in these respects than friendship may be peculiar to our age and cultural ways. If it is, then love would not be more demanding than friendship by its "nature."

A second argument for love's exclusivity emphasizes love's conceptual, not practical, aspects that make love exclusive: intimacy, trust, and privacy. One cannot be intimate with many people, trust many people (in deep, meaningful ways), or conduct a private life with many people, because intimacy, trust, and privacy thrive only among members of small groups. Telling a deep secret to twelve people makes it really no longer a secret. Because romantic love requires these elements, it is exclusive.

Although it is true that for romantic love to succeed it needs trust, privacy, and intimacy, the argument does not show love's exclusivity; instead it shows that love's non-exclusivity cannot mean having *too many* beloveds, a claim different from that love is confined to one and only one person at a time. Consider friendship. Aristotle, in discussing the number of friends one can have, offers the correct insight that "those who have many friends and treat everyone as close to them seem to be friends to no one" (1999, 1171a16). Aristotle gives for friendship an argument similar to that for the exclusivity of love: spreading yourself too thinly defeats the very requirement of love. Yet friendship is not exclusive to only two friends. So the above argument does not show that love is exclusive, only that love, like friendship, cannot have too many beloveds.

A third argument for the exclusivity of love relies on the concern found in love. When x loves y, x's concern for y's well-being is so deep and strong that x cannot love another person. This argument can be about practical issues: because of the time and energy x needs to promote y's well-being, x has no time for another person. It could also be conceptual: that, somehow, romantic love requires that x be concerned for the well-being of y and only of y.

Both forms of the argument are unconvincing. Friends are concerned for the well-being of their friends, yet they manage to practically pull this off with multiple friends. Moreover, there is no good reason to think that romantic love conceptually requires that the lover be concerned with only the beloved's well-being. Does the welfare of strangers have no claims on the lover? What about the lover's friends? If the lovers have children, can they not show concern for them because, somehow, they can only show concern for each other, as this argument requires? Clearly, we are able to show deep concern for more than one person (though, again, not to too many), so this third argument fails.

In arguing for romantic love's exclusivity, we should not make four assumptions that could skew our conclusions. First, we should not assume a love *relationship*: there is a difference between romantic love as an emotion and romantic love manifesting itself in a relationship. The first two arguments conclude that non-exclusive love is impossible because they assume that the lover is (or tries to be) in more than one love *relationship*. If he were, say, in a love relationship with y but *only felt* love for z, the alleged practical and conceptual difficulties with multiple loves would not be convincing.

Second, we should not assume that the love is reciprocated (Soble 1990, 190). Chapter 1 showed that we know that a generally necessary feature of love is that the lovers move toward marriage (a relationship), but only if the love is reciprocated. The practical arguments for love's exclusivity assume reciprocity, and although the conceptual arguments need not assume it (x can love z, share intimate moments with z, and be concerned for z's well-being, even if z does not love x back), doing so skews these arguments' conclusions because reciprocity allows for deeper and more pervasive forms of intimacy and concern.

Third, we should not assume whatever requirement or feature we think is part of love to exist to the highest degree (Soble 1990, 190). For example, if concern is a feature of love, we should not assume that it exists to the highest degree in any case of love. If sharing intimate moments is a requirement, we should not assume that the sharing is thoroughgoing. Depending on the case, it may or may not be. If we assume this, we tip the scales unfairly in favor of exclusivity by making it virtually impossible for a lover to show concern for or be intimate with more than one beloved.

Fourth, we should not assume a particular cultural idea of how love is or should be conducted. In many cultures romantic love is both very much valued and elevated as one of the best types of relationships people can have. Indeed, the alleged exclusivity of love may be part of such a cultural picture, a picture that fuels and supports ideas of love requiring much of the lover's time and energy to be spent with the lover's one and only beloved, and much of the lover's concern to be directed toward the beloved. Yet it may be that love works in different ways.

Although the arguments for romantic love's exclusivity fail to show that love is exclusive, they show its *limited number* of multiple instances. Like sexual desire, romantic love is not exclusive, but unlike sexual desire, its objects are not as many.

I end this section with a warning. It is one thing to conclude that arguments for love's exclusivity fail, but it is another to present convincing cases of non-exclusive love (Soble 1990, 174). This exercise, however, I leave to the reader.

The durability of romantic love. If sexual desire for our beloveds usually wanes or dies, what is it that sustains the love between the lovers? In Chapter 1, I claimed that a non-generally necessary feature of love is that it is a long-term emotion. This is the durability of love, sometimes also called "constancy" (a stronger term). The idea is that for love to be real or genuine it must endure, last for a long time, or even be constant. On one view (Soble calls it "strict constancy"), if x loves y, then x continues to love y as long as y (and x, of course) is alive (I set aside the difficult issues raised by loving the dead); that is, if x's love ends before y dies, then whatever x felt toward y was not love (Soble 1990, 207). Another view – "indefinite constancy" – requires only that x's emotion for y last for *some* time for it to be love (Soble 1990, 207). This view does not specify the length of time, only requiring that it last for some time.

Constancy and exclusivity are not the same. If love is constant but not exclusive, x can simultaneously love y and z and do so constantly (either for the rest of y and z's lifetimes or for an indefinite period). If love is exclusive but not constant, x's loving y means that x loves y and only y, but x may stop doing so before y dies (strict constancy) or after only a few months (indefinite constancy).

To evaluate the two views of strict and indefinite constancy, let us return to sexual desire. We know that sexual desire and activity play a crucial role in generating and cementing love. However, we should distinguish between the *causal* and the *conceptual* roles that sex plays. To see the difference, consider the following example. Sexual desire can help generate and cement the love between Ringo and Star. Suppose we ask Star *why* she loves Ringo (not *how she came to* love him). She answers, "Because he's smart, he's funny, and he really gets along with my mother." Note the absence of any sexual reasons (e.g., Ringo's sexual prowess) or sexually based reasons (e.g., his physical features), which indicates that even though sexual desire and activity may play a role in how a love starts and in how it is strengthened, it may not play a role in providing reasons for why Star loves Ringo. The first is a causal role, the second conceptual. Of course, sex may also play a conceptual role; after all, Star could have mentioned sex as one of her reasons for loving Ringo, but she didn't, and that's the point.

The distinction between sex's causal and conceptual roles is key to answering the question about love's durability. Indeed, the key is the *general* distinction between the two roles that any love-relevant feature has. For example, much as sex can play a causal role in generating Star's love for Ringo, his wit can play a similar role. But it may not be a reason why Star loves him. Or it may. That is, any love-relevant feature can play a role in generating and cementing x's love for y, as a reason for why x loves y, or both.

How is this distinction key to addressing the durability of love? Star loves Ringo because he's smart, funny, and gets along with her mother. If these are the only reasons why she loves him and they *endure as the reasons for her love*, then

Star's sexual desires (for Ringo) dying or not dying are irrelevant for why her love for him endures, because the duration of her love depends on her *reasons* for loving Ringo, among which sexual desires do not figure. As long as these reasons endure, so does her love. To generalize, what is crucial in addressing the constancy or durability of love is not the causal role the features play, but their conceptual or reason-providing role. Along these lines, had sexual desires for Ringo played a reason-providing role for Star's love, they will play a role in whether her love for him endures.

The danger is when x's love for y is based *only* on sexual desires. Because sexual desires for our beloveds usually wane and eventually die, the love will also die. If Star loves Ringo *only* because he has a large penis, because he has a nice hairy chest, and because he talks dirty to her during sex, then once Star's awe for Ringo's penis goes away, his hairy chest looks to her more like an ugly carpet, and she loses interest in Ringo's sexual dirty talk, her love dies, too.

There is no need for despair. The fact is that people's love for each other is usually based on features other than only sex. So even if sexual features figure as part of the set of reasons why x loves y, they are not the only ones. If they wither away, the remaining reasons will sustain the love. Ringo's being smart, funny, and getting along with Star's mother will (hopefully) do the job.

But what if Ringo becomes stupid (or Star realizes that he never really was smart)? What if he stops being funny or keeps repeating the same old, by-now-tired jokes? What if he and Star's mother no longer get along? Well, we can hope that after being together for a while, Star starts to love Ringo for additional reasons. Perhaps Star now loves Ringo because he helps around the house, because he's a good father, and because he entertains well when they have guests.

But there are no guarantees. Star may not have reasons additional to, or that replace, the old, defunct ones. When this happens, and unless Star's love for Ringo is either *agapic* or not based on reasons (see Chapter 3), then the love dies (which is not the same as the relationship ending; many couples stay together out of dependency, need, lack of strength to break up, or even sheer habit).

If romantic love lasts as long as the reasons on which it is based last, strict constancy would be true only if the reasons for love are themselves strictly constant. Whether a reason for love lasts or is strictly constant depends on the reason – some last and some don't. Perhaps a more interesting issue is whether there are any reasons for love that are immune to change. It is hard to see how there are any, especially if reasons for love are tied to our contingent, changing nature; if they are not, they are probably irrelevant. For example, if Star loves Ringo because "triangles have three sides" or because "two plus two equals four," then her love is "based" on non-changing reasons (triangles will never stop having three sides). But then it is virtually impossible to see *how* these reasons *can be the basis* of her love for Ringo: what does the fact that triangles have three sides have to do with him?

We can conclude, tentatively and conditionally, that strict constancy is false: if romantic love is based on reasons, and if these reasons are subject to change, it is implausible to logically require that for an emotion to be love it must last as long as the beloved (and the lover) lasts – unless we agree that few people have ever loved.

What about indefinite constancy? One advantage of this view is its recognition that love need not last for as long as the beloved lives, and that it might end once the lover's reasons for loving end. But one obvious problem with this view is that because it does not tell us how long a love must last for it to be love, it is empty and uninformative, rendering it useless in helping us decide in which case *x*'s emotion for *y* is love and in which case it is not: if Star's love for Ringo died after two years, was it love? What if it died after one year? Three months? Suppose, however, that even an emotion of very short duration can be love. It follows that indefinite constancy (and strict constancy) is false, because if an emotion of short duration can be love, the idea that love is constant would be false, so both strict and indefinite constancy go out of the window.

If love is an emotion like other emotions, there is no reason why it *must* be of long duration. If love, like other emotions, is reason-based, it will last as long as the reasons do. But it is also crucial to remember that the reasons for love do not descend on us from the sky like manna; they come packaged in *beliefs*. Star loves Ringo because she *believes* that he is smart. Although most of the time these beliefs are true, sometimes they are false, even from the get-go, and sometimes they turn false when the features of the beloved change. For example, Star's belief that Ringo is funny becomes false when he is no longer funny. If this is true, once a lover discovers that her beliefs about her beloved are not (or are no longer) true, the love will not continue. So if love can be of short duration, it is also not necessarily constant.

When love is constant it is usually not because of its nature, but because (1) the lovers' original reasons for loving each other endure, or (2) they do not endure but the lovers have new reasons for loving each other. And if (3) their reasons for love end and are not replaced by new reasons, they either break up or stay with each other but without the love. In (1) and (2), love is constant not because it is love, but because the reasons keep sustaining it. In (3), love is not constant. Whichever way, constancy loses.

Perhaps we think love is exclusive and constant because we *want* it to be so. If my lover loves only me, that makes me feel good and special. If my lover loves me for ever and ever, no matter who I am or who I become, that makes me feel good and secure. So we may want love to be exclusive and constant because this makes us feel special, wanted, or tolerated. There is nothing necessarily wrong with this – we are, after all, erring human beings – but we shouldn't pretend that romantic love is something it is not.

Summary and Conclusion

Rich accounts of union that attempt to leave room for individual autonomy – such as Nozick's – are untenable. They are in tension with robust concern, a notion indispensable to understanding love; thus two features of love – union and concern – are incompatible. We opted for concern, showing that not only is it not ultimately selfish, but that it often requires heavy sacrifices on the part of the lovers. Two other features of love – exclusivity and constancy – are not really features of love, certainly not necessarily or logically. It is interesting that out of the four features, only the three that romanticize romantic love – union ("two hearts as one"), exclusivity ("I love you and only you"), and constancy ("I'll love you forever and ever") – encounter severe objections. My guess is that this is because they are not really features of romantic love. We want them to be because this makes us feel good and secure, but the sooner we demythologize love, the sooner we see it for what it is and stop it from having a strong grip on our lives.

Notes

1 Chapter 5 in Soble (1990) contains an excellent discussion of Aristophanes' speech, to which I am very much indebted.
2 Of course, this may not be possible on Aristophanes' view: *we* exist because of sexual intercourse between males and females, so *our* forefathers were heterosexuals and should not expect male or female homosexuals to exist. For them to exist, (1) some males of a male–male half had to have sex with females, (2) some females of a female–female half had to have sex with males, and (3) some of their children carried the "genes" of their homosexual parents – three claims about which Aristophanes had nothing to say.
3 This 1997 essay by Soble discusses various accounts of union given by past and contemporary philosophers, and the tension between these views and the idea of concern.
4 To Jean-Paul Sartre, love is inherently contradictory because it involves the desire to *possess* your beloved *and* the desire that the beloved *freely* love you back (Sartre 1956, 474–493). This tension might mirror that found in union: how can one love *another* being but also desire to merge with him or her?
5 Solomon believes that the *goal* of shared identity is impossible to attain, because attaining it is a never-ending process given the lovers' individual differences: "no sooner do we approach this goal than we are abruptly reminded of our differences" (1990, 269). On my interpretation of his view the goal is not impossible, but it is never fixed and always subject to amendments, changes, and tinkering.
6 Some philosophers – most famously perhaps Vlastos (1989) – argue that Plato's view of love is also selfish. I discuss Plato's views in Chapter 3.

Further Reading

For an interesting interpretation of Aristophanes's speech, see Nussbaum (1986, ch. 6). On second-order desires, see Frankfurt (1971). Bloomfield (2008) contains excellent selections on the relationship between ethics and self-interest; another good anthology on self-interest is Paul, Miller, and Paul (1997). Fisher (1990) and Hunter (1980) adopt and develop union views of love. Hannay (1991, ch. 7) develops and evaluates Kierkegaard's arguments about the selfishness of love. Soble (1990, chs 9 and 10) contains detailed discussions of exclusivity and constancy, as well as essential references to other writers on these two topics.

3 The Basis of Romantic Love

Socrates's Speech in Praise of Love

In the *Symposium*, Socrates gives a startling view of love. He begins by convincing another attendee of the symposium, Agathon, that love is desire for beauty. Love itself is not beautiful, because, to Socrates, we only desire things we don't have (Plato 1997g, 199e–201c). His reasoning is that I, for example, desire chocolate because I don't have chocolate; if I did, I wouldn't desire it. That is why Socrates thinks that to desire something is to lack that thing (strictly, Socrates should have argued that if someone desires something, then he *thinks* that he does not have it; I could certainly desire chocolate even if I have some already, so long as I *think* I do not have any). As to the other idea that love desires beauty, Socrates relies on the common view that we do not love what is ugly. To make Socrates sound plausible, we should understand his claim to mean that we don't love what we *perceive* to be ugly. Put differently, we can love or desire ugly objects as long as we perceive them to be beautiful. In general, this claim sounds correct, especially if we think of it in terms of *value*, in that it is hard to see how one can love something if one does not value it in some way. Since beauty is a type of value (others include knowledge, goodness, and health), Socrates insists that we love what is beautiful, not what is ugly.

Then something curious happens. Instead of giving his own speech on love, Socrates relays a view of love – one he accepts – that Diotima, "a woman who was wise about many things" (201d), had earlier told him.[1] Diotima says that people not only love "the good," but they also want it forever, so she defines love as "wanting to possess the good forever" (206a–206b). The idea here is similar to that offered by Socrates: people love what they find to be valuable, not just any old thing. Since goodness is a value, people love the good. Yet why claim that people also want the good *forever*? The reason is unclear, but it is probably because it would not make sense *otherwise*: if one gets to possess something good, why would one want to give it up? It is more plausible to want it forever. Having made this claim, Diotima then argues that love not only desires the good, but also desires immortality: "A lover must desire immortality along with the good, if what we agreed earlier was right, that Love wants to possess the good forever" (207a).[2]

According to Diotima, we mortals can possess the good forever in one of two ways. First, some possess it through biological reproduction, "because it always leaves behind a new young one in place of the old" (207d). Second, others become pregnant in their souls with "wisdom and the rest of virtue," especially "moderation and justice" (209a). When a man has such ideas, especially in rudimentary form, and when he encounters a beautiful male youth, the youth "makes him instantly teem with ideas and arguments about virtue … In my view, you see, when he makes contact with someone beautiful and keeps company with him, he conceives and gives birth to what he has been carrying inside him for ages." Indeed, such children-ideas are "more beautiful and more immortal" than biological, human children (209c).

At this point Diotima introduces the famous ladder of love. A lover who wishes to go about loving correctly will not be content with loving one beautiful body, because he will grasp the truth that all bodies have the same beauty (210b). From loving one beautiful body he moves up to loving all beautiful bodies. But he realizes that the beauty of souls is even more valuable than that of bodies, so he moves up to loving that. From this he moves up to loving the beauty of laws and "activities," and from there to loving the beauty of knowledge. Then something amazing happens. The lover is "turned to the great sea of beauty … all of a sudden he will catch sight of something wonderfully beautiful in its nature; that, Socrates, is the reason for all his earlier labors" (210b–211a). What is this thing? It is worth quoting Diotima at some length:

> First, it always *is* and neither comes to be nor passes away, neither waxes nor wanes. Second, it is not beautiful this way and ugly that way, nor beautiful at one time and ugly at another, nor beautiful in relation to one thing and ugly in relation to another; nor is it beautiful here but ugly there, as it would be if it were beautiful for some people and ugly for others. Nor will the beautiful appear to him in the guise of a face or hands or anything else that belongs to the body. It will not appear to him as one idea or one kind of knowledge. It is not anywhere in another thing, as in an animal, or in earth, or in heaven, or in anything else, but itself by itself with itself, it is always one in form; and all the other things share in that, in such a way that when these others come to be or pass away, this does not become the least bit smaller or greater nor suffer any change. So when someone rises by these stages, through loving boys correctly, and begins to see this beauty, he has almost grasped his goal. This is what it is to go aright, or be led by another, into the mystery of Love … But how would it be in our view … if someone got to see the Beautiful itself, absolute, pure, unmixed, not polluted by human flesh or color or any other great nonsense of mortality, but if he could see the divine Beauty in itself in its one form? Do you think it would be a poor life for a human being to look there and to behold it by that which he ought, and to be with it? … Only then will it become possible for him to give birth not to images of virtue (because he's in touch with no images), but to true virtue (because he is in

touch with the true Beauty). The love of the gods belongs to anyone who has given birth to true virtue and nourished it, and if any human being could become immortal, it would be he.

(211a–212b)

Note the contempt that Socrates (through Diotima) shows for the usual erotic or romantic love that human beings have for each other: the Beauty that crowns the lover's ascent is "not *polluted* by human flesh or color or any other great nonsense of mortality." Socrates says that the correct method of love is to dump one's beloved in favor of Beauty. This need not mean that the lover abandons the beloved, because Diotima explicitly states, "this is what it is to go aright, *or be led by another*, into the mystery of Love." The one who is being led could be the has-been-beloved, who is now merely the companion of the lover.[3] Socrates's view of the correct method of love is not one we normally accept (his view is as surprising to us as it was to his fellow attendees at the symposium). So should we accept it? I tackle this issue in Chapter 4, where I discuss the place, rationality, and value of romantic love in our lives (as we will see, Socrates's view is tempting).

Note also the characteristics of Beauty, the final object of the ascent. It is a hyper-objective type of beauty. Ordinary beauty – the beauty of youth, of art, of sunsets, of majestic mountains – is fleeting. The youth grows old and ugly, the art and the mountains will eventually wither, and so will the sun and therefore sunsets. But not this Beauty: it is eternal (it neither "comes to be nor passes away"). Ordinary beautiful objects are beautiful in one way but not in another. A painting is beautiful only if (usually) seen from a distance and a particular angle. Looked at very closely or by having it lie flat on its back, it loses its beauty. Not so with Socrates's Beauty. Ordinary things are beautiful at one time but not at another: a rose is beautiful in its full bloom, not when it is dying. Not so with Socrates's Beauty. Ordinary beauty is often a matter of taste: some find sunsets beautiful, others don't (in one episode of *The Simpsons*, the comic-book guy asks sarcastically about a sunset, "Can it *be* any more orange?"). Not so with Socrates's Beauty. Ordinary beauty is embodied: we find it in a person's face, hands, or in a cat or a tiger. Not so with Socrates's Beauty. In all these ways, it is "objective."

But it is *hyper*-objective in that it is *hyper-real*. Socrates's Beauty is actually the Form of Beauty. Plato is famous for his theory of Forms. While we cannot get into its intricacies, a brief explanation is worthwhile. According to Plato, even though, for example, there are lots of different houses (they come in different shapes, colors, sizes, materials), they are all houses in that they all "share" a common element that we can call "house-hood," an element in virtue of which a house is a house. A tree is not a house because it does not "participate" or "share in" house-hood, but because it shares in "tree-hood." So, to Plato, there are essences or forms in virtue of which the diverse and sensory objects of our space–time world exist. The forms do not exist in space–time and are eternal (uncreated). They are inaccessible to the senses and we cannot travel to them.

Indeed, we cannot causally interact with them in any way. While ordinary objects exist and are real enough (although in later works Plato sheds doubts on this idea), the Forms are ultimate reality and the ultimate objects of knowledge. That Beauty is one of the Forms is evinced not only by its having their usual characteristics (eternality, lack of change), but also by Diotima's remark that all the other beautiful things "share in" it.

Most important for this chapter's purposes, note also Socrates's potentially worrisome view of the object of love, the beloved. Who – or what – does the lover love? We know that, if the ascent is successful, it is the Form of Beauty, but before that, Socrates seems to hold one of two views (or perhaps a combination): either the object of love is the youth, the boy himself, including his beauty, or it is the beauty, and only the beauty, embodied in the youth. Our concern is not with the nature of Greek homosexuality – why the object of love is a *male youth* (as opposed to a woman or an adult male) – but whether it is a human being at all.

First, if the object of love is the youth, not merely the youth's beauty, Socrates would have a view of love similar to ours, simply because he and we would agree that love is of individual human beings, not only their beauty. This is all fine and good, were it not for the following point: Socrates thinks that if we love the youth at all, we do so *because* of his beauty – his beauty is the reason or cause for the lover to love him. This raises a couple of disturbing possibilities. First, there are lots of beautiful youths. Does this mean that the lover should love them all? Would his love then not be exclusive? Would the beloved not be unique or irreplaceable? Diotima thinks so: at one stage the lover loves all beautiful bodies, eventually leaving them for higher forms of beauty. Moreover, these issues are not confined to youths or beauty. We romantically love all types of people for all sorts of reasons; with any type or reason, the same worries arise.

Second, if Socrates thinks that the object of love is not the youth but only his beauty, this raises a different philosophical worry: we normally think that we love the person, not only his beauty (or wit, humor, vulgarity, money, status, or comic book collection). So we don't agree with him on this point. Worse: What if Socrates is right? What does it mean, anyway, to love the person and not (only) parts of her (e.g., her beauty)? Does such a view make any sense?

This chapter addresses these two sets of issues. My concern is with the implications of Socrates's views for our beliefs about love, not with his arguments.

Loving for Reasons

Suppose that Socrates thinks we do love (prior to ascending the ladder) individual human beings, not just their beauty. People popularly and commonly hold a number of entrenched views about romantic love, three of which are on a collision course with Socrates's view of love.[4] First, we believe (or wish?) that love is constant. Because Socrates believes that the correct way of loving is to move away (and up) from loving a particular human being, he seems to think that love is not – or should not be – constant (Socrates retains constancy when loving the Form of Beauty).

Second, we believe (or wish?) that love is exclusive at a time: when x loves y during a stretch of time, x loves *only* y during that time. Because Socrates believes that if x loves y, x loves y for y's beauty, his view implies that x should also love z, who is as or more beautiful than y (Socrates must retain exclusivity when loving the Form of Beauty; it has no other contender).

Third, we believe (or wish?) that our beloved is unique: when x loves y, x seems to think that no one else is like y. Because Socrates believes that if x loves y, x loves y for y's beauty, and because he believes that many people are beautiful, he implies that our beloveds are not unique (Socrates retains uniqueness with the Form of Beauty).

Do not confuse constancy, exclusivity, and uniqueness with each other. To love y constantly is to love y until you or y dies. To love y exclusively (at a time) is to love y and only y during that time (but you need not do so constantly). To think that y is unique is to think that no one else is like y (but you may think that z is also unique, in which case you can love both y and z, either non-exclusively or serially, constantly or not constantly). So there are different combinations of these three possibilities (eight in all).

Recall also that x loves y for reasons (and that when these reasons no longer hold, the love goes away). This is the "reason-based" or "property-based" view of romantic love (Soble (1990) calls it the "erosic" view of love). When x loves y, x does so *because* y has features, qualities, or properties that x finds valuable. More accurately, when x loves y, x does so because x *believes* that y has properties that x finds valuable. It is the existence of these properties in y – or x's belief in their existence – that explains why x loves y. This view is opposed to the *agapic* one – discussed below – that flips the order of explanation around: x finds certain properties of y valuable because x loves y. It is the love that explains why x finds some or all features of y valuable (that is why it is difficult, under this view, to answer the question of why x loves y, given that y's properties are not candidates for answering the question).

Socrates's view of love is reason-based. This is clear in his claim that we love something because we don't have it: x loves y because x finds y's beauty desirable. It is complemented by Diotima's view that the lover falls in love with the youth for his beauty. So if we ask Socrates why he, Socrates, loves Alcibiades (a young Athenian general who was himself madly in love with Socrates), he would answer that Alcibiades is beautiful. Of course, we are assuming that Socrates accepts a view of love according to which the lover loves another human being as an individual, not only the beauty found in that human being (I suspend this assumption later in this chapter).

Note five things. First, the Socratic view may be generalized to properties other than beauty: x need not love y only because y is beautiful (y's beauty need not be a reason at all for why x loves y). X could love y because y is witty, knowledgeable, makes for a good companion, is a sexual dynamo, wealthy, or politically well connected. *X* could love *y* for any one or more of these reasons (or ones not on this list). In any of these examples, *x*'s love for *y* is reason- or property-based. It is a Socratic view, but one not limited to the two properties of beauty and goodness.

Second, in principle, one can love another for a large number or type of reasons, but not any reason will do if *x*'s love for *y* is to be comprehensible. Compare the following two lists. Under List A, *x* loves *y* for the following reasons: *y* likes cats, *y* is a brilliant mathematician, and *y* owns two yachts. Under List B, *x* loves *y* because cats are cute, mathematics inspires awe, and yachts signify wealth. With List A, we can understand why *x* loves *y*: perhaps *x* is a cat lover and wants that in a beloved; perhaps *x* is attracted to smart people and being a good mathematician is a sure sign that *y* is smart; and perhaps *x* is also shallow and is attracted to rich people. We may not like all these reasons, and maybe some would not be *our* reasons for loving someone, but they are comprehensible reasons; they make *x*'s love for *y* *rational*. Not so with the reasons under List B: it is virtually impossible to see any connection between the cuteness of cats as such, and *x*'s love for *y*. Ditto for the rest of the reasons. If *x* stares us in the face and says, "There's no further connection; I love *y* because cats are cute. There's no more to it," we'll think *x* is bonkers. The point is that the view of romantic love as reason-based does not entail that any reason will do; it allows placing limits on what reasons can explain *x*'s love for *y* and how they do so.

Third, some of *x*'s reasons for loving *y* may not be another's reasons for love, which indicates that reasons for love might be subjective, and different individuals might have different reasons for loving (cf. Soble 1990, 11). Here, reasons function differently from the way they do in moral thinking: murder is wrong, for example, for reasons that apply to *any* murder (whether reasons operate also differently in art criticism and appreciation is more debatable). This does not mean that we have moved far from the Socratic view. On the level of articulating specific reasons for love, it *seems* to be a departure: Joanna loves Bill for Bill's big nose, whereas big noses simply don't move Sarah. Socrates, on the other hand, simply does not get into big noses and, generally, the specificity of reasons. But on a deeper level on which we discuss value in general, it is not a departure: whatever the reasons for Joanna and Sarah's loving, neither one will love someone for a property or quality they don't find valuable. In this way, they both love another for his "beauty" or "goodness," thus falling in line with the Socratic view.

Fourth, the reason-based view of love assimilates romantic love to other emotions, because in being dependent on reasons, it would be, in this respect, similar to almost all other emotions. When *x* hates, envies, is angry with, feels sad for, or is jealous of *y*, *x* (typically) has these emotions for reasons. "I hate *y* because he's so damn arrogant"; "I envy *y* because he has the first issue of *Superman*"; "I'm angry with *y* because he didn't give me back my money like he promised"; "I feel sad for *y* because his dog just died"; and so on. With almost any other emotion, asking for reasons for the emotion makes perfect sense.

If the person feeling the emotion cannot give an answer, something could be wrong. The reason-based view, then, allows love to conform with other emotions. We are thus able to evaluate it as rational or justified (Soble 1990, ch. 7).

Fifth, it is *possible* for an emotion to *not* be based on reasons: "I can't stand Nick! I can't even bear to look at him!" "Why?" "I don't know; he just rubs me up the wrong way." "There must be something! Search deep within yourself, go back to your encounters with him; surely there's a reason." "I tried all that; I couldn't find anything. I just hate him for no reason!" Now it could be that the hater is not searching deep enough in her self and a good psychiatrist might help. But it is also possible that she's correct and that there is no reason, really, for her hatred. We shouldn't rule out this possibility for any emotion, including love. The reason-based view of love does not require that *every* case of romantic love be based on reasons or properties of the beloved, only that romantic love is *typically* – like other emotions – reason-based (Soble 1990, 121).

It is a good thing that the reason-based view of love assimilates love to other emotions, thereby opening it to evaluation in terms of rationality and justification. So why discuss a rival view of love according to which love is not reason-based? Answer: Because the reason-based view clashes with the above-mentioned three beliefs about love.

Difficulties with Reason-based Love

The clash between our belief in constancy and reason-based love is the most straightforward: unless the properties on which the love is based cannot be lost, constancy is always in danger when it comes to reason-based love, because of the possibility that the beloved loses these properties. If this happens, we expect the love to end (the only properties that cannot be lost are those that are essential: being a person, being made of molecules, and – if God exists – being God's child, for example; I discuss these below). It is difficult to see how this tension can be avoided. If we love others for properties they can lose, then constancy cannot be a necessary feature of romantic love.

Let us turn to thornier issues: exclusivity and uniqueness.

The problem arises from the clash between, on the one hand, some entrenched beliefs about romantic love, and, on the other, what is called in philosophy the generality or universality of reasons. We have already seen what these entrenched beliefs are: we tend to think that the beloved is unique, and that romantic love is exclusive. Let us look into the generality of reasons; we can then better see how the problem arises.

If we have a reason to do something in one set of circumstances, then, when relevantly similar circumstances come up, we have the same reason to do the same type of action. A reason to do action A in circumstances $C1$ is also the reason to do action A in circumstances $C2$, as long as $C1$ and $C2$ are relevantly similar to each other. Consider first an example from everyday life. If one day on my walk to work I decide to buy a newspaper because I should stay informed, then as long as things keep happening in the world, staying informed is a "valid" reason, so I should buy a newspaper every day. If I *don't* buy a newspaper or seek other sources of information, either I am being inconsistent or other circumstances provide a different reason for not buying a newspaper (e.g., I don't have enough cash on me to buy a newspaper *and* coffee, and I want coffee). Consider now an example from morality. If one day on my way to work I decide to give money to a homeless person, then I ought to do so every day as long as this is beneficial to that person. If I don't, I'm either being inconsistent or different circumstances have come up (e.g., I happen not to have cash on me, or I realize that being beneficial is not something I need to do on a daily basis).

Consider now how the collision between our beliefs about love and the generality of reasons gives rise to problems. To simplify things, suppose Adam loves Eve because she's beautiful and good – her beauty and goodness are Adam's reasons for loving her. Because Eve is not the only person or woman who is beautiful and good, then, given the generality of reasons, Adam has as much reason to love these other women as he has to love Eve. Moreover, if Eve loses the properties on which basis Adam loves her, Adam would no longer have reason to love her. This means, first, that Eve is not unique: the qualities that make her lovable for Adam are not qualities that only she possesses. Second, Adam's love for Eve is not in principle exclusive: if another woman comes along who has the same qualities, Adam has reason to love her also, at the same time as he loves Eve. Thus, the generality of reasons is incompatible with these two beliefs about romantic love. (The generality of reasons does not threaten the irreplaceability of the beloved: the same reasons that make Adam love Eve and that should make him love women other than Eve would still operate in Eve's case, thus making him love all of them; Eve is thus not replaced.)

This is a *conceptual*, not necessarily a *factual*, problem. Here is what I mean: suppose that Adam meets Delilah, who is beautiful and good. However, he is, for some reason, not attracted to her and does not fall in love with her. Somehow, she does not move him to love her. But even though, in fact Adam does not love Delilah, he still has reason to, and the problem – that this clashes with the exclusivity of love – still exists.

There are four ways by which to solve the problem. The first is to offload our entrenched beliefs about love: we declare them false, unjustified, irrational. The second is to tweak the generality of reasons to remove the inconsistency between our beliefs about love and how reasons function. The third is to offload the view that reasons are – or are always – general. The fourth is to adopt a non-reason-based view of love. Let us look at the second, third, and fourth attempts first before we decide to give up on our beliefs on love.

Tweaking the Generality of Reasons

There are two ways to tweak the generality of reasons to save our beliefs about love: make them more specific or make them relational.

Making reasons specific. Suppose that Rose asks Jeff why he loves her. He says he loves her because she's smart and beautiful. He adds, "It's more complicated, actually. It's not only because you're smart, but also because you have a way of seeing things, of connecting the dots, that make you smart in a very specific way, like the time you noticed how Ted avoids eye contact with Michael. And it's not simply because you're beautiful, but because you have an amazing smile that makes your eyes twinkle, and because your teeth are just so white without looking fake!"

Is Jeff's answer satisfactory? Let us begin by asking whether these properties about Rose for which Jeff loves her make her unique. The answer is that they do not, although they might make her somewhat rare (even here I wouldn't be too confident), because there are – and certainly could be – other women who have these more specified properties; there are women who see things and connect the dots in just the same ways that Rose does, whose eyes twinkle when they smile in just the way Rose's do. So Rose is not unique. We can also see why Jeff's love for her is not exclusive: the same reasons he cites for loving Rose are reasons why he would, or should, love another woman who has the same properties as Rose.

Might it be that if we specify our reasons more we can avoid finding other women who have the same love-inducing properties as Rose? There are three reasons for thinking that further specificity won't solve the problem. The first is that people are not really unique in a way that is interesting or love-relevant. People are certainly unique in some ways: each person (except for identical twins) has her own genetic make-up and each person has her own, unique fingerprint (including identical twins), but these are not reasons for why people love others (Soble 1990, 55). They are certainly not typical reasons, and if, by some chance, x loves y because of y's unique fingerprint, we would want a more detailed explanation to make x's love comprehensible. We would certainly want to know what it is about y's fingerprint – as opposed to z's – that has x smitten. However, when it comes to the usual reasons or properties why people love each other, they are not unique, and their further specification won't make them unique either; at best, it makes them rare. People love others for their wit, knowledge, physical beauty, money, and fame, to give a few examples. Specifying these traits further – for example, wit when it comes to cat–dog relationships, knowledge about plant species, the physical beauty of the nose, money made (not inherited), and fame due to a history of speaking truth to power – helps a bit, but it is not going to make the beloveds unique and it won't secure exclusivity.

Second, the further we specify the properties, the more we may be able to make the beloved unique, but the price may be incomprehensibility: it becomes harder to see why x would love y based on such highly detailed properties. Suppose that Jeff loves Rose because of the way she walks; specifically, how she walks in flip-flops, on a particular sandy beach somewhere in Hawaii, between seven and eight o'clock in the evening, on the first day of June. Now maybe Rose's walk in these specific circumstances is indeed unique – no other woman, clad in flip-flops, on that day, at that time, walks quite like Rose. That's great for Jeff and even more so for Rose. The problem is that it is hard to see why *that* walk serves or even can serve as the reason for Jeff's love. We might as well go with the unique fingerprint. So the more we specify – and we must be very specific to render the beloved unique – the harder it is to understand someone's love.

Third, even if somehow Rose is unique in that there is no *actual* woman who has the same properties that serve as Jeff's basis for loving Rose, it is always *possible* for there to be such a woman. We might be able to secure Rose's uniqueness and make Jeff's love for her exclusive in actual fact, but not conceptually. If both Rose and Jeff were super-duper scientists who have access to a worldwide database that lists every single individual's (past, present, and future) properties, they might run it through some super computer that cranks out the result that no other woman has those properties on which basis Jeff loves Rose. Rose might then be content that until his or her death, Jeff has no reason to love another existing woman. But Rose also knows that being special is an accident: *had* the world been different such that there were other women who had the same properties, her uniqueness and Jeff's exclusive love for her go out of the window.

So further specification won't quite do. Let us try the other solution.

Making reasons relational. Suppose that Jeff answers Rose's question why he loves her by saying, "Because you make me happy, because you're patient with my mood swings, because you can sleep next to me even though I snore like a hippo, because your brown eyes mesmerize me, and because your wit dazzles me." There is a crucial difference between the reasons Jeff gives in this answer and those he gives in the previous one. His new reasons are *relational*: they all incorporate how Rose's properties relate to *him* ("Because you're patient with *my* mood swings"; "Because your brown eyes mesmerize *me*"). This is crucial because it blocks the generality of reasons. To see this, consider another example: John is the son of Micah, and Jonathan is the son of Mike. Both John and Jonathan have almost the exact, non-relational properties: they were both born on the same day and time, both weigh the same, both are equally tall, equally intelligent, both are heads of their respective classes, and so on. Micah, however, loves John, not Jonathan. Suppose we ask him why, even though both have almost the exact same qualities. He answers, "Because he's *my* son." This reason seems to not be general: Micah is not forced, on pain of inconsistency or irrationality, to love every other boy who has the same properties as John, because one crucial property – a relational one – sets John apart from other boys. Similarly with Jeff's answer: Rose makes *Jeff* happy, Rose is patient with *Jeff's* mood swings. So can relational properties solve the problem, as some philosophers believe (e.g., Newton-Smith 1989; Nussbaum 1997)?

Go back to John and Micah. We ask Micah, "What happens if, somehow, you find out that Jonathan is not really Mike's son but yours?" Micah will probably (and reasonably) answer, "I'm not sure how this can be, but if he is my son, well, then, I'll love him, too!" Here lies an important lesson: relational properties can also be general. That is, if *x*'s reason for loving *y* is that *y* is *x*'s son, then *x* has reason to love *z* if *z* is also *x*'s son. Now go back to Jeff: if Flower can make Jeff happy, if she can tolerate his mood swings, and if she can sleep next to him while he snores like a hippo, then Jeff has as much reason to love Flower as he does Rose. Relational properties do not secure Jeff's love for Rose exclusively. They also don't make her unique as an object of love: people other than Rose can also have, for example, the relational property, "Makes Jeff happy."

Are we overlooking the fact that it is Rose who is related to Jeff in these ways, that what might be important to Jeff is not simply that *someone* tolerates his snoring, or that *someone* mesmerizes him with her brown eyes, but that *Rose* does? After all, we are talking about her and only her: Jeff loves Rose because *her* eyes and wit have these effects on him, not just *anyone's* eyes and wit, even with these effects. These relational properties, then, are not general; they cover neither other *actual* people nor even *possible* ones, since no other person can be Rose. Rose is Rose and is necessarily Rose, even if she went by some other name. And she's the one related to Jeff in these ways.

Would this solve the problem of uniqueness? The relational properties, those that incorporate the beloved, not the lover, make the beloved unique in a special way: if it is important to the lover that he or she experience these properties and their effects (being dazzled, mesmerized) not just at the hands of anyone but at the hands of that specific beloved, then that beloved is indeed unique.

What about exclusivity? Relational properties incorporating the beloved would secure the exclusivity of Jeff's love for Rose, because it is these effects as produced only by Rose that form the basis of Jeff's love for her. This locks in exclusivity almost by definition, by the very way we have characterized the properties. There's a heavy price to be paid, however. Remember that giving reasons for loving someone is meant to explain (and sometimes justify) one's love. But when Jeff says he loves Rose because of the way *she* dazzles and mesmerizes him, we ought to press him: "But Flower can do that to you, too, you know. Why not love her?" "Because Flower is not Rose and I love Rose because *she*, not Flower, does that to me." "Um … But what is it about *Rose* that makes you love *her* instead of *Flower* when *either one* can affect you in the same way?" In other words, incorporating the beloved in a relational reason secures exclusivity but at the price of lack of explanation: it pushes the question of why *x* loves *y* one step back, but does not answer it (Soble 1990, 56–59).

So tweaking the generality of reasons won't do. Let us consider the third attempt to solve the problem: doing away with the very idea that reasons have to be general.

Non-general Reasons

Why might we think that reasons are not general? If the only answer is to save our beliefs about love, it would be contrived, made up just to fix the problem. As long as love seems to be reason-based, and as long as we have no independent arguments to raise doubts about the generality of reasons across the board (in love matters and in non-love matters), claiming that in love they are not general is indeed contrived and so unconvincing.

There are philosophers who argue that some reasons are not general. Some do so in areas that are not surprising – in art and aesthetics. But some do so in areas that *are* surprising – in ethics and moral philosophy. Considering them might provide independent grounds for thinking that reasons in love might also not be general.

Let us begin with art, focusing on painting. Suppose that any time there's a painting with the color red in it, we have reason to believe that the painting is good. The color red is always a good-making feature in paintings. It follows that having the color red is a property that provides a general reason for good-ness: if red is a good-making feature in painting, then a painting with red in it is good. In short, redness in paintings is a general reason: it makes good all paintings that have this feature.

But it is evident that there are – and certainly could be – paintings with red in them that are mediocre or bad. Is red then not a good-making feature? It depends on which of two options we accept. The first is that even though red is a good-making feature in paintings, it is not the only one and can be defeated (overridden, overpowered) by other features, some of which can be so powerful that they make the painting, overall, quite bad. This argument does *not* deny the generality of reasons; instead, it claims that these reasons can be overpow-ered by other reasons. For example, suppose that painting P has red in it but is also badly executed, has no good idea or conception, and has too much gray. It is a bad painting, not, however, because red is not a good-making feature, but because redness is overpowered by the other features. Thus, its generality as a reason for thinking paintings good is not in doubt.

The second option is to deny the generality of red as a good-making feature in paintings, and to claim that red is, in and of itself, neither a good-making nor a bad-making feature. Whether it is good or bad depends entirely on the particular painting, especially the painting's other features and how they inter-act with each other to form the particular painting that it is. In short, we have no reason to think that red – or any other artistic or aesthetic property – provides a general reason for whether a work of art is good, bad, or mediocre. Everything depends on how that feature figures in each work of art. Obviously, the second option denies the generality of reasons in art.

In ethics, a similar picture exists. Suppose that being pleasurable is a good-making feature of an action. If someone were faced with a situation in which she can provide pleasure to others, this would be a morally good thing to do, thus giving her a reason to do the action. However, the provision of pleasure is sometimes overridden by other considerations, such that, overall, what a person ought to do in a situation is not to provide pleasure but something else. For example, letting a rapist off the legal hook and not penalizing him would give him, his friends, and his family members pleasure, but we ought not to let him go free because justice requires that he be punished.

As in the case of art, there are two options. The first is that in situations in which one ought not to act by providing pleasure, providing pleasure is still a morally good-making feature but one defeated by more powerful features (e.g., administering justice). Under this option, providing pleasure is still a general reason. The second option – known as moral *particularism* – denies that pleasure-giving or any other feature is always a morally good- (or bad-) making feature of situations. Whether it is depends *entirely* on the particular situation, on how the features of a situation interact with each other to determine what one should do in the situation. Moral particularism – as its name indicates – is thus a theory that rejects the generality of reasons in moral decision-making.

Can these two models support the idea that when it comes to love, reasons are also not general? On the one hand, if the models are convincing, then not all types of reasons are general. Indeed, if in ethics and moral philosophy – areas in which the generality of reasons has been an anchor for many moral theories – reasons are not general, our confidence in their generality in other areas will be seriously undermined. On the other hand, if the two models are false, then we should not lose confidence in the generality of reasons, including love-related ones. I will not argue that these two models are false. I assume that the art-related one is true, but that it should not make us doubt the generality of reasons when it comes to love because it is irrelevant. I also argue that we should not doubt the generality of reasons in love on the basis of moral particularism.

Why accept particularism in art? The main reason is the *uniqueness* of works of art. If each work of art is unique in an interesting way (not just trivially, as in "each work of art is different from another"), then what makes one work of art good (or bad) is going to differ from one work of art to another. If a painting by Kandinsky and a painting by Pollock are each unique in a deep and interesting sense, then even though both may contain the color red, there is reason to believe that the color red behaves differently in each painting, interacting with other elements to yield the overall unique quality of each. The basic idea is that *the uniqueness of each work of art provides the basis for thinking that reasons in art are not general.*

But with love, individual people are not unique in deep and interesting ways. Moreover, basing love on properties that do make individual human beings unique (e.g., genetic code) won't provide reasons that are adequate to explain one's love for another. Basing love on specific properties won't work either, because if they are not specific enough they don't make the beloved unique, and the more specific we make them, the harder it is to see how they can be the basis of love (remember the example of Rose walking in her flip-flops in that unique way in Hawaii). So the model of the non-generality of reasons in art is irrelevant to love.

Consider next particularism in ethics. Although I am sympathetic to the theory, two considerations should give us pause. First, there are plausible examples of features that are *always* good- (or bad-) making features of actions, such that when they are not acted upon in a particular situation this is because other reasons override them, *not* because they are neither good- (nor bad-) making features in these particular situations (as the particularist contends). Examples are benefiting others, promoting justice, keeping freely made promises, and not harming others (Hooker 2000, 8–11). Each seems to always be a good-making feature of a situation. Again, in many situations such features might be overridden by others such that the overall right thing to do would not be to benefit others, promote justice, keep a promise, or not harm others. But this claim, one in keeping with the generality of reasons, is different from the particularist claim that none of them is always a good-making feature.

Second, and related to the first reason, it is difficult to see how the particularist can convince us of her view. Consider the following example (adapted from Plato's *Republic*; Plato 1997f, 331c). Suppose that John gives Smith a gun for safekeeping while John is away on a trip. In fairness, Smith should return the gun to John when he returns. But suppose that John comes back stark-raving mad. Should Smith return the gun to him? Probably not, because there is no telling the amount of harm that John could do with it given his newly acquired lunacy. The generalist would say that this is a case in which returning the gun to John is the fair thing to do, but that fairness is outweighed by other crucial features (e.g., clear and present danger to others). The particularist would say that in this case fairness (would he even call it that?) is not a good-making feature of the situation. But how to determine whether it is or is not such a feature? It seems that the particularist has no convincing argument that fairness is bad in this case. Indeed, what if the generalist, by providing a built-in exception, fine-tunes his reason, stating that returning things to their rightful owners, *except in cases when doing so brings great harm*, is always a good-making feature? How would the particularist then convince us that this is actually not so in the case at hand?

For these two reasons, moral particularism is controversial; it is not a moral theory that commands wide assent when it comes to its tenet of denying the generality of reasons. To be sure, no other moral theory commands wide assent either. But all other moral theories agree on the generality of reasons, none denying such a bedrock principle of reasoning in ethics. If moral particularism is highly controversial, it should not be a model on which to base the non-generality of reasons for love.

We should, then, inquire into the rival view of love – the one that claims love is not based on reasons – to see whether we have a more plausible view of love that can get around the difficulties we have encountered so far.

Is Love Not About Reasons?

Let us ask why such a view exists. One philosophical answer is that it is a possible way to get out of the difficulties faced by the reason-based view of love. A non-reason-based view of love might preserve our beliefs that love is exclusive and that the beloved is unique. There is a historical reason also: the non-reason-based view of love developed on its own over the years, especially in Christian thought. In the words of St. Paul in the Bible, "Love bears all things, believes all things, hopes all things, endures all things" (1 Corinthians 13). In other words, love does not target individuals based on desirable properties (St. Paul does *not* say, "Love bears *some* things as long as other things love finds desirable"). Let us begin by looking at the views of two Christian authors.

In *The Four Loves*, C. S. Lewis makes a basic distinction between two types of love: need-love and gift-love. The first is based, as its name indicates, on our needs: we love others because of their ability to meet certain needs of ours (1960, 11–21). Gift-love is modeled on God's love for us; it is not based on need because in God "there is no hunger that needs to be filled, only plenteousness that desires to give" (1960, 175). In us, this divine gift-love allows us to "love what is not naturally loveable; lepers, criminals, enemies, morons, the sulky, the superior and the sneering." It is the type of love that is "wholly disinterested and desires what is simply best for the beloved" (1960, 177). According to Lewis, many find this love difficult to receive because we want to be loved for our desirable or good qualities (1960, 179).

Gift-love, exercised properly, should mirror, as best as possible, the love that God has for us. This type of love does not respond to our attractive properties, but is directed at everyone, even at those who have no attractive properties (or ones strong enough to overpower their attractive ones). Lewis states, "No sooner do we believe that God loves us than there is an impulse to believe that He does so, not because He is Love, but because we are intrinsically loveable" (1960, 180). To Lewis, we should avoid this impulse. We *may* have the property of being intrinsically loveable, but this is irrelevant, because God's love is not based on it. God loves us because "He is Love." Thus God's love for us – a love on which *our* gift-love for others is to be modeled – is emphatically not based on the properties of the beloved. It is a gift that flows from God's own nature.

Anders Nygren, another Christian thinker, adopts a similar view in his book, *Agape and Eros*. He lists several features of *agape*, two of which are crucial to our discussion. First, *agape* is unmotivated: "We look in vain for an explanation of God's love in the character of the man who is the object of His love… the only ground for it is to be found in God Himself … When it is said that God loves man, this is not a judgment on what man is like, but on what God is like" (1953, 75–76). Connected to this is the idea that God's love is indifferent to value; God's love for us is motivated not by whatever value we have, but simply by God's own goodness: "When God's love is directed to the sinner, then the position is clear: all thought of valuation is excluded in advance; for if God, the Holy One, loves the sinner, it cannot be because of his sin, but in spite of his sin" (1953, 77). Second, *agape* creates value in its beloved: "God does not love that which is already in itself worthy of love, but on the contrary, that which in itself has no worth acquires worth just by becoming the object of God's love" (1953, 78).

Note, first, that unlike romantic or erotic love, which both authors agree is based on reasons, *agapic* love is reason-less or, more accurately, not based on the properties of the beloved; its reasons are not based on *these* properties. Second, unlike property-based love, in which the lover finds value in the beloved and on its basis loves her, in *agapic* love God *creates* value. Nygren states, "The man who is loved by God has no value in himself; what gives him value is precisely the fact that God loves him" (1953, 78). Nygren explicitly warns against thinking that God loves us because our souls have infinite value, claiming that this idea is not really central in Christian doctrine (1953, 78–79). Third, God loves the sinner not because, to God, but not to us, being a sinner is a valuable property. As Nygren explicitly claims, God loves the sinner *in spite* of his sin, not because of it (if the Christian view were that being a leper is somehow an attractive property, the view would be a reason-based view of love). Fourth, we should not confuse non-reason-based love with disinterested (not selfish) love: love can be based on reasons or properties and still be disinterested, and love can be reason-less and still be selfish (a Christian can love the leper in the hope of attaining heaven in the afterlife).

Is agape *really not based on reasons?* In addressing this question, we should keep in mind that *agape* is a kind of love that God has for us *and* that we as human beings should have for each other, modeled on God's love for us. Although I find the idea of God loving us gratuitously, because it is His nature to do so, mysterious, when it comes to the Judeo-Christian-Islamic God (and, indeed, other gods), mysteries abound. So I consider God's gift-love for us another mystery better left to the theologians to figure out.

But *we* are supposed to love our neighbors (everybody else, really) *agapically*. Is *this* form of *agape* also not based on reasons? Here we have to be careful. There is a sense, of course, in which even God's love for us is based on reasons. The answer to the question, "Why does God love us?" "Because it's in His nature to do so," provides a reason, though one based on His nature, not on the properties of the objects of His love (us). When it comes to *our agapic* love for others, there is an obvious way in which it is indeed reason-based: being loved by God, we as human beings acquire value. According to Nygren: "The man who is loved by God has no value in himself; what gives him value is precisely the fact that God loves him" (1953, 78). So even though when God loves us He does so by *creating* value, when *we* love each other *agapically* we do so by responding to the value found in ourselves, a value we acquire in virtue of God loving us. Examples of properties on which we base our *agapic* love for each other could include "being created by God," "being God's children," or "being loved by God."

The idea that our *agapic* love for each other is based on our properties is supported by two thoughts. First, a main idea in the commandment to love our neighbor is to love all humanity, not preferring particular individuals (as we do with romantic beloveds and friends). This idea emphasizes not so much the nature of our love (baseless or not baseless), but its universality. Second, human *agape* would still be contrasted with romantic love as far as reasons for loving are concerned, but the contrast would not be between non-reason-based and reason-based-love, but between the *types of reason* invoked. In romantic love, the reasons or properties are not universal: not everyone is beautiful, witty, smart, or famous. With human *agape*, the properties are universal: we are *all* God's children, we are *all* loved by God. So there is a way in which human *agape* is a form of reason-based love (Soble 1998, 100–101).

But does this sound plausible? After all, when it comes to *agape* we are to *fully* mirror God's love for us and to love each other not based on our properties, but on *our* nature to love, much like God loves us because it's in His nature to. If so, we shouldn't think of human *agape* as reason-based. Here we have to be careful, however. Our nature to love is not like God's under the Christian conception, according to which God *is* Love, in that this is His nature. There is a sense, then, in which God cannot *but* love (which raises issues about God's free will). We are different: if it is in our nature to love, it is so only in the sense that we are *capable* of loving, just as we are capable of hating, envying, and so on. Unlike God, we need not love, and when we do love, we do not do so automatically. To us, loving *agapically* must come with an effort of will or from character cultivation. Either way, an act of will (or a series of such acts) at some stage is needed for us to love each other *agapically*.

This is why we are *commanded* to love each other *agapically*; if we can do it because it is in our nature to do it, we wouldn't need to be ordered to do it.[5] But then if we are commanded to love *agapically*, the natural question to ask is: *Why* should I love my neighbor in this fashion? Why can I not pick and choose whom to love? If the answer is, "Because God said so" or "Because God commands us to," this would give us a reason for love similar to God's reason for loving us, in that it is *not* based on the properties of the objects of love. But this does not mean that it is a satisfactory reason: just because God tells us to do something does not mean that we should.[6] We need to know *why* we should love others *agapically*, and it seems that whatever answer we come up with, it is going to have *something* to do with the properties of the objects of love: "Because we are God's children," "Because we are loved by God," or "Because we have worth (bestowed on us by God)." Whereas God can love us for reasons that have nothing to do with our nature or properties (although I still think this is a mystery), when we love each other *agapically*, there is no escape from the properties of the objects of love. These will be properties that all human beings have, but this does not make them any less the beloveds' properties.

This discussion has taken a particularly Christian form of non-reason-based love according to which we are meant to or should love others in this way. Philosophically speaking, non-reason-based love need not have this form; *x* can love *y* in a non-reason-based way even if *x* does not love everyone else this way, is not commanded to, or is not a Christian. Is this form of love plausible? This brings us to our second question.

Does non-reason-based love avoid the problems of reason-based love? Christianity aside, one reason why we might want to opt for a non-reason-based love is to avoid the problems faced by the reason-based type, thus preserving our beliefs about love (that it is exclusive, that the beloved is unique, and so on). Can baseless love do this?

It is hard to see how. Indeed, it poses more of a danger to these beliefs. Non-reason-based love does not offer any guarantee for constancy. Just because x loves y for no reason (or no reason having to do with y), it does not follow that x's love for y will last. Just as it "magically" came into existence, it might also "magically" go out. At least with reason-based love, as long as y continues to contain the properties on which basis x loves y, we expect x's love to endure. With non-reason-based love, if x later comes to find value in y and his love for y continues on its basis, x's love would have become reason-based. Thus non-reason-based-love provides no guarantee for constancy.

One interesting twist here is this: accepting a form of *agape* as reason-based would secure constancy, because the properties on which it is based are ones that no beloved can lose. For example, no one will lose the property "Being God's child" or "Being loved by God"; we are all God's children until our death (and probably after). If *agape* is based on such properties, constancy is guaranteed. But, of course, this type of *agape* is reason-based (cf. Soble 1990, 232–236).

What about exclusivity? With reason-based love, if x loves y on the basis of property P that y has, then as long as z has P, x has reason to love z also. Non-reason-based love does not fare any better. If x loves y for no reason having to do with y, what is to stop x from loving z also for no reason having to do with z? It is very possible that x will also love z, w, and a few more. At least with reason-based love, we can see *some* conceptual limits on x loving people other than y: it is likely that what x finds valuable in y are not properties that every other human being has (not everyone is witty, charming, or a fantastic chess player). With non-reason-based love, the sky is the limit.

There is another twist: accepting a reason-based form of *agape* gets rid of exclusivity: If x loves y because "y is God's child," then, since everyone has this property, there are no limits at all on the exclusivity of x's love for y (cf. Soble 1990, 195–198).

Might non-reason-based love secure uniqueness? If x loves y but not on the basis of any of y's properties, then the fact that y has no interesting uniqueness-making properties should *not* be a source of worry, so that perhaps y's uniqueness can be secured in a different way. Perhaps if x, in virtue of his love, confers value upon y, then y becomes unique in virtue of having this value. What, however, would be the property in virtue of which y is unique? It must be "being valued by x." But then y's uniqueness will be preserved *only if* x *does not love another* person. If x does, x would confer the same value, and then z would have the property, "loved by x," in which case neither y nor z is unique. Moreover, since non-reason-based love does not secure exclusivity, we have no good reason to believe that x won't love z (and w, etc.).

So non-reason-based love fares no better than reason-based love as far as securing our beliefs about constancy, exclusivity, and uniqueness is concerned. Indeed, it fares worse (if the lover loves another, in the case of the latter). Moreover, non-reason-based love is difficult to accept on its own merits, regardless of how it compares with reason-based love. First, it is insulting. People want to be loved for a reason, because they think that there is something about them on which to base that love. Being loved for no reason having to do with them makes them feel unworthy of the love; it is one step below telling someone, "I love you because you're you." At least this answer provides a reason of sorts that has *something* to do – no matter how murky – with the beloved (cf. Soble 1990, 145).

If our desire to be loved for who we are were irrational, the above would not be a problem for non-reason-based love, because we can shrug our shoulders and say, "Big deal. People want all sorts of things, but that doesn't make what they want rational or acceptable." But the desire to be loved for who we are *is* rational: it gives us a sense of self-worth, and makes us feel good about ourselves and deserving to be the recipients of such an important and positive emotion as love. There is nothing obviously irrational about this. Perhaps few people actually have any worth – humanity has not exactly been a shining specimen of excellence – but the *desire* to have self-worth might still be rational.

Second, non-reason-based love is anomalous: it violates our canons of rationality and makes love a bizarre emotion. With every emotion, people are able to provide reasons for why they have it. Non-reason-based love is an exception. Although it is possible that sometimes an emotion, including love, is not based on reasons, this is not the norm. Accepting non-reason-based love turns love into an emotion that *typically* (not exceptionally) does not respond to reasons, thus making it anomalous. We have seen no good reason to do so. The clincher is when we reconcile (to some extent) reason-based love with our beliefs about love, thus showing that we really do not need non-reason-based love to salvage these beliefs.

Reconciling the Two Views?

There is a way to make reason-based romantic love more palatable as far as our beliefs about love are concerned, allowing for some reconciliation between the two. It works as follows: it "starts" with the lover finding the properties of the beloved (or some of them) valuable. The lover then goes on to endow or bestow on the beloved more value (on bestowal, see Singer 1984, ch. 1). Let us consider an example.

Like many others, William values and is attracted to people who are physically beautiful, witty, and knowledgeable about all sorts of things. One night, he meets Olga in a bar and they strike up a riveting conversation. Soon they are dating: he finds her to be amazing, especially when it comes to her beauty, wit, and knowledge. He falls in love with her (and she, too, with him – I give a one-sided account to keep things simple). As their relationship grows, William does two things: first, he tolerates or turns a blind eye to those properties of Olga that he generally cannot stand (e.g., that she chews her food with her mouth open, and that she likes to watch reality TV). Second, he endows other properties of Olga – properties to which he is usually indifferent when found in people other than her – with value and comes to find them charming and endearing. For example, he never really thought one way or another about people singing in the shower. Olga likes to do a lot of that – especially opera. He comes to find this adorable. Third, he endows with *more* value Olga's properties that attracted him to her in the first place. In general, then, as time goes by, William endows more and more properties of Olga with value. Soon she becomes his "special baby."

Note that the properties that William initially finds valuable in Olga are ones that he continues to find valuable in her (and in others). But by endowing them and others of Olga's properties with value, Olga becomes very special to him. When this happens, her uniqueness to him increases, and so does her irreplaceability. Moreover, because she has become so special, there is a higher probability that – as long as nothing drastic happens or changes – his love for her becomes more and more durable. Finally, and for the same reasons, his love for her becomes more and more exclusive. The main reason is that as William endows Olga with more value, his attachment to her increases. With the increase in attachment, chances that his love will not be constant, that she ceases to be unique to him, or that he will also love another woman, decrease.

However, we have to be careful how to state the point. Consider exclusivity: because, first, other women have the properties that attracted William to Olga in the first place, and because, second, William, in all likelihood, finds valuable *other* properties that Olga does not have but that other women do, his love for Olga is *not* exclusive in a conceptual sense. That he adds value to her *increases the probability* that his love is exclusive. Logically speaking, the addition of value is a bar neither to non-exclusive love nor to non-constant love. The point is that the creation of value can help retain constancy, exclusivity, uniqueness, and irreplaceability in *real-life* cases, because people who are strongly attached to their objects of value *tend* not to part with them and tend to be awed by them, leaving room for less and less attention to and love for others with similar properties. So if we are content to maintain constancy, exclusivity, and uniqueness only at the level of our actual love lives, the creation of value goes a long way to secure them. But if we insist on exclusivity, constancy, and uniqueness at the conceptual or logical level, we are asking for the impossible.

Let us close this section by revisiting the Jeff and Rose example. Here is how Jeff should answer Rose's question why he loves her: "I love you because you're beautiful, witty, and know a lot about European history! Although, conceptually speaking, I do have reason to love other women with these same properties, ever since we've been together I have come to love everything about you. I even adore the fact that you never put enough salt in the food or that you never rent a decent movie for us to watch! What I'm saying is that because of the traits for which I love you, I have come to also love these other ones; I have come to consider them valuable. I have bestowed value on you. But I don't love any other woman *for* them, because bestowing value on you made me attached to you. So you see, the time we spent together allowed me to see you and to consider you as my special girl. No one else can take your place, no one else is quite like you, and the way things are going now, I figure I'm going to love you forever – not conceptually, but as a matter of fact."

Philosophical and highfalutin as it sounds, Jeff's answer is probably the best he – or we – could come up with if we want to neither romanticize love nor completely drain it of its exclusivity, constancy, and uniqueness.

What Do We Love? Properties of the Beloved

There is a case to be made that Socrates thinks the object of love – what or whom we love – is not the person, but the person's beauty. Recall that Socrates claims, first, that we desire beauty, and he identifies love with the desire for beauty. Second, he advises that we move up the ladder of love from an individual human being to the Form of Beauty. Third, he seems to assume that the beauty found in human beings, in souls, in laws and activities, and finally in the Form of Beauty itself, is all of the same *type*, albeit more valuable as we go up (cf. Nussbaum 1986, 178–179). That is, if the beauty of bodies, of souls, and so on were all of different kinds, it would be difficult to compare them on a single scale of value. If we cannot make this comparison, it is difficult to see how Socrates could justify the ascent from loving individuals to loving the Form of Beauty. If, fourth, Socrates considers the Form of Beauty to be the main embodiment and "paradigmatic instance of [Beauty]" (Vlastos 1989, 106), the implication is that the object of love is beauty as such, whether found in human beings, in souls, or in the Form of Beauty itself.

If we interpret Socrates as claiming that we love *both* the individual and the beauty found in him, this would not be (very) controversial, because we seem to agree with him. Lovers do tell their beloveds how much they love their eyes, smiles, charm, wit, and so on, so to claim that we love other people's attributes is a problem only if we assume that we love *only* people's attributes, *not* also the people themselves. But so what if the belief that we love individual people is false? Why is this a problem? To find out, we need to figure out what it means to love someone as an individual.

Let us begin with the view of Gregory Vlastos.[7] Commenting on Plato's (Socrates's) theory, he writes,

> What needs to be stressed most of all ... is that Plato's theory is not, and is not meant to be, about personal love for persons ... In this theory persons evoke [eros] if they have beautiful bodies, minds, or dispositions. But so do quite impersonal objects ... as objects of Platonic love all these are not only as good as persons, but distinctly better.
>
> (Vlastos 1989, 107–108)

He adds,

> As a theory of the love of persons ... we are to love the persons so far, and only insofar, as they are good and beautiful. Now since all too few human

beings are masterworks of excellence, and not even the best of those we have the chance to love are wholly free of streaks of the ugly, the mean, the commonplace, the ridiculous, if our love for them is to be only for their virtue and beauty, the individual, in the uniqueness and integrity of his or her individuality, will never be the object of our love. This seems to me the cardinal flaw in Plato's theory. It does not provide for love of whole persons, but only for love of that abstract version of persons which consists of the complex of their best qualities.

(Vlastos 1989, 110)

Vlastos is accusing Plato of giving us a view of love according to which the object of love is not the whole individual. But he seems to be attributing two views to Plato. The first is that we love not the individual, but his or her good *properties* (the last sentence in the above quotation indicates this). I address below whether it is possible to love *properties*. The other view is that we love *part* of the individual. Let us assume, correctly, along with Vlastos, that few people (if any) are perfectly good and beautiful, and that most of us have defects. If Plato's view is that "we are to love others so far, and only insofar, as they are good and beautiful," then we are able to love only that part of someone that is good and beautiful. Loving only a part of the person means that, somehow, we love not the whole person. If there is someone who is flawless, who has no defects at all, then, on Vlastos's understanding of Plato, this person *would* be the object of love, whole and complete.

Because he wants a theory that allows us to love an individual as a whole, Vlastos *faults* Plato for giving us this theory of love. Although noble, Vlastos's position is troubling. First, Plato's theory presents no conceptual or logical difficulty in loving individuals as a whole. If, by some miracle, the majority of people were perfectly good and beautiful, then, on Vlastos's own rendering of Plato, we will be able to love them as wholes. It is only an accident, so to speak, that we happen to be defective. Vlastos may reply – convincingly – that a good theory of love should accommodate the fact that we are defective. It should not make it a condition of loving a person as a whole that he or she be perfect. Although this claim is correct, it is not the same as Vlastos's original criticism of Plato: it is one thing to accuse a theory of not allowing us, logically, to love persons as whole, but quite another to accuse it of not allowing us to do so contingently.

Second, what would be Vlastos's alternative view to Plato's? If Vlastos faults Plato for offering us a theory of love that, given our defects, allows us to love only those parts of us that are good and beautiful, an alternative view would have to tackle how in loving others we are to approach their not-so-good-and-beautiful parts when we love them as wholes: if I am to love Steve wholly, do I also love his incessant snoring? We have two options. Either the alternative view would ask us to tolerate these properties, or it would ask us to love them. The first is a plausible alternative, but not one that Vlastos can adopt. The second is implausible.

When we love others, it sounds silly, not to mention strange and possibly unachievable, to *require* that lovers love not only the good parts of their beloveds, but every other part as well. It is a tall order to require me to love – not merely tolerate – the grapefruit-sized goiter on my beloved's neck, his undulating layers of fat, his stinking feet, or his habit of constantly harping on about some point or other. Not only is such a requirement a tall order, it also does not cohere with how people actually love (sad to say, we *do not* usually love our beloveds' goiters or their leprosy). So the most to ask of a theory of love is that it requires us to tolerate the nasty parts of our beloveds, not love them. But Vlastos cannot take this way out, because Plato's theory of love accommodates tolerating the bad parts of the beloved. The only option left to Vlastos is to require that we love those bad parts – an implausible idea, as we have seen.

So to love a person as a whole, not in part, is to love the person in virtue of her good properties and to tolerate the bad ones. This still does not tell us what it *means* to love *the person* as a whole or in part (to love the person, period). Who or what is this person that we are meant to love wholly, for her self?

There is no denying that we have properties. For example, I have the properties of having been born in 1967, of being five feet, eleven inches tall, of being a philosopher, of being of Arab origin, of liking to have Coco Puffs for breakfast, of having three brothers, of living in Chicago, and of being a fan of *The Simpsons*. Any aspect of a person (or object for that matter) can be captured, using the right language, in terms of a property. So in a sense each of us is a "bundle of properties," a collection or a list of all his or her properties. The issue is whether there is something over and above – or rather, underlying – these properties: a *person*, a soul, or a transcendental self, something in which all the properties inhere or to which they all attach. Imagine a ball of wax with thousands of pins stuck in it, covering its entire surface. The pins would represent the properties, while the ball of wax would represent the soul or the self. It is what underlies and unifies all the properties (the pins) as the properties belonging to *one* entity. If we were a bunch of properties, to *what* would they attach? Either there must be *something* to which they attach, or there isn't, in which case we are *nothing but* a bundle of properties.

Suppose that there is something that unifies the properties, a "soul," say, or a transcendental self: would loving the person mean loving his soul (in addition to his properties)? Suppose that we do not have a soul or a transcendental self: what, then, would it mean to love the person?

Let us start with the second question. Suppose that we do not have a soul or a transcendental self; we are nothing but a bundle or collection of properties. Loving the person *y* would then mean loving that particular bundle of properties that is *y* or that constitutes what *y* is (to see this, just substitute "bundle of properties" for "person," as if it is a mathematical equation, since they both refer to the same object). Is this a troubling answer as far as love is concerned? Not really. For if *each one of us* is nothing but a bundle of properties, there is really nothing more to aspire to. It is not as if *y* can complain to *x*, his lover, "*You* love me as nothing but a bundle of properties, but *Sarah* loves Micah as more than that!" And should x rhetorically (even sarcastically) ask y, "More than what, exactly?" x would be right, because we are all in the same boat, x, y, Sarah, and Micah. On this view, each of us is nothing but a bundle of properties, and there's no more to it than that. Moreover, there's nothing bad or demeaning about being a bundle of properties: this is a purely metaphysical view with no repercussions to morality or any other social or political matter (some might worry that without souls or selves we would have no inherent dignity, but dignity could have other sources).

More important, if the objects of love – what we love – are, metaphysically speaking, nothing but collections of properties, it does not follow that when we love the person as a person we love *each* of the person's properties, *individually*. Consider: Micah is nothing but the collection of properties $P1$ to Pn. Sarah loves Micah, the person or the individual. This means that Sarah loves the collection of properties $P1$ to Pn. This does not mean that she loves each property individually or on its own. For one thing, to love a collection is not to love the individual members of that collection (I love the human race, but I don't love Margaret Thatcher, Ariel Sharon, or George W. Bush, let alone Adolf Hitler or Joseph Stalin). For another, if Micah is nothing but his collection of properties, some are probably downright nasty, like having a grapefruit-sized goiter on his neck or smelly feet. Does Sarah love these too? Probably not. "Hence, x can love y in virtue of y's attractive properties that outweigh y's defects, and the object of x's love is the collection of properties that y is, yet none of these properties is necessarily also an object of love for x" (Soble 1990, 308).

There is a third reason: strictly speaking, properties cannot be objects of love. Suppose that Rose has the property of having blue eyes. What would it mean for Jeff to love this property? Does Jeff *love* Rose's having blue eyes? Or does he love, simply, her blue eyes? The latter makes sense, at least as far as common sense is concerned. When lovers whisper loving things to their beloveds, they do not say, "I love your having blue eyes"; they say, "I love your blue eyes." This indicates that the appropriate object of love is an object, not a property (which is a modification of the object), either the whole person or part of the whole person. And just because persons might be collections of properties, they are still objects: a collection of properties is not itself a property.

A brief digression is worthwhile at this point: Does the above mean that properties are also inadequate as the basis for love? Is it Rose's blue eyes that are the basis of Jeff's love for her? Or is it Rose's having blue eyes the property? The answer is that it is the property, because objects, as such, cannot be reasons, since reasons are a bridge between an object, on the one hand, and an attitude, emotion, or action regarding the object, on the other. Rose as such, as an object, is not a reason; it is something *about* her that would provide the link between Rose and Jeff's love for her, such as Rose's having blue eyes. It is here, moreover, that Socrates (or Plato) may have made a mistake: if I am correct that properties can be reasons for, but not objects of, love, then we can love someone *for* having black eyes and we can love his black eyes, but we cannot love his having black eyes. Socrates, seeing that beauty as a property is shared among different bodies, souls, activities, and the Form of Beauty itself, notices that we have reason to love all these objects, that we have reason to love all these objects *for* their beauty (this is the tension with our belief in exclusivity). But he ends up recommending that we drop everything and stick only with the Form of Beauty as the *object* of love. In short, Socrates seems to confuse the *basis* of love with the *object* of love.

Back to our pre-digression point: even if we don't have souls or transcendental selves, and even if we are nothing but bundles of properties, there is nothing in this view to endanger the idea that we can love a person as a person or wholly. (What it would mean, however, to love a *part* of the person, *a la* Vlastos's Plato, is more difficult to fathom; perhaps it means to love a smaller bundle of the person's properties but still as a bundle; that is, instead of loving Micah (P1 to Pn), you love part of Micah, the *collection* P3–P17, which is subset – a smaller bundle – of Micah's properties.)

Let us now tackle the first question: Suppose that we did have a soul or a self, over and above our properties, what would it mean to love the person as a person? One hurdle here is that we don't have a good idea of what the soul or the self is, apart from manifesting itself in the individual whom we love and with whom we interact in physical space. I suppose the answer to the question would be that to love the person as a person is to love her soul or self, but this might not withstand much scrutiny. Consider our options. Either it means that we love the person's soul in itself, *apart* from its manifestation in the (physical) individual, or it means that we love the person's soul as it is manifested in the (physical) individual. The first option is hard to understand: If I love Nora's soul in itself, how can I have access to it in order to love it? I cannot "grasp" her soul so that I can love it. Moreover, if I love her soul apart from how it is manifested in her person, it is not clear that it is *Nora's* soul as opposed to anybody else's or – for that matter – nobody's soul. And if nothing makes it Nora's soul in particular, what happens to my love for *Nora*? I cannot love *her* by loving a soul that is not connected to her in any significant way. So it is difficult to understand the idea that we can love someone as a person if it means that we love her soul in itself, apart from its manifestation in the person's properties.

If you reply that I love Nora's soul because I can see it in her gleaming eyes, her relaxing smile, and her tender touch, we are back to the second option, namely the soul's manifestation in (the embodied, physical) Nora. We can say that I love Nora's soul in how it manifests itself in different ways in her. But then talk of souls adds nothing informative. If we know, on independent grounds (that is, metaphysical grounds, having nothing to do with love), that souls exist, then talking about loving souls as they are manifested in people would make sense and would make discussing the object of love more accurate and truthful. But we don't have such knowledge, so I suspect that talking about the soul or the self adds nothing.

The picture we emerge with, then, is one in which we love an individual *for* (on the basis of, for reasons of) some of his properties, and we tolerate him for having others. With *some* other properties – those that we value in general, to which we are indifferent or even dislike – we come to endow them with value in the beloved. In all this, we love the person as a person in that we love him as the collection of properties that he is, without loving each and every subset of properties (those containing the nasty ones), and without having to decide whether there is a soul or a self that underlies this collection.

However, there is one more point I have so far glossed over: Is there a distinction between loving a person *as a whole* and loving a person *as a person*? The first seems to be about a mode of love such that when we love *y*, every aspect of *y* must be loved or at least accounted for. The second seems to be about loving some *core* or essence of *y*, instead of loving the totality of *y*. Talk of souls or selves might make us think that these two are the same, because if we view the soul as constituting the core of someone (as is common) and as somehow pervading every aspect of someone (as is also common), it is easy to see how the two issues can be run together. But if the two were different, we would have so far addressed only the one about loving the whole person, not about loving the person as a core or for who he really is.

To love the person as a person in the sense of loving the core of the person means to love the person for whom he or she really is. This, in turn, means to love that collection of properties, those parts of the person that the person has, such that, without them, the person is no longer the same person. For example, if the crucial properties that Omar has are his wit, sense of humor, and joyfulness, to love Omar for whom he really is, is to love this set of properties. If something were to happen to Omar that causes him to deeply change and become morose, depressed, and joyless, in a sense he is no longer the same person. For if wit, humor, and joyfulness are the properties that define who Omar is, the properties that described his basic character, to lose them is to lose this basic character. But to lose this basic character is to become a different person (as we will see below, this change is not a metaphysical type of change).

As a corollary to the above, to *not* love the real Omar could mean two things. It could mean that Layla, Omar's lover, loves those properties of his that do not define his core or basic character. Or it could mean that Layla loves someone other than who Omar really is. If, by some chance, Layla has completely mistaken beliefs about who Omar is – if, for example, her beliefs that he is witty, has a sense of humor, and is joyful are wrong – then whatever Layla loves, "it" is not really Omar. She loves an imaginary person whom she thinks is Omar. So we have two ways in which *x* might not love the real *y*. First, *x* loves that set of properties of *y* that does not define *y*'s core. Second, *x* loves that set of properties that *x* mistakenly thinks defines *y*'s core.

Different Types of Properties and Love's Durability and Depth

We have seen that the beloved's properties play the crucial role of forming the basis of love: *x* loves *y for* such-and-such properties; they provide *x* with reasons for loving *y*. But properties come in different types, and this raises an important question: Are there properties on which basis it is, in some sense, *better* to love? Before we explain this question, let us distinguish between the different types of properties.

Properties can be distinguished from each other in at least five different ways: (1) essential and accidental properties; (2) important and unimportant properties; (3) mental, character-related properties and physical properties; (4) innate and acquired properties; and (5) properties for which we want to be loved and properties for which we do not want, or prefer not, to be loved (cf. Soble 1990, 228). Some of these distinctions intersect: for example, an innate property can be one for which a person wants to be loved, but it can also be one for which the beloved does not want to be loved.

Essential vs. accidental properties. I use the term "essential" in the metaphysical sense to mean "a property without which the object ceases to be what it is." For example, if the property of being odd is an essential property of the number three, the number three *cannot* be the number three without its being odd. The Judeo-Christian-Islamic God, to give another example, has the essential property of being morally perfect (in addition to being omnipotent, etc.); remove this property and God is no longer God. An *accidental* property is one that an entity can lose without its ceasing to exist. For example, that I own 4,476 books is an accidental property of mine. If I lose it – say, three books get lost – I am still the same person. I also have the property of having ten fingers; if I lose this property (I get one finger chopped off), I am still the same person.

Philosophers are frugal when it comes to people's essential properties, leaning toward the view that most people's properties are accidental: Could Socrates have been a shoemaker instead of a philosopher and still be Socrates? Yes! Examples of essential properties of people include: being a person, being made of molecules, and coming from a particular sperm and egg (if another person has every property I have, including the same name, except that he came from a different sperm and egg, he would not be me, but someone else).

Important vs. unimportant properties. Even though being a philosopher is not an *essential* property of Socrates, it is an *important* property of his. In some sense, he would not be the same person had he not been a philosopher. He would still be the same person in a *metaphysical* sense – we still point to him and say, "There goes Socrates" – but he changes deeply – we point to him and say, "Poor Socrates. He's never been the same since he lost his ability to teach philosophy." Note that whether a property is important is not up to the person to decide, but on whether it defines who the person is. Some of his *unimportant* properties might be wearing an off-white toga for most of his life, or gesticulating while speaking. Other properties are not so clear: Socrates had a snub nose, and Nietzsche made fun of him for it; is it an important or unimportant property?

These two distinctions cut across each other. A property might be essential but not important to who one is (e.g., being made of molecules); it might be essential and important (being a person); it might be accidental but important (being a philosopher); and it might be accidental and unimportant (preferring chocolate over vanilla ice cream).

Mental vs. physical properties. Examples of mental properties include being smart (or stupid), imaginative (or dull), and witty (or slow). They also include personality and character traits, such as being vivacious, courageous, forth-coming, a dullard, just, and temperate. Examples of physical properties include being of a certain height, weight, and mass, of having a large nose, of having high cheekbones, and of having large feet.

Again, this distinction cuts across both of the first two. A mental property might be important to whom one is (being smart) and it might not (being bored with postmodern documentary films). I will let the reader come up with examples of the other intersections.

Innate vs. acquired properties. Examples of innate properties include having brown eyes, having the disposition to be afraid of snakes, and having an aver-sion to heights. Examples of acquired properties include being a good gymnast, being an excellent chess player, and having a PhD in philosophy. There are some unclear cases, such as the property of salivating over lasagna. Part of the problem is lack of clarity of the meaning of the terms "acquired" and "innate." For example, does "acquired" include the condition that the person exercised effort or will to possess the property, or is the mere role of the environment enough for a property to be acquired?

Fuzziness aside, this distinction again cuts across all the above four distinc-tions. For example, the property of being a philosopher is mental, acquired, (probably) important to its owner, and accidental. The property of being able to lift over 200 lb is physical and acquired, but it is accidental and may or may not be important for the one who has it. I leave it to the reader to go through the combinations (sixteen in all).

Properties for which we desire to be loved vs. properties for which we do not desire to be loved. This is a subjective distinction: each person has (some) preferences for which properties he or she wants to be loved. Mary might want to be loved for her skill at outwitting people, whereas John might want to be loved for his buns of steel. Again, this distinction cuts across all the above four distinctions, and, again, I leave it to the reader to go through each combination (thirty-two in all).

The above distinctions raise an important question about love: Is there a type of property on which basis it is better to love a person than another type of property? "Better" can mean (1) "a type of property that makes the love *more comprehensible* than another type of property"; (2) "a type of property that allows the love to be more constant or more exclusive than another type of property"; (3) "a type of property that makes the beloved more unique or more irreplace-able than another type of property"; or (4) "a type of property that makes the love *more moral or more prudent* to have than another type of property." I won't go through the first three in detail (and I leave the fourth until Chapter 4), but a few remarks are helpful.

First, can *any* property, no matter of what type, be a basis or a reason for *x* loving *y*? Yes, but not any property can make the love comprehensible (how is Martin's love for Nelson because the number three is odd comprehensible?). (1) Essential properties tend not to make a love comprehensible (x's love for y because y is made of molecules or because y is a person is puzzling), unless they are endowed with value, such as being a child of God, having inherent dignity, and being valued by God. Accidental properties run the gamut from the silly to the important, from the normal to the abnormal, and whether a love based on them is comprehensible depends on the property in question. (2) Almost any important property can make love comprehensible, because important properties are identity-conferring (being a chef, a philosopher, a model, good at ice-skating, or a stamp collector), which means that they tend to be valuable to human beings, so that people's love on their basis is comprehensible. With unimportant properties, things stand in much the same way as they do with accidental properties: it depends on the property. (3) There are good (being clever, being courageous) and bad (being stupid, being a coward) mental properties. Ditto for physical properties, though individual taste plays a larger role here. People tend to think more highly of loves based on (positive) mental properties than of loves based on physical properties ("Hrmph! He loves her for her huge breasts. God only knows what she does with them to keep him drooling like a puppy"). Whether we like it or not, it is understandable why someone can love another on the basis of a physical property (negative or positive) and how someone can love another on the basis of a positive mental property. The hard cases involve loving someone on the basis of a negative mental property ("I love him because he's such a bimbo"). But they can be explained: perhaps being a bimbo ensures that her friends won't find him a catch and so she won't have to worry about being jealous (cf. Armstrong 2003, ch. 12). (4) Whether an innate or acquired property makes a love comprehensible depends on the property itself. (5) The fact that someone wants to be loved for a certain property is not a reason, in and of itself, that makes the love comprehensible (Ito's wanting to be loved for the fact that he lives 300 miles away from Tokyo is incomprehensible). The same goes for *not* wanting to be loved for a particular property.

Second, are there types of property that allow the love to be more constant or more exclusive than another type of property? (1) Whether a love is exclusive as far as its basis is concerned depends on whether the properties are shared with ones other than the beloved. Some essential properties are shared (being a person, being made of molecules, and being God's child) and some are not (having come from a particular sperm and egg). Non-shared essential properties secure exclusivity, but they cannot make the love comprehensible (a difficulty, as we have seen, with all essential properties). Essential properties also secure constancy because they are unchanging – an empty victory, because essential properties are incomprehensible as the basis of love. Whether accidental properties secure exclusivity or constancy depends on whether the property in question is, respectively, shared or constant. Most accidental properties are shared, and the more specific we become in describing each property, the more we secure exclusivity but the more incomprehensible the love is. Securing constancy depends on the accidental property in question and on how long-lasting it is. Having a flat stomach and being a brilliant architect are both accidental properties, but the first is of much shorter duration (usually) than the second, so a love solely based on it should be expected to last as long as it does. (2) A property being important or unimportant has nothing to do, as such, with guaranteeing exclusivity, because the issue is whether the property is shared, and both important and unimportant properties can be shared. Important properties help secure constancy because they tend to define who a person is and so are likely to be stable. However, love's constancy based on unimportant properties depends on the specific property (some are durable, others are not). (3) Basing love on mental and physical properties secures exclusivity insofar as these properties are not shared. However, it is likely that they are, but the narrower we define them, the less likely they can be the basis of love. With constancy things are more nuanced. If mental, but not physical, properties tend to be durable, basing love on the first makes it more constant (but remember that some people do shed them, some mental properties are not durable, and some do not base love understandably). Physical properties tend to change, so a love based on them would change also. And among those that do not (having blue eyes, having two arms, and having a face), some cannot comprehensibly ground love. (4) Whether an innate or an acquired property secures exclusivity depends on whether it is a shared property, and, it seems, innate and acquired properties tend to be shared. Securing constancy depends on the durability of the property in question; some innate properties are durable, some are not; some acquired properties are durable, some are not. (5) Whether a love based on properties for which the beloved wants to be loved is exclusive or constant depends on the property. But we can confidently claim that such properties tend to be shared and durable, because people often want to be loved for those properties that define them, which tend to be common and to last for a long time. Such loves would not be exclusive, though they would tend to be constant. Whether a love based on qualities for which the beloved does not want to be loved secures exclusivity depends on the property. But such a love is likely not to be constant insofar as the beloved might come to refuse or reject it.

Third, is there a type of property on the basis of which the beloved is more unique or more irreplaceable?

Except for some essential properties, *types* of properties do not provide good grounds for making the beloved unique or more unique than another object of love. The essential properties that do provide such grounds are those that make the beloved unique: her genetic code, her coming from a particular pair of sperm and egg, and so on. But these are hard to fathom as grounds of love. The other types of essential properties – those shared with others (e.g., being a person, being made of molecules, having consciousness, being God's child) – do not provide for the uniqueness of the beloved precisely because they are shared. This leaves us with accidental properties and the rest of the types of properties. Everything depends on the property in question, because talk of uniqueness does not sit well with talk of types. After all, the main purpose of having types is avoiding individuality. We should not, then, expect that a love based on a *type* of property is going to make a beloved unique; whether it does depends entirely on the *particular* property on which it is based, not on its type. Even here we should not be too hopeful, because almost all love-relevant properties are shared, and the more we refine a property, the more difficult it will be to understand how it can base a love.

What about irreplaceability? The notion of irreplaceability is laden with value: whether something is irreplaceable is connected to the value it has to someone. Love is not different. Whether the beloved is irreplaceable depends not on the properties on which the love is based, but on the value with which the lover endows the beloved. Because most properties that can adequately base love are shared, the beloved's irreplaceability is not going to depend on them. Even if a property makes the beloved unique, she will not be irreplaceable unless she is endowed with value, because something's having a unique property does not mean it has value to its owner or lover. Of course, that she is a beloved means she is valued to some extent by the lover, but this does not ensure irreplaceability, because the value needs to be quite high to do so. This might happen as the love progresses: the more value the lover endows her with, the more valuable she becomes to him; the more valuable she becomes, the more irreplaceable.

Summary

It makes sense to speak of loving the whole person: we love the person as a collection of properties, whether there is or is not a soul or self underlying or unifying this collection. This does not mean that we love everything about the person; those nasty bits of him are more likely to be tolerated than loved. It also makes sense to speak of loving the person for who he is, those parts of him that define his identity.

There are also a few advantages to regarding love as reason-based. We can evaluate it rationally, like we do other emotions, and assimilate it to other emotions, making it less anomalous. The price we pay is a conceptual clash between this type of love and some of our beliefs about love's constancy and exclusivity, and the beloved's uniqueness. However, we are better off attenuating these beliefs and accepting that romantic love is not *by its nature* constant and exclusive, and that the beloved is not *necessarily* unique. We should weaken these beliefs for two main reasons. First, as we have seen in Chapter 2, love is neither exclusive nor constant by its nature. Second, a non-reason-based view of love has a more difficult time securing these beliefs. We are better off accepting a reason-based view of love that is more rationally assessable.

There is a third reason: attenuating such beliefs might spare us much heartbreak and cushion the shock when we are no longer loved. This is a topic for Chapter 4.

Notes

1 This is strange because, to convey his own views, Socrates does not usually rely on others, especially *women*.
2 Diotima's conclusion seems to be that love desires *two* things: the good *and* immortality. But it does not follow from her claim that love desires the *possession of the good forever*, which is *one* thing, not two. In other words, the "forever" describes *how* the good is possessed; it is not an additional desired thing, over and above the good.
3 Or it could be the lover, who is being led by Socrates's wisdom and teaching. For the first interpretation, see Price (1997).
4 I say "Socrates," not "Plato," because even though Socrates is usually Plato's mouthpiece, it is not clear that he is in the *Symposium*.
5 The philosopher Immanuel Kant once said that to us human beings moral demands take the form of commands because we have to fight our desires and inclinations to act morally; not so with God, who does what is moral because it is His nature to do so (Kant 1981, 414).
6 Compare this with Plato's question in the *Euthyphro*: "Is the pious being loved by the gods because it is pious, or is it pious because it is being loved by the gods?" (Plato 1997a, 10a). Consider also: Does God command us to do what is good because it is good, or is something good because God commands us to do it?
7 The discussion of Vlastos's view that follows benefited immensely from Soble (1990, 300–301).

Further Reading

On loving for reasons, non-reason-based love, exclusivity, constancy, uniqueness, and irreplaceability, Alan Soble's 1990 book is detailed and a must-read. The *Phaedrus* is another extensive treatment of love by Plato. On why Plato chose a woman to be Socrates's teacher of love, see Halperin (1990, ch. 6). Plato expounds his Theory of Forms in many of his works, but the *Phaedo* and the *Republic* are two starting points. The *Timaeus* presents Plato's later treatment, and in the *Parmenides* Plato subjects his theory to criticism. For secondary sources on the Theory of Forms, see Vlastos (1978). See Gosling (1983) for a treatment of Plato's philosophy. Kosman (1989) raises some issues regarding exclusivity and other related topics. On the generality of reasons in art, see Goldman (2006), and Sibley (2004a) and (2004b). On moral particularism, see McNaughton (1988, ch. 13), and Hooker and Little (2000). On *agape*, see also Kierkegaard (1962). Singer (1984, 2001a) offers a reason-based and non-reason-based view of love. On essential and accidental properties, see Kripke (1972). A good introduction to the metaphysical issues raised in this chapter is van Inwagen (1993).

4　Love and Morality

Love and Morality

"All's fair in love and war" is a common saying. We know very well that in war, not "all" is fair – some actions are plain wrong and are rightly prohibited (e.g., targeting civilians). Is "all" fair in love? Answering this question is the task of this chapter.

Morality divides actions into right and wrong, and subdivides right actions into permissible and obligatory. Wrong actions are ones we should not do, permissible actions are ones we may do, and obligatory actions are ones we must do. To which category does romantic love belong? And does this question even make sense since love is an emotion, not an action? Suppose that envy is a bad emotion. Suppose also that Rajiv is an envious person and that Sanjay is neither envious nor not envious. Sanjay should take steps to ensure that he won't become an envious person, and Rajiv should take steps to expunge envy in him. Morality requires them to act in these ways. So morality prohibiting or permitting an emotion makes sense, including the emotion of romantic love. If morality prohibits it, we should act to either expunge or not cultivate it. If morality permits love but does not consider it obligatory, we may have the emotion and act on it. If morality considers love obligatory, we must take steps to cultivate it in ourselves.

This is not all. If morality considers romantic love permissible or obligatory, there is still the issue of which actions are right and which are wrong when done for love or because of love, to beloveds and those not part of the love relationship. "All's" indeed not fair in love.

Is romantic love morally obligatory? To be sure, there have been injunctions that we love each other. Christ commanded us to do so, and so has Cher in her song "Love One Another." But Christ did not have romantic love in mind, and Cher's words can be chalked up to poetry. Besides, romantic love cannot really be obligatory, because it violates the important principle in moral philosophy of "ought" implies "can." If we are obligated to do action A, we would have to be able to do A. For example, if I have an obligation to visit my ailing father in hospital, then I am able to do so (I am not in a coma, I am not in a far away continent). If, somehow, I am unable to visit him, I cannot have an obligation to do so. Romantic love is not under people's control. If people cannot just decide to fall in love, whether with a particular person or in general (this is true of all emotions; we cannot just decide to hate, envy, or be jealous of so-and-so), then romantic love is not under our command, which means it is not something we are able to do at will. It violates the "ought implies can," so it cannot be obligatory.

But can people not control, moderate, even extirpate or cultivate an emotion, given time and focus? Emotions may not be under our *direct* control, but surely they can be *indirectly* controlled. Why can't this be true also of romantic love?

Although it is plausible that emotions can be controlled or moderated once they exist (even here it is doubtful that everyone can control his or her emotions), it is a different matter whether they can be extirpated or cultivated from scratch. For example, if Khaled hates Rami, it is possible for him to moderate his hatred or control it in different ways. But it may not be possible for him to get rid of it altogether or, if his hatred does not exist, that he can bring himself to hate Rami. Remember that emotions are typically reason-based. If Khaled has no reason to hate Rami, it will be virtually impossible for him to hate him out of nothing. If Khaled has reasons to hate Rami, it will also be virtually impossible for him to stop hating him unless these reasons are addressed. Love is similar.

There is a more important reason why romantic love is not obligatory. Usually, if x has an obligation to y to do A, then y has a right against x that x do A. For example, if William has an obligation to Mary to look after her plants while she is away, Mary has a right against William that he look after her plants. If the rich have obligations to help the poor, the poor have rights against the rich to help them. If parents have obligations to tend to their children, the children have rights against their parents that they are looked after. And so on. Once we consider rights – the flipside of obligations – we can better see why there is no obligation to romantically love another. No y has a right against x that x romantically love y. No person can demand of me that I love him. Even if y has every property x considers necessary to love someone, x would still have no obligation to love y, even if y were not a stranger but someone who, in addition to having desirable properties, has a history with x (though y may have rights against x to considerate treatment, gratitude, and generosity, for example).

So we have no obligations to romantically love other people (though, once in love, couples may have obligations toward each other).

Is romantic love morally prohibited? There are at least two reasons to believe that it is. The first is that love is selfish, a reason with which we have already dealt (Chapter 2). The second is that romantic love involves preferential treatment. The Danish philosopher Kierkegaard thought so: "Insofar as you love your beloved, you are not like unto God, for in God there is no partiality ... Insofar as you love your friend, you are not like unto God, because before God there is no distinction. But when you love your neighbor, then you are like unto God"

(1962, 74–75). The contemporary philosopher Robert Ehman also thinks that romantic love is preferential:

> The fundamental requirement of love is to raise the beloved above all others and to give her a privileged status in our life ... The fundamental requirement of morality in contrast is to treat all persons as having equal worth and to justify all special treatment of a person by reference to universally valid principles.

He adds, "there is always something immoral in the privilege and attention that the lover gives to the beloved at the expense of others who might have an even higher claim on the beloved" (Ehman 1989, 260; the last word in the quotation is a mistake; it should be "lover").

Ehman's reasoning would apply not only to romantic lovers, but also to any intimate relationship: friendship, parents–children, and sibling relationships. If romantic love were morally abhorrent *because* it involves the preferential treatment of the beloved, then any other intimate association would also be morally abhorrent if it involves such preferential treatment. Since we usually treat our children, siblings, parents, and friends preferentially, these forms of love will be morally dubious unless radically reformed. This point is important because it shows – to some, anyway – that there is a mistake in Ehman's (and Kierkegaard's) reasoning: that because a relationship involves preferential treatment it is morally wrong. Perhaps the truth in reasoning such as Ehman's is that such relationships are morally wrong when the privileging is excessive or when it comes *at the expense* of our obligations to others. We shall return to this point below.

Others, however, might find Ehman's reasoning compelling: Why not radically transform these intimate relationships so that we treat everyone equally? Why should morality allow *any* amount of preferential treatment at all? This is a difficult question to answer, but a rough one goes as follows. We, as human beings, are not cold, rational creatures that relate to each other merely on this basis. We are, first, biological creatures that perpetuate ourselves through bearing and rearing children; we are, second, emotional beings with the full spectrum of emotions and desires; and we are, third, social and political animals, living in communities and as parts of networks of relationships. So we relate to each other not only rationally, but also emotionally and socially. To thrive, we need friends, children, and social networks (whether we need romantic love is a more debatable issue; see below). And without some preferential treatment, we cannot have friends or lovers, or raise our children properly. If Rachel is *my friend* and Juan is *my lover*, then almost by definition I will need to relate to them preferentially, because we need to spend additional time, energy, money, attention, among other things, to cultivate and maintain friendships and love. And in order to raise my children and take care of my parents, I need to devote extra time and attention to them, too. In short, *the very idea* of having friends, lovers, children, siblings, and parents becomes empty without the notion of preferential treatment. So morality will either have to accept this fact and monitor it to ensure that the treatment is not excessive or at the expense of obligations to others, or it will have to ask us to eschew intimate relationships altogether. The second is not an option, because without friendships and love in all their forms, we lose our ability to thrive as human beings, perhaps even our very humanity. So the thought that romantic love is morally suspicious because it involves preferential treatment is misguided. Morality should allow preferential treatment.

But this does not show that romantic love is morally permissible. Just because morality allows preferential treatment, it does not follow that *any* type of preferential relationship is morally allowed. Is a relationship between a Mafioso and his privileged clients morally permissible just because morality *generally* allows preferential treatment? No. What needs to be shown, then, is either that the relationship is a basic good, one needed for a minimum standard of decent living (the Mafioso–client relationship does not satisfy this requirement), or that it is otherwise morally in the clear (again, the Mafioso–client relationship does not meet this requirement), for then morality would allow people to choose their lives as they see fit, including the cultivation of romantic relationships.

Romantic love is not a basic good (see below), but, unlike the Mafioso–client relationship, it is not morally suspect either (at first blush, anyway). So its involving preferential treatment seems to be on a par with other morally permissible relationships also involving preferential treatment. Morality, then, should treat romantic love as it treats other things that are neither obligatory nor prohibited: it is up to individuals to decide whether to have it in their lives, subject to some moral regulations.

Romantic love, then, is neither morally obligatory nor morally prohibited; it is morally permissible. The main moral theories agree.

Love and Moral Theories

I focus on the three major moral theories – consequentialism, Kantian ethics, and virtue ethics – and conclude with a discussion of "commonsense" morality.

Consequentialism. As its name indicates, consequentialism's organizing concept is that of consequences. It claims that an action is right if, and only if, it yields the best possible consequences from among the available options. For example, faced with the options of saving a drowning child and of doing nothing, consequentialism requires that I save the drowning child because it yields the better consequences (a child is saved, his family is happy, only a minor inconvenience to me). But what does "consequences" mean? Consequentialists differ in how they cash in this notion. Classical utilitarianism – a type of consequentialism founded by Jeremy Bentham and championed and ably defended by John Stuart Mill – understands consequences in terms of happiness or, what is (to them) the same thing, pleasure. So to utilitarians, the best consequences are those that yield the greatest net amount of pleasure ("net" because almost all actions yield some pain that needs to be "subtracted" from the amount of pleasure produced).

How would consequentialism justify romantic love? The predictable answer is that it depends on romantic love's general effects: does it yield good or bad consequences in general? The expression "in general" reflects the idea that consequentialism is in principle willing to prohibit *particular* instances of romantic love if they have deleterious effects (on the lovers, their friends, their families). But as long as romantic love has no bad effects *in general*, consequentialism would consider it permissible.

Does romantic love generally have good or bad effects? Perhaps an obvious answer is that it does not have bad effects; if anything, it has good effects. It makes people happy and euphoric, gets rid of loneliness, it provides (when applicable) a decent atmosphere for raising children, to give a few examples. But this answer tells only part of the story, because romantic love also leads to pain when one of the lovers dies, gets sick, cheats, lies, or leaves the other; and it leads to often unwanted co-dependency and loss of autonomy. The issue is whether its good results are on balance greater than its bad results, an issue difficult to settle without proper empirical research, because we need to trace the actual effects of love. The research will also be fraught with pitfalls: How are we to determine the effects of love? By asking people? How then do we formulate the questions? Should we trust people's answers? If we get a mix of answers, how do we actually decide whether love has *overall* good or bad effects? Indeed, how do we understand the notions of "good results" and "bad results," objectively or subjectively, and how do we allow for self-deception, since people are sometimes self-deceived about how happy they are or about whether their love lives are working? This is only a sample of questions that any reliable empirical research needs to address. The research is likely to be unwieldy, with results that in all likelihood would not garner widespread agreement.

Perhaps we can adopt a non-empirical approach and say that since people have sought and fallen in love throughout the ages, it must on balance be better to have loved than not to have loved. If love were overall a bad thing, it would have died out a long time ago, so it is generally a good thing. If this reasoning is plausible, consequentialism would consider love to be morally permissible.

But consequentialism has a better reason for declaring love permissible. It is always a good thing to allow people to pursue their individual lives as they see fit and according to their own lights (unless they cause others harm). If we attempt to push people into what we think are good lives for them to lead, more harm than good would result.[1] Since romantic love is not obligatory, and even if it tends to have bad consequences (overall or in many cases), we are better off letting people decide whether they want to be in love and with whom. We thus treat love much like we treat other individual projects that people have: it is better to let them decide what careers they want to have, how many children to have, what to wear, what to read, where to travel, and so on, because even if some of their choices turn out badly, letting people do what they want produces more good consequences than otherwise. Love, then, is in general morally justified according to consequentialism on grounds of liberty or autonomy, which, in turn, is justified on grounds of happiness or good consequences (allowing people liberty is more productive of happiness than not).

Kantian ethics. Kantian ethics is a moral theory that follows closely in the footsteps of Immanuel Kant's moral teachings, though it need not (and usually does not) accept every claim made by Kant (hence "Kantian ethics" instead of "Kant's ethics").[2] Kantian ethicists favor the concept of motive.[3] What matter are not the consequences of one's actions, but the motives from which a person acts.

Suppose that Anastasia, a young, rich heiress, has been kidnapped for ransom. Her parents offer a handsome reward for finding her. Suppose that both Ivan and Alexander find her tied up in a chair in a shack somewhere on the outskirts of St. Petersburg. They both intend to rescue her. Although they both have the same intention, each has a different motive or reason. Ivan's motive is the reward, Alexander's to save a human child. According to Kantian ethics, only Alexander's motive is fully morally right. (Both their *actions* are right – they both saved a child – but only Alexander's *motive*, as Kant himself would put it, has moral *worth*.)

Kantians emphasize motives because motives tell us whether people act out of respect for the moral law. For we ought to do what morality requires of us *because* morality requires it, not because of other reasons (that is why Kant claims that morality is *categorical*, leaving no leeway in terms of doing something because we feel like doing it or because it profits). This point is usually captured by the concept of *duty*. What morality requires is a matter of duty, and if something is a duty, we must do it, period. So whereas Ivan rescues Anastasia because he wants the money, Alexander does so because it is his duty: morality demands that when we are in a position to save a child, we should.

Some critics think that Kantian ethics requires us to act for the *sake of* duty; it is as if Alexander thinks to himself, "Here we go again, yet another duty. Well, I guess I should save the damn child for its own sake." But this is a travesty. What Kantians have in mind is Alexander thinking along such lines: "A poor, helpless child! I *must* help her." Alexander need not actually think of the word "duty" as he saves Anastasia, let alone think that he must save the child for duty's sake. Instead, Alexander, as a morally decent man, recognizes that a child must be saved and he saves her, thus acting from the motive of duty and showing his commitment to morality.

Here comes the crucial part. Kantians (including Kant) divide duties into two types: perfect (or narrow) and imperfect (or wide). Perfect duties leave the agent no leeway in terms of when, how, and to whom to discharge (act on) the duty. If I promised Firas that I will meet him tomorrow at Dunkin' Donuts at three in the afternoon, it is my duty to do so, and I have to discharge it in exactly those ways: meet *Firas* (not someone else), tomorrow at three (not some other day or time) at Dunkin' Donuts (not some other place). Imperfect duties leave room for how, when, and to whom to discharge them (don't let the term "imperfect" mislead you; imperfect duties are as real and as binding as perfect ones). For example, according to Kant, we have the imperfect duty to help others to be happy, and the imperfect duty to improve our talents. But this does not mean that I have to help everyone to be happy or that I have to improve my every talent. I can choose whom to help, how, and when, and I can choose which of my talents to improve, how, and when, even if I choose a talent that is less helpful than another to humanity at large.

There is one more issue to delve into before turning to what Kantian ethics has to say about love. Kant is famous for his Categorical Imperative, which to him is morality's basic and ultimate principle. He gave different versions of it, but we shall be concerned only with the following one: "Act in such a way that you treat humanity in others and in yourself not only as a means but also as an end." There are four crucial aspects to this principle to note (see also the example in the next paragraph). First, Kant speaks of actions and treatment, not motives. Second, he does not say, "treat human beings, including yourself ..." but "treat humanity *in* others and yourself ..." Without being too pedantic, "humanity" is a term of art that refers to our capacity to set goals, including moral ones, for ourselves and to act on these goals (see Hill 1980). Third, I should treat humanity as an end in others *and* in myself. Fourth, Kant does not deny that we treat others as a means and does not think this is a bad thing. Instead, we should not treat each other *only* as a means; *as* we treat each other as a means, we should also treat each other as ends.

Consider a college philosophy teacher and his students. When he lectures in class and raises questions for debate, and when his students ask him questions, each party uses the other: he uses his students to stimulate his thinking about his field and to make money, and they use him to gain knowledge and achieve good grades. But they should also treat each other as ends: the teacher respects the students' goals of learning and receiving good grades, and he acts to help them attain these goals (he prepares well for his classes, he grades them fairly); in short, he *adopts* their goals as his own. When the students treat him as an end, they respect the fact that teaching is his job and that he is there for them but that he also has other things to do (so they hand in their assignments on time, they study hard so as not to frustrate his desire to teach them); they, too, adopt his goals as their own. This is, roughly, treating the humanity in others as an end: helping them to attain whatever (morally permissible) goals they have adopted for themselves, and doing so *minimally* by not frustrating these goals. Similarly, when I treat the humanity in myself as an end, I do not act in ways to frustrate my goals, but in ways to promote them. If my goal is to be a successful writer, I should not get drunk every night, and I should devote the time necessary for writing. Thus, there are two ways to treat someone as an end: negatively, by not acting in ways to frustrate or impede the person's goals, and positively, by acting in ways to help the person attain his or her goals. Although Kant speaks of treatment and action, motives are still present: in acting in ways that treat humanity as an end, we ensure that we are acting from motives of duty. We cannot treat others as an end from immoral motives. "Scratching your back" and you "scratching" mine might help us to attain our goals, but it does not carry the proper moral *attitude* because we are treating each other's goals only as a means.

Let us join these points together. To act from duty is to act from the motive of respecting morality or intending to act in such-and-such a way *because* morality requires it. To act from the motive of duty is to treat the humanity in others both as a means and as an end, because no proper or moral motive allows us to treat others only as a means. When we help promote the happiness of those people we choose to help, we treat the humanity in them as an end. That is, if we help them from the proper motives, we treat their humanity as an end.

What about romantic love? There are three ways by which Kantians can argue that romantic love (in general, not particular instances of it) is permissible. First, if romantic love involves robust concern, whereby each lover is attentive to the needs and the desires of the other for her own sake, lovers do not use each other merely as a means but also as ends. Whether love does not violate the Categorical Imperative is a different question, because the Categorical Imperative applies not only to how lovers treat each other but to their treatment of everyone else, requiring them to not treat others merely as a means. But if love involves the elevation and the preferential treatment of one person (the beloved) over others, there is a serious moral risk that the lovers might neglect their duties to others. If love tends to make lovers excessively attentive to each other, it would be morally suspicious in Kantian eyes. The word "tends" is important. The issue is not particular cases of love, whereby in some cases the lovers neglect others but in other cases they don't, but whether love pushes the lovers to be engrossed with each other to the point of neglecting others. But even if love has this tendency, it would not necessarily mean that love is morally prohibited according to Kantians, but that lovers should be on their moral guard to ensure that their attention to each other does not come at the expense of their duties to others. Thus one, though not ultimate, justification for love is that it *need not* violate the Categorical Imperative.

The second reason why love is permissible on Kantian ethics is best seen through a comparison with utilitarianism. One (mistaken) criticism of utilitarianism is that it is too demanding: in its zeal to maximize happiness, it requires agents to always select the option that maximizes happiness. If by not going to the movies I can better spend my money on a charitable organization, that is where my money should go. So I can only go to the movies when I reach a point at which *not* going prohibits me from maximizing happiness (because "I need a break").[4] Kantian ethics is not as demanding. We see this in the idea of imperfect duties. The imperfect duty to help others attain their happiness does not mean that I have to constantly do so and with everyone. The leeway I have in deciding whom, when, and how to help implies that I have time or space to attend to "personal" matters; in slang, "I have a life" (but I cannot do immoral things). I am free to engage in hobbies, to choose what career I want, to decide where and when to travel, and, most pertinent, to cultivate personal relationships with others, including friendships and romantic love.

It is important not to misunderstand this point. It is not about whether Kantians make "room" for romantic love in their moral hub, but about whether love is morally affordable. If the above criticism of utilitarianism is correct (and it is not), utilitarianism does not make love morally affordable, because the time, attention, money, and energy spent on my beloved may be used in better ways to increase overall happiness. Love becomes a moral luxury on this criticism of utilitarianism. Not so with Kantian ethics: morality permits us to have romantic love in our lives. So perhaps *the* justification for love on Kantian ethics is grounded in autonomy: the ability of individuals to chart their lives as they see fit so long as they attend to their duties to others and to themselves.

The third (and tentative) reason why love is permissible according to Kantian ethics has to do with the imperfect duty to morally perfect ourselves. Each of us has the duty to cultivate in ourself those character traits and emotions that allow us to act from the motive of duty, such as sympathy, compassion, courage, benevolence, and generosity. For example, a sympathetic person is likely to be attentive to the needs of others; she notices things – an elderly person needing help crossing the street – while a not-so-sympathetic or self-absorbed person might not. Now *if* (this is a big "if"; hence the "tentative" above) romantic love has the tendency to make us better people, as some say, it would be one way to cultivate the above-mentioned character traits. For example, if I am a timid person by nature, and if the sight of my beloved being treated unjustly makes me speak out in his defense, being in love pushes me to be more courageous. If, then, love pushes us to acquire those good traits, being in love is one way by which I can morally perfect myself.[5] This *might* be a third justification for love on Kantian ethics, but it might be a double-edged sword: love can make us, say, less generous toward others because it makes us want to spend our money mostly on our beloveds.

Virtue ethics. Virtue ethics is a type of moral theory whose central and organizing concept is virtue, which is a trait of character that disposes the person who has it to judge, act, or feel rightly in the relevant situation. The virtue of patience, according to Aristotle, moderates the emotion of anger. Some people feel excessively angry in traffic jams (road rage), and some people do not feel angry at all at the wholesale slaughter and ethnic cleansing of a people. A virtuous person would feel anger in the right "amounts," depending on the situation and on what "amount" of anger it calls for. Aristotle also claims that the virtuous person would experience the emotion "at the right times, about the right things, toward the right people, for the right end and in the right way" (1999, 1106b20–23). Note how many things the virtuous person gets right so that her emotion is properly experienced, and note that she can go wrong with respect to any one of them: expressing her anger at a friend at his wedding would not be the right time; being angry at him about something silly would not be about the right thing; taking her anger out on her friend's sister would not be toward the right person; expressing her anger at her friend just to make him feel bad would not be for the right end; and being angry at him by smashing his favorite china set would not be the right way. (Aristotle should have also added, "for the right duration.")

A virtuous person has all the virtues. They include courage, temperance, justice, generosity, patience, and care. It is not necessary that they all moderate emotions. Courage and patience do; the first revolves around fear and confidence, the second around anger. But the virtue of temperance moderates *desires* (for food, drink, and sex), whereas the virtue of justice need involve neither emotions nor desires; it moderates our judgments regarding what is fair to others. Moreover, a virtuous person would likely not display any or all virtues all the time. Whether she does and which virtue depends on the circumstances. Finally, a right action is one that is performed by a virtuous person; if the person happens not to be virtuous, a right action is what a virtuous person *would* perform. The main idea is that the virtues are moral excellences; they are opposed to the vices. A virtuous person is a morally good, even excellent, person.

A second crucial concept for virtue ethics is the good life – a life good for human beings, given their characteristics, to lead. It is a flourishing life; it is a happy life, so long as "happiness" does not mean only pleasure or pleasurable sensations. The view that there is a proper life for humans to lead is called "naturalism," because it relies on the idea that the right way for us human beings to live accords, somehow, with our nature. A wolf, for example, that does not hunt with the pack and a male king penguin that does not shelter its eggs are not leading proper lives, because a good life for a wolf and for a male king penguin include hunting with the pack and sheltering its eggs, respectively. The issue is whether this is also true of human beings. It is difficult to settle: human beings don't merely act on instinct or as nature dictates but also on reason, which means that human beings can lead different types of lives because they can *decide* what lives to lead.

Our purpose is not to evaluate the truth of virtue ethics, let alone a naturalist version of it, though we do need to retain the idea of a good life for human beings. The distinctness of virtue ethics lies in the idea that there is a strong connection between having the virtues and leading a good life: being virtuous is necessary for the good life. This means that those who are vicious or who are neither vicious nor virtuous cannot lead a good life.[6] But because it is *possible* that someone who is vicious can lead a good life, perhaps we should say that the virtues are a person's *best bet* to lead a good life (Hursthouse 1986). For example, being courageous allows the courageous person to fight for important things. Being honest allows the honest person to have better dealings with people. If she succeeds in these endeavors, she would likely lead a good life.

Before we turn to love, we should clarify one important idea. The claim that the virtues are necessary or the best bet for a good life is not a causal claim or a process. It is *not* that a person becomes virtuous and then, later, she reaps the benefits of a good life. It is not like working hard for a month and then receiving a paycheck. Instead, *in* leading a virtuous life the person is also leading a good life. The virtues *constitute* the good life. Moreover, just because the virtues are needed for a good life does not mean that when we act virtuously we are always asking, "What's in it for me?" This confuses two levels. At the basic level is why anyone should be virtuous – why we have the need for the virtues – the answer to which is that the virtues are needed for the good life. But – this is the second level – once we become virtuous, our life goes on automatic pilot, so to speak. The issue is no longer *why* we should be virtuous, but a set of questions concerning how we act and feel *given that* we are virtuous: Should I be honest or should I spare her feelings? Should I forget what he did to me or should I confront him about it? Once a person is virtuous, her concern is with doing the right thing (but remember: acting bravely or justly can be costly; that's why the virtues are not sufficient for a good life).

Does virtue ethics consider romantic love permissible? I argued in Chapter 1 that romantic love is not a virtue because love itself is neither good nor bad, whereas the virtues are excellences. Here is another argument why it is not a virtue: if the virtues are needed or even necessary for the good life, someone who is not romantically in love is not leading a good life. But this is false; obviously, people can lead good lives without romantic love (this is one reason why I wrote above that love is not a basic good). According to virtue ethics, being morally defective is one crucial way for someone to not lead a good life. Although lacking courage, patience, or temperance makes someone defective – makes her a poor specimen of a human being – things are not that way with romantic love. Someone might be defective if she shuns intimacy altogether – if she has no friends, for example. But merely rejecting romantic love or, more commonly, happening not to fall in love, does not imply that there is anything wrong with her. So romantic love is not a virtue.[7] This is a good thing, too, because if romantic love were a virtue, we would be morally obligated to acquire or cultivate it – a counter-intuitive result.

Of course, people who *do* have romantic love in their lives are not defective either. The good life is compatible with both having and not having romantic love. This means that the only other reason why virtue ethics might consider romantic love impermissible is if it were incompatible with one or more virtues. Justice is the only virtue that romantic love might be at odds with. But though romantic love involves preferential treatment, so do other types of love (we treat our siblings, children, parents, and friends preferentially). If justice denies us this way of living, something has gone wrong with our conception of it. A proper conception of justice requires us to not violate others' rights, and preferential treatment does not necessarily do this (with one caveat; see the second paragraph from the next).

So the existence of romantic love is compatible with virtue. But how would virtue ethics justify it? Although virtue ethics cannot justify romantic love on the ground that it is needed for a good life, so long as love does not violate virtue we should be free to pursue it. Virtue ethics, like consequentialism and Kantian ethics, justifies romantic love on the grounds of liberty or autonomy.

The three main moral theories, then, justify romantic love on the grounds of liberty. This claim needs two important qualifications, regardless of which moral theory we prefer. First, the claim is true only when people generally have true autonomy; under certain social conditions many might not. For example, in societies in which women have few options other than attaching themselves to a man for social and economic support, many women may marry men and (perhaps) eventually love them, simply because they have no other real choices. Sometimes bad social conditions limit autonomy by steering people *away* from love: in societies in which homophobia runs deep, many gay men and women may *not* love other men or women out of the (conscious or unconscious) fear that it would bring disaster on their heads (e.g., legal persecution, social condemnation). Thus, ideally justifying love on grounds of autonomy is plausible; in practice, the conditions allowing for genuine autonomy must exist for the justification to function.

Second, the moral justification of love is general, meaning that *particular cases* of love might be unjustified. Much depends on how lovers behave when in love. Lovers often go to great lengths to shower their beloveds with attention and other forms of loving. The danger is that they act in ways contrary to the dictates of the virtues or morality. For example, in giving my beloved too many gifts, I go too far. I should spend some of the money on other important things. My actions go against the dictates of the virtues of justice and benevolence. In sparing my beloved's feelings too much, I go against the virtue of honesty (this is the caveat mentioned three paragraphs above). So while romantic love in general can co-exist with morality, much depends on how each couple behaves toward the other. I discuss this claim in the next section.

Commonsense morality. Unlike the first three, "commonsense morality" is not really a theory, but what people think about morality at a pre-theoretical level. On the one hand, commonsense morality supplies many philosophers' intuitions about how to think about morality and against which to test moral theories (intuitions are pre-theoretical judgments considered to be true). For example, the idea that happiness is important is common sense, and supplies utilitarianism with its basic concept. Any moral theory that gives happiness no place is going to have a hard time being convincing.

On the other hand, commonsense morality comprises a hodge-podge of beliefs, many of which have dubious or unclear origins. The extent to which commonsense morality should be trusted (think of audiences at *The Jerry Springer Show* espousing all sorts of views) and used as a measuring yard for evaluating moral theories is tricky. Romantic love provides an excellent example.

In societies that consider romantic love to be a good thing, commonsense morality often gives lovers a *carte blanche* to act in any way they want. Indeed, according to commonsense morality, invoking love as a way to explain what would otherwise be clearly bad behavior is considered *justification* of the action in question. If John spends tons of money on wining and dining Rachel, even though they are surrounded by poor people, commonsense morality thinks nothing wrong with such behavior. Sometimes commonsense morality accepts lying, cheating, stealing, and even killing if done in the name of love. Although many people don't accept such behavior, generally people tend to have a very permissive attitude toward actions done out of love. In this regard, commonsense morality considers love to be permissible with a vengeance.

Ehman may be reflecting popular views about love and commonsense morality's stance on love when he writes,

> In asserting our love for a person, we single out the person and raise her above the field of social relations and obligations in terms of which we comport ourselves toward others. The assertion of love implies that the beloved has a value for the lover above that of others and that the lover regards his relation to his beloved as more important than his other relationships.
>
> (Ehman 1989, 256)

But this cannot be correct, even if Ehman is only registering people's attitude toward love. For surely not all lovers value their beloveds above everyone else; certainly, most would consider their children to be at least as valuable, if not more so (luckily, we usually don't have to choose). Nonetheless, Ehman makes an interesting, if exaggerated, point: popular opinion – often reflecting and reflected in commonsense morality – considers love to be supremely important and considers virtually any loving behavior toward the beloved to be morally permissible.

This not only answers the question of what commonsense morality has to say about the permissibility of romantic love, it also illustrates a problem: if philosophers use commonsense morality to test moral theories, and if commonsense morality is permissive when it comes to love, should we believe commonsense morality or a moral theory that places restrictions on love? I argue in support of moral theories, starting with the example of John and Rachel.

John spends too much money on Rachel, even though Rachel doesn't need so much money spent on her and there are lots of people in need of help. If John were to use some of his money to help the poor, he would make a big difference in their lives. Suppose that commonsense morality finds nothing wrong with John's actions, and suppose that we ask a defender of commonsense morality, "Isn't John being extravagant? Shouldn't John *not* spend as much money on Rachel but use some of it to help those in need?" What answer could the defender of commonsense morality possibly give to morally defend John's actions? I cannot think of a single, convincing answer. The answer, "It makes John and Rachel happy" is unconvincing because (1) John and Rachel are not the only people whose happiness is at stake; (2) others will be made happy by John's benevolence; and (3) spending less money on Rachel is not likely to make John and Rachel *un*happy, but only slightly less happy (things get worse for commonsense morality if it attempts to shield John when he *harms* others in making Rachel happy). Think of it this way: Who are these characters John and Rachel anyway? What is so special about them? And why should their being in love mean that they can morally "screw" the rest of the world? To neglect morality's requirements, we need a convincing reason; since commonsense morality has no adequate justification for its permissive attitude toward romantic love, we should accept moral restrictions on lovers' behavior. I discuss these restrictions in the next section.

Moral Restrictions on Love

Moral restrictions on love apply to two areas: the behavior and actions of the lovers, and the basis on which love is based.

Moral Restrictions on Lovers' Behavior

Let us begin with a few facts. First, desires and beliefs prompt us to act. My desire for chocolate, coupled with my belief that I have some, prompts me to eat it, so long as the desire is not defeated by other desires and considerations, such as my stronger desire not to add more fat to my love handles. My desire to see Yemen, coupled with the belief that I can afford a vacation, prompts me to plan a trip there.

Second, while some desires are easy to resist (e.g., desire for chocolate), other desires are powerful and have a stronger pull on us. One main example of a very powerful desire is sexual desire. People who get under its sway (and we all do) often do silly things to satisfy it. Worse, they often convince themselves of things they know to be false in order to rationalize why they should act on their sexual urges. Here's Sam, who has only $1,200 dollars in his savings account: "Sure I can afford a classy call girl; $500 won't make much of a dent in my bank account; anyway, I'll work hard and make up the money fast." Here's Angela, who knows that her air-headed albeit hot and swarthy pool-boy is the biggest bragger in town: "I'll just have sex with him once and make him promise not to tell anyone; I'm sure he won't tell if he promises."

Third, desires are morally neutral. There is no type of desire that comes with a stamp of moral approval or disapproval. Whether acting on a desire is morally good or bad depends not only on the desire but also on the context in which it is felt. Acting on my desire to have chocolate is perfectly fine if I already have chocolate in my kitchen or if I go out and buy it with legally obtained money. But satisfying my desire by stealing chocolate from a store or snatching it from a child's hand is morally wrong. Acting on my desire for sex is perfectly fine if I were to masturbate or do it with another consenting adult, but not if I rape someone or fondle a child.

The point is that desires in general, and powerful ones specifically, require moral monitoring. Ideally, we would all feel just the right desires, at the right times, toward the right people. Unfortunately, we are not all virtuous people (far from it). Instead, we have to curb our desires when it is morally impermissible to act on them.

What has this got to do with romantic love? First, romantic love, as an emotion, is made up of desires and beliefs. Second, love is an especially powerful emotion, exercising its pull on us in powerful ways. Thus, it is especially in need of moral monitoring. Let us look at these two claims in a little more detail.

Love's desires are many. The lover desires (1) to protect and promote the well-being of his beloved; (2) to make the beloved happy (this second desire sometimes clashes with the first when what makes the beloved happy – eating loads of chocolate – does not coincide with her well-being – maintaining decent health); (3) to be in the company of his beloved; and (4) the beloved to reciprocate (if she doesn't already) or to continue to reciprocate the love (if she does already). Each of these four desires can be complex, and each affects other people. For example, no one, including lovers, can protect and promote another's well-being without affecting others (positively, negatively, or neutrally). If my beloved has become chubby owing to all the chocolate he ate and I decide to promote his well-being by buying him a year's membership at a gym, that money is going to have to come from somewhere, and the spot he gets at the gym is one less spot for another person. Similar reasoning applies to the other three desires.

This point is bland: virtually anything we do – to our beloveds, to acquaintances, to strangers – affects others. It becomes less bland if we recall that love is an especially powerful emotion. In its initial stages, when the passion is at its highest, lovers are famous for their frenzied behavior of neglecting their friends and family members, being distracted at work, losing their appetite, and so on. Thinking that if they cannot have their beloveds their world is going to crash, they are liable to do all sorts of things to attain their happiness. Lovers who have been together for a while, who have built lives together, are as susceptible to doing all sorts of things to heed the desires of love.

So romantic love is an especially powerful emotion and seems not to vary in this respect from lover to lover. This means that morality must place restrictions on love, because otherwise lovers have moral license to act in any way they want to satisfy love's desires (ditto for any intimate relationship with very intense desires and emotional components). Incidentally, this is why I am unconvinced that love makes us morally better. Love's tendency to make lovers self-absorbed, pulling them away from others and their moral dues, can only contribute to making the lovers morally worse.

The restrictions boil down to the idea that lovers need be to careful to fulfill their moral obligations in the face of love's tendency to make them neglect or ignore them. The obligations come in two distinctions that cut across each other. The first is between negative and positive obligations, the second between obligations to the beloved and obligations to others (including the lover). The first distinction is difficult to make but contains a fairly intuitive idea. Negative obligations are obligations to *refrain* from doing things to others: to not harm or lie to them, to not put obstacles in their way, and so on. Positive obligations are obligations to *do* certain things to others: to keep our promises, aid the needy, help others in general, tell the truth, act justly, make amends for past wrongdoing, express our gratitude to good things done to us, and so on.

The second distinction recognizes that when it comes to love we have obligations to the beloved and obligations to other people. Just because y is x's beloved does not mean that x has no obligations toward y and to other people. Moreover, x's obligations toward y and other people are both negative and positive. So the two distinctions intersect.

Go back to the example of John and Rachel (to simplify things, I discuss this only in terms of John's obligations to Rachel). First, John has obligations of honesty to Rachel, which can sometimes be painful to act on since honesty often hurts the person hearing difficult truths. Because lovers typically not only don't want to hurt their beloveds' feelings but to also make them happy, being honest is difficult. If Rachel wears a dress in which she looks ridiculous, John has an obligation, especially if she asks him, about how she looks, to tell her the truth. Being honest does not mean that he can tell her the truth in any way ("You look like a heifer, dear"), because we, including John, have an obligation to spare people unnecessary pain. Of course, John and Rachel's obligations of honesty to each other cover not only such mundane areas as their appearance, but other areas as well: their habits, personal hygiene, the way they relate to others, and so on.

Another obligation that John has to Rachel is to not harm her. If Rachel is eating way too much fried chicken, John should encourage her to stop eating it, even though eating it makes her happy. Here, his obligation conflicts both with his desire to make Rachel happy and, possibly, with other obligations he has toward her, such as the obligation to keep his promises (e.g., to help her satisfy her desires and to make her happy).

Another obligation is to keep his promises: if John promised Rachel sexual fidelity, cheating on her is a moral no-no. Once again, this obligation can go against his desires for Rachel or against other obligations. If he promised to make her happy in any way he can, acting on this promise may go against his desire to persuade her to change her life (because, say, he thinks her life is not going anywhere). But this obligation may also go against another obligation he has toward her, say, the obligation to be honest.

Yet another obligation is to be fair: unless they have mutually agreed to this effect (which itself should be fair), John should not be the one to do all the housework or to decide all the time what to watch on TV, where to go for dinner, and where to travel. John may want to make all these decisions because he thinks Rachel will enjoy his choices, but being fair may mean curbing this desire. It may also go against other obligations such as any promises he made to make her happy (if Rachel is a control freak, she may be unhappy with any arrangement that cedes some control to John, but fairness may require that she should not do all the household work or make all the decisions).

Another obligation is to help Rachel attain her goals. If John thinks that a particular goal is not good for her, he has an obligation to discuss the matter with her and try to dissuade her from it (but always leaving room that he might be wrong). If Rachel does not change her mind, John should not put obstacles in her way of attaining her goal, because she is an autonomous individual and he ought to respect her decisions. Again, this obligation might go against John's desire to see Rachel happy and against his other obligations, such as respecting her decisions.

If John has wronged Rachel in the past, he has the duty to make reparations or amends. He also has the obligation to show her gratitude for good things she has done for him. These two obligations are special because they are usually not in tension with other obligations or desires if both parties are psychologically healthy. But if Rachel likes to be the victim, and if John desires to make her happy, acting on the obligation to make reparations may go against his desire, since he knows that Rachel won't be happy if she no longer feels the victim. If Rachel always likes to be the martyr, being shown gratitude would not sit well with her, so again the obligation to express gratitude may conflict with John's desire to make her happy.

Note, first, that some obligations are easy to act on, especially ones that accord with John or Rachel's desires to do the thing the obligation requires. If Rachel does look good in that dress, telling the truth is not only easy, but a pleasure, since it accords with John's desire to make Rachel happy. Second, all these obligations stem from general moral considerations, not from the fact that John and Rachel are lovers. But *how* they are asserted and acted on might be a matter left to the lovers. Indeed, they may decide to release each other from some obligations if this strengthens the love between them. Third, it is an interesting question – one I do not pursue here – whether treating our beloveds preferentially is a matter of *obligation*, stemming from the special relationship between the two, be they lovers, siblings, parent–child, or friends, or is merely morally *permitted*, but not required. My hunch is that there are such special obligations, generated by the type of relationship in question – a business rela- tionship, a doctor–patient relationship, friendship, lovers – as long as the relationship itself is of a type that is morally permissible – not, e.g., a Mafioso– client relationship.

John and Rachel also have obligations to others. There are obligations that, first, stem from their work and other intimate relationships (e.g., with their families, friends, or work colleagues). Rachel wants to spend the evening with John, but spending time with her estranged sister, a few extra hours at work, or helping a friend might be a priority. Second, there are obligations stemming from their relationships to other human beings in general (e.g., neighbors, near and distant strangers): Rachel wants to buy a present for John, but she bought him one last week, so her money is better spent on something more worthy. If John and Rachel are involved in a car accident and John is only in mild shock, Rachel has an obligation to attend to the injured stranger rather than comfort John, even though she wants to. Rachel has an obligation to be honest, even if this sometimes makes John look bad ("I'm so sorry; yes, it was John who ran over your cat. Please let us know what we can do to make things better"). Rachel has an obligation to keep her promises, even if she prefers to be with John instead ("I do want to go to the movies with you, but I promised Leila I'd go shopping with her"). Rachel has an obligation to be fair to people, even if at John's expense ("John! You've had your share of chicken breasts. Leave some for David" – David is the neighbor's son). And Rachel has obligations to not harm others, even if the expense is of some benefit to John ("I know you want me to help you with your project, but if I don't spend these hours painting the new shelter, it won't open in time").

John and Rachel's obligations toward others might conflict not only with their desires for each other, but also with their obligations to each other. Rachel's promise to help her friend Sarah move may conflict with her promise to John to help him with his project (if she mistakenly made these promises for the same days and times). John's obligation to spend time with his dying father may conflict with his obligation toward Rachel to tend to her while she is sick. How these obligations are resolved depends on the context and on the strength of each obligation. For example, Rachel's promise to Sarah to have lunch with her "to catch up" may be overridden by her obligation toward John to tend to him while he is sick. Even Rachel's obligation to help Sarah move house may be overridden by John's getting sick if the sickness is serious. Note that resolving these conflicts applies to *all* Rachel and John's obligations: if Rachel comes across a stranger in need of help, she may also violate her promise to have lunch with her friend, because assisting someone in need is more important than keeping a "let's catch up" lunch promise.

There is an interesting issue here: Does morality permit violating our obligations toward others even when the reason is not as important as is normally required, so long as it is love-related? For example, may Rachel violate her lunch promise to Sarah to comfort John even if he is only in a bad mood, when normally someone's being in a bad mood is not enough justification to override a promise? If yes, is it because it involves comforting John, who is Rachel's beloved, not just anyone? I do not pursue this point here.

If John or Rachel neglect their obligations toward each other, they are behaving immorally, toward each other. If they neglect their obligations toward others, they also behave immorally, even if their reason is their love for each other.

Finally, John (and Rachel) has obligations to himself; they, too, can conflict with his obligations to or desires for Rachel. For example, there are obligations for self-improvement, including moral self-improvement. If his relationship with Rachel is not only not going anywhere but is bad for John and adversely affecting his life, he may have an obligation to himself to abandon ship. He may still love Rachel deeply, so acting on this obligation goes against his desire to be with her. Even if his life is not deteriorating, John may still need to leave Rachel if his continued love for her means ongoing humiliation and lack of self-respect for himself. Rachel may be someone who is simply not worthy of his love and affection, and every minute he spends with her is a minute he pays for in loss of self-respect and dignity. (I shall let the reader give examples of conflict between duties of self-improvement and duties to Rachel.)

The point so far is to illustrate the various obligations that lovers have and how they can conflict with each other and with lovers' desires. There is a larger point: when in love we are not on a moral holiday, and lovers' moral obligations remain in full force. They do so not in virtue of the lovers being lovers, but in virtue of being human beings with standing and potential moral relationships to each other and to other people.

Further Moral Restrictions

We have seen that romantic love is reason-based. Strictly speaking, x loves y because x *believes* that y has such-and-such properties. But beliefs can be false, and x may be mistaken that y has property P on the basis of which x loves y. Interesting in itself, this also raises the further point that love can be morally assessed depending on how the beliefs are arrived at. Because beliefs prompt us to action, it is important – for pragmatic and, certainly, for moral reasons – to be careful about how we form our beliefs. Even if we don't act on some of them, we do care about what type of person we are; and we don't want to be the type of person who forms beliefs recklessly or who has false beliefs.

When two people fall in love after having been friends, they already know each other quite well, so it is not an issue for either to be careful about the beliefs he or she has about the other. But when people fall in love with others whom they barely know, caution about belief formation is crucial. It works in two ways: on the part of the lover forming his or her beliefs about the beloved, and on the part of the beloved saying or doing things that lead the lover to form beliefs about him or her. To be cautious about the beliefs they form doesn't mean that lovers have to be certain about the beliefs' truths before they can act on them, but they must arrive at them based on proper evidence (unless it's a special case, in which extra caution is required).

Suppose that Kamal and Rani meet at the beach. They are attracted to each other and come to like each other very much (to simplify, I discuss only Rani's responsibilities). First, Rani should be diligent in not misleading Kamal into believing things about her that are not true. At one extreme, she should not tell him lies about herself. Less extremely, she should not let Kamal acquire certain beliefs about her when she can dispel them by being clear. For example, if he asks her whether she is married, a simple "no" is misleading: she should clarify that she has a boyfriend, especially if she suspects that Kamal understands her "no" to mean she is single. Rani need not disclose every important thing about herself upon first, second, or even later encounters with Kamal. She needs to exercise prudence. If she thinks that Kamal might flee were he to know that she has only one kidney, she need not disclose this fact during their early encounters, since someone's having one kidney is usually irrelevant for the morality of social and personal relationships. The point is that it is immoral for Rani to get Kamal to love her under false pretenses regarding things that are usually pertinent to love or, as the case may be, pertinent to the two individuals concerned: if Rani knows that Kamal is an ardent advocate for animal rights, she should not tell him she is a vegetarian (or, worse, a vegan).

It is important to not mislead potential lovers because, love or no love, people need to be able to plan their lives and to make decisions, both of which depend on correct information and are undermined by false information. There is a *special* reason pertaining to love: falling in love is potentially life-changing; if the two form a relationship, their lives do change. To discover that the basis of one's love is a sham is not only immensely painful, it can also – depending on the age and duration of the love – undermine one's entire life. This is also true in the case of young love: lying to or misleading someone whom you know is interested in you is morally wrong. It leads him to form beliefs, make plans, and rearrange his life to accommodate what he thinks is a new love. Realizing otherwise is, or could be, crushing. At the least, it is a major nuisance.

Moreover, sometimes people are entitled to know the truth. If I am offered a job somewhere, and I ask about particular policies at my potential new job, I am entitled to know what they are, and not to have a fake version of them fed to me to accept the job. Similarly, people who have been in love for years are entitled to know certain things about each other. If one of them is having an affair or is abusing drugs, the other is entitled to know. Even in young love such entitlement exists: if it is clear (it usually is) to both Rani and Kamal that they are interested in each other "in that way," expectations are formed, and each person is entitled to know basic truths about the other that are crucial for his or her ability to decide whether to continue with the love. Kamal needs to know, for example, that Rani is really not a meat-eater for him to forge ahead with the relationship.

But Kamal cannot just relax and let Rani take all the responsibility. He, too, needs to be diligent about what he believes about her. If in talking to her he begins to suspect that she is needy and lacks self-confidence, he may want to allow for the possibility that she might lie to him to get him to love her. If she tells him she's a vegan, he should not go wild, hugging his pillow at night thinking, "Finally! I've met a gorgeous, non-Birkenstock-wearing vegan!" He should have the presence of mind to suspect the truth of what Rani tells him.

In short, Kamal, too, must responsibly arrive at whatever beliefs he forms about his beloved, because, first, the lover's ability to plan ahead and make decisions hinges on his having correct beliefs. In addition, having erroneous beliefs about his love can have disastrous effects on his dignity and autonomy; he can do without the humiliation and suffering that come from a false love. Second, arriving at his beliefs negligently might negatively affect the beloved: if Kamal leaves Rani, this will cause her to suffer too, and to undermine her plans and decision-making abilities. Here also lies another moral role for the beloved: if Rani knows that Kamal has carelessly arrived at his beliefs about her and she does not correct them, she shares part of the responsibility for any pain and suffering both undergo upon any possible breakup (cf. Soble 1990, 284–285).

Of course, at some point lovers cannot be responsible for what the other believes. If Rani had told Kamal more than once (or even only once) that she is *not* a vegetarian, let alone a vegan, it is not her fault that Kamal, in the frenzied throes of love, continues to believe that she is. He cannot, a few years later, accuse her of lying (her response, "But you see me stuff my face with mutton every friggin' night! What the hell is your problem?" would be perfectly justified).

This brings us to a crucial point. Much like desires, what we believe when in or falling in love can be difficult to resist because it is tempting to believe what we want to believe. For example, if Kamal finds Rani sexy and is mesmerized by her laugh and wit, he can bring himself to believe things just to convince himself that she is right for him; and he can do this despite Rani's protests (e.g., "Read my meat-filled lips: I am *not* a vegetarian"). Even if they have been together for a long time and are still very much in love, he can easily bring himself to believe all sorts of things to hide from himself some ugly truths (e.g., "What?" he says to himself, "Ali? He's just a good friend of Rani. Sure they spend way too much time together, spoon-feed each other mutton chops, and she comes home every night smelling of his cologne. But they're *not* having an affair!"). Like love's desires, its beliefs can be very seductive. Moral monitoring is especially needed.

Morality and the Basis of Love

Are there properties on the basis of which love can be morally better? This can mean one of two things: first, that depending on the property or reason for the love, it can reflect well or badly on the lover; second, that depending on the property or reason for the love, it can make the love itself – the relationship – more moral or immoral.

Consider the first point: if Kamal loves Rani on the basis of her good looks or the fact that she has lots of money, this may tell us that Kamal is shallow or greedy, indicating he has a morally defective character. If Kamal loves Rani because she is courageous, caring, or just, this reflects well on him. It is not only moral properties that reflect well on the lover's character. If, for example, Kamal loves Rani on the basis of a non-moral (not the same as immoral) property *generally* considered valuable, though not necessarily a virtue, such as intelligence, ambition, and having considerate judgment, this also reflects morally well on him because it shows he has the wisdom to love someone on the basis of non-shallow or non-fleeting properties. Moreover, if Kamal loves Rani on the basis of a non-moral property, this, although not *generally* considered important, is important to who Rani is (an identity-making property), such as being able to memorize a large number of historical dates (she's a historian); this also reflects well on Kamal because it shows that he loves Rani for her identity-making properties (but what if he loves her because of the identity-making property of being a powerful yet evil politician?).

The above distinction is between loving someone on the basis of a shallow property and on the basis of an important, non-shallow property. Loving someone on the basis of the second property reflects morally well on the lover because it indicates that he seeks what is valuable in a beloved. Three points are in order. First, this distinction cuts across the distinctions we made in the previous chapter: some shallow properties are essential, important to who one is, mental, innate, and wanting to be loved on their basis. Other shallow properties occupy the opposites of the above types of properties; similarly for non-shallow properties (I won't go through a whole listing).

Second, while there can be general agreement that, in love, some properties are shallow while others are not, others are not so clear. If Kamal loves Rani because she is an excellent cook, would this be shallow on his part? Perhaps it would be if it reflects his sexist views that any woman worth her salt must be able to cook. But what if he himself is a great cook and wants the same quality in his beloved? And what if he is neither a great cook nor sexist, but just happens to be attracted to that property found in Rani? What if Kamal loves Rani because she is astoundingly beautiful or because she is great in bed? We do consider beauty to be a crucial value, but many would say that Kamal's love is shallow. Moreover, sex and sexual pleasure are important components of who we are and of successful relationships, yet many would also denigrate Kamal's love as shallow on their basis. So there are many properties that are hard to qualify as shallow or non-shallow as the basis of love. Context is crucial: loving y for property P may reflect badly on x in one context, but may not reflect badly on z in another.

Third, someone might fall in love on the basis of a shallow property yet come to love the person later on the basis of a non-shallow property. Kamal might initially love Rani on the basis that she has well-shaped breasts, but later come to love her because she is witty, charming, and able to diffuse family conflicts. Does this reflect well or badly on Kamal? People do usually fall in love based on physical attraction but then love each other for other reasons. If falling in love initially on the basis of good looks is enough to indict the lover as shallow, most of us are in deep trouble. Perhaps, then, loving someone on the basis of a shallow property does not reflect badly on the lover so long as he also loves the beloved on the basis of non-shallow properties.

Loving someone on the basis of some types of properties can also make the love better by making the love *relationship* morally better (or if the love is unrequited, *would* make the relationship better were the love to be requited). Moreover, the only sense we can make of this idea is that the lovers relate to each other in morally proper ways, an issue we discussed in the previous section. That is, a love relationship that is morally good or superior is one in which the lovers relate to each other by acting on their moral obligations and any other moral requirements (of course, if they *only* relate to each other by fulfilling their obligations, we question whether they truly love each other).

If you think this is easy, think again. *X* may have a bizarre or warped conception of how to make *y* happy or of how to secure *y*'s well-being. If *x* acts on such misconceptions, *x* may act in morally wrong ways. Even worse, *x* may have erroneous views about what constitutes honesty, bravery, kindness, fairness, and other moral concepts. For example, *x* may think that honesty requires him to tell *y* every fleeting thought he has about other women: "I just saw the hottest chick on the beach, honey," or, "Ooh, look at the ass on that one!" Infuriated, *y* says to him, "Look, I understand that you find other women sexually desirable, but do you have to tell me about every single one?" If *x* replies, "I'm just being honest!" he has the wrong idea of what honesty is. He probably also has a moral blind spot when it comes to kindness, where he simply cannot see that such silly comments hurt *y*. *X* might also have the wrong idea of fairness: "I earn the money, sweetie-pie, so you cook, breed, and clean, okay?" Such mistaken moral views translate into a morally bad relationship, no matter how intense the love is.

So for a love relationship to be superior, it should be based on moral properties or, more simply, on the virtues. No matter what other properties the love is based on, none will have built-in moral guarantees. Even identity-making properties won't do the trick: they may guarantee that the love is durable, but not that it is moral. Only loving someone because she is fair, kind, brave, caring, patient, temperate will carry such guarantees, because only virtuous people are able to act correctly on their moral obligations and to treat each other morally correctly. Aristotle has come back to us with a vengeance:

> But complete friendship is the friendship of good people similar in virtue; for they wish goods in the same way to each other insofar as they are good, and they are good in their own right. [Hence they wish good to each other for each other's own sake.] Now those who wish goods to their friend for their friend's own sake are friends most of all; for they have this attitude because of the friend himself, not coincidentally. Hence these people's friendship lasts as long as they are good; and virtue is enduring.
>
> (1999, 1156b6–14)

It doesn't matter which conception of virtue we accept (Socratic, Aristotelian, Humean, or Kantian), because any conception will be one of *virtue*, of moral excellence, and so secures the idea that the love is morally superior. Those who are virtuous and in love have it all: a moral *and* an enduring love (a point to which I return below). Alas, they are rare.

The Prudentiality of Love

Philosophers often distinguish between the moral and the prudential (but some question the distinction; e.g., Foot 1995). Roughly, the prudential is what is in a person's *interest* to do. Thus, it is thought, what is prudential is not always what is moral. It may be moral to help the person being mugged, but not be prudent, seeing that I may be seriously injured in the process. Sometimes what is prudent is not moral: it is in my interest to pocket the stack of dollar bills on the counter while no one is watching, but it is not moral. (Those philosophers who wish to assimilate the prudential to the moral argue that it is, broadly speaking, in my self-interest to be moral.)

To ask about the prudentiality of love is to ask whether it is in our self-interest to romantically love another. This question is ambiguous, however, between whether it is prudent for x to love y or to love z, and whether it is prudent for x to have love in x's life, period. Under the first meaning, x *wants* love in his life but needs to decide *whom* to love. Under the second, the issue is whether x should have romantic love in his life, given how his life is going or given what we know about romantic love.

Choosing between Y *and* Z. Usually, when we try to choose between two or more objects, we rely on specific criteria. If I am choosing which novel to read, I might rely on the criteria of which novel is more likely to (1) be pleasurable to read, (2) be intellectually enriching, and (3) allow me to keep up better with the field. But the criteria are not objective; they depend on my *purposes* for reading novels.

If choosing between two options requires a purpose, how can one decide between two loves if love has no purpose? As Alan Soble puts it,

> "Whom should I love?" seems incomprehensible. The question seems far removed in logical space from "Should I have sex with y or z?" "Should I go to the movies with y or z?" and even "Whom should I marry?" – all of which are similar to "Whom should I hire?" These activities have a specifiable purpose that indicates the properties of persons to be taken into account ... Love seems to have no purpose, either by its nature or by assigning one to it, but is something whose point resides in itself.
>
> (Soble 1990, 280–281)

But, as Soble recognizes (1990, 281), just because love has no purpose does not mean that the question "Whom should I love?" cannot be answered. Put differently, even if love does not have an *external* purpose and that its "point resides in itself," we can still ask about whom to love by deciding what characteristics we want the love to have: do we want a durable or a brief love? Do we want a moral love or do we not care? If we want the love to be durable, we should love on the basis of durable properties, such as identity-making properties or even essential properties. If we want the love to be moral, we should love on the basis of moral properties. Thus, the answer to the question I raised in the previous chapter, "Is there a type of property on which basis the love is more prudential?," depends on, if not the purpose of love, the desired *characteristics* of love, such as its durability, morality, and compatibility between the lovers.

This won't take us far in deciding whether to love y or z. For every person has identity-making properties and many people have moral properties or properties that make the beloved compatible with the lover; durability, morality, compatibility, and other such properties are not going to narrow down the criteria to clearly decide whether to love y or z. It may then be that no clear choice can be made and something of a mental counterpart to a coin toss is the only option (or just letting circumstances and luck play their role). X's criteria for love may be durability and compatibility, yet both y and z have identity-making properties which x finds attractive, and they both have properties that make them compatible with x. In such cases – likely to be common – x has no clear answer as to whom he should love. Perhaps he ought to make an "existential leap" and just "decide" to love y, not z, or go on dates with each and then "listen to his heart."

However, love may, after all, have an external purpose such as happiness or contributing to a well-lived life. It is likely that most people would answer the question, "Why do you want to be in love?" or "Why do you love Pia?" by saying something like, "Because it'll make me happy," "Because it'll make my life richer," or "Because she makes me happy." Although these purposes might be too vague to help answer the question "Whom should I love?" (Soble 1990, 281), they can help narrow down the choices somewhat. If x realizes that he is incompatible with y, it would not be prudent for x to love y if x wants happiness or a richer life. So, as purposes of love, happiness or a richer life may help us to select some criteria, but not all. If we want a happy or richer life, compatibility in love might be a must. Not so with durability: a life could be happy with a series of short-term loves, so long as the lovers can predict the short-lived-ness of their love (this helps to lessen the pain of breakup if not completely eliminate it) and decide to enjoy it while it lasts. A richer life is also compatible with a series of short-lived loves.

This still does not narrow down the choices enough. If either a rich or a happy life is compatible with long- or short-term love, then wanting either life is not going to help x decide between a short-term love and a long-term love, let alone help x choose between y and z, even if x knows that y's love will be short- (or long-)term and that z's love will be short- (or long-)term. Things are slightly – but only slightly – better with compatibility: I know that if I want a happier or a richer life through love, I should love someone with whom I am compatible. But that's about it: if I am compatible with either of y or z, I still need to choose between them.

What about morality? Morality certainly won't detract from a rich life (some philosophers believe, mistakenly, that moral people tend to be boring; see Wolf 1982), and it may or may not make it richer. But lovers are certainly better off seeking beloveds with moral qualities, because this lowers the chances of the beloved acting immorally toward them and others. This is important: watching our beloveds treating others badly or even horribly is painful and shameful. So if y has the morals of a yeti but z is morally decent, happiness through love would tell x to go for z. If both are morally decent, x has to rely on other criteria or on that coin toss.

So we can develop some criteria to help in choosing between y and z. But they only go so far, because even if love has purposes, they are too vague or general to narrow the choices in decisive ways. Ultimately, the choice has to be made without their help.

There is another important point to consider. Making a life richer may be an undisputed general purpose of love, because even painful, lousy, or failed loves can enrich life ("Well, *I* certainly learned from this big mistake"; "It was a wild ride while it lasted"). But whether happiness *is* such a purpose is debatable. If love involves robust concern for the beloved, this concern should track what is objectively good for the beloved, not (or not always) what makes the beloved happy or what satisfies the beloved's desires. If we add Aristotle's view that the virtues are necessary for happiness, we reach a troubling conclusion. According to John Armstrong, "Much of the time we will be unable to make another person happy, because that person lacks the essential characteristics [the virtues] which make their own happiness possible." Armstrong adds,

> On this view it is futile, and worthless, to love someone who is not virtuous ... For in that case the aim of love will always be frustrated: the desire to make the other happy will never come to fruition, not because one is insufficiently ardent or self-sacrificing but because the character flaws of the other cut them off from happiness.
>
> (Armstrong 2003, 111)

There is some truth to these claims. If Aristotle is right, our happiness does not lie – or mostly lie – in the hands of *any* other. If all is going well – we live in decent democracies, our parents and co-workers are decent people – individual happiness mostly lies in the individual herself. If she is not virtuous, no other person, including her beloved, is going to make her happy, certainly not in a robust, deep sense. Happiness, then, does not provide even vague criteria to help us decide whom to love. For the answer to *x*'s question, "If I want to be happy through love, whom should I love, *y* or *z*?" is, "Neither. Your happiness does not lie in the hands of *y*, *z*, or anyone else. It lies in your own hands, *x*." Indeed, Aristotle or no Aristotle, virtues or no virtues, it is itself an interesting question to what extent a person's happiness is in the hands of romantic love.

Is it prudential to love? Aristotle's view that the virtues are necessary for happiness might of course be wrong, and even a modified version of it – that the virtues are one's best bet for happiness – might be wrong, too. Even if Aristotle is correct, it may be that in practice his view is mostly inapplicable: since very few people are virtuous, their happiness is not in their hands but in the hands of others. How my life goes is *only partially* up to me, and others have a big say in it: my parents, children, friends, colleagues, neighbors, politicians, and even perfect strangers. This raises a crucial question: If romantic love is an especially powerful emotion, and if, because it is a powerful emotion, having it in one's life means having the possibility of immense pain (to use a blanket term for a range of bad things), should one have it in one's life? Is it prudent to have love in our lives given its negative consequences?

Annette Baier offers a powerful and succinct account of the dangers of love to the lover: "paralyzing grief or reckless despair at the loss or death of loved ones, retreat into a sort of psychic hibernation when cut off from 'news' of them, crippling anxiety when they are in danger, helpless anguish when they are in pain, crushing guilt when one has harmed them, deadly shame when one fails them" (1991, 433–434). This is not to mention the dangers to others: Baier cites the aggressive emotions attendant to love against rivals, such as fear, hate, and jealousy (1991, 433). There is also the potential moral danger of the lovers excluding themselves from the rest of the world, neglecting their friends, family, and even strangers. Is romantic love worth it? This question bifurcates into two: (1) Is it prudent for *x* to have love in his life given love's negative consequences? And (2) is it prudent for *humanity* to accept romantic love and to even encourage it among its "members" (as most societies do today)? Answering the second question negatively answers the first negatively also, because if it is not a good idea for human beings to have romantic love in their lives, it is not a good idea for virtually any individual human being to have love in her life. I say "virtually" because there are always exceptional cases, such that it makes perfect sense for *some* individuals to have romantic love in their lives (e.g., someone who has never known the meaning of love or intimacy in any of their forms – filial, parental, friendship). But answering the second question positively does *not* answer the first, because even if in general the pain of love is worthwhile, other considerations may make it imprudent for *particular* individuals to have love in their lives (e.g., their lives are so busy that they simply have no room for it).

Let us begin, then, with the second question. Baier herself, despite listing the above dangers of love, does not argue that it is imprudent to love. Instead, she argues,

> If safety is what one values most, the womb or the grave are the best places for one, and, between them, one will want the best approximations one can get to these places where one is sheltered from or beyond hurt. One will opt for places where one cannot respond emotionally to the emotions and other states of mind of others … There is no safe love.
>
> (Baier 1991, 446)

To Baier, there is no such thing as a safe love, and if we want safety we should shun love altogether. If she is right, and if it is safety we want, we should lead life in such a way that we are utterly emotionally detached from others.

This sounds harsh. We don't want to live such a life, and, anyway, it is not a life fit for human beings. But because Baier's point applies (as she intends) to *all* types of love, her conclusion does not show that it is prudent to have *romantic* love in one's life. Sure, we would be stupid to refuse *all* love, but the issue is romantic love: why have *that*?

Consider that (1) with any type of love other than romantic love either (a) its risks and dangers are not as severe as romantic love's; (b) they are as severe but the love is clearly worth it; or (c) we have no choice about it so the issue of its prudence is moot. But, (2), when it comes to romantic love, (a) its dangers are severe; (b) there is no clear necessity for it; and (c) we do have a choice about whether to have it in our lives. So why have it?

Here is the argument in a more expanded form. The main types of love between human beings are five: the love of parents for their children, the love of children for their parents, the love of friends for each other, the love of siblings for each other, and romantic love. The first type of love is as emotionally intense, if not more so, as romantic love. All the dangers Baier mentions apply to the love of parents for their children. But we should not doubt the prudence of this type of love. First, having children tends to make life much richer, even though this is not necessarily true, since there are many childless couples (by choice or necessity) who lead sufficiently rich lives. Second, we need to have children if we are to continue as a species (but some philosophers question the need to; Schopenhauer 1958, ch. 46, and, more recently, Benatar 1997).

The love of children for their parents could be as emotionally intense as romantic love, though it is usually not as intense as the parents' love for their children (especially if the relationship has been difficult). In any case, the prudence of this love is moot because children have no choice about having parents. Once born and raised by them, children love them back. Although children can choose to dampen their love for their parents or even crush it entirely, this is not a general issue about this type of love but one that touches on *particular* child–parent loves (the same may be said about the parents and siblings and other types of love). The same reasoning applies to sibling love.

Friendship is different. Its prudence lies in the fact that we need forms of intimacy – people whom we can trust with our woes and pleasures, people on whom we can rely, and people whose company we enjoy – that are not familial because, first, they function as an important source of affection and refuge from family members from whom we often need to distance ourselves if we are to grow up in mature, healthy ways, and, second, because we normally do not spend our entire lives with other family members. We need intimate, non-familial relationships to carry us through the rest of our lives. Moreover, friendships, at least in today's world, tend not to be as emotionally intense as romantic love, so the dangers that Baier enumerates are not as deep with friendship as they are with love. In addition, friendships, unlike romantic love, tend not to be exclusive. The loss of a friend is cushioned by the presence of other friends, either practically (the friends offer comfort and solace while grieving) or – for lack of a better term – mentally: knowing that we have other friends is a major source of comfort for not feeling bereft. Not so with romantic love: given its usual exclusivity and its emotional intensity, the loss of the beloved is crushing.

Because there are other forms of intimate relationships, we need a powerful justification for having romantic love in our lives given its attendant dangers as enumerated by Baier. Here we should recall a crucial point: romantic love leads, by its very nature, to a severe loss of autonomy. While some philosophers have distinguished between more and less autonomous forms of romantic love (see Lehrer 1997), all cases of romantic love lead to a serious loss of autonomy owing to the very deep emotional, mental, and physical dependency that constitutes its very core (see Halwani and Jones 2007). In this respect, it differs from other forms of love. With parental love for children, children's love for their parents, and sibling love, the relationships are not expected or meant to last for the duration of the lives of the parties to the relationships: children eventually lead their own lives; parents know this and plan their lives; and siblings, of course, lead their own lives apart from each other. As the parties to these relationships grow physically and mentally apart, the emotional dependency weakens. Friendships are not usually as emotionally intense as romantic love, so do not create the deep loss of autonomy that romantic love does.

In short, the exclusivity, durability (constancy), and emotional intensity of romantic love set it apart from other types of love, creating great potential for pain and suffering, and a deep loss of autonomy. Without a good explanation, it is a live issue whether or not it is prudent to have it in our lives.

Another way to think of the main idea in this argument is that romantic love is not among the basic goods – goods needed for a minimally decent life – such as good physical health (including lack of chronic pain), some measure of political freedom, basic education, and, most pertinent for our purposes, intimate relationships. We can easily imagine cases of people leading good, rich lives without it. It also has severe negative consequences. What is the rationale, then, for having it in our lives?

I can think of three. The first is happiness. Despite the pains and risks of love, its resultant happiness can be so powerful, unique, and long-lasting that the risks are worth it. The second is pleasure and intensity: romantic love brings the lovers intense and unique moments of pleasure, so the risks are also worth it. This second explanation is different from the first: lovers can be, due to their very love, generally unhappy. That is, their lives are not as contented and smooth as they can be; they fight a lot, they are bitter at each other much of the time, and so on. Nonetheless, their love can give them intense moments of pleasure (sexual and non-sexual) rarely produced by other events and things. The sheer joy of spending a few hours watching a movie together, walking together on the streets of their favorite neighborhood or city, having a hearty laugh at the folly of their pets, children, or friends, the very sight of each other after a long absence, and other such moments can be worth the risks of love. Romantic love's emotional intimacy and intensity – the same one that sets it apart from other forms of love – can be the very explanation for romantic love's prudence.

The third explanation is that romantic love can make life very rich and give it meaning. It can take the lovers on the emotional equivalent of a roller-coaster ride. Both the good and the bad are included, because even love's painful experiences enrich life at least in that they allow lovers to learn from them, to gain some wisdom. Either way, by loving another person, caring for him, empathizing with him, the lover is able to have meaning in her life (among other sources of meaning).

One might object that other things, including other types of love, can bring us happiness, can be intensely pleasurable, and can be life-enriching. Why should romantic love be prudent, then, given its risks? But just because there are other things that make us happy, provide us with intense moments of pleasure, and make life rich (or richer) and meaningful, does not mean that having romantic love is imprudent. Indeed, love is one of those things; if the others are prudent, why not romantic love, especially since most of them have their own attendant risks?

There is a more powerful objection: the above explanations sound silly when it comes to prudence. Consider again the example of a bitter, fight-filled love punctuated with moments of intense pleasure and joy. What's so *prudent* about having such a love in one's life? Or consider examples of loves gone wrong; yes, they might make life richer, more meaningful, but not all such lives are *prudent*. If I had the choice between a rich, meaningful life with a love gone awry (and thus painful), and a rich, meaningful, life with one of those lucky loves that go well, it would be prudent to choose the second. There's nothing prudent about the first.

This objection sounds right. Romantic love is a wonderful thing in many ways, but trying to explain how it is generally prudent for human beings to have it in their lives is a "tough call." However, this is where the defenders of romantic love (and I'm still not sure whether I'm one of them) step in with a forceful point: "Okay, okay. When it comes to morality, we're with you that it needs to temper love, since morality is crucial to our lives and we need it to live properly. But it's difficult to see why prudence is so important. It isn't everything. People who build careers doing highly risky things – rock climbing, car racing, sword swallowing, joining the army and fighting – are not very prudent. But so what? We don't usually condemn them for these lives – we sometimes even encourage and applaud them. So we don't consider prudence to be everything. Maybe morality is an overarching value, but prudence certainly isn't. It is one value among others, and if it doesn't go well with love, so much the worse for prudence."

This rejoinder sounds right: prudence isn't everything. But the rejoinder contains the seeds of its own destruction. If you go back and consider all the dangers of romantic love we have discussed, you should be struck by the fact that all of them are moral, not only prudential (another strike in favor of assimilating morality with prudence). Baier's paralyzing grief, reckless despair, psychic hibernation, crippling anxiety, helpless anguish, crushing guilt, and deadly shame are not merely prudential issues; they are also (even only) moral concerns. Neglecting friends, co-workers, and strangers when in love are also moral actions. The necessary loss of autonomy that lovers undergo and the humiliating, demeaning behavior they sometimes go through to attain, main-tain, or hold on to their loves are also moral phenomena. Thus, the dangers of love are moral. If they are also prudential, it's not their prudentiality that makes them so cutting and weighty. The idea that it is not prudent to have romantic love is now replaced with (or strengthened by) moral considerations. The rejoinder, which conceded the importance of morality but not prudence, would have to contend with this strengthened version of the objection to romantic love. I leave it to the reader to decide the issue.

However, even if it is both prudent and morally wise to have romantic love in general, we should still take steps to minimize its negative consequences. Two steps are crucial: (1) lovers should have other (non-romantic) sources of affection and intimacy, such that if love should go wrong, they are left with other avenues of support; (2) some pernicious and (most likely) false beliefs about love should be shed, especially the beliefs in love's exclusivity, constancy, and in the beloved's irreplaceability. Although lovers should not behave as if any day they will find an additional beloved, replace the ones they have, or end the love they have, they should also not conduct their loves as if these beliefs are true. This just might help cushion the pain when or if they come to find out that the love is not working out or that the beloved has fallen for someone else.

One final point: even if it is prudent to have romantic love in general, this would not settle the question whether a *particular* person should have romantic love in his or her life. Consider Matt and Martha. Matt has had such a bad experience with love that having another love in his life fail would be emotionally and psychologically detrimental to him. For Matt, having love in his life contains tremendous risks. It is imprudent and irrational for him to be in love. Martha, on the other hand, has not been stung by love, at least not severely. But in her case there are factors that make it imprudent for her to be in love. Suppose that she dedicates her life to a very time-consuming career or to being a "people person" (such as a revolutionary and a prophet).[8] If Martha really wants this career or to be a "people person," then, given that romantic love will divert much of her energy toward one person (maybe down the road also to children) and might consume her mind with anxiety, fear, worry, and the rest of the risks of love, it is not prudent for her to be in love. Some individuals, then, have to choose between a life with romantic love and one without it.

Summary and Conclusion

Romantic love, like other intimate relationships, involves preferential treatment. So long as this treatment does not come at the expense of the lovers' violation of their duties and decent treatment of others, it is morally permissible, and all the main moral theories concur. Love is an emotion; as such, it has no built-in moral guarantees, and lovers need to monitor their treatment of each other and of others. Finally, although love is morally justified on grounds of autonomy, it does not seem to be necessary for a good life, and it is an open question whether it is prudent. Love might be a great thing in general, but when it goes bad it goes *really* bad.

Notes

1 This is how John Stuart Mill defends individual liberty on utilitarian grounds.
2 Like consequentialists, Kantian ethicists also disagree about how to properly formulate their theory, so Kantian ethics is a *type* of moral theory, not "a moral theory," period.
3 Kantian ethics is, to my mind, a much more complex theory than consequentialism. In what follows I will be simplifying a little.
4 This is a mistaken criticism because in utilitarianism happiness is better maximized by agents doing "their thing," not by telling people how to run their lives.
5 In his speech in Plato's *Symposium*, Phaedrus claims that both the man (lover) and the boy (beloved) are ashamed to do bad, especially cowardly things, in front of each other, and that is why an army of lovers would be the most courageous (Plato 1997g, 178E).
6 Aristotle believed that the virtues are not sufficient for a good life because we need "external goods": friends, money, and a dose of good fortune. In this, Aristotle departs from some other Greek philosophers (e.g., Socrates and the Stoics) who believed that the virtues are both necessary and sufficient for a good life.
7 For a more elaborate argument along these lines, see Halwani 2003, 158–168.
8 Compare what Nozick says on this (1991, 430).

Further Reading

On morality in general, two fairly easy introductions are Gensler (1998) and Rachels (1986). Two more involved but highly readable works are Darwall (1998) and Kagan (1998). On rights, see Campbell (2006) and Thomson (1990). On partiality, preferential treatment, and special obligations see Blum (1980), Graham and LaFollette (1989), Jeske (1998), and O'Neill and Ruddick (1979). A general introduction to the three moral theories is Baron, Pettit, and Slote (1997). On utilitarianism and consequentialism, see Mill, *Utilitarianism* (any version) and Darwall (2003). On Kantian ethics, see Kant, *Grounding for the Metaphysics of Morals* (the Ellington translation, published by Hackett, is good), Baron (1995) and Wood (2008). On virtue ethics, Aristotle's *Nicomachean Ethics* (the Irwin translation, published by Hackett) is a must, and Hursthouse (1999). On common-sense morality, see Slote (1992). On romantic love and virtue, see Solomon (1991). On universal love and virtue, see Swanton (2003, ch. 5). On morality and belief formation, see Zagzebski (1996). On love and sexism, see de Beauvoir (1952, esp. ch. 23), Firestone (1970, esp. chs 6 and 7), and Morgan (1991). On basic goods, see Feinberg (1984, esp. chs 1 and 5). On the value of love, see White (2001, ch. 2).

Part II

Sex

5   What Is Sex?

Greta Christina, a freelance writer who writes about sex, grappling with the question of what sex is, writes the following:

> I'm having trouble here. Even the conventional standby – sex equals intercourse – has a serious flaw: it includes rape, which is something I emphatically refuse to accept. As far as I'm concerned, if there's no consent, it ain't sex. But I feel that's about the only place in this whole quagmire where I have a grip … At what point in an encounter does it *become* sexual? If an encounter that begins nonsexually turns into sex, was it sex all along? What about sex with someone who's asleep? Can you have a situation where someone is having sex and the other isn't? It seems that no matter what definition I come up with, I can think of some real-life experience that calls it into question.
>
> (Christina 2008, 27–28)

Christina's questions point to a crucial issue: it is difficult, if not impossible, to define what "sex" is. Specifically, it is very difficult to define particular concepts of sex, such as "sexual act" or "activity" (I do not distinguish between "sexual act" and "sexual activity"), "sexual desire," and "sexual pleasure," and it is difficult to define types of sexual practices, such as "adultery," "casual sex," and "prostitution." Of course, we can usually *identify* some acts as sexual: intercourse (vaginal or anal), fellatio, cunnilingus, and masturbation are examples (others we may have trouble with). But the issue is not whether we can *identify* *some* acts as sexual, but whether we can *define* "sexual act," including types of sexual acts (e.g., "adultery").

Defining Sexual Acts[1]

What is a sexual act? We are not after a rough idea of what a sexual act is, but a definition – necessary and sufficient conditions that capture all and only sexual acts. This is important for two main reasons. First, it is an interesting philosophical question in itself, one that can teach us about how to think about sex, and which we need to define other types of sexual categories. For example, to know whether *x* committed adultery with *z*, we need to know whether *x* committed a sexual act with *z*. If we don't know what a sexual act is, we might not know whether *x* committed adultery.

Second, knowing whether an act is sexual helps, among others, with (1) legal issues (settling disputes among participants to the act); (2) social issues (understanding how to relate to each other and to society in general; constructing social scientific surveys about sex and sexual behavior); and (3) personal issues (knowing whether what happened between me and Jim last night was sex).

There are a number of possible criteria for defining a sexual act.

Behavior. Suppose that we define "sexual act" by saying that any act that has sexual behavior in it is sexual. So, for example, if penile–vaginal intercourse is sexual behavior, any act that has that in it is sexual.

This won't do, because we don't always know what counts as sexual behavior. The same behavior is sometimes sexual, sometimes not. Whether two men kissing each other on the cheek, close to the lips, is sexual depends on, for example, their culture. If they come from a culture where it is customary for men to greet each other this way (e.g., the Middle East and Eastern Europe), chances are that the kiss is not sexual. If they come from, say, North America, they are likely to be gay and the act is likely to be sexual.

Consider another example: inserting one finger (or more) into a vagina is a behavior often found in sexual activity, but by itself it does not tell us whether the act is sexual. If the man or the woman doing the inserting is a doctor, chances are that the act is not sexual (what if the doctor is turned on by the act?). If the person doing the inserting is the woman's sexual partner, chances are the act is sexual. If a woman inserts a finger in her own vagina, this, too, might or might not be sexual. If she is doing it because she is masturbating, it is sexual. If she is doing it as part of an artistic performance (think Annie Sprinkle), it need not be sexual (but it might be, depending on the woman and the performance), though it might *represent* a sexual act. If a man inserts one or more fingers into his anus, this also may or may not be sexual. If he does it to massage his prostate gland while masturbating, it is sexual. If he does it to give himself a prostate examination, it is not (but what if it makes him ejaculate?).

Or suppose that someone sticks his tongue into the ear of another and whirls it around. If I do it to my friend to drive him crazy and annoy him, it is not sexual. If I do it to a guy I pick up in a bar, it is sexual. Or consider a simple, yet firm, handshake: whether it is sexual depends again on the context, the history of the two people shaking each other's hand, and the two people themselves.

Thus, mere behavior is not going to *always* tell us whether an act is sexual. Of course, sometimes it does. If two people engage in sexual intercourse on stage, as an artistic performance, their act is sexual, not merely representative of a sexual act, because intercourse (and oral sex) is a standard sexual act, such that even if the people engaging in it do not think of themselves as having sex or do not enjoy it, their behavior is enough to make their act sexual (compare this to a couple having intercourse in a routine, non-pleasurable way: it is still sex even though they don't enjoy it).

Contact with sexual body parts. Let us try the following. An act is sexual if it involves contact with a sexual body part, one's own or another's. If Jim puts John's penis in his mouth, he makes contact with a sexual body part of John, and by this criterion their act is sexual. This sounds right. But some of the above examples show that this criterion also won't do. The vagina is a standard sexual body part, but whether contact with it is sexual depends on factors other than the contact itself. This means that contact with a sexual body part is not enough (sufficient) to classify an act as sexual. It may not even be necessary: Suppose that Elmo calls one of those 900 numbers and talks to a sex worker, having a fantastic orgasm by the end of the conversation. The act is sexual, at least for Elmo if not also for the sex worker, yet no physical contact was made with each other's sexual parts. (Here's an interesting question: Can the same act be sexual for one person but not the other? How, if it's the same act? Or should we say that one and the same *behavior* is a sexual act for one but not a sexual act for another?)

One might object that even though Elmo did not touch another person's sexual parts he touched his own; after all, he masturbated. Okay. Here's another example: suppose that prior to having sex with his girlfriend, Elmo likes to get himself hot and randy by calling one of those 900 numbers and talking to a sex worker. By the end of the conversation, during which he never touches himself because this is how he gets himself sexually worked up, Elmo is ready for sex with his girlfriend. Elmo had sex without physical contact with a sexual (or any other) body part. You might think that Elmo did not have sex. Fair enough. But you need to say why. Is it because there was no orgasm? This can't be right because many sexual acts are orgasm-free. Is it because there was no touching of anyone? But then what about going to a strip show, gazing intently and enjoyably at the stripper without touching yourself? Is this also not a sexual act?

The second criterion won't do for another reason: like "sexual behavior," we don't know what a sexual body part is independently of knowing whether the act is sexual. With the exception perhaps of penises and vaginas, there are no sexual body parts as such; whether a body part is sexual depends on what it is doing or what is being done to it. So this criterion gets things the wrong way round. As Soble puts it, "instead of saying … that whether an act is sexual depends on the sexual nature of the body part it involves, we should say that whether a part is sexual sometimes depends on the sexual nature of the act in which it is involved" (1996, 119).

Sexual pleasure. Perhaps an act is sexual if it involves or produces sexual pleasure. If two people who, without taking off their clothes, kiss, rub, and tug at each other, all the while feeling sexual pleasure, their act is sexual. This sounds correct. But it won't do if it means that producing sexual pleasure is *necessary* for an act to be sexual. First, many acts that are clearly sexual do not produce sexual pleasure (though they may produce other types of pleasure).

Suppose that Christopher and Marissa, both young, sexually inexperienced high school students, badly want to have intercourse with each other, but neither really knows what to do. They engage in intercourse, but it is painful, awkward, and blundering, and the experience frustrates both. Their act is sexual, but it does not produce pleasure of any kind. Or suppose that Christopher wants to have intercourse with Marissa because she is the girl-friend of his arch-enemy John, and Marissa wants to have intercourse with Christopher because she wants to get back at John, who's been treating her badly. They have sex but don't feel any sexual pleasure, though they do feel the pleasures of revenge and conquest at "screwing" John.

Consider a couple who have been having the same old, tired, routine sex. Another Friday night comes by and once again they go to bed to do their thing ("Let's go honey; it's nine o'clock"). Neither is stimulated enough and neither reaches orgasm. They have sex, as always, but there is no pleasure in it.

As a final example, consider all the prostitutes (male or female) who perform oral sex on men (many of whom are not sexually desirable), but feel no pleasure in doing so. Have they not, then, engaged in sexual acts? Clearly they have, so this criterion won't do if it means that producing or involving sexual pleasure is *necessary* for an act to be sexual.

Is the criterion successful as a sufficient condition for an act to be sexual – if an act produces sexual pleasure, then it is a sexual act? In the usual cases it succeeds (e.g., a gay man giving another man a blow job and both of them enjoying it). It works even in some non-standard cases. Suppose that I stick my tongue in my friend's ear, thinking that this will annoy him. Instead, he gets tremendous sexual pleasure from it. Or suppose that a gynecologist feels sexual pleasure while examining his patient, or a lifeguard feels sexual pleasure while he gives mouth-to-mouth resuscitation to a beautiful girl (Soble 1996, 130). The criterion tells us that the acts are sexual, which sounds right.

But there are less clear cases. Consider Soble's example of a man who, while driving his car, sees someone out walking and "as a result feels a twinge of sexual pleasure" (1996, 130). Soble thinks that this is not a sexual act. Had the man continued to look at the person, then, according to Soble, the act might be sexual: "passively experiencing sexual arousal or pleasure can in this way amount to the performance of a sexual act" (1996, 130). But what accounts for the difference? Not passivity and activity, because one can enjoy sexual pleasure and engage in a sexual act either passively (lie down and enjoy the cunnilingus) or actively (giving cunnilingus). Duration does not have much to do with it either. A penis sucked for only a second, a man penetrating a woman for a second, and a woman nibbling on another woman's clitoris also for a second are all sexual acts, albeit brief ones (pleasure or no pleasure).

Intention, as Soble suggests, is likely what explains the difference. If I am driving my car and feel a twinge of sexual desire, not only does this happen to me passively, I also do not willingly initiate the event or continue to partake in it. But if I decide that I like the appearance of this person and take another look, I initiate the event. Given that actions, as opposed to mere reflexive bodily behavior or events that people undergo, are intentional, that to *act* is to intend to do something, something producing pleasure is not enough to make it an act; the person experiencing the pleasure must somehow initiate it.

So is producing sexual pleasure sufficient for an act to be sexual? All sexual acts are sexual experiences, but not all sexual experiences are sexual acts, and this is where the trouble begins. Although feeling a twinge in the groin because of accidentally seeing a good-looking person is a sexual experience and not a sexual act, not all cases are as clear. One of Greta Christina's questions is, "What about sex with someone who's asleep?" Suppose – as many a scenario in pornography has taught us – a guy enters a room where a woman is sleeping naked under the sheets. The man slowly removes the sheets and goes down on her – as gently as possible so as not to wake her up. The woman, moaning with pleasure, sleeps through the whole thing. If intentions are necessary for an act to be sexual, then the man has a sexual experience *and* performs a sexual act, but the woman has *only* a sexual experience, because she had no intention of having sex with the man. Perhaps this explains Christina's reluctance to consider rape as a sexual act; she may agree that the raped woman has undergone a sexual experience (without the pleasure), but not a sexual act. Perhaps our intuitions are not firm about whether such cases count as only sexual experiences or both sexual experiences *and* acts.

Consider, however, this case. Suppose that Matt is gay but, as a devout Christian, has vowed never to have sex with a man. He accepts a dinner invitation from Hani, a gay colleague of his to whom he is attracted. After dinner, Hani begins kissing Matt's neck, sticking his tongue in his ear, pinching his nipples, and then begins fellating him (Matt does not touch Hani at all). Up until then, Matt's will was literally divided: part of it tells him to continue, and part tells him to stop (the second part wins when the oral sex begins). Did Matt have a sexual experience or a sexual act? If intentions or the will are our guide, the answer is not clear, since Matt's will is literally divided.

The point is that it might be plausible to say that producing sexual pleasure is sufficient for an act to be sexual, as long as we are clear on the distinction between acts and experiences. If the distinction is fuzzy – as the above cases indicate – we cannot be confident that a sexual experience is *only* an experience, not also a sexual *act*.

Intentions. Perhaps we can use the concept of intention as a criterion by which to decide whether an act is sexual. If physical behavior, body parts, and sexual pleasure fail to provide necessary and sufficient conditions to define "sexual act," we are left with intentions, though we still need to figure out what the intention is for.

It won't do to say, "the intention to have sex" or "the intention to engage in a sex act," because we want to define "sex" or "sex act," and relying on the concept of "having sex" or "sex act" is to use the very same terms to define what we set out to define (this would be a circular definition). We need to define "having sex" or "sex act" if we are to understand what it is to intend to do these things. So suppose that instead we say, "the intention to physically touch or interact with someone else." This also won't do because not all physical interactions are sexual (e.g., boxing, hugging a sibling), and not all sexual acts involve physical contact with another person (e.g., phone sex, watching pornography).

One reasonable candidate is "the intention to produce sexual pleasure in oneself or in another." This accounts for some cases. A doctor's inserting his finger into a woman's vagina is a sexual act if he intends to produce sexual pleasure for himself or the woman, but it is not sexual if he intends to examine the woman (what if he has both intentions?). The man feeling sexual pleasure by glancing briefly at a good-looking person does not have a sexual act because he did not intend to derive sexual pleasure from looking. But the man who continues to look at the good-looking person does undergo a sexual act because he intends to (continue to) derive pleasure.

However, the intention to produce sexual pleasure gets many cases wrong. If two people have sexual intercourse intending to procreate, they engage in a sexual act. Although they experience or may experience sexual pleasure, this is a *by-product* of the action (Soble 1996, 132). So this criterion does not give us a necessary condition for an act to be sexual. It is also not sufficient. Suppose that John is sexually aroused every time he hears the word "chipmunk." Daisy, intending to get him sexually aroused, says the word "chipmunk" over and over with increasing intensity. Daisy acts intending to produce sexual pleasure in John, but her act is not sexual (cf. Soble 1996, 132).

Sexual desire. One other (perhaps obvious) criterion by which to define sexual acts is sexual desire. Here is a definition offered by the philosopher Alan Goldman in his essay "Plain Sex": "sexual desire is desire for contact with another person's body and for the pleasure which such contact produces; sexual activity is activity which tends to fulfill such desire of the agent" (2008, 56). We will return to the part of the definition that defines "sexual desire." For now, our focus is on defining a sexual act (or "activity," in Goldman's terms) as activity "which tends to fulfill" sexual desire.

The definition sounds right. After all, what *else* is sexual activity if not activity that satisfies or "tends to" satisfy sexual desire? What else is a sexual act if not an act that satisfies or "tends to" satisfy sexual desire?[2] "Eating activity" is activity that satisfies desires for food (which could, but need not, include hunger), so we should expect something similar for sexual activity. But, alas, the definition faces two difficulties. The first is that we need to know what sexual desire is if the definition is to be helpful or informative, an issue we will address in the following section.

The second is that the definition faces obvious counter-examples. Two people can have sex to reproduce without the desire to have sex. A prostitute performing fellatio on a man does it (typically) not to satisfy or fulfill her sexual desire, but to make money. She engages in sexual activity yet without a sexual desire to be fulfilled. Thus satisfying sexual desire is not necessary for an activity to be sexual.

Whether fulfilling sexual desire is sufficient for an activity to be sexual depends on what we mean by "satisfaction" or "fulfillment." If we mean something like "the desire is no longer felt for the time being" or "the desire is gone," satisfying sexual desire would *not* be sufficient. Consider: popping one of those "food" pills is enough to quench the desire for hunger, but popping these pills is not an eating activity. Similarly for sex: injecting myself with a medicine designed to quell sexual desires, taking a cold shower, taking a powerful sleeping pill, or even just focusing on something other than sex might be sufficient to get rid of the sexual desire, yet none of these activities is sexual.

If by "satisfying sexual desire" we mean something like, "the desire achieves its goal" (which is sexual fulfillment), then satisfying a sexual desire by a particular activity *would* be sufficient for that activity to be sexual. But then the problem of circularity arises again: "sexual activity is that activity which satisfies sexual desire by means of a sexual activity." This is circular reasoning and is not going to take us anywhere. The criterion of sexual desire, then, does not succeed in defining sexual activity.

It seems that all the plausible criteria, taken individually, fail. What if we combine them? Right off the bat, however, two criteria – sexual behavior and sexual body parts – cannot be included in such a combination-definition, because, as we have seen, they get things back to front: whether a behavior or a body part is sexual *depends on* whether the act is sexual, not the other way around. This means that we are left with the two other criteria. They can be combined in at least one of two ways.

- An act is sexual if, and only if, it produces pleasure, is intended to produce pleasure, *and* satisfies sexual desire.
- An act is sexual if, and only if, it produces pleasure, is intended to produce pleasure, *or* satisfies sexual desire.[3]

The first requires that for an act to be sexual it satisfy *all* three criteria, the second that it satisfy *only one* of the three. Therefore, if we find an example of a sexual act that satisfies none of the three criteria, it would show that neither formulation succeeds in defining what a sexual act is. Not surprisingly, there are sexual acts that do not produce pleasure, are not intended to, and that do not satisfy a (pre-existing) sexual desire. Suppose that a couple have sexual intercourse with the intention of procreating, not to experience pleasure. Suppose that they are both also tired, under pressure to have children, and do not, at that moment at least, really feel like having sex with each other. The sex ends up being boring, awkward, and painful, with neither of them achieving orgasm. This would be a sex act but one that does not produce pleasure, that is not intended to, and that does not satisfy sexual desire. Another example: two people perform sexual intercourse on stage, at a sex club, or as an artistic performance. The act does not produce pleasure, is not intended to produce pleasure, and the performers have no sexual desires to do it.

Thus, both types of the above combinations won't do. Indeed, they fail in the face of common examples.

By the above criteria, a definition of "sex act" is not forthcoming. My hunch is that the reason has to do with the fact that what we commonly think is a sexual act does not depend on one criterion. Sometimes we rely on behavior, sometimes on intentions, sometimes on contact with body parts, and so forth. We should probably just give up on finding a definition or – more valiantly, but less plausibly – stick to a favored definition and heroically reject or argue against whatever plausible counter-examples it faces.

Let us look at another crucial concept in sex, that of sexual desire.

Defining Sexual Desire

Goldman defines "sexual desire" as "desire for contact with another person's body and for the pleasure which such contact produces; sexual activity is activity which tends to fulfill such desire of the agent" (2008, 56). Goldman's main motive for adopting this definition is to liberate sexual desire from a "means–end" analysis of sexual desire, which is any analysis that understands sexual desire in terms of an *external purpose* such as procreation and love. Goldman's point is that if sexual desire has any purpose it is internal, namely contact with another's body and the pleasure of this contact.

As worded, the definition gives the wrong results. Suppose that after I have an angry argument with one of my colleagues, I say to him, "You know what? It'll give me great pleasure to punch you in the face right now!" I desire contact with my colleague's body (I want to punch him) and the pleasure the contact will give me. But unless I'm a complete pervert, the pleasure I derive from punching him is not sexual. So wanting to punch my colleague fulfills the left-hand side of Goldman's definition but not the right-hand side. As worded, then, the definition is off-track.

Goldman, I suppose, can amend his definition by adding the word "sexual": "sexual desire is desire for contact with another person's body and for the *sexual* pleasure which such contact produces." Setting aside the issue that the definition won't be informative until we know what sexual, as opposed to other types of pleasure is, Goldman intends the phrases "desire for contact with another person's body" and "desire for the sexual pleasure such contact produces" to constitute *one* condition in the definition, because separating them into two makes it appear as if the desirer wants two things, physical contact plus sexual pleasure, whereas Goldman intends that one desires sexual pleasure *in* or *through* contact with another person's body. The physical contact is desirable in and of itself because it produces the pleasure (but see below). Let me explain.

Suppose Grace lusts after Travis. She wants to have sex with him because she believes it would give her sexual pleasure to have sex with him. Suppose we offer Grace a very sophisticated machine – the "Travis-Orgasmatron" – such that if she uses it she will experience the same sex-pleasure sensations as if she were having sex with Travis. Chances are that Grace would decline and would prefer the actual sex with Travis. The point is that most people's sexual desires are not usually desires for only sexual, pleasurable sensations. Although they want them, they want them by actually having sex. As Goldman states, "it is not a desire for a particular sensation detachable from its causal context, a sensation which can be derived in other ways" (2008, 57). To him, the goal of the desire is the contact itself; that's why he says that even though in contact sports there is a desire to touch another player's body, the desire is not ultimately for the sake of physical contact, but for winning (2008, 57).

Alluring as it sounds, Goldman's definition is not plausible. There are types of sexual desire that do *not* involve the desire for contact with another person's body. Indeed, any such contact deflates the desire entirely, as if the desirer has cold water poured over him. Voyeurism and exhibitionism are two such desires. While there are voyeurs who peep because the opportunity to see someone stripping or having sex is just too good to ignore, "real" voyeurs enjoy their sexual acts *precisely* because they are able to look without touching (whether the voyeur minds that the person being looked at knows or does not know she or he is being looked at depends on the voyeur). Voyeuristic sexual desires may be morally wrong or perverted, but they are sexual desires nonetheless. Thus, what Goldman says about voyeurism (which is not much) is plain wrong: "Voyeurism or viewing a pornographic movie qualifies as a sexual activity, but only as an imaginative substitute for the real thing (otherwise a deviation from the norm as expressed in our definition)" (2008, 58). That is, either voyeurism fits his definition but it's not real voyeurism (because it's a "substitute for the real thing") or it's real voyeurism (not a substitute for anything) but it's not really sexual desire.

In addition to voyeurism, two other sexual desires falter on Goldman's view. The exhibitionist "gets off" on being watched by others getting naked, having sex, masturbating, and so on; he does not desire to be touched by or to touch those to whom he exhibits himself (not initially, at least). Like voyeurism, Goldman's definition renders this type of desire non-sexual (and what would be the "real thing" for which exhibitionism might be a substitute?). It thus rules *out* a crucial type of sexual desire as sexual. In addition, those who have bestial desires – desires for sex with animals – also fare badly on Goldman's definition (bestial desires need not be a matter of sexual *orientation*, and they are typically not; instead, someone, feeling randy, sees, say, a sexy horse or a Norwegian elkhound, and desires it). They do not desire to have contact with another *person's* body, though they do desire contact with an animal's body. Again, bestial desires may be perverted or immoral, but they are not any less sexual for that.

Goldman's definition also rules out another crucial – and much more common – type of sexual desire, the desire for (solitary) masturbation. I assume that when Goldman uses the phrase, "watching a pornographic movie" in the above quotation, he assumes someone who masturbates while watching. This means that either Goldman thinks all masturbators masturbate only because they can't get the "real thing" or that even though there are masturbators who don't masturbate as a substitute for the real thing, their desires don't count as sexual. Either way, Goldman is wrong.

If there are "non-substitute" masturbators, this means that they masturbate for reasons or desires that have nothing to do with lack of access to a man or a woman with whom to have sex. *If* there were such masturbators, it would be implausible to rule out their desires as sexual. Thus the second option is a non-starter. *Are* there non-substitute masturbators? Clearly, many people masturbate because they don't have sexual access (then or ever) to another person's body. Even guys who have a quickie masturbation before they go to work might gladly substitute that for a real quickie. But surely there are non-substitute masturbators: men and women who are utterly faithful to their spouses, who would never dream of cheating on them or of having sex outside the relationship; men and women who have perfected masturbation as an art – with whom it is almost a ritual. They are non-substitute masturbators. At the very least, it seems strange – not to mention close-minded – to somehow think that it is *impossible* that there be non-substitute masturbators. On Goldman's definition, if there are such masturbators, their desires to masturbate are not sexual – a false claim.[4]

There is another potential problem for Goldman's definition. What does "substitute" exactly mean? We can classify those who masturbate due to lack of access to a sexual partner into two groups. The first are those who masturbate because they cannot or do not have access to a *particular person*. For example, Grace might masturbate while fantasizing about having sex with Travis, because he is sexually unavailable to her (then or ever). Or Diego masturbates while thinking about Ryan because Ryan is also sexually unavailable. In such cases, the unavailability may be due to various reasons: Travis might be gay; Ryan, whether straight or gay, might be sexually uninterested in Diego. But the reasons could also have to do with the masturbator: Tony might masturbate to the image of Rizzo – a 10-year-old boy – but would never dream of actually touching the boy because it is wrong. Grace doesn't want to touch Travis because, being gay, this might ruin their friendship. Or Jackie might masturbate while fantasizing about Wade, but would never even think of actually having sex with him because he is married and she would not want to be part of any adulterous affairs.

In all these cases, Goldman might convincingly maintain that the people still desire contact with those they desire, but would not act on it. This brings us to the second group of masturbators, who masturbate without fantasizing about anybody specific while masturbating. Suppose that both Leo and Leonard are masturbating while watching pornography. Leo is utterly turned on by the women he sees, and he really wants to have sex with one of them. When he masturbates, he does so as a substitute for having sex with her. Thus, Leo falls under the first group. But Leonard is not turned on by any specific woman, and he is not masturbating because he wants to have sex with one of the women but cannot. Instead, he is turned on by the action on the screen: the fellatio, the intercourse, the screams, and the moans. He has no desire to touch any of the actors he sees, but enjoys the action unfolding in front of him. Is there a person here for whom Leonard substitutes masturbation? In a sense yes – all these actors on screen – but in another sense no, because there is no specific person with whom Leonard wishes to have sex.

Or consider Sylvia, who imagines a woman she would really like to have sex with. The woman isn't real and is purely a figment of Sylvia's imagination. There is no substitute woman here (if there is, it's a weird one: the woman who would have existed had the world been different). So the issue of having sex as a substitute for the real thing bears careful thinking, because the notion of "substitution" in such cases is not all that clear.

Of course, even though Goldman might successfully account for some types of masturbation given his views on sexual desire, his views on sexual activity don't fare so well. If sexual activity is activity that "tends to fulfill" the desires of the person, masturbation does not fulfill such desires. Even if the person is masturbating as a substitute for the real thing, masturbation does not fulfill, or even tend to fulfill, the desire. Masturbating while fantasizing about y is not the same at all as having sex with y. At best, masturbation can abate the sexual desires for y, but this is not the same as fulfilling them (see Soble 2008a, 80–83).

One other issue remains. It is worthwhile to think about what "body" in "person's body" refers to in Goldman's definition. Consider necrophilia – the desire for having sex with the bodies of dead human beings. Whether it is a sexual or non-sexual desire on Goldman's view depends on how we understand "body." If it refers only to the bodies of living human beings, necrophilia is off the sexual chart. If "body" refers also to the bodies of dead human beings, it is not. But then Goldman's definition of "sexual desire" becomes strange indeed: it would rule out bestiality, voyeurism, and other types of sexual desires as sexual, but rules in necrophilia.

Generally speaking, it might also be that Goldman has things back to front. Just as whether a body part or a behavior is sexual depends on the activity in question, perhaps whether a desire is sexual depends on what it is a desire *for*, specifically, what kind of activity it is a desire for. Perhaps we should not define "sexual activity" *in terms* of "sexual desire" and give an independent definition of "sexual desire," as Goldman does. We should define "sexual desire" in terms of "sexual activity," and give an independent definition of "sexual activity," something that has so far proven elusive.

There is a different type of criticism of Goldman's definition given by the philosopher, Seiriol Morgan, who accuses it of *under-describing* sexual desire. Morgan states that, according to Goldman's definition and other similar ones, the *essence* of sexual desire is "a desire for bodily pleasure … But this is a mistake, because it assumes without argument that sexual pleasure is a simple phenomenon which manifests a uniform essentially physical character in all its instances" (2003a, 4). To Morgan, sexual desire is not mere appetite, as Goldman's view makes it out to be, but something more complex because it is infused with *intentionality*, meaning that bodily urges and appetites are transformed through "mentality" (2003a, 9). When we sexually desire someone, our desires are often shot through with beliefs about the person or activity we desire. For example, *x* might desire *y* not (only) because *y* is another attractive human being, but because *y* is *y*:

> the devoted lover wants the pleasure of contact with *her* body, which he experiences as *pleasure at contact with her body*. Bodily pleasure as such is not what he wants – this kind of lover would find a sexual experience with another unsatisfying or even downright unpleasant. Because of her significance for him, the physical experiences he has with her have a particular nature for him – it is these he wants and he can have them with no other.
>
> (Morgan 2003a, 6)

A man could be attracted to a woman because she is a police officer and what sexually arouses him about her is precisely this fact; his sexual desire is constituted or strengthened by the belief that she is a policewoman (Morgan 2003a, 7–8). A woman's sexual experience and pleasure could be heightened by the fact that she is having sex with a man on the same bed on which he made love to another woman for whom he left her (Morgan 2003a, 8). Morgan's intentionality view also explains the "highly impersonal and anonymous sex engaged in by some gay men," because "in some cases their behaviour is such that it can only be adequately understood if we see their sexual pleasure as mediated by their arousal at the sheer anonymity of their sexual partners, an essentially intentional arousal" (2003a, 8–9).

Morgan is correct that Goldman's definition under-describes many sexual phenomena, because in many cases sexual desires are pervaded by the kind of beliefs, attitudes, and mental states of which Morgan gives examples. So to characterize them as simply for contact with another person's body and the pleasure this brings would be to give a very minimal – under-described – account of these desires. But whether Morgan's criticism is damaging to Goldman's view depends on whether Goldman offers a *definition* of sexual desire (in terms of necessary and sufficient conditions) and on what we expect a definition to achieve.

I have assumed that Goldman does give a definition of sexual desire, not a full-blown theory of its workings and nature. In this sense he would not deny that sexual desire could be complex in the ways on which Morgan insists. But he might argue that a definition does not need to go into such detail and complexity. If we define "human being" as "rational animal," we offer two necessary and jointly sufficient conditions for what a human being is, without denying that actual human beings, individually and socially, are much more complex (indeed, Goldman says, "sexual desire can be focused or selective at the same time as being physical" (2008, 65)). At this point, we can either claim that both Goldman (assuming his definition is correct) and Morgan are right, in that Goldman offers a decent definition of "sexual desire" that underlies both complex and simple ones, but agreeing that in the case of many sexual desires a more nuanced account needs to be given. Or we can reject Goldman's definition on the ground that a good definition should be more informative and have more explanatory power to account for the kinds of complexities that Morgan discusses. I leave the issue open.

Once again, we have failed to define another crucial concept in sex, that of sexual desire. Let us turn to another concept, that of sexual pleasure.

Defining Sexual Pleasure

The concept of sexual pleasure is crucial because it is an essential ingredient in other concepts; without a clear understanding of it, those other concepts would remain unclear. For example, we have seen that one way of defining "sexual act" is that it either produces or is intended to produce sexual pleasure. Even if this definition of sexual acts were true (it is not), we would still need to know what sexual pleasure is for the definition to be informative. Another example is this: the liberal philosopher Igor Primoratz, in attempting to get around the difficulties faced by Goldman's definition with masturbation, redefines "sexual desire" as "the desire for certain bodily pleasures" (1999, 46). If we don't know what these bodily pleasures are, we cannot understand what sexual desire is, according to this definition. So one reason why it is important to define "sexual pleasure" is that the clarity of other definitions relies on it. Another reason is that the definition can help tell us whether a particular pleasure is sexual or some other type.

There are basically two approaches to defining "sexual pleasure." The first relies on the way the pleasure *feels*. The second forges links between the pleasures and things intimately connected to them, such as sexual organs, sexual acts, and sexual desires.

The feeling approach. If a pleasure feels this or that way, it is sexual. If it does not, it is non-sexual. This approach sounds plausible. After all, this is how we usually tell whether we are feeling pleasure or pain. Moreover, we are talking about pleasures – sensations of sorts – and if we don't define them by the way they feel, how else are we to do so? A third reason why this approach is plausible is that, if successful, we can define "sexual pleasure" without tying it to sexual activity or another sexual phenomenon, so that a pleasure might be sexual even if obtained through non-sexual activity, such as a man ejaculating during a wet dream.

The approach works in some cases. The pleasures of an orgasm are unique in how they feel. Orgasms have a distinctive feel and quality about them not found among other pleasures or easily confused with them. Perhaps the sensations of having one's nipples caressed, massaged, licked, and so on are also somewhat unique. But our confidence ends here, because sexual pleasures are not confined to pleasures obtained through the usual sexual organs (penis, anus, clitoris, vagina, nipples); virtually any physical area or region in one's body can be a source of sexual pleasure depending on the context and the individual involved: from toes, to fingers, ears, necks, belly buttons, and thighs. Because pleasures obtained from these areas need not have a distinctive feel to them, they cannot be relied on to provide a criterion for what is a sexual pleasure and what is not.

Moreover, even if they did have a distinctive feel – e.g., having one's toes sucked always feels the same way – it might be that the same sensation or feel is sexual in one context but not in another. Having a dog lick my feet might feel the same way as having Brad Pitt do so, but the first is definitely not sexual (to me, anyway), while the second is. This point indicates something else: it may be that the sensations themselves are not as such pleasures or not pleasures. Let me elaborate.

Two sensations might feel the same way and both be pleasurable, but such that only one is sexual. The dog licking my feet feels exactly the same way as Brad Pitt doing it, and they are both pleasurable, but only the second is sexual. This is one possibility. Another possibility is that both sensations feel exactly the same, but are such that the dog's is not pleasurable (maybe even painful) while Brad Pitt's is. If these two possibilities exist, this means that the feeling approach can fail in one of two ways: depending on the context, the sensation may either not be pleasurable, period, or may not be *sexually* pleasurable.

That's not all. Many sexual pleasures – as Morgan insists – are mental. Suppose that it's been my fantasy to have sex with Justin Timberlake. The thought, "I'm having sex with Justin Timberlake," provides me with no pleasure on its own. But suppose that on a trip to Los Angeles I stumble upon him and manage to seduce him. Then, as we go at it like two cats on heat, the thought, "I'm having sex with Justin Timberlake," provides me with tremendous pleasure, heightening whatever sexual pleasure I am experiencing already. This means that sexual pleasures are not only physical, but mental as well. Since thoughts as such have no particular feel to them – no reliable ones, at least – whatever feel they might have depends on the context. Suppose that Justin Timberlake turns out not only to be horrible in bed, but also to have a bad odor. Then the thought, "I'm having sex with Justin Timberlake" fills me with nausea, not excitement.

So the feeling approach won't succeed.

Non-feeling approach: genital organs. One suggestion is that sexual pleasures are those produced by, or associated with, the genital organs. Although this works in obvious cases, it also won't do. For one thing, we have already seen that not all sexual pleasures have to do with the genitals. For another, not all the pleasures produced by, or associated with, the genitals are sexual. The relief produced by urinating or defecating is a pleasure, though it is not sexual (Freud notwithstanding). The pleasure women sometimes feel when their infants suckle their breasts is not (or need not be) sexual.

Non-feeling approach: sexual activity. Another suggestion is that pleasures are sexual if produced by sexual activity or if they occur during such activity (including foreplay). This is promising because it covers more than the usual suspects (orgasms and nipple sensations) and includes the pleasures of having one's neck kissed and licked, of feeling one's thighs intertwined with another's, and so on. But it is still defective as a definition, because it includes things that should not be included and excludes things that should not be excluded. Suppose that I have a date with P. Diddy in two hours' time; it is a sex date that we have every Friday at four in the afternoon. We have been having these sex dates for only four weeks, so the novelty and excitement of sex has not yet worn off. As I sit trying to read Plato, my thoughts keep wandering to P. Diddy and the eventual things I plan to do to him. These sexual thoughts fill me with *sexual* pleasure. Yet they are not produced by any sexual activity, nor do they occur during one; if a penis gets erect or a vagina secretes juices because of these thoughts, this would still not count as sexual activity. So this definition excludes some sexual pleasures.

It also includes non-sexual pleasures. Suppose that as I am having sex with P. Diddy I suddenly remember that tomorrow I'm going to go to Disney Land with my best friend. The thought fills me with pleasure, but the pleasure is not sexual, even though it occurs during a sexual act. Perhaps we should drop "occurs during" and retain only "produced by," because this maintains a strong link between the sexual activity and any pleasures resulting during the activity by making the activity the cause of these pleasures. But this still won't do. Suppose that, after being with P. Diddy for fifteen weeks, I become bored with him. During the sex, my thoughts wander to all sorts of other things. On one particular Friday afternoon, as we're having sex, I solve a philosophical problem that's been nagging on me. The thought fills me with non-sexual pleasure, but it is caused by the boring sex with P. Diddy. So either claiming that the pleasures have to be caused by the sexual activity won't work or we must tighten the causal links to ensure that *only* sexual pleasures are caused by the sexual activity. I am not clear on how to do the latter.

Non-feeling approach: *Primoratz's view*. Primoratz defines "sexual pleasure" as "the sort of bodily pleasure experienced in the sexual parts of the body, or at least related to those parts in that if it is associated with arousal, the arousal occurs in those parts" (1999, 46). The pleasures of a kiss can be sexual without being experienced in the sexual parts of the body (the genitals) – without being accompanied by genital arousal. But if the pleasure of the kiss is sexual, then *were* it to be connected at all to arousal, the arousal would have to be in the genital parts of the body. In other words, because the pleasures of a kiss can be sexual and not *actually* connected to genital arousal, the way to distinguish the sexual from the non-sexual pleasures of a kiss (and other activities) is to ask a *hypothetical* question: If we are to connect these pleasures with arousal, where would this arousal occur? If we answer, "In the sexual parts of the body," the pleasures are sexual. If we answer, "In the non-sexual parts of the body," the pleasures are non-sexual.

This is an ingenious definition. It explains a lot of things. Suppose that two men shake hands and they feel pleasure. Whether their pleasure is sexual depends on whether it is "associated with the sexual parts of the body. If yes, it is sexual." The pleasure I felt during sex with P. Diddy from solving the philosophical problem is non-sexual, because, even though caused by the boring sex, it is not connected to arousal in the genital parts of my body. Primoratz's view, then, can sort most, maybe even all, instances of pleasure between sexual and non-sexual.

Before evaluating this definition, let us note three things. First, insisting on associating sexual pleasure with the genital parts of the body makes sense: we are biological beings and our sexual pleasures eventually have to have something to do with our genital parts; these are, after all, the loci of our sexual and reproductive basic functions.

Second, we have seen that, except for the genitals, whether a body part is sexual depends on the use to which it is put. Does Primoratz's view suffer from this problem? No. Primoratz is specific in what he means by "sexual body parts," namely "the genitals and other parts that differentiate the sexes" (1999, 46). If he is right, the definition does not suffer from the problem of being uninformative, because it relies on a specific list of what the sexual body parts are, not leaving the idea of it open.

Third, if successful, Primoratz would not only have defined "sexual pleasure," but also "sexual desire" and "sexual activity," because he defines sexual acts in terms of sexual desires, and sexual desires in terms of sexual pleasure: "Sexual activity ... [is] activity that tends to fulfill sexual desire" and "sexual desire" is "the desire for certain bodily pleasures" (1999, 46). So we define "sexual activity" in terms of sexual desire. If we ask what sexual desire is, we define it in terms of sexual pleasure. And if we ask what sexual pleasure is, we define it (partly) in terms of sexual bodily parts, by providing a closed list of what they are, not by leaving it undefined.

Ingenious as it is, the definition faces three difficulties. The first is that the notion of arousal is vague: Is it a mental state, a purely physical state, or sometimes both? If I have a sexual dream while I am asleep, eventuating in ejaculation, am I aroused? If after much poking by my doctor in my anus I ejaculate, am I aroused? Depending on the answers, the definition may or may not succeed. For example, if arousal is never only a physical state but is also always mental, then when I ejaculate during an anal examination I experience sexual pleasure but without being aroused. (The notions of being "linked to" and "associated with" arousal bear some scrutiny also, because they, too, are vague.)

Second, the definition is hard to apply because it relies on hypothetical questions. Suppose that I always feel a weird type of pleasure whenever I see Oprah Winfrey on television (without any arousal). Is this pleasure sexual or not? The only way to know, according to this definition, is to figure out whether, *if* it is associated with arousal, the arousal is genital. But since my pleasure is not *actually* associated with any arousal, it is virtually impossible to know whether it is sexual (Primoratz seems to acknowledge this problem, though his statement of it is too brief; 1999, 46–47).

Third, the objections that Morgan raises against Goldman's views also apply to Primoratz's (Morgan's essay explicitly targets them), so it may also be that they suffer from the same defects that, according to Morgan, Goldman's do (I leave it to the reader to decide how these objections apply to the views of Primoratz and whether they succeed).

Let us now turn to defining some particular types of sexual activities.

Casual Sex, Adultery, and Prostitution

There are many types of sexual activities: casual sex, promiscuity, sex with prostitutes, sex between friends, adultery, rape, cyber-sex, masturbation (with or without aids, while and while not watching or reading pornography), sex between two people who love each other, orgiastic sex, sex with animals, sex with corpses, sex involving fetish objects, and so on. Some cut across each other: casual sex can be had with a friend or a stranger; it can be promiscuous but it need not be; it can be orgiastic but need not be. Someone can have sex with a prostitute he loves. Sex between two people can be "merely" masturbatory. Adultery can be committed with a friend. And so on. I cannot attempt to define each item on this (non-exhaustive) list of sexual activities, but attempting to define some items highlights the issues involved in arriving at such definitions.

Casual sex. Basically, casual sex is sex for the sake of sexual pleasure. However, no definition of "casual sex" that states, "sex for the sake of sexual pleasure" can succeed. First, couples that are in love often have sex for the sake of pleasure (and for other purposes as well, such as to procreate or to make up after a fight), but it is not casual sex. Second, sex with prostitutes is a type of casual sex, but prostitutes (typically) don't do it for the sake of pleasure at all, but for money. So even if the definition states, "sex *merely* for the sake of sexual pleasure," it still won't do, because it would run afoul of prostitution (although it may be that one and the same sexual activity can be done for pleasure for one party and for other purposes for the other party), and it would run afoul of loving couples: they often also have sex merely for pleasure, but it is not casual.

Relying on behavioral criteria to define "casual sex" also won't work. For example, performing oral sex and engaging in intercourse do not, on their own, differentiate casual from non-casual sexual activity, because they are standard sexual activities that any two or more people can engage in. Other behavioral suggestions are also unlikely to succeed. Although behavior that describes what goes on in orgies or sex with animals might capture the idea that these sexual activities are casual (as orgies and sex with animals tend to be), it excludes other types of casual sexual activities that do not conform to this behavior, such as non-orgiastic casual sex and casual sex with other human beings (rather than animals). For example, merely knowing that two people are masturbating each other or in front of each other does not tell us whether their sex is casual. It could be (if they are two strangers who picked each other up), but need not (if they are two lovers who sometimes or always have sex this way).

The example of lovers engaging in sex for pleasure suggests that casual sex is not so much sex for the sake of sexual pleasure or sex that conforms to particular behavior, as much as that it does not involve a deep commitment. Anthony Ellis defines it ("roughly") as "sex between partners who have no deep or substantial relationships of which sex is a component" (1986, 157). In other words, if Homer and Marge have a substantial relationship of which sex is a component – as lovers have – the sex between them is not casual. Sex between two colleagues or two friends can be casual even if they have a deep relationship (friendship or work colleagues), so long as this relationship does not have a sexual component. And, of course, sex can still be casual if the two people have no relationship at all. Moreover, sex between two people who have merely a sexual relationship with each other is still casual despite the fact that the two have a relationship, because the relationship is not "deep" or "substantial" (if it is or becomes deep, we then question whether the sex between them is casual).

What Ellis's definition captures about casual sex is that it is sex without prior or the promise of future attachment. In online cruising for sex, for example, the abbreviation "NSA" – "no strings attached" – is often used to describe the desired sex. However, the definition does not fully capture what we mean by "casual sex." Suppose that Ken and Laurie, after meeting online for purposes of dating (not casual hook-ups), go on a first date. After the date they have sex. On Ellis's definition, the sex they have is casual, because they have no deep relationship of which sex is a part. However, it is plausible that it is not casual because of Ken and Laurie's intentions and beliefs: they intend the sex to be the first of many more encounters to come because they intend or at least hope to have a relationship (whether they end up having a relationship is irrelevant). Because of these beliefs and intentions, it is arguable that the sex between them is not casual, even though Ellis's definition classifies it as such.

This indicates that a correct definition of "casual sex" requires mentioning something about the beliefs or intentions of the parties involved. Suppose that we define casual sex as "sexual activity engaged in with the understanding or belief that it will not lead to emotional commitments" (Halwani 2006a, 136). The words "understanding" and "belief" are crucial because they countervail other types of mental states that would make a sexual act non-casual. For example, if Laurie and Ken *hope* or *desire* that their sexual activity will lead to a deep relationship, this likely makes the sex non-casual. However, if they also believe or understand, despite their hope, that the sex will not or is likely not to lead to a relationship, then it is plausible that the sex is casual. It might even be a better definition if we define "casual sex" as "sexual activity engaged in with the intention that it not lead to emotional commitments." This makes it clear that casual sex is indeed NSA sex.

But the definitions still won't do. First, the "intention" version of the definition is too strong. It rules out instances of casual sex as not casual if the parties have no such intentions. What if Ken and Laurie have no such intentions but only the understanding that the sex will not lead to a commitment? The sex between them would still be casual despite the lack of these intentions. Second, even the "understanding" version of the definition rules out possible cases of casual sex: What if the parties have *no* beliefs or understanding one way or another? The definition is silent on such cases. Third, what if the sex occurs between a human being and an entity that cannot have beliefs, intentions, and so on, such as an animal or a corpse? Worse, what if one party believes or intends the sex to not lead to a commitment but the other party either has no beliefs or intentions about the activity or beliefs or intentions that it *will* lead to a commitment? Would this mean that the sexual activity is casual for one but not for the other (a not so implausible result)?

Perhaps what is needed is a more expansive definition, coupled with the realization that one and the same sexual activity could be casual for one party but not for the other. Here is one final attempt: casual sex is sexual activity engaged in between people with no prior deep commitment of which sex is a part and with no beliefs, intentions, or desires that it should lead to such a commitment. This sounds promising. It emphasizes that the sex occurs between people (not with animals or corpses); it requires the people to not have a deep commitment *and* to not want the sex to lead to such a commitment. If two people have sex without such a commitment and without any beliefs one way or another, the definition classifies the sex as casual – a plausible result. If two people have sex without a deep commitment and with the belief that it will not lead to such a commitment, the definition classifies their sex as casual – also a plausible result.

One counter-intuitive result of the definition, however, is that it classifies many instances of rape as casual sex, because the rapist and the victim do not have a deep relationship of which sex is a part, and neither of them desires the sex to lead to such a relationship. But rape is not usually considered casual sex. I leave it to the reader to decide whether we ought to tolerate or even accept this counter-intuitive result or whether we should amend or even reject the definition. I also leave it to the reader to decide whether this definition faces other counter-examples. (Note how the definition contains the concept of "sexual activity," a concept we have not yet been able to plausibly define.)

One final point before moving to another type of sexual activity: the above definition mentions nothing about the frequency of sexual encounters and whether it has anything to do with casual sex. This is important because it is sometimes thought that people who have casual sex are bed-hoppers. However, we should leave frequency out of the definition, because it has more to do with promiscuity than with casual sex as such. On the one hand, a person might have promiscuous sex without all the encounters being casual (serial monogamy). On the other hand, there is nothing in the concept of casual sex that ties it to frequency; a person can have casual sex only once in his lifetime. Again, I leave it to the reader to differentiate more fully between casual sex and promiscuity.

Adultery. Defining "adultery" is important for many reasons: it is an interesting philosophical issue in itself; it raises fascinating questions about whether a sexual act is adulterous and whether a non-sexual act is adulterous; and sometimes we need to know whether a person's sexual act is adulterous to know whether he or she has wronged his or her spouse. I take the following, seemingly obvious, definition as my starting point: "adultery can be defined as extramarital sex: sex a married person has with someone other than his or her spouse" (Primoratz 1999, 78; see also Wasserstrom 1998, 140). Although it sounds sensible, it glosses over issues that make defining "adultery" a complicated task. Let us use the example of Ken and Laurie, a married couple.

(1) Suppose that Ken engages in solitary masturbation. This is adultery according to the above definition, because Ken, a married man, has sex with himself; and because he is not married to himself, he has sex with someone other than his spouse. Although some people might accept that Ken's masturbation is adultery, most won't because they simply don't consider masturbation to be adulterous. The definition needs to be amended. So let it state for now that adultery is "sex a married person has with someone other than his or her spouse, excluding solitary masturbation."

(2) But suppose that Ken masturbates (a) while watching a pornography movie; (b) while inserting his penis into an inflated doll; (c) while watching his next-door neighbor Lisette undress; (d) while talking dirty with a phone-sex worker; or (e) while talking with someone on his computer in a chat room. I doubt whether there would be consensus that none of these cases is adulterous. I bet that while some people would not count (a) and (b) as adultery, they might not be sure about the others. The difficult task is figuring out whether there are any relevant differences between them. The issue *could* be that we need to decide which of (a) through (e) are cases of solitary masturbation. We can then argue as follows: "Well, since engaging in solitary masturbation is not adultery, then those cases that are solitary masturbation are not cases of adultery." But things are not so simple. Even if we agree on which cases are solitary masturbation, someone might retort that solitary masturbation is sometimes adulterous. If Ken masturbates while watching Lisette, he commits adultery, whether it counts as solitary masturbation or not.

I think this is correct. Consider case (e): suppose that the other person with whom Ken is chatting in virtual reality is really a woman (not a computer nerd with nothing better to do than pretend to be a hot woman on the sexual hunt). Throughout the chat, the woman does not masturbate but Ken does, finally reaching orgasm. He engages in solitary masturbation and he commits adultery – actually, he commits adultery *by* engaging in solitary masturbation. So some cases of solitary masturbation are adulterous. Our amendment to the definition thus fails.

(3) The "someone" in the definition also raises some complex issues. We may be confident that it is meant to exclude inanimate objects such as dildos and inflated dolls, but it is not clear whether it should include only living

human beings. Suppose that Laurie walks in one day on Ken to find him having sex with their female border collie, Edwina. Since animals are not people, on this definition Ken's having sex with Edwina is not adulterous. But I suspect that some would contest this claim. The reason why it is not adulterous cannot be because the dog does not consent, because if Ken had raped another woman we would think of his act as adulterous (though not the most serious moral problem with it). It cannot be because sex with a dog is casual, because if Ken had picked up a woman and had sex with her for half an hour in a hotel room, this would be adulterous. Besides, what if Ken and Edwina have been having an affair? Many zoophiles have long-term sexual "affairs" with animals. So it is unclear whether a married person having sex with an animal would, or should, count as adultery. It probably depends on the context, including the type of animal in question.

Suppose that Laurie walks in on Ken to find him sodomizing a human corpse. If the corpse of a human being is not a "someone," Ken's behavior would not be adulterous according to the definition. Whether we agree or not that human corpses are "someones," however, is not going to settle the issue, because it could be argued that even if having sex with a human corpse is not having sex with "someone," when a married person does it he commits adultery nonetheless. This means the "someone" in the definition raises two questions: What types of things count as "someone"? And if "someone" includes only living human beings, *should* it?

(4) The "other than his or her spouse" also raises issues. Suppose that Laurie and Ken have a threesome with their neighbor Drew. Both Ken and Laurie would be having sex with someone other than their spouse. According to our definition, both commit adultery. But it is not obvious that they do, one reason being that "adultery" is often understood to involve cheating, and threesomes that include both spouses do not. There is another reason. Suppose that Ken and Laurie have an open marriage. One day, Ken leaves the house, telling Laurie, "Okay dear. I'm off to have sex with Lisette. Be back by six for dinner. Love ya!" Not only does Laurie know about this, she also doesn't mind. Again, according to the definition, Ken commits adultery. But if Ken does not commit adultery in his threesome with Laurie and Drew, why does he when he has sex with Lisette if Laurie knows and agrees to it? Perhaps the reason has nothing to do with whether Laurie knows, but with whether she is present during or partaking in the sex act. This might work. But suppose that Laurie watches Ken having sex with Lisette without her own participation (say she videotapes them having sex). Does Ken still commit adultery? If we say yes, the answer sounds contrived. After all, Laurie knew about it and was present, filming the whole thing. If we say no, why would he commit adultery if Laurie is not present but knows about it? Perhaps the answer to all three cases – the threesome, the mere knowledge on Laurie's part, and Laurie's knowledge, presence, but non-participation – is that Ken commits adultery in all three, but his adultery is morally permissible given Laurie's consent. This might do the trick, though I suspect that many would disagree.

(5) Our working definition also glosses over intentions. Suppose that one night, while Laurie is at her sister's, Lisette, who has a total crush on Ken, comes into his bedroom pretending to be Laurie. She sounds like Laurie, in the dark *seems* to be Laurie, and Ken swallows the story that "I couldn't sleep at my sister's, got to thinking of you, got to feeling hot and heavy, couldn't sleep even more, and decided to come in for a quickie with my wonderful husband." Ken has sex with Lisette thinking she is Laurie (cf. Scruton's example (1986, 78–79)). According to our definition, Ken commits adultery. But if to commit adultery a person has to intend to or to do so knowingly, it is not clear that Ken does.

(6) Our definition is vague on the word "married." Suppose that Ken and Laurie are not legally married to each other, but have a substantive marriage. If Ken cheats on Laurie with another woman, does he commit adultery? If, for some reason we think that for someone to commit adultery he has to be in a legal marriage, the answer is no. It used to be, and still is, that adultery is illegal in many states, so that only legally married couples can commit adultery. This implies that gay couples cannot commit adultery as long as they are not allowed to legally wed, which sounds wrong.

These six points indicate that a number of hurdles need to be overcome for a successful definition of "adultery." Specifically, should the following be part of the definition and how? (1) Sexual acts not involving animals, human corpses, or another human being at all; (2) sexual acts with another human being but that do not involve direct physical contact with him or her; (3) sexual acts involving animals or human corpses; (4) sexual acts involving a human being who is not the spouse but done with the knowledge, presence, or even participation of the spouse; (5) the intentions or knowledge of the person having sex; and (6) the type of marriage. I cannot settle these questions, but will offer a few general remarks.

We need to decide whether particular *sexual* activities count as adulterous and whether particular activities are to count as sexual. Depending on the answers, three views can be carved. The first is that some sexual activities – such as solitary masturbation – are not adulterous. It may even be that only sexual *affairs* are adulterous, not one-time sexual encounters, such as sex with a prostitute or a one-night stand with a stranger.[5] The second view is that *all* sexual activities that are extramarital are adulterous, but quibble with what counts as sexual and what doesn't. Thus one can claim – implausibly, to my mind – that solitary masturbation is not sexual activity and so get it off the adulterous hook. One can also claim (also implausibly), as Bill Clinton once did, that oral sex is not really sex, thus getting blow jobs (and cunnilingus) also off the adultery hook. The third view is a hybrid of the first two: it claims that we need to be clear on what counts as sexual activity and what doesn't, but that, even once this is cleared up, not all sexual activities count as adulterous just because they are extramarital.

Each view has its merits and demerits. The first might be correct if the particular list of extramarital, non-adulterous sexual activities with which it comes up coheres with our intuitions on the matter (and our intuitions themselves are probably not very clear anyway). However, it needs to also give a convincing defense of why solitary masturbation is not adulterous, but oral sex with a non-spouse is: Why is a man's masturbating to pornography not adulterous but lying back and *only* getting fellated by someone is?

The second view does not sound so implausible when it comes to activities other than masturbation and other standard sexual activities. For example, a married woman's flirting at a party with a man who is not her husband does not count as sexual activity, so is not – plausibly enough – adulterous. A man's calling a 900 number and having phone sex with a sex worker (without masturbating) might not count as sexual activity and so not count – somewhat plausibly – as adultery. But the second view falters on solitary masturbation: it either considers it sexual activity and so adulterous, or it does not consider it sexual activity, period. Either option is unconvincing.

The third, hybrid view might avoid the pitfalls of the second view in its willingness to refuse to consider adulterous some forms of sexual activities. Thus, in following in the footsteps of the first view, it might agree that solitary masturbation is sexual activity but refuse to consider it adultery. But, like the first view, it must provide defensible reasons why some sexual activities are adulterous and why some are not.

Moreover, all three views have to contend with another issue: Is it only sexual activities that can be adulterous? If the first and third views allow some types of sexual activities to not be adulterous, would they consider adulterous some forms of non-sexual activities? If the second view considers all extramarital sexual activities adulterous, would it consider some non-sexual ones also adulterous? The philosopher Richard Taylor gives the case of a husband who, though he never sexually cheats on his wife (because he has a weak sexual drive), keeps secret from her eight savings accounts containing a hefty sum of money. Taylor raises the question whether the husband has been faithless to his wife (1982, 59–61). Taylor does not claim that the husband has committed adultery, but that if the idea behind the wrongness of adultery is faithfulness, there are many ways to be unfaithful besides sexually cheating on one's spouse: "What must be remembered by those persons who wish to condemn adultery is that the primary vow of marriage is to love ... The first and ultimate infidelity is to withhold the love that was promised, and which was originally represented as the reason for marriage to begin with" (1982, 139).

The point that Taylor makes is brought out beautifully in the film *Thou Shalt Not Commit Adultery* (volume six of *The Decalogue*), directed by Krzysztof Kieslowski. The teenager Tomek, using his telescope, daily peeps at his beautiful neighbor Magda, watching her undress and have sex and do whatever she does, sexually and non-sexually, in her apartment (the film gives no evidence that Tomek masturbated while peeping). Eventually Magda finds out. After overcoming her anger she becomes intrigued by Tomek and sees more of him, finally allowing him to take her on a date. After the date, they go to her apartment. She crouches in front of him as he sits in an armchair and lets him – and he seems reluctant to do this – caress her thighs as she guides his hands all the way to her vagina, at which point Tomek ejaculates. She makes slight fun of him and tells him that this is what love is – it is sex pure and simple and nothing more (somewhat echoing the views of the philosopher Schopenhauer (1958), who thought that love was simply nature's way of getting people to procreate). Tomek runs out of the apartment in shame and bewilderment, and later tries to commit suicide. Magda, not seeing him for a long time, gets worried sick, apparently also falling in love with him. She finally finds him back at work at the post office, having been released from hospital. But he says to her that he no longer peeps at her – a metaphor for the cessation of his love. The movie ends there.

The film's point is that one need not cheat on one's spouse in order to commit adultery, that adultery can take the form of a betrayal of love. Indeed, Kieslowski seems to be one up on Taylor in the idea that Magda commits adultery by betraying the very phenomenon of love, telling Tomek that love is nothing but sex (she doesn't really betray her love for Tomek since she had no love for him at that point, though she may have betrayed his love for her by making these remarks – an intriguing idea in its own right).

The idea that adultery is ultimately a form of faithlessness or betrayal of love is interesting in itself, but it also suggests a way to define "adultery." Roughly speaking, all those activities that betray love are adultery. This suggestion solves a number of our issues. First, we don't need to worry about whether the couple is legally married; the issue is love, not marriage. Second, any activity that does not betray love is not adulterous, and any activity that does betray love is adulterous. None of these activities is usually a betrayal of love, so none is adulterous: solitary masturbation, buggering a goat (unless one is in love with the goat), having sex with a prostitute whom one does not love, having a threesome with one's spouse and a third person, and having sex with someone you mistakenly think is your spouse. But stashing away money while one's spouse thinks there are no such secret bank accounts, falling in love with someone other than one's spouse (with or with no sex), and so on are all betrayals of love, so all are adulterous.

Interesting as this suggestion is, it faces three difficulties. The first, perhaps most obvious, one is that it is revisionist and goes against many cases usually considered adultery. It claims that if Ken has a sexual affair with Lisette, then as long as this does not betray his love for Lauric, it is not adultery. This is highly counter-intuitive. Perhaps this is why philosophers such as Richard Taylor shy away from discussing adultery as such and broaden the topic to include faithfulness and faithlessness. A defender of this view may claim that as long as the non-adulterous spouse accepts the sexual affair, it should not be considered adultery. Yet this is not so obvious: this answer might make the adultery morally permissible or not a form of cheating, but it is adultery nonetheless. Moreover, what if the spouse does not even know of the affair? Would it be a betrayal of love and thus adulterous?

This brings us to the second difficulty. It is not always clear what counts as faithlessness and betrayal of love. And is it something that should be up to the individual couples to decide or is it an objective issue? For example, if Laurie knows about the sexual affair between Ken and Lisette, does not mind it, and is even happy that Ken is getting some extra spice in his life, would this count as a betrayal of their love? It should not be if Ken and Laurie are happy with the arrangement and continue to love each other. But what if most couples have not thought these things through and have not agreed on what counts as betrayal of love and what does not? Setting aside some obvious cases, how is it to be decided that an action by a spouse counts as betrayal? If Ken has sex with a prostitute whom he does not love, is this "meaningless" sex a betrayal of his love for Laurie? Some might think so because they see a strong connection between sex and love, but others won't agree so easily. Moreover, if betraying love is not – or is not always – left up to the couple to decide, it is unclear whether some activities amount to a betrayal of love: If Ken fantasizes about Katie Holmes while having sex with Laurie, is this betrayal? If Laurie flirts with Ben at a party, is this also betrayal?

The third potential problem is that in identifying adultery with faithlessness or betrayal of love, this view makes adultery morally wrong automatically or by definition, which means we can longer sensibly discuss the ethics of adultery; "justified adultery" becomes at best a bad joke, at worst an oxymoron. However, as some philosophers have maintained, it makes perfect sense to speak of, and to distinguish between, justified adultery and wrongful adultery. Indeed, "extramarital sex" might be a better definition because it does not prejudge the moral issues. (A defender of the view might reply that even if adultery is identified with betrayal of love, this does not necessarily make adultery wrong by definition, because some instances of betrayal are morally justified.)

We have failed to define "adultery," but at least we have a good idea of the hurdles that need to be overcome in future attempts.

Prostitution. In defining "prostitution," one thing that should be obvious by now is that no merely behavioral criterion will do. Handing money over to someone before or after a sex act does not show that the person receiving the money is a prostitute or that the transaction is one of prostitution. It could be an artistic representation of prostitution or just a mere coincidence of events (a boyfriend giving his girlfriend, just before they have sex, the money he owes her for paying his ticket to the movies the night before).

Suppose instead that we define "prostitution" broadly as "sex for money" or "the provision of sexual services in return for money." Whether this definition succeeds depends partly on what we have in mind when we think of prostitutes. It covers those sex workers who receive payments for direct, physical, sexual interactions with a client, such as oral sex, intercourse, and hand jobs. But if we wish to exclude, because we don't think of them as prostitutes, phone-sex workers, strippers who do not engage in sex with their customers, and men and women who perform at peep shows, for example, the definition won't succeed because all these people provide sexual services for money.

One option is to accept that the above are indeed prostitutes and to be happy with the definition. Another option is to amend the definition to exclude them. The first option won't yield a true definition. Young, beautiful women who marry older husbands for their money, and young, beautiful men who marry older women for their money provide sex and sexual pleasure to their older spouses (among other things, including, I suppose, some sort of prestige in having them be seen with such pretty young things) in return for money and other goods for which money is usually needed (food, shelter, clothing) or that can be easily converted into money (jewelry, an apartment in Manhattan, or a villa in Tuscany). Those women, who out of financial and other needs, marry and stay with men for economic reasons provide (among other things) sexual services for money. Are they all prostitutes? They are not – at least we don't think of them as such – so we need to amend the definition to prevent this implication.

This brings us to the second option. In addition to fixing the definition to block the implication that many spouses are prostitutes, we also need to fix it to exclude sex workers we don't regard as prostitutes (e.g., strippers, phone-sex workers, porn actors).

Primoratz defines prostitution as "the provision of sexual services usually involving physical contact and catering indiscriminately to those willing to pay the price" (2006, 849). Primoratz intends "usually involving physical contact" to rule out sex workers who we don't consider as prostitutes, but "physical contact" is too vague to do this. Many strippers, for example, allow the client to insert money in their g-string; gay male strippers, especially, often allow the client to feel their buttocks, thighs, penis, and so on. This is physical contact. And many female strippers perform lap dances, often to the point when the client orgasms. This is not just any physical contact, but one involving actual orgasm on the part of one person in the transaction. Perhaps we could say, "Okay. Strippers are in! They're prostitutes! That's not so implausible, is it?"

Perhaps not, but it is hard to see then why strippers should be allowed into the category of prostitution but not other types of sex workers. Is it only on account of the physical contact? Suppose that John is at a peep show. The woman behind the glass, finding him attractive, enjoys giving him a show and even starts to masturbate herself as he masturbates himself. John, being a veteran of peep shows and adept at knowing when a dancer is really aroused and when she is faking, realizes that the dancer before him is actually enjoying herself. He masturbates himself into a frenzy. Is not what occurred between them a sexual act for which John paid money? If John did the same thing with his wife – glass partition and all – as a form of role-playing, would this not be a sexual act? The point is that on the one hand, it is not clear that actual physical contact is necessary for someone to be a prostitute as opposed to a mere sex worker; on the other, phone-sex workers don't seem to count as prostitutes.

The reason why I insisted that John and the woman at the peep show engage in a sex act is to emphasize that what might differentiate a phone sex worker from, say, a call-girl in being a prostitute is not so much actual physical contact as the occurrence of a sex act. It may be that our reluctance to think of phone-sex workers as prostitutes is not because there is no physical contact between her and the caller, but because we doubt whether what occurs between them is a sexual act (she says to the caller, "Oh, yes, Kevin, I would love it if you went down on me; I'm coming just at the idea!"; but she's faking it, ironing clothes or solving a jigsaw puzzle as she says these words).

So it might be that although engaging in physical contact in exchange for money is not necessary for somebody to be a prostitute, engaging in a sex act is. However, Primoratz's definition includes another type of sex worker that Primoratz, sensibly, wishes to exclude: pornography actors. They, too, provide sexual services with full physical contact for money. And they, too, are indiscriminate as long as the money is right (if one thinks that pornography actors are not *that* indiscriminate, that's fine; but then we should remember that many prostitutes are also not *that* indiscriminate). Yet they are not – or we tend not to think of them as – prostitutes (although some do engage in prostitution on the side). It is not clear why, however, they are not or should not be thought of as prostitutes. The main difference that I can see is that pornography actors do not engage in sexual activities with clients, but with each other.

At this point, perhaps we can amend Primoratz's definition as follows. "Prostitution" is "engaging in sexual acts, many of which involve physical contact, with anyone who is willing to pay the price." I got rid of "indiscriminately" because "anyone who is willing to pay the price" covers it. Using "sexual acts" allows us to include only those sex workers about whom it makes sense to refer to as prostitutes. The word "with" rules out pornography actors, since they don't have sex with the one who pays the money (the viewer). Finally, the word "anyone" rules out gold diggers and economic wives, a welcome result.

There are two more issues with which to contend. Suppose that Jackie likes to have a lot of casual sex with many men. She picks up guys wherever she happens to be, in bars, coffee shops, supermarkets, Macy's. She is so good in bed that guys often like to leave her some money as a token of gratitude or appreciation. Jackie likes this ("Hey! I can buy myself a nice bottle of perfume!"). Is Jackie a prostitute? If she is, she is one by default, not by design, because she does not intend to make her sexual services conditional on receiving money for them. This raises the issue of whether intentions to receive money for sexual acts are necessary for prostitution. Note that our amended definition is silent on intentions, and is compatible with both their presence and their lack. *If* we insist on intentions, we can further amend the definition as follows. "Prostitution" is "engaging in sexual acts, many of which involve physical contact, only with those who are willing to pay the price." The word "only" implies that engaging in sex is intentional: the person targets only those who are willing to pay.

The second issue is whether prostitution can be defined at all. The feminist philosopher Laurie Shrage states that, "there is no single thing as 'prostitution' that can be evaluated apart from a cultural framework. Instead there are many particular prostitutions that have varying social origins and social consequences" (1994, 119). Shrage gives examples of different types of "prostitutions" from across cultures and ages, including ancient Babylon, Kenya during colonial times, West Nepal, and medieval southern France. She argues that they differ from each other in important ways. For example, prostitutes in medieval southern France were "not socially marginal" and "were active participant[s] in public life" (1994, 114). They were also "legally free and socially eligible for marriage" (1994, 115). Similarly, "in colonial Kenya it was not uncommon for prostitutes to be recruited by their clients to be their full-time, legal wives, and thus some prostitutes eventually entered legal, monogamous marriage" (1994, 109). The prostitutes served the social function of supporting their families (1994, 107–108). Compare now both these types to that of ancient Babylon: being a religious form of prostitution, it celebrated the sexual powers of Mylitta, the fertility goddess, by having women have sex with strangers in return for silver coins. This was necessary for the land and the people to be fertile (1994, 100–101). Thus we reach the suspicion that "prostitution" as such cannot be defined because there is no core or shared essence to the various types of prostitution across cultures and ages.[6]

If Shrage means that any thorough discussion of prostitution must take into account prostitution's various incarnations in different cultures and ages, she is correct. No proper discussion of any phenomenon can be complete if it reduces that phenomenon to a few aspects. However, if Shrage means that "prostitution" as such cannot be defined because there is no single core or essence to prostitution given its different types, her argument fails, because from the fact that a concept has multiple, different instances or examples, it does not follow that it cannot be defined. Indeed, those philosophers who attempt to define concepts know full well that concepts usually have multiple instances but realize that to define them is (partly) to go beyond these variations to find a common core. Tigers, for example, come in different types, colors, and sizes, but this does not mean that the concept of "tiger" cannot be defined. The concept of "art" is similar but closer to home because art, unlike tigers, is a cultural phenomenon. So granted that prostitution (and pornography, casual sex, adultery, and so on) has many variations, has been understood differently in different cultures, and has served different functions, it does not follow that it cannot be defined.

Let us, at this point, survey the main issues that have come up in our attempt to define "casual sex," "adultery," and "prostitution."

1   Intentions and other mental states: we need to decide in a convincing manner whether intentions or other types of mental states should figure in the definitions of "casual sex," "adultery," and "prostitution."

2 Behavior: we need to decide whether any behavioral criteria should be used in these definitions.

3 Sexual acts: in the cases of both adultery and prostitution, figuring out what a sexual act is, is crucial. One view regarding adultery considers adulterous any type of extramarital sexual act, but we need to know what a sexual act is. Moreover, if prostitution is to include only sexual acts, we also need to know what they are. (This is not likely to be an issue with casual sex since we know that it is a sexual act; we just need to figure out what kind of a sexual act it is.)

4 Particular sexual practices, such as masturbation, rape, bestiality, necrophilia, and others, are all particular sexual practices that we have to look out for when defining other sexual practices (and vice versa), because, for example, if we don't think of rape as a form of casual sex, we should not define "casual sex" in such a way to imply that rape is casual sex. If we think that solitary masturbation is not a form of adultery, we need to define "adultery" in such a way to not imply that solitary masturbation is adultery.

5 Finally, there are particular issues that come up for each specific sexual practice we are trying to define. For example, deciding what we mean by "marriage" is crucial for a definition of "adultery" (also for "prostitution"), and deciding on the role of sexual pleasure is crucial for defining "casual sex."

Notes

1 This section has benefited much from Alan Soble's discussion (1996, ch. 3).

2 I do not discuss the "tends to" part of Goldman's definition (which poses problems for it; see Soble (2008a, 81–82) for discussion). I use instead "fulfills" or "satisfies" instead of "tends to fulfill" or "tends to satisfy."

3 There are actually two sets of four combinations: the first set uses "and" to combine the three together and two of each three; the second set uses "or" to combine all three and two of each. The reader should evaluate whether any succeeds.

4 Goldman says that desires for only looking or touching items of clothing are abnormal or perverted (2008, 69). He also says parenthetically in the quotation I offered: "(otherwise a deviation from the norm as expressed in our definition)." Perhaps Goldman – he is unclear on this – intends his definition to be really of "normal sexual desire," by which he would have to mean "normal in the statistical sense," given that in his essay he is opposed to moralizing analyses of sex. However, given that masturbation falters on his definition and that masturbation is statistically normal, the definition still won't do.

5 Many philosophers in discussing adultery implicitly assume that it takes the form of an affair. See, for example, Steinbock 1991; Martin 1998.

6 This type of argument can be made about any form of sexual activity (and, indeed, about any cultural practice whatsoever), because they all differ from one culture to another, including pornography, casual sex, and adultery (Shrage applies a similar argument to the last (1994, ch. 2)). My replies to Shrage's argument regarding prostitution apply in principle to other forms of sexual practices.

Further Reading

Soble's (2006b) encyclopedia of the philosophy of sex is an indispensable tool and resource for all the issues discussed in this and later chapters. For more on defining sexual concepts, see Berkowitz (1997), Gray (1978), Harding (1998), Primoratz (1999, ch. 5), Shaffer (1978), Soble (1998, ch. 1), Soble (2006a), and Vannoy (1980, 97–101). For some skepticism about whether we can define certain central concepts in sex, see Hamilton (2008). LeMoncheck (1997) attempts to define a number of sexual practices, including promiscuity and prostitution.

6 Sex, Pleasure, and Morality

Sexual Pleasure and Other Values of Sex Acts

One way to evaluate sexual activity is by relying on values such as pleasure, excitement, being rewarding, and satisfaction. Before we delve into these values, we go on a short detour.

The philosopher Janice Moulton claims that that there are at least two models of sexual behavior. The first is sexual anticipation (which includes flirtation and seduction) and the second is sexual satisfaction. The first is not about "physical contact" (or sexual acts), but about what occurs before: _→foreplay_

> Flirtation, seduction, and traditional courtship involve sexual feelings that are quite independent of physical contact. These feelings are increased by anticipation of success, winning, or conquest. Because what is anticipated is the opportunity for sexual intimacy and satisfaction, the feelings of sexual satisfaction are usually not distinguished from those of sexual anticipation.
> (Moulton 2008, 46)

The second model of sexual satisfaction "involves sexual feelings which are _how well a partner knows what we want sexually._ increased by the other person's knowledge of one's preferences and sensitivities, the familiarity of their touch or smell or way of moving, and not by the novelty of their sexual interest" (Moulton 2008, 46). The idea is that although sexual anticipation may be present when a person knows she is going to have sex with a familiar partner, anticipation is definitely heightened by the knowledge or expectation of having sex with someone new (that's why it includes courtship, flirtation, and seduction). On my first sex date with Mario Lopez, my (and hopefully his) sexual expectations and anticipation will be quite high. If he and I have been having sex for years, I may no longer be thrilled by the idea of having sex with him, but the sex might be satisfying since he knows my body and what sexually pleases me.

The two models of anticipation and satisfaction are often in tension with one another:

> A strong feeling of sexual anticipation is produced by the uncertainty, challenge or secrecy of novel sexual experiences, but the tension and

excitement that increase anticipation often interfere with sexual satisfaction. The comfort and trust and experience with familiar partners may increase sexual satisfaction, but decrease the uncertainty and challenge that heighten sexual anticipation.

(Moulton 2008, 47)

The more one knows one's sexual partner, the more one can count on satisfaction, but the less on excitement and anticipation. The less one knows one's sexual partner, the more one can count on anticipation and excitement, but the less on satisfaction.

Note that, strictly speaking, while sexual satisfaction occurs during the sexual act, sexual anticipation occurs prior to it (though this depends on how broadly or narrowly we define "sexual act"). Might anticipation and excitement then not be part of the evaluation of sexual acts since they occur prior to them?

Not necessarily, because they can also occur during the act. Beginning a sexual act with kissing, necking, and oral stimulation but knowing that intercourse is to follow, one gets sexually more excited and anticipatory of the action to come (if one is into intercourse). Sexual acts could, and often do, include sexual excitement and anticipation. So the tension of which Moulton speaks between anticipation and satisfaction sometimes exists, but sometimes it doesn't, during the sexual act. For example, a couple who have been having the same type of sex for years would probably have little or no anticipation even if they know that the sex is satisfactory. Their knowledge of the ensuing satisfaction is not the same as anticipation, because *expecting* the orgasm is not the same as *anticipating* or being *excited* by it. Of course, the sex between them can sometimes fail in both respects: it is routine so lacks excitement, and, because of some quirk that day, they also fail to be satisfied by it. Moreover, if the partners know each other but the sex between them has not lost its magic, they will feel both anticipation and satisfaction. If the partners don't know each other, they will feel anticipation and may or may not feel satisfaction, depending on whether they sexually click. That is why Moulton's claim that anticipation often "interferes" with satisfaction is puzzling. For *anticipation* need not adversely interfere with satisfaction (though I think it helps motivate the partners to please each other); what does interfere – for better or worse – is the partners' knowledge or ignorance of each other's sexual proclivities and bodies.

We can now evaluate a sexual act on the basis of at least two dimensions: satisfaction and excitement (or heightened anticipation). Because the two can come apart during a single sexual act, one and the same sexual act can be sexually good in that it is exciting (or satisfactory) but sexually bad in that it is unsatisfactory (or unexciting). Of course, a sexual act can also be good in both ways.

Where is pleasure in all this? Pleasure is tricky, because it can mean different things. One is "sensation": to feel pleasure is to feel a particular sensation in some body part or other. Under this meaning, some obvious examples of sexual pleasure are orgasm, the pleasure of nipple massaging, the pleasure of ear licking, and so on. I suppose that by "satisfaction" Moulton means (given her emphasis on physical contact) pleasure-as-sensation. The two partners to a sexual act who know each other can rely on each other to provide the right kinds of touching, rhythm in sex, and so on, thus achieving satisfaction by providing each other with pleasure-as-sensation. But the feelings of anticipation and excitement that people can feel during sex are also pleasurable, though they are not pleasures-as-sensations. There are no particular regions of the body where one experiences these feelings and are "felt" throughout the whole body. The upshot is that we cannot, in a discussion of the "pleasures" of sex, use the word "pleasure" in an indiscriminate and vague way.

Suppose that (for now) we use "satisfaction" to mean pleasure-as-sensation. Then every satisfactory sexual act is a pleasurable one. But there are degrees of pleasure. A routine sexual act may be satisfactory, producing the expected pleasures, but it may not be *very* pleasurable. Note how the more pleasurable a sex act is, the less inclined we are to call it "satisfactory," a term that usually denotes a moderate or even minimal amount of pleasure. To avoid confusion, I suggest we drop the term "satisfaction" and use instead "pleasure." We can then speak of somewhat pleasurable, moderately pleasurable, and highly pleasurable sexual acts. We can also use "enjoyable" to refer to those pleasures that are not sensations but pleasures of excitement and anticipation occurring during sex. Again, sex acts can then be minimally, somewhat, moderately, or highly enjoyable.

Are there ways to evaluate sexual acts other than pleasure and enjoyment? A sex act can be enriching (or rewarding), impoverishing, or neither enriching nor impoverishing (it can be anywhere on this spectrum) in ways that go beyond being pleasurable (painful) or enjoyable (unenjoyable). Sexual acts can be rewarding in a number of ways. They can be sexually instructive in that they teach the participant(s) new sexual techniques or positions; they can leave the participant(s) with wonderful memories about the act itself; they can result in a baby; they can result in acquiring money (if one participant is a sex worker); they can lead to new friendships; and they can cement a new or current love. Sexual acts can also be impoverishing. Although participants cannot "de-learn" sexual techniques or positions, they can leave with lousy memories of a sexual act – a bad taste in their mouth. Sex acts can lead to diseases, to breaking up a good friendship, or, perhaps most important, they can fracture the participant(s)' moral integrity: "I can't believe I just had sex with …" and then fill in the gap with the inappropriate person, animal, thing, or method ("my best friend's wife," "a 10-year-old child," "a dog," "I can't believe I just had sex with Hannah by lying to her," "by raping her," "by allowing him to tie me up," "by drinking his urine"). All are examples of how sexual acts can leave one or more participant feeling shame and disbelief about what they are capable of. Depending on the act, its effects may be long-lasting.

However, these all seem to be *consequences* of sexual acts. If our concern is with evaluating sex acts *as* sex acts, not in terms of their results, it's hard to make sense of the idea of a sex act being rewarding or impoverishing *apart* from its being pleasurable (non-pleasurable) or enjoyable (non-enjoyable). Any additional suggestion is bound to be a consequence of the sex act. So it seems that there are only these two ways of evaluating sex acts as sex acts (in addition, as we will see in Chapter 8, to evaluating them as natural or perverted, and as moral or immoral in this chapter).

One crucial question is: Who or what decides whether a sexual act is pleasurable, frustrating, or enjoyable? Is it the participants themselves and their sexual tastes? Or is it something more objective? For example, it's silly to claim that chocolate is "objectively" better tasting than vanilla; the decision is left to individual taste. Not so, however, with morality – whether murder or stealing is right or wrong is not up to the tastes of individual people. That is why we debate such issues as abortion, euthanasia, capital punishment, and eating the flesh of non-human animals; if we believe that they should be decided by individual tastes, we wouldn't debate them. So is whether sex is pleasurable like eating ice cream or like morality?

There's a deceptive answer to this question that goes like this: it depends on the type of evaluation of sex. If it's moral evaluation or whether the sex is perverted, it's not up to the participants. But if it's whether the sex is pleasurable, then it is up to the individuals. After all, we are talking about *pleasure*, which is a matter of individual taste: what pleases one person, another might view with indifference, and a third might find painful or disgusting. If John likes anal sex, good for John. If Katie likes the doggie-style position, good for Katie. End of story.

This might be the end of the story but for two considerations. First, many philosophers believe that some pleasures are superior to others. John Stuart Mill, for example, claims that there are higher and lower pleasures, the second of which includes sexual pleasures (Mill 1987, ch. 2). Moreover, even though sexual pleasures have been typically lumped together in the category of lower pleasures, once we accept or even entertain the idea that there are higher and lower pleasures, it is possible that within types of pleasures there are also higher and lower types. This is easily seen in connection to art. Although we may agree that there is such a thing as artistic pleasure (pleasure derived from, in, or by contemplating art), if there is a distinction between low art and high art, we can distinguish between higher and lower pleasures within the category of artistic pleasures: the pleasures derived from reading Nathaniel Hawthorne or listening to Beethoven are higher than the pleasures derived from reading comic books or listening to Hannah Montana. If we can make this distinction with respect to art, why not also with respect to sex? Why not say that heterosexual intercourse is more pleasurable than anal homosexual intercourse? Why not also say that sex after a night of deep sleep is more pleasurable than sex after a long day at work?

Connected to this point is a second consideration: suppose that Randy has tried to read literature but just could not enjoy it; he prefers Sidney Sheldon and Harold Robbins to Jane Austen and Leo Tolstoy. He has tried listening to

Beethoven and Bartok, but he prefers Abba and the soundtrack from *Cats*. He has tried watching Matthew Barney films, but he prefers *Alien vs. Predator* and *High School Musical 3*. Randy just does not enjoy high art and enjoys low art. Is this the end of the story? Not quite. Once we distinguish between higher and lower pleasures, we can claim that Randy is missing out on a higher type of pleasure, even though he cannot attain it. And he is, indeed, *missing out* on reading Austen and Tolstoy, because we have agreed that they are *higher* pleasures.

Can something similar be said about sexual pleasure? Yes, but only *if* there is a distinction to be made between higher and lower sexual pleasures. This distinction usually refers to the *quality* of pleasures, not their *quantity*: pleasures derived from reading Tolstoy are *better* or qualitatively higher than those derived from reading Sidney Sheldon. We can make a similar distinction in sex, but it will have to be one about *quantity*, specifically its intensity and duration. There are sexual techniques that could help in making a sexual act last longer, in sexually exploring new areas of the human body, in intensifying the intensity and duration of an orgasm. So one way of cashing in on the idea of higher and lower sexual pleasures is that one and the same type of sexual act can be more pleasurable or enjoyable if the participants know what to do. But note that making the distinction this way cuts across all types of sexual acts; heterosexual and homosexual sex, including oral sex and intercourse, can be more or less pleasurable (or enjoyable) depending on how good the participants are; ditto for any type of sexual act, natural or perverted, moral or immoral, involving or not involving fetishes. So not only does the "higher" versus "lower" distinction have to do with the quantities, not qualities, of pleasures, it is also not confined to any type of sexual activity.

There's another way of making the distinction, also along quantitative lines. As is well known, due to various influences, people internalize taboos against some sexual proclivities. Examples include not only obvious ones such as repressed homosexuality, but also acts that someone might be ashamed of, thinks are wrong, or even does not know about. A foot fetishist may be too shy to ask his sexual partner to indulge him. A woman who likes to be tied up may think it politically unacceptable to do so (out of, say, feminist considerations). A pedophile may not have sex with minors because he knows it is wrong. A well-bred woman may be too genteel to have sex doggie-style. A man may be excited by smelling dirty underwear yet not know this about himself. These people do enjoy sexual acts not involving their sexual preferences, but were they to act on their preferences they would enjoy sex a lot more. Thus, sex tends to be more pleasurable the more it involves acting on one's favored acts, positions, fantasies, and fetishes, and the less it is accompanied by negative emotions such as guilt and shame.

So we have two ways by which to distinguish between higher and lower sexual pleasures, neither of which corresponds or is confined to a type of sexual activity, such as heterosexual sex, homosexual sex, oral sex, natural sex, and sex involving fetishes. This is not surprising. A type of sexual activity is not, *because* it is that type, more sexually pleasurable than another type of activity. Oral sex is not, because it is oral sex, more pleasurable or painful than another type of sexual activity. Sometimes it is, sometimes it isn't, depending on all sorts of factors. We also all have similar biological bodies and points of pleasure. Where we differ is in our sexual tastes. So if Joan prefers intercourse to oral sex, it doesn't make sense to say that she is missing out on a superior type of pleasure (oral sex). After all, she prefers intercourse – by what criteria is oral sex more pleasurable? Nor would it make sense to say that a male homosexual is missing out on a superior type of sexual pleasure (heterosexual sex). After all, he prefers homosexual sex – by what criteria is heterosexual sex more pleasurable?

Evolutionary biology won't be of much help here. Even if we have evolved in such a way that Mother Nature made sex pleasurable to get us to procreate (which sounds plausible), she need not have made heterosexual intercourse the *most* pleasurable or pleasurable in the highest quality to attain her purposes. Making it pleasurable enough to get people to enjoy it would have been sufficient. Furthermore, we now know that women derive the greatest sexual pleasure from the clitoris. But the clitoris's evolutionary function as far as procreation is concerned is controversial.[2] In any case, we are both biological *and* cultural creatures. Our tastes and proclivities – sexual and non-sexual – are as much the product of nature as they are the product of culture. Nature or biology should not be the arbiter about which sexual pleasures are higher in quality.

There is another (tentative) reason why there is no qualitative distinction between higher and lower sexual pleasures. Usually, this distinction is made (and makes sense, perhaps) in connection to complex objects that require sophisticated responses to yield the requisite higher pleasures. For example, the reason why reading Tolstoy yields higher pleasures than reading Sheldon is that Tolstoy's literary works are more sophisticated than Sheldon's. To enjoy them fully (and so attain the higher pleasures), the reader must engage with their complexity. Sheldon's works, by contrast, contain no such complexity, so their pleasures are not that sophisticated. Similar things may be said about music, painting, food, and any culturally produced object or event that admits of higher and lower kinds (e.g., artistic paintings vs. hotel room paintings, classical music vs. pop music).

But sex may not be like this. Although there are techniques in sex and a wide variety of positions and acts, sexual activity may not require complex mental and emotional responses to be appreciated. Our bodies may also not be complex when it comes to sexual activity. We know roughly what the pleasure zones are and we can explore a few more, but none requires the kind of mental engagement that, say, listening to Tchaikovsky does. At most, it requires some techniques (some of which require in turn certain bodily regimens). No wonder few conservative philosophers claim that heterosexual sex is superior to other kinds of sex as far as *pleasure* or enjoyment is concerned, confining their claims, instead, to its moral superiority.

However, even if no type of sexual activity is superior in pleasure to another, it is often claimed that sex with love is more pleasurable than sex without love. Russell Vannoy presents a number of arguments for this view (all of which he rejects). Let us look at some of the crucial ones (the second is mine, not Vannoy's).

One argument is that sex with love is "deeply personal. One forms a unity not only with the body, but also with all the other aspects of what constitute a complete experience: the mental, emotional, spiritual" (Vannoy 1980, 13). Sex without love can be at most only pleasurable. Sex with love, however, has meaning or significance (Vannoy 1980, 14).

Evaluating this argument requires making a distinction. "Sex with love" can mean (1) "sex with someone with whom you are in love or have a love relationship," or (2) "expressing your love *during* sex with the person you love." Under the first meaning, there is no reason to believe that sex with love is necessarily meaningful or has these unifying aspects. Think of all the routine sex that couples have with each other after years of being together. It might be minimally pleasurable in that they rely on the "tested and tried" methods that the couples have used over the years (Moulton's "satisfaction model"), but it need not be powerful in the ways that the argument claims.

If "sex with love" means "expressing your love *during* sex with the person you love," the argument is on to something, because each body gesture is meant to show the love and emotion the lovers have for each other. However, as Vannoy points out, if the sex is good, the lovers are bound at some point to surrender themselves to lust, and when they do, they are no different from two strangers surrendering to their lust (1980, 14). Vannoy's point, I think, is that it is easier said than done to unite sex with love. For while the lovers, as lovers, communicate their passions to each other at *some points* during the sex act, at *other points* the sex takes over. Although well taken, Vannoy's point does not defeat the argument, because if it is the entire sex act being evaluated, then a sex act that alternates between lust and tender emotions might be, on the whole, more pleasurable than one that is merely lustful.

The main problem with the argument is that it presents a false dilemma: we are asked to choose between sex with love and sex without love, meaning, "cold, mechanical fucking," without any tender emotions. These are not the only options. Two strangers can have sex with each other – even rough sex – while at the same time kissing, hugging, relishing each other's bodies, and being attentive to each other's needs. The presence of these emotions can make sex much more pleasurable and exciting. So if the argument in favor of sex with love includes the range of emotions that lovers often exhibit to each other during sex, sex between strangers can come close to that in many ways.

A third and final thought: there is no doubt that sex with love (in the second sense) or sex between strangers accompanied by tenderness and attention is quite enjoyable, but some people may always prefer emotionless sex, while others may like it only sometimes. If their preferences are for the type of sex without love, it is hard to see how sex with love is more pleasurable, period, regardless of the preferences involved, especially if there is no reason to qualitatively distinguish between higher and lower types of sexual pleasure.

A second argument is that lovers know how to please each other sexually better than sex between strangers. This means that sex with love, as sex, is more pleasurable than sex with someone who is not one's lover. This may be true. But as we have seen with the above distinctions, it might mean that the sex is pleasurable in that it is satisfactory, but not pleasurable in that it is enjoyable, since it is routine, expected, and so on. Moreover, sex without love might score higher points by the anticipation and excitement criteria. Sometimes, also, strangers sexually click: they know how to please each other, especially if they're assertive about it, telling each other (nicely) what to do and how to do it. Remember also that knowing someone sexually is not confined to lovers, but includes any two people who have only a sexual relationship: they, too, know each other's bodies and pleasures and should be able to know how to satisfy each other.

A third argument is that lovers go to greater lengths to sexually please each other than strangers or non-lovers will (Vannoy 1980, 15). This means that sex with love has a higher chance of being pleasurable than sex without love, since lovers wouldn't give up so easily on pleasing each other. This may be correct, but, again, it depends on a few factors. If the lovers have been together for a while, they might rely on routine sex. Moreover, think of all the husbands, as the cliché goes, who come home tired and just want to have quick sex with their wives. Whether lovers make such efforts depends on how new they are as lovers and how they are as individuals: "the key factors depend more on the partner's *sexual sophistication* and *innate generosity* than it does on whether that person happens to be one's beloved" (Vannoy 1980, 15).

Moreover, if it is generally true that people enjoy sex more when they sense that their sexual partners are aroused and enjoying the sex, then people have an incentive to be attentive to each other's sexual needs during the sex act, simply (and selfishly, I suppose) because this heightens their own arousal. This is true, by the way, regardless of whether the sexual partners are lovers or non-lovers.

A fourth argument is that the superiority of sex with love shows why we don't just masturbate: if all we wanted were just sex for the sake of sex, we would just masturbate. So we desire another person when we want very pleasurable sex "because we want to unite with, relate to, communicate with another human being" (Vannoy 1980, 15–16). Although most people generally prefer sex with another person over masturbation because they desire to relate to someone, clearly, the other person does not have to be a lover. It could be a total stranger, a friend, or a cousin. Moreover, "relate to" is ambiguous. It could refer to the partners' desire for an emotional exchange during the sexual act, in which case it is not obvious that all sexual partners want this. Instead, they could desire a sexual partner, rather than masturbate, because they want, literally, a new *touch* (Soble 1996, 86–87). How else to explain the shepherd's occasional preference for sex with a sheep to masturbating? Or does he wish to relate to the sheep?

A final argument is that "sex with a lover is … more likely to lead to future emotional security; men and women don't have to worry constantly about whether or not they will find a new 'one-night' stand" (Vannoy 1980, 14). This may be true, but it does not show that sex with love is more pleasurable than sex without love. All it shows is that people are often willing to agree to a sure-thing and forgo the ups and downs of finding new sexual partners, even though, if successful, such one-night stands might be highly pleasurable or enjoyable.

So there seems to be no good reason to think that sex with love is generally more pleasurable or enjoyable than sex without love.[3] This should not be surprising. As I argue below (Chapter 8, in connection with Scruton's views), sex and love are very different (it would be more surprising if sex with love were more pleasurable than sex without love).

Let us now turn to the moral evaluation of sex.

Consequentialism and Sex

In the discussion of romantic love, I stressed that romantic love has the tendency to lead lovers to be absorbed with each other, to neglect their duties to others, and to sometimes demean themselves to attain or preserve their love. Sexual desire has a similar power. The nineteenth-century German philosopher, Arthur Schopenhauer, writes the following:

> It is the ultimate goal of almost all human effort; it has an unfavorable influence on the most important affairs, interrupts every hour the most serious occupations, and sometimes perplexes for a while even the greatest minds. It does not hesitate to intrude with its trash, and to interfere with the negotiations of statesmen and the investigations of the learned. It knows how to slip its love-notes and ringlets even into ministerial portfolios and philosophical manuscripts. Every day it brews and hatches the worst and most perplexing quarrels and disputes, destroys the most valuable relationships, and breaks the strongest bonds. It demands sometimes the sacrifice of life or health, sometimes of wealth, position, and happiness. Indeed, it robs of all conscience those who were previously honorable and upright, and makes traitors of those who have hitherto been loyal and faithful.
>
> (Schopenhauer 1958, 533–534)

Alan Soble, explaining Kant's worries about sexual desire (which I discuss in the next chapter), writes,

> Sexual desire is inelastic, relentless, the passion most likely to challenge reason and make us succumb to *akrasia* [weakness of will], compelling us to seek satisfaction even when doing so involves the risks of dark-alley gropings, microbiologically filthy acts, slinking around the White House,

or getting married impetuously. Sexually motivated behavior easily destroys our self-respect.

(Soble 2008b, 261)

If half of what Schopenhauer and Soble (on Kant) say about sexual desire is true, it is especially in need of moral control, to protect ourselves, and others, from its dangers.

Consequentialism

Jeremy Bentham, the founder of modern utilitarianism, was born in 1748 and died in 1832. Some time in the 1780s he wrote an essay on homosexuality that was published after his death. "An Essay on 'Paederasty'" (1984) tackled the morality of homosexual sex by looking at its consequences, specifically the pleasure and pain it tends to produce. He surveyed every argument known to him which tried to show that homosexuality leads to bad consequences and rejected each. For example, addressing the objection that homosexuality, if widely practiced, leads to the demise of the human race, Bentham makes the following points. First, this result would follow only if those who engaged in homosexual sex did so exclusively (1984, 360). Second, not much effort and time are needed to impregnate a woman; the probability that men would be so disinclined to have sex with women to the point of not even being willing to impregnate them is close to zero (1984, 360). Third, historically speaking, there is no evidence that in societies where homosexuality was practiced the population decreased (1984, 360). Fourth, for the sake of consistency, celibacy should be criticized more vehemently than homosexuality: "If then merely out of regard to population it were right that paederasts should be burnt alive monks ought to be roasted alive by a slow fire" (1984, 360–361).

Not only does Bentham find no bad consequences to homosexuality, he finds good ones:

It is evident that it produces no pain in anyone. On the contrary it produces pleasure, and that a pleasure which, by their perverted taste, is by this supposition preferred to that pleasure which is in general reputed the greatest. The partners are both willing. If either of them be unwilling, the act is not that which we have here in view: ... it is a personal injury; it is a kind of rape.

(Bentham 1984, 355)

Homosexual sex generally produces pleasure, not pain, since its practitioners prefer it and are willing to engage in it. If one of them is unwilling, it is no longer homosexual sex but rape.

Consequentialism evaluates homosexual sex based on its consequences. Roughly speaking, actions are morally right if they produce good consequences.

If an action produces both good and bad consequences (as any action is likely to do), the good consequences have to outweigh the bad ones for the action to be right. Moreover, if there are a number of actions each of which produces more good than bad consequences, we choose the action that produces the most *net* good consequences. If each action produces good and only good consequences, we choose the one with the best consequences. If each produces more bad than good consequences, we choose the one with the least *net* bad consequences. If each produces only bad consequences, we choose the action with the least bad consequences.

Preliminary Points

There are a few additional issues that must be kept in mind when evaluating actions consequentially. Let us discuss them specifically in connection with sexual practices and actions.

Notion of consequences. What is meant by "good" and "bad" consequences? Classical utilitarians, like Bentham and Mill, understood them to mean pleasure and pain. Other consequentialists understand them differently – for example, "satisfying desire" (not every pleasure takes the form of satisfying desires, and not every satisfied desire takes the form of a pleasure – so the two are not the same). I do not adopt any specific view of consequences, but assess sexual acts in terms of their tendency to lead to children, foster love and friendship, and maintain or promote the well-functioning of society in general (good consequences), and their tendency to lead to diseases, the breakup of marriages or friendships, the enhancement of patriarchy, and offense to the public (bad consequences). So I rely on a commonsense list of what good and bad consequences are, leaving it to consequentialist theorists to decide how their goodness and badness are to be understood.

Consequences affecting whom? We need to also ask about whom the consequences affect: The immediate parties to the sex act? Their friends and family members also? Their colleagues at work? Society at large? All humanity? Future humanity? Other sentient creatures (e.g., some animals)? It is often difficult to trace the consequences of singular acts to humanity at large, let alone future generations (it is easier when we talk about universal, scientific phenomena, such as global warming). Here, we should not confuse *knowledge* of the consequences with how far into the future and how far across people and species the consequences *should* matter. If someone does something today that has horrendous effects on the future of humanity, of course these consequences matter. But normally our daily actions' effects become less and less important as time goes by (this cannot be said for the actions of high-level politicians). So the decision as to how far into the future and across people the consequences should matter likely depends on the nature of the action or practice itself: Is it of the type that will have serious ripple effects across all society or even humanity? If yes, then the consequences matter. If no, even if its effects go into the far future, they may not matter.

Even with grave actions, our knowledge about their effects may be limited, so we must make as accurate a prediction as possible about them. Incidentally, making accurate predictions is necessary not only for actions whose consequences are far-flung, but for any action whatsoever, because we are never in a position to know (with certainty) what an action's consequences are. We have to consider each sexual action or practice on its own merits and make as accurate as possible a prediction about its effects.

What sexual acts? We need to distinguish between a particular sexual act and a sexual practice: it may be that heterosexual intercourse in general has good consequences, but that heterosexual intercourse between Jeff and Joan has bad ones. Indeed, most moral discussions of sex have addressed practices, not singular actions: masturbation, prostitution, pornography, homosexuality, bestiality, incest, pedophilia, and all sorts of practices often considered perversions. I discuss prostitution below as an example once we have dealt with these preliminary points.

Private vs. public, secretive vs. public. Sexual activity is usually private, not public, and its ins and outs are usually secret, not public knowledge. Do not confuse privacy with secrecy; many of the things we do in private – sleeping, eating, watching television – are not secretive, although certain details of some private activities are secret. It is no secret that Mary got pregnant by having had sex with her husband Martin, but the details of their sexual acts are usually kept secret. The two dimensions of privacy and secrecy are crucial in evaluating the morality of sexual acts. If Heather and I have sex in public, this would have consequences far beyond what they would have were we to have sex in private. Furthermore, even if we had sex in private but told the world about its details, this would also have consequences different from keeping our sexual gymnastics secret.

Offense. Sex has always offended, and is likely to continue to offend, many people in all sorts of ways. This raises the question of how we are to weight the reactions of the public to specific or general sexual acts. If the public were to be offended or shocked by the knowledge of my sexual shenanigans with Paula Abdul, should we give any moral weight to this offense and shock? If yes, how much? If the public are dismayed by the mere knowledge that homosexual sex goes on in their midst, how much weight, if any, should we give this dismay? Similar questions may be asked about all sorts of sexual practices that are likely to offend or dismay one section of the public or other.

Keeping these points in mind, let us delve into a consequentialist discussion of the morality of sex.

Consequentialism and Sex

Generally speaking, sexual activity gets (or should get) a two-thumbs-up from consequentialism. It gives pleasure to the participants (and causes little or no pain to its participants and others), including the pleasures of orgasm and sensuousness, of passion, and of emotional intimacy. Heterosexual intercourse is the usual way by which children are conceived, and having children is a good thing. It is our usual way of continuing the species, which – I suppose – is also a good thing. Sexual activity often leads to new friendships or loves, or to cementing old ones – another good consequence.

However, once we move away from the general level, things quickly become complicated. Sometimes, heterosexual sex has bad consequences: literal pain (the man's penis is too big for the woman's vagina), transmission of sexual diseases, unwanted pregnancies, and the breakup of good friendships (Lisa and Paul are good friends; had they not had sex they would have remained so). So just because a type of sexual act generally has good consequences does not mean that every instance of it has. The opposite is also true: some types of sexual acts generally have bad consequences (e.g., adultery, bestiality, necrophilia), but some of their instances have good ones.

Here we need a crucial distinction. *Act consequentialism* evaluates the morality of actions by considering each act itself; it asks whether *this* act is right or wrong by looking at the consequences of *the act in question*. *Rule* consequentialism evaluates an action by considering whether it violates some moral rule or other, whereby the moral rule is justified consequentially: it is a rule that, if conformed to by everyone or almost everyone, would lead to good results. For example, an act consequentialist would check whether a particular act of stealing is right or wrong by looking at the consequences of that act: Who benefits by it? Whom does it harm? A rule consequentialist would (probably) claim that stealing is wrong because it violates the rule, "Do not steal," a rule that, if followed by most or all people, has highly beneficial results.

When it comes to sex (and other areas perhaps), rule consequentialism (and other rule-reliant theories) would have strange and unacceptable results if it formulates moral rules that *require* sexual actions, such as "Have homosexual sex!" Unlike rules such as "Be honest," "Be kind," and "Be charitable," no one is required to have any type of sex at all during his or her life, not even heterosexual sex. (Possible exceptions are rules requiring sex with people to whom we have sexual obligations – a tricky idea which I discuss in the next chapter – but this is not a type of sexual activity.) This means that rule consequentialism will have to issue mostly negative rules, such as "Do not have gay sex," "No sex with animals," and "Adultery is prohibited."

Bearing these points in mind, let us address the evaluation of singular sexual acts. Suppose that Bob and Bonnie have sex. An act consequentialist would evaluate their action on its own merits, tracing its consequences to Bob, Bonnie, and other relevant parties. A rule consequentialist would have to see whether the sex between them violates a rule that, if followed, is conducive to good consequences. However, we won't know whether the sex violates this rule until we know more about the sex between Bob and Bonnie: Are they strangers and is the sex between them casual? If yes, does the sex have the necessary precautions? Are they married, and to each other? In any case, does the sex involve anything weird, like urine, feces, or an animal? Are they brother and sister or related in other close ways? Do they have oral sex, anal sex, penile–vaginal sex, mutual masturbation, or two or more of these? Do they consent to the act? Do they perform the act in private? The answers to these questions are important because, for example, if Bob and Bonnie are brother and sister, their sex violates the rule prohibiting incestuous sex (a plausible rule given that most or all people's having incestuous sex leads to some very harmful results). If Bob did not consent to the sex, the sex violates the rule against rape. If there's a rule against bestiality, and both Bob and their dog, Tonguey, perform oral sex on Bonnie, the sex violates the rule, and so is wrong.

There are some factors that a rule consequentialist would insist be part of *any* rule about sexual behavior: consent, the private performance of sex, the use of necessary precautions, and anything else needed to avoid serious harm or damage not covered by the first three factors. Rules prohibiting sexual acts involving lack of consent, that are performed in public, that have a high probability of transmitting serious diseases, or that involve other types of serious harm would be endorsed by the rule consequentialist, because these rules have highly beneficial consequences (and because the wide practice of these acts would lead to serious damage or harm). For example, non-consensual sex is likely to lead to harmful consequences for the non-consenting party in the form of physical damage and psychological trauma whose effects can be long-lasting. It may even lead to harmful effects to the consenting party in the form of guilt that can be long-lasting. Sex in crowded public places likely leads to major disruptions of daily life, especially since sex always captures people's attention (Riley 1998, 180). Since there is rarely ever a reason to perform sex in public, rule consequentialism is likely to also prohibit it (sex on stage in sex clubs is sex in front of *a* public, but the space itself is private in that it is not forced upon people who do not wish to see it, so it is not the same as public sex). Sex that does not involve precautions where such precautions should be used (e.g., anal sex) would be prohibited, and sex that has a high risk of transmitting diseases but that could not involve precautions (e.g., sex involving ingesting urine or feces) would also be prohibited, because sexual diseases are obviously bad and, if left unchecked, have a multiplying effect. There are also consensual, private sexual activities (incest and some forms of pedophilia) that would also be banned by rule consequentialism for similar reasons.

The rules in rule consequentialism can change depending on changes in technology, medicine, and other transformations. For example, if we evolve to the point of developing a natural immunity to any and all sexually transmitted diseases, any rule against having unprotected sex would be dropped, because having unprotected sex would no longer carry the dangers it carries today. A more realistic example is premarital sex: prior to birth control, rules against premarital sex made sense because of the harmful effects on children and on a society containing many children born out of wedlock. With birth control, such rules are no longer needed, at least not as blanket prohibitions (they can be amended to "Do not have heterosexual sexual intercourse without using birth control if you are not married to each other"). Consider a third example: in most societies, sexism has had a strong cultural presence. In most societies, also, most prostitutes have been women. How we evaluate the morality of prostitution on consequentialist grounds depends on these two factors. If prostitution promotes and abets sexism (an issue I discuss below), rule consequentialism might prohibit it. Change one of these two factors and the rule might change, too: if most prostitutes are no longer women but men, promoting sexism may no longer be an issue, in which case the rule prohibiting female prostitution would no longer be needed. Or if sexism were to somehow disappear from society, prostitution could no longer promote it, in which case the rule prohibiting it would also no longer be needed. This raises an interesting point about rule consequentialism. I will illustrate it by an example.

Suppose that there is a society the majority of whose members are so dismayed by homosexual sex (or interracial sex) that they have recourse to mob violence whenever they hear that a homosexual sexual activity has occurred ("What? David and Jonathan did it *again*? To the streets, people! Smash, break, and plunder everything in sight! We'll show those homosexuals what we're capable of!"). Even though such mob action is stupid and silly (not to mention destructive of life and property), rule consequentialism would have to prohibit homosexual sex based on these consequences, because such a rule would be highly beneficial to society. Yet something strange has happened in this case: a moral theory declaring an action immoral based on the *bigoted* or wrong reactions of people. No doubt rule consequentialism would also declare the actions of the mob wrong, but this does not change the fact that they are a consequence of homosexual sex. We have two options: either rule consequentialism goes by the consequences of actions as these consequences are embodied in *ideal* or *decent* people (to rule out such bigoted reactions), or we must distinguish between consequences that should morally count and consequences that shouldn't. I am not hopeful of either option.

This raises another crucial point about consequentialism. Suppose the reactions toward homosexual sex are not extreme, but confined to offense: people are offended, even shocked, by the occurrence of privately conducted homosexual sex among them or by any kind of sex that does not fit their mores (we can even imagine a society of homosexuals that perpetrates itself by conceiving of children in test tubes, and that is horrified, shocked, dismayed, and deeply offended by the knowledge of any heterosexual sex that occurs in its midst). The people are so offended that they feel disgust and nausea. The question is not so much whether such consequences should be factored in any rule (or even act) consequentialist judgment about the morality of such acts, because, obviously, they should be factored in (they are consequences, after all). The question is how much weight they should be given.

Although the people seem genuinely bothered by homosexual sex, reactions of offense, shock, and nausea are not detrimental or seriously harmful (they are usually temporary). Moreover, the reactions are often a function of taste and changing social norms: what people yesterday considered offensive and disgusting, today they don't even think twice about. There is also the thought that the nausea and disgust are really the fault of the people who feel them: nobody forces them to dwell in their minds on homosexual sex; if this sex is not causing any other type of harm or damage to society, why mentally linger on it? If they insist on doing so, it's their own fault. Perhaps because of these reasons, the disgust and nausea of the people of this society should not be given much weight when discussing the morality of homosexual sex on consequentialist grounds.

Nonetheless, the above discussion again underscores the idea that the notion of consequences needs careful handling, because not all consequences should have much of a role to play in morally assessing actions. This vigilance is especially needed when it comes to issues – like sex – that have proven to raise people's ire and to tickle their sensitivities. How much weight we give to these sensitivities could decide whether we have gone down the right or the wrong moral path.

Let us turn briefly to act consequentialism. Because it evaluates each action by tracing its consequences, does it then leave no room for rules? Not quite.

In *Utilitarianism* (ch. 2), John Stuart Mill (1987) addresses the objection that we often have no time to decide what to do by calculating the foreseeable consequences of the action. There is some truth in this objection. We sometimes have to make quick decisions and have no time to figure out the possible good and bad consequences of our actions before we decide what to do. Mill responds to the objection by arguing that the accumulated wisdom of the past has taught us that certain actions are wrong and others right precisely because we generally know to what effects they lead. If you have to quickly decide whether to lie, chances are that you should not, because, as experience has shown, lying usually has bad consequences that outweigh – at least in the long run – its good ones. Act consequentialism, then, could rely on *rules of thumb* that are the product of accumulated wisdom. Of course, act consequentialism sometimes counsels to break these rules and to assess the action on its own merits. Thus it is hospitable to making exceptions to these rules of thumb.

That act consequentialism allows for exceptions to the rules of thumb raises the interesting issue of what role consent, private sex, precautions against diseases and against any serious harm or damage whose source is not the first three play in act consequentialism. Because act consequentialism merely allows for rules of thumb, violating them if a particular action leads to overall good consequences, it has to consider these factors defeasible were such an action to occur. For example, if somehow *x* raping *y* leads to highly beneficial consequences, with minimally bad ones, act consequentialism would have to consider this act of rape right. If having sex with Mario Lopez in public leads to highly beneficial consequences, the action would be right. And so on. (This rule violation is not confined to sex acts, but to any type of act: murder would be deemed right if it leads to overall good consequences.)

Many people would balk at this, finding it highly disturbing, for example, that an act of rape or pedophilia is morally right simply on the grounds that it can lead to highly beneficial effects, especially if the recipients of these effects were people who are not party to the sex act. They would claim that no matter how good the results are, rape is wrong. Act consequentialists may reply that we need to be careful in constructing our cases. It is one thing to say in the abstract that there can be a case of rape with highly beneficial results, but another to provide the details of this case. Details are crucial because they might show that no convincing case can be made of a rape that leads to highly beneficial results. And even if such cases can be made, they will likely be theoretical, not real. Finally, if such a case does actually occur, and if its benefits were really quite high and its bad effects quite low, is it so inconceivable that the act is right?

Whether these replies are convincing I leave to the reader to decide. Either way, act consequentialism does take the factors of consent, privacy, protection against diseases, and other harms seriously. But there is another issue: I claimed that for rape, for example, to be justified according to act consequentialism, the benefits have to be quite high and the costs quite low. Why "quite high" and "quite low"? Why not say that the overall benefits have to be higher than the costs or harms? After all, act consequentialism (and consequentialism in general) does not place limits on how high or low the benefits and costs should be. All it claims, really, is that there should be an overall net amount of benefits for an action to be right. So if an act of rape yields slightly more pleasure or benefits overall, then it should be right. Why, then, the qualifications "high" and "low"?

One answer is this: our intuitions tell us that for such usually horrendous acts to be justified at all, their benefits must be quite high and their costs quite low. But a consequentialist cannot adopt this answer, because it considers these acts *wrong to begin with* and goes on to claim that if it so happens that they yield such a high amount of benefits, maybe they are justified. But for a consequentialist, because the act's rightness or wrongness is decided by looking solely at its consequences, we cannot assume that the act is wrong to begin with, so this answer is not an option.

The consequentialist has another answer: a sexual *practice* (for lack of a better term) is a kind of sexual activity in which many people actually engage, such as rape, pedophilia, prostitution, and foot fetishism. With some sexual practices, the fact that many people engage in them means little as far as harmful consequences are concerned. For example, foot fetishism is a popular sexual practice, but it is usually conducted in private, and it is has virtually no harmful effects on the participants. So whether we consider acts of foot fetishism singularly (action-by-action) or as an aggregate (a practice) is of no consequence, literally speaking. If anything, the consequences are good: they bring pleasure to the participants.

Not so with other practices such as rape and pedophilia. Perhaps some individual acts of rape or pedophilia could have more good than bad effects, but this does not mean that an act consequentialist would not prohibit them, because *as an aggregate*, acts of rape and pedophilia have very harmful effects.

So the reason for prohibiting acts of rape or pedophilia, except perhaps for those that have astronomically good benefits and very low costs, is to avoid a slippery slope: allowing some might encourage others and this could lead to a sexual *practice* in which many members of society engage. Of course, we do prohibit rape and pedophilia, and this has not made them any less of a practice. Nonetheless, not prohibiting them would probably make them more wide-spread. So act consequentialism can prohibit some sexual acts because of their tendency to spread among many members of society. Let us consider the example of prostitution.

Consequentialism, Feminism, and Prostitution

Even if two (or more) adults consent to a sex act and the other caveats are satisfied, it may still be that the sex act, as a practice, has pernicious results. This is where prostitution comes in, because even if prostitutes and their clients consent to sex, practice safe sex, and so on, female prostitution in general might nonetheless abet and help the bad consequence of entrenching sexism. It would then be morally wrong according to consequentialism. Let us consider one attempt at such an argument.

Laurie Shrage argues that because of the way prostitution is understood, practiced, and, generally speaking, culturally framed in the Unites States and similar Western societies, its continued practice leads to pernicious results, namely the perpetuation of "the marginalization of people of color and women in the U.S. and elsewhere" (1994, 125). If prostitution has these effects in U.S. society, and if not offset by beneficial ones, prostitution would be condemned on consequentialist grounds (in what follows I discuss issues pertaining to women in general, not to women of color in particular).

Shrage argues that there are four cultural "principles" (or "beliefs") that "shape commercial sexual transactions and condition our attitudes to them" (1994, 127). Because these beliefs are false and support prostitution (prostitu-tion, in turn, supports them) and imply the lower status of women, they are a serious moral strike against prostitution.

The first is the belief in a universal, powerful sex drive, especially in men. Shrage argues that this belief is false because other peoples do not experience sexual desire as powerful and hard to control. She gives the example of the Dani in New Guinea, who, after the birth of a child, forgo sexual activity for a number of years without distressing about it. She concludes that one rational-ization for tolerating prostitution – the belief in a powerful sex drive – is "a purely cultural phenomenon" (1994, 129).

Before considering the other beliefs, there are three crucial issues in under-standing and evaluating Shrage's complex argument. The first is whether it is true that our culture (but not others) has these beliefs and whether, if we have them, they are indeed false or bad. The second is how these beliefs help support prostitution and how prostitution helps support them. The third is whether the beliefs are really pernicious to women. Shrage's argument against the belief in a universal sex drive is inconclusive, because citing the Dani as an example is not enough; we need additional examples of peoples who don't experience the sex drive as Westerners supposedly do (or think they do), because the Dani could have a powerful sex drive but, for cultural and other reasons, control or repress it better than Westerners do (Shrage acknowledges this; 1994, 129). Moreover, that the Dani do not fuss about their lengthy post-partum sexual abstinence tells us little about what they feel on the inside. Perhaps many masturbate privately and do not brag about it (much like Westerners do). After all, masturbation allows many men and women to go years without sex with another person.

But whether the belief in a universal, powerful sex drive is true or false is somewhat irrelevant, because, according to Shrage, we here in the U.S. do believe it, and the belief helps rationalize the existence of prostitution: given men's powerful libido, prostitution provides an outlet for it. We may even think this is good, because without prostitutes all the horny men would be ravishing honest and chaste women. As the English author Bernard Mandeville noted in his famous *The Fable of the Bees*, "There is a Necessity of sacrificing one part of Womankind to preserve the other, and prevent a Filthiness of a more heinous Nature" (quoted in Primoratz 1999, 97). The belief in a powerful sex drive also helps prostitution in its turn prop up the belief itself: its continued presence leads us to think that prostitution exists because of a powerful sex drive continuously seeking an outlet (Shrage's reasoning about the connections between the four beliefs and prostitution is brief; I am supplying what I think are the connections).

Is the belief in this powerful sex drive pernicious for women? Shrage is right in that if we believe that it is mostly men who possess this powerful sex drive, society is likely to treat men and women unequally when it comes to sex. Other serious consequences include the socialization of women into devaluing their sexual desires and preferences and depriving them of sexual power. But the more important question is this: Is the best – or even good – way to combat these beliefs by prohibiting prostitution? Shrage does not argue that prosti-tution should be banned or prohibited, but deterred by regulation (1994, 158–161). Nonetheless, if prostitution does lead to these bad effects, it is, according to consequentialism, wrong (setting aside whether it has good effects that offset the bad ones). If this means that it should be prohibited, we face obvious difficulties. In the U.S., it is already illegal in most parts of the country, but this has not stopped it from flourishing. Cracking down on it even more is likely to be much more costly and to make it go further underground. In the past, this didn't seem to work:

> King Louis IX of France [1214–1270; known as Saint Louis] tried … exile. By banishing large numbers of ladies of the night from the Kingdom he did manage to empty the brothels for a month or so, that is until they were filled by a generation of new recruits. The king's edict was repealed. There was another attempt to clamp down in 1635. Pimps were to be

condemned to the galleys for life; prostitutes were to be whipped, shaved and banished. This didn't work either. The supply of prostitutes did not diminish, and the laws were manipulated by men wishing to settle scores with their mistresses by accusing them of being prostitutes. The law banning prostitution remained in full force till the eighteenth century – and was, in fact, the means by which the Canadian colonists were supplied with wives from the dregs of Paris.

(Gordon 2004, 56)

Moreover, the cultural belief in a male powerful sex drive is not only fueled by prostitution but by other practices: straight pornography (the gay male pornography industry, and the lack of a lesbian counterpart, indicates further that we believe in this drive to exist mostly among men), the cosmetic industry for women that encourages them to continuously look good, the flourishing of plastic surgery (especially for women), and so on. Perhaps, then, a better way to combat this pernicious belief is not by banning prostitution, but by combating the belief directly, either by arguing that there is no such *universal* sex drive or by showing that the sex drive is indeed universal, in *both* men and women, but that women had had to repress and control it more, or exhibit it in non-sexual ways. A glimpse at today's popular culture indicates that society increasingly believes that the drive is indeed universal: especially the explosion of so-called reality TV shows and the frank portrayal of women's powerful and demanding sexuality seems to show that women are catching up with men in exhibiting as powerful a sex drive.

The second belief is that men are naturally dominant. According to Shrage, that men are often the consumers of sexual services (women are rarely clients of male or female prostitutes) reflects this view since the role of consumer usually carries with it a type of authority. Women, even as consumers, are usually not thought to have this authority, since sales people prefer to deal with women's male companions in business transactions (especially for traditionally non-women-related products such as cars and building tools). This gets worse when women buy sexual services, because they are not supposed to have sexual knowledge even about their own sexual needs and desires (Shrage 1994, 129–130). Shrage adds, "The role of sex consumer is an especially awkward role for women, since the transaction they assume the right to lead is a sexual one – an activity where women are socialized to follow their partners, not lead" (1994, 130). She concludes that if we hope to see more equality between sexual partners, we need to abolish the roles of sex provider and sex consumer (1994, 130).

But the belief in the natural dominance of men is not as widely accepted anymore, at least outside some highly conservative religious circles. It is also a mistake to discuss this belief in general terms and about culture at large. For example, there may still be a large segment of the U.S. population, conservative and non-conservative, that thinks that a woman is not fit to be president, for direct military combat, or for construction work (except for the presidency, which admittedly includes being Commander-in-Chief, all these areas involve physical stress). But few people today believe that women cannot be excellent lawyers, doctors, artists, college teachers, and virtually any other profession considered in the past to be a man's domain. Nor do sales people prefer to talk to a man if it is a woman who is making a purchase, including when the woman is buying a product traditionally marketed for men, such as cars and power tools. And although women still rarely purchase sexual services, it is unclear what this shows about the belief in the natural dominance of men, especially given the changes in our beliefs about the other areas just mentioned. Again, however, a glimpse at popular culture indicates that women are almost taking as much charge as men are when it comes to sexual encounters, so the belief in men's dominance in this area is also changing, and quite rapidly.

Second, even if the belief about the dominance of men is still in cultural circulation, we need to see how it helps prop up prostitution and vice versa (Shrage is unclear on this point). I think the reasoning is that being a buyer of sexual services reflects the view that the buyer is in charge. Since it is mostly men who purchase sexual activities, this reflects that view that they are in charge. Thus, prostitution is kept alive because men continue to buy it. In turn, prostitution feeds our belief that men are naturally dominant (at least in sexual transactions) because of the background belief that the purchaser is the powerful party (he has, after all, the money).

Here we have to be careful. First, this reasoning, even if true, does not show that we have the belief that men are *naturally* dominant. All it shows is that we believe they are dominant, because they have the economic, political, or social power. So it is unclear what "natural" means in this argument. Second, it is unclear why being a buyer reflects a belief in his dominance. Although it means having the ability to purchase something (this ability is a form of power), this is half the story, because sellers also have power: they have the goods (a wealthy Arab can have all the money in the world and yet be refused a transaction because the seller does not want to sell to Arabs). Many prostitutes are in a psychologically powerful position: they have what the client wants and many can refuse him particular services or any service, period. Shrage might agree but insist that the power of the prostitute is not usually found in our beliefs about prostitutes. That is, our cultural beliefs when it comes to dominance and submission tilt, respectively, toward the male and female. She might be right, but it is hard to figure out what our cultural beliefs are in such general ways (a moot point since these beliefs are changing).

The third principle or belief is that sex pollutes women. This is the old idea that the more a woman has sex (especially with different men), the more people think of her as a "slut" or a "whore." Our culture prizes the sexual innocence of women (Shrage 1994, 134). Perhaps because we connect too closely moral with sexual concerns, a woman who has too much sex is seen as loose and immoral. In this way, too much sexual contact "pollutes" women (1994, 135). Shrage sees this belief reflected in the way we talk: women are "fucked," "banged," and "screwed," whereas it is the men who do the fucking, banging, and screwing. The idea is that women "are 'had' sexually, suggesting that they can be used up; women are 'screwed,' suggesting that they can be twisted on their threads; and women are 'banged,' suggesting that, in intercourse, they can be bumped and bruised" (1994, 135–136). Prostitutes, of course, are the most "polluted" because they have sexual contact with a large number of men.

I do not doubt that many believe these connections between sex and women's purity. I can imagine sexual conservatives who hold such beliefs and maybe many teenage boys and men who think this ("Yeah, man, that Susan is a total slut; she fucked all the guys in the neighborhood" – note here the ease with which many people today use the terms "fuck," "bang," and "screw" in the active sense to describe women's sexual behavior, indicating that how we use these terms is changing; see Primoratz 1999, 108). But note two points. This belief may not be as widespread as it used to be. Once again, popular culture provides evidence: many women are sexually aggressive or at least not sexually demur, but pass uncensored by the people who watch such popular shows (do not confuse this with people lamenting the lower standards of television shows). Interesting here is that few men today (in the Western world, at least, Shrage's object of discussion) consider a woman's active sexual history to be an obstacle to her being eligible for marriage – with the general exception, that is, of female prostitutes.

This brings me to the second point. It may not be that we believe that too much sexual contact as such pollutes women, but that too much sexual contact with *many* men pollutes them, or, more pertinently, that the *kind* of sex that women have pollutes them (Shrage acknowledges this point; 1994, note 24, 207–208). That is, Jane can have lots of sex with John, her husband, without our thinking any less of her. But if Jane has sex with John, Jim, Jerome, and so on, we might change our minds. Or, if we find out that when she has sex with her husband she is into some kinky stuff, this may also make us think less of her. It may be our belief that prostitutes are willing to do just about anything sexually for the right price that makes them fallen human beings. In other words, the (false) image of the prostitute as a fallen woman is an exemplary paradigm of the belief connecting sex with pollution (no wonder Sigmund Freud (1912) claimed that the more a man respects a woman, the less enjoyable his sex with her will be). Whether we continue to believe that sex pollutes women, who the "we" is who believes this, and what the content of the belief is are complicated matters. Sweeping claims about this "culture believing this" and that "culture believing that" are not helpful, let alone true.

More important, perhaps, is the issue of how the belief that sex pollutes women props up prostitution and vice versa. I think that the idea is this: combined with the first two beliefs about the powerful sex drive in men and their natural dominance, we realize that men, alas, are just going to have too much sex. So it is better to keep prostitutes around because if women are going to be polluted by sex, it is better to have one segment of them (the prostitutes) polluted rather than all of them. We accept (or tolerate) prostitution as a necessary evil. In its turn, prostitution props up the belief that sex pollutes women by sending the cultural message that there are special women who are willing to do this "sort of thing."

Of course, the belief that sex pollutes women, coupled with the lack of belief about men (if anything, sexual experience in men is often considered a good thing, though conservatives don't think this) spells trouble for women, because it leads to all sorts of social oppression of women's sexuality and sexual desires. Moreover, it may very well be that as it exists in America, prostitution lends support to this belief. But the final question is crucial: Would prohibiting prostitution get rid of these sexist beliefs? It might help, but the ban is going to be costly and probably counter-productive. So, again, we are better off fighting this belief more directly. Thankfully, as women make strides in society, fewer people believe that sex pollutes women (though negative beliefs about prostitutes persist, which should be puzzling on Shrage's analysis).

The fourth and final cultural principle or belief is that our society reifies sexual practices. This means that we place people into sexual categories: heterosexual, homosexual, pervert, prostitute, pedophile, rapist. We also "mark women in terms of the number of partners with whom they have sex, e.g., virgins, harlots, sluts, and whores ... When we identify someone in one of these ways, we often think we have learned something important about them" (Shrage 1994, 137). Shrage correctly notes that such categories are often hollow because they smooth over complexities, such as that many lesbians have slept with men, many straight people are actually confused about their sexuality, and many women successfully undertake male roles (1994, 137–138).

Shrage is right that we categorize people sexually and believe they fall into different sexual and gender types, but how does this belief help maintain prostitution and vice versa? These sexual categories do not function scientifically, as, say, taxonomies in science, but socially: belonging to a certain category gets you associated with other beliefs and roles about who you are. Being a prostitute means that you have a certain (low) status in our society, and *not* being a prostitute might mean that you have a (higher) status (it depends on under what other categories you fall). "Prostitute" and other categories function partly to divide women between bad and good ones. This is an irrelevant, so pernicious division: as people, some women are bad and some are good depending not on whether they are prostitutes, but on their moral characters. So the category "prostitute" partly serves to maintain a false view about who the good and the bad women are, thus perpetuating erroneous views about women (Shrage 1994, 140; cf. Garry 1984, Halperin 1990, chs 1 and 2).

This may be true (see the next paragraph), but prohibiting prostitution may not be the best way to combat it. Moreover, we should not exaggerate how much thinking that someone belongs to a sexual category tells us about him or her: how many people really think that someone's being gay tells them much about him, or that a woman's not being a prostitute tells us much about her, let alone that she's good?

In the final analysis, Shrage's view is hostage to whether our society has the beliefs she says it has and the extent to which they support and are supported by prostitution. I have shed some doubts about the accuracy of this account. I am also skeptical about Shrage's – or any other – analysis of prostitution in our society that implicates it in directly or fully helping maintain sexism and the oppression of women. There are, of course, connections. Chances are that female prostitutes would not have the low status they have were it not for sexism, and the fact that it has existed and continues to exist in a sexist society means that it will have to conduct itself in such a way to thrive in society. So it has to adopt the mantle of its social environment, which means that it will adopt many sexist views and modes of behavior, and cater to male sexual desires (e.g., to have sex with women in high heels), which often come garbed in sexist beliefs.

However, the low status of prostitution does not merely reflect sexist views, but views about sex in general. If, somehow, sexism were to disappear entirely from society, prostitution would not be greeted with welcoming arms and prostitutes' lives would not much improve. Male prostitutes – who cater to mostly male clients – also don't have high social status. The fact that the gay male community largely views them with indifference, perhaps even acceptance, is mostly a function of the highly liberal views about sex among the community's members. So whether female prostitution becomes accepted is not only a matter of sexism, but also of our views about sex. As long as we think that sex should not be sold, should only be with love, or, in short, should not only be special (it is, after all, special), but special in a prudish way, prostitution will continue to occupy a low status in society. If so, the *extent* to which prostitution is the culprit in maintaining and promoting sexism and pernicious views about women is not clear. Thus, a consequentialist argument such as Shrage's is inconclusive.

While Shrage's argument is a consequentialist one based in a feminist framework, there are other anti-prostitution consequentialist arguments. For example, it may be argued that prostitution is bad because it leads to rampant sexual diseases, to unwanted children, to abusing drugs and crowded jails, to cheapening sexual experiences, to a loss of a decent sexual life on the part of the prostitute (doing something over and over again makes us bored with, even sick of, it), or to the breakup of good families. Like Shrage's, these arguments depend on contingent factors. If there were better protection of prostitutes and their rights and better regulation of their work conditions, they might not contract and spread sexual diseases; they might not have to abuse drugs to make more money; they might not crowd already crowded jails; and they might have more control (and charge more) over whom they will have sex with, thus not ruining their sex lives.

Moreover, for the above arguments to succeed, we must factor in two things. First, we should not criticize prostitution by abstractly claiming that it leads to this and that bad consequence. The consequentialist critic must do his homework and offer a more or less accurate picture of these consequences: To what extent *does* prostitution break up homes, spread sexual diseases, lead to unwanted children? These cannot simply be asserted but must be shown, and it is not enough to produce one or two cases of hapless men who caught syphilis by sleeping with prostitutes. If the case against prostitution is to be convincingly made, the extent of these consequences has to be deep and far-reaching.

Second, consequentialists cannot merely tabulate prostitution's bad consequences; they must also trace its good ones, because what matters is prostitution's *overall* consequences. And prostitution does have potentially good consequences. These include: (1) pleasure for clients and income for prostitutes, income often higher than what they would earn as cashiers at Walmart or McDonald's (a lower income not compensated for by a much higher work status); (2) sexual outlets for people who have a hard, if not impossible, time finding sexual partners (the old, the fat, the ugly, the crippled, the sick); (3) sexual outlets for people with specific sexual needs (e.g., fetishes); (4) sexual outlets for those who are too busy to have sexual or love relationships or for those who just prefer anonymous, quick sex; (5) keeping spouses sexually happy by providing them with a sexual outlet with a professional; they don't have to worry about three-way sex with someone who will favor one more than the other, who will go "fatal attraction" on them, or who will blab about it to others (cf. Califia 1994).

The reader should use consequentialism, feminism, or both together to evaluate other sexual practices, such as adultery, casual sex, bestiality, gay sex, oral sex, cyber-sex, masturbation, pedophilia, and looking at pornography. It may turn out that solitary masturbation that does not involve pornography, Fluffy the cat (or any other animal), a cadaver, or peeping at your neighbor (or anyone else) ends up winning the Consequentialism Prize in Sexual Behavior: it involves consent, does not involve the exploitation of anybody else (hammering yourself with a dildo is not exploitation, mind you), and it yields great pleasure – as long as, that is, it does not take up too much time that could be spent on another activity more beneficial to you and others.

Virtues, Vices, and Sex

Roughly speaking, according to virtue ethics a sexual act is wrong if it goes against one or more virtues or stems from one or more vices. A sexual act is right (permissible) if it stems from one or more virtues or does not go against one or more virtues.

Virtue ethics, like consequentialism, considers consent to be crucial. Respect is a virtue (though not a particularly Aristotelian one), and respecting others' autonomy and ability to make their own decisions requires that we seek their consent to what we propose to do to or with them. Rape is wrong because it is forced, non-consensual sex. Sexual acts obtained by deceiving someone or by manipulating her decisions are examples of sexual acts obtained without her consent (or genuine consent). If Tom lies to Lisa by telling her that he plans to marry her knowing this is the only way he can get her in the sack, Tom deceives Lisa. The sexual act is wrong because it is disrespectful (in a deep way, not as in "rude"). Thus consent is necessary for a sex act to be right.

But virtue ethics is not content merely with securing consent. The sex between Tom and Lisa is wrong not only because it is disrespectful to Lisa, but also because it is dishonest. It contravenes the virtue of honesty or stems from the vice of dishonesty. Note that not all dishonest sexual acts are also non-consensual. Suppose that Tom is John's best friend. Tom has his eye on Luisa, John's wife. Luisa has her eye on Tom. They each tell John a lie about where they are going to spend the afternoon, but they are having voracious sex in a cheap motel. Their sexual act secures their consent but is wrong because it is dishonest to John, someone who has the right to know about his wife and Tom's whereabouts when these include sexual antics with each other (is the sex act wrong if they told the same lies to Bernard, a mutual friend with no rights to know about their whereabouts?). Actually, the act involves two kinds of dishonesty, lying and unfaithfulness: Luisa has an obligation to John to not sexually cheat on him and Tom has an obligation to John to not violate the bonds of friendship between them.

That's not all. Suppose that Judy, knowing that Marianne loves Peter, and wanting to hurt her, seduces and has sex with him. Her motive for having sex with him is vengeance or humiliation: she wants Marianne to suffer. Her sex act with Peter is wrong because it is vengeful, despite the fact that both she and Peter consented to it.

Suppose that William is a male prostitute who needs the money to pay his college expenses. Being good looking he has many clients, enough to meet his financial needs, but he keeps taking more bookings because he's greedy for more money. The later sex acts are wrong because they stem from greed. Or suppose that he books more appointments because he is vain. His sex acts are wrong because they are vain.

Suppose that Hal looks down upon many people, thinking them to be miserable cockroaches, lucky to be even around him. Out of utter pity and contempt for some, he consents to have sex with them: "Let these fools have a taste of heaven. What do I have to lose?" His actions are wrong because they stem from arrogance.

Disloyalty, unfaithfulness, dishonesty, vengefulness, humiliation, greed, vanity, and arrogance form a partial list of reasons why sexual acts can be wrong *even if* they were consensual (see also Morgan (2003b) on how dark sexual desires can be). Consent is necessary for a sexual act to be morally permissible, but it is not sufficient. Note, however, that the *severity* of the wrongness need not be the same in all these cases; an act's being wrong because it is arrogant or vain is not as wrong because it is forced or even greedy.

Is the consent in the above cases genuine? If it is not, perhaps the problem with these cases does, after all, have to do with lack of consent. Although it is difficult to distinguish between genuine and apparent consent, there are clear cases. The example above of Tom and Lisa is of apparent consent. Lisa consents to sex with Tom believing that he intends to marry her. Had she had the correct information needed for a proper decision, she would not have consented.[4] If someone consents to sex under the influence of alcohol, hypnotism, or even mind-altering bad arguments (manipulation), the consent is also not genuine. The other cases, however, involve genuine consent. Consider again Peter. He says to himself, "I know that Judy wants to have sex with me because she wants Marianne to suffer. But you know what? I don't care about how Marianne feels and Judy is *hot*! So I will have sex with her!" Peter genuinely consents to the sex act. Suppose that I am William's client and I say to myself, "I know William agreed to accept me as a client out of greed (or vanity) and he doesn't need the extra money. But I don't mind paying the money and William is *hot*!" I genuinely consent to the act. Finally, suppose that I agree to have sex with Hal. I say to myself, "I know he pities me and that's why he's having sex with me. What an insufferable loser. But what do I care, as long as he does a good job in bed? Besides, he's *hot*!" I may be pathetic to have sex with him, but I genuinely consent. Ditto for Judy, William, Hal, and others in similar situations.

Let us discuss sex and the virtues, instead of the vices. The virtues of respect, fairness, and faithfulness play a crucial role in honoring sexual commitments, part of which are *sexual obligations*: if I promised Jet Li to have sex with him, then being faithful to my word and having sex with him would be the right thing to do, even if at that moment I didn't particularly feel like having sex with him. Spouses, including boyfriends and girlfriends (in a culture that has no problems with premarital sex), also have sexual obligations to each other. Although when, how, and where to have sex should not be spelled out in advance, there's an expectation that spouses should "put out." Indeed, it is reasonable for a girlfriend to leave her boyfriend (or girlfriend) if he constantly refuses to have sex. Even in long-term marriages, which are built on many foundations other than sex, a spouse would be perfectly within her rights to leave the marriage if her husband refuses her sex *and* does not allow her sex outside the marriage (things get complicated if the spouse demanding the sex refuses to have sex outside the marriage for religious or moral reasons). The virtues of being faithful to one's word or of respecting one's commitments play a role here, especially in cases when the spouse does not particularly feel like having sex. This does not mean that a spouse has to have sex whenever the other spouse wants or demands it, only that on some occasions he or she should.

Other virtues play a role, too. In sexual encounters between strangers or between sadomasochists, trust is crucial. Imaginativeness – if it's a virtue – is also crucial for sexual acts to be pleasurable or adventurous. Justice or fairness requires that we please our sexual partners as much as they please us, unless the partners agree otherwise. Generosity might require that we please our sexual partners even if they sometimes don't go out of their way to please us or to indulge their sexual tastes even if we don't share them. Patience requires us to be, well, patient with our sexual partners' habits, quirks, or sexual tastes. Even compassion plays a role, as when a male or female nurse might masturbate to orgasm a hospital patient in hospital unable to do so him or herself.

As important, virtues play a crucial role in getting us to *not* have sex: respecting John's being a priest, Kasia's being my student, and Heather being my wife's sister, I refuse to have sex with them even if I know that they want to or that I can seduce them (fairness and faithfulness to my wife come into play, too!). Virtues that play a role in relationships, such as those between friends, family members, colleagues, teachers and students, and co-workers, often require us to not initiate or undertake sexual relationships. Respect requires us to maintain the boundaries of these roles, which sexual relationships usually destroy. Fairness or justice plays another crucial role in maintaining teacher–student relationships free of sexual contact, since such relationships often involve potential abuse of power, subjecting both the student in the sexual relationship and the other students to unfair grading and other unfair treatment. The virtue of honoring relationships between siblings requires them to not have sex with each other (similarly for parent–child relationships).

The above virtues and vices are pervasive and regulate all our social interactions, not just sexual partners. We need to turn to a special virtue (and vice) when it comes to sex, the virtue of temperance and the vice of intemperance, *the* virtue and *the* vice of sex and sexual desire.

Temperance and Intemperance

Temperance is the virtue that moderates our desires for food, drink, and sex. Traditionally understood, it is about *amounts*: a temperate person is someone who consumes neither too much nor too little food and drink, for example, whereas the intemperate person eats and drinks too much (the glutton) or eats and drinks too little (there is no common term for this). This makes sense for food and drink (though even here I have doubts), but it's mostly nonsensical when it comes to sex, because, first, it is difficult to figure out what constitutes too much sex and too little sex. Is having sex once a day daily too much? What about sex twice a day daily? And is having sex only once a week or once a month too little? Of course, someone who desires to and actually has sex five times a day every day might be an obvious case of too much, and someone who never desires sex and never has it (or has it once every two or three years) might be a case of too little. But there's a gray area between them that is too large to be philosophically tolerable.

Second, even if we can agree on the amounts, it is not clear why they should *matter*. They matter with food and drink, because eating loads of food or drinking gallons of liquids every day endangers one's health, no matter what one eats or drinks (one cannot take "precautions" by eating only vegetables, for example). But what is wrong with having sex fifteen times a day if the person takes precautions (e.g., uses condoms, undertakes no oral or genital sex)? Any wrongness that such actions have is not evident merely by looking at the *amount* of sex engaged in.

To be temperate about sex must mean something other than amounts. If amounts matter, they are secondary or implied by more important issues. Aristotle does discuss temperance in terms of amounts (1999, 1119a15–20), but he also states that the temperate person does not desire the wrong things or those that deviate from the fine or noble (1119a15–19), and that the intemperate person enjoys things to excess (too much) because he enjoys wrong or hateful things (1118b25). So the temperate person enjoys *the right things*, whereas the intemperate person enjoys *the wrong or hateful things*. If Aristotle is right, temperance and intemperance are about wrong and right, not amounts.

Let us illustrate these points. To rape someone because of sexual desires (as opposed to, say, assertion of power, in which case the rape would be wrong for other reasons) is to commit an intemperate act, even if the person committing the rape did it only once (a small amount). If someone can only (or prefers to) attain sexual gratification through rape, he would be intemperate, even if he actually raped only a few times a year (small amounts). To have sex with children is wrong. If one desired this type of sexual activity, one is intemperate – not because one desired it all the time or because one acted on it frequently, but because the *kind of thing desired* – sex with children – is wrong or "hateful." But if someone who likes "traditional," non-kinky sex has it with her husband twice a day daily, she has too much sex, but it doesn't seem to be wrong sex.

The virtue of temperance and the vice of intemperance are *the* virtue and *the* vice when it comes to sex and sexual activity because they hit at the core of the issue of sex, namely sexual desire itself. In the above discussion of other virtues and vices, the motives and intentions that made the sexual acts right and wrong were not, as such, about sexual desire, but about other things: the male prostitute was greedy for *money*; the arrogant and vain were arrogant and vain about their personalities; the woman who desired to inflict pain on her friend slept with the man out of vengeance. Although these motives make the sex acts wrong, none of them is about, or only about, sexual desire. Similarly for the virtues: it is compassion, not sexual desire, which leads the nurse to masturbate the patient. Even if these virtues are about sex – I trust that the stranger's sexual desires won't lead him to harm me – they are, as mentioned, not confined to the sexual domain. But temperance and intemperance are. The intemperate person commits a wrong sexual act out of a *sexual* motive or desire, not a non-sexual one. And a temperate person does the right thing because her sexual desire is properly directed at the right objects. In this respect, the "field" or "area of operation" of temperance and intemperance is narrow, applying to our appetites, unlike the field of other virtues and vices, such as justice and trust, which are pervasive in our social relations.

What sex acts or objects are hateful or the wrong things to desire? They fall into two kinds. The first consists of sexual activities that are, in their "nature," wrong, such as bestiality and necrophilia. The second consists of sexual activities that are not by their "nature" wrong, but that can be wrong in particular instances. For example, heterosexual sexual intercourse and oral sex are not wrong, but heterosexual rape is wrong; some cases of heterosexual adultery are wrong; heterosexual pedophilia is wrong; and heterosexual sex between siblings or between parents and children is wrong (similarly for homosexual sex). People who sexually prefer or desire these activities are not temperate (but whether they are intemperate is more complicated; see below). Note that we might agree that temperance and intemperance are about right and wrong things to sexually desire, but disagree on what they are. A religious conservative and a liberal might agree with the first point, yet disagree that, say, desiring homosexual sex is morally okay.

Note also the distinction between intemperate acts and intemperate people. A lonely Greek shepherd's sex with one of his sheep makes his act intemperate, but it does not make *him* intemperate if he has no sexual preference for sheep and has sex with one only on the spur of the moment or out of frustration or boredom. His *act* is intemperate, because it is the kind of act that a bestial, intemperate person would do in a similar situation. Being forced at the point of a gun to have sex with a sheep, however, makes neither the act nor the person intemperate, because the cause of the action is not sexual desire, whether occasional or a matter of preference. All this implies that someone can be intemperate – for example, he prefers to have sex with human cadavers – without even acting on this preference a single time, because being temperate and intemperate is primarily about sexual desires and preferences, not acts.

However, things are more complicated. Suppose that Buck, Chuck, and Huck's sexual preference is to masturbate while watching their unsuspecting neighbors (or whoever) undress, have sex (including solitary masturbation), shower, use the bathroom, or whatever excites Buck, Chuck, and Huck. Buck has no problem indulging his preference: every day at 7 p.m. he sits by his living room window, with one hand holding his telescope and the other his penis. He peeps at all the apartments in the high-rise building across from his own, searching for good-looking women who are doing whatever turns him on. Chuck is slightly different. He is able to resist the temptation to act on his preference, so he never actually peeps at anyone. However, he spends quite a lot of time fantasizing about peeping at this or that person (some imaginary, some real people), and he spends quite a lot of time planning all sorts of peeping schemes. Although he goes to all this trouble, he can never bring himself to actually peep because he knows it's wrong and this knowledge is enough to deter him from undertaking the final step. Finally, not only does Huck not actually peep at people, he also does not fantasize about or plan it. He simply does not want to be that kind of person and has been able to train himself to not dwell on his preference, to not cultivate it. Occasionally, when it crosses his mind to peep at someone he finds especially good looking, he feels a twinge "down there," but he does not give it a second thought.

Are there moral differences between these three people? Yes, according to virtue ethics. Buck is the worst: he is a full-fledged intemperate person (if he regrets his actions, however, he would be merely incontinent, someone who does what is wrong but also feels bad about it). Chuck is what Aristotle would call a continent person: he has the desires but is able to resist acting on them. It is Huck who is the temperate one among them, because he is able not only to not act on his desires (continence), but to more or less banish them into the basement of his soul: they play no role in how he conducts his life in general or his sexual life in particular. Someone might object that he is not really temperate because he, somewhere in his soul, still has this preference. However, because sexual desires are often deeply ingrained in us (possibly since childhood) by processes over which we have little control, and because they tend to be difficult and even impossible to expunge completely, the most we can ask for – if we are to be realistic and if we are to make temperance within our reach – is someone like Huck, someone who has these desires and preferences but who banishes them to a place from where they cannot rear their heads. Of course, if someone does not have these bad desires and has "normal" sexual desires, he or she would also be temperate.

What roles sexual desires are to play in our lives is part of the larger issue of what role sex is to play in human lives. Someone who spends too much time and energy purchasing and watching pornography with little time or room for anything else is giving sexual activity a disproportionate role in his life. Moreover, someone need not spend too many hours a day on sex for this to be a problem, because even only a few hours a day can come at the expense of other things the person should be doing (either obligations he has to other people or things he needs to do to get his life into shape or not waste it). Sexual activity is highly pleasurable and enjoyable, and orgasm might even be a unique pleasure, but its pleasures are fleeting and its experiences (except for traumatic ones, such as many instances of rape) do not leave their mark on the individuals – even incredible sex with someone we love or someone with whom we sexually click does not leave deep marks. Sex is like food and drink in this respect: you enjoy it while you do it, you later yearn for some more, you do it again, and so on, but in between these periods, no deep or enriching marks are left; even sweet memories are just that – sweet. So we should not elevate sex and sexual activity to a high status in our lives. Doing this is misguided, especially if we are capable of more worthwhile things. This is why someone who has too much sex is intemperate: he gives sexual desire a place in his life it should not have.

If this is correct, then whether too much or too little sex is temperate or intemperate depends not so much on how we define "too much" or "too little," but on why and how the person does so. A Christian nun who trains herself to subdue the itch of sexual desire and to eventually not feel it is not likely to have sex – she is someone who has too little sex (an understatement). But she has good reasons for this – religious reasons, even from an atheistic perspective, provide justification for refraining from sex. However, someone who trains his desires in the same way as the nun does but for the reason that sex is too messy and too filthy shows a mistaken understanding of sex and sexual activity – his "too little sex" is intemperate. On the opposite side, someone who has sex with strangers twice or three times a week because he likes sex has sex "too much"; but he is temperate if his sexual activity falls in line with an overall acceptable life project – if he is able to do other things with his life that are worthwhile, not allowing sex to disrupt them. But if he does it because he likes sex yet is unable to harness his sexual desires, he is not temperate and shows weakness of will (he is incontinent). And if he has too much sex and thinks that this is how his life *should* be, he is intemperate – he shows a mistaken conception of life.

Of course, a lot depends on what we mean by a "worthwhile" life or "acceptable" life project. We can agree on some candidates – being an artist, a scientist, a writer, a farmer, a journalist, an athlete, an astronaut, an architect, a full-time parent, a doctor, a nurse, an academic. But what about people who have nine-to-five humdrum jobs with which they do not identify or about which they are not passionate – a bank clerk, a secretary, a traffic police officer? Or people who have difficult jobs – such as mining and policing? Or those who have jobs considered lowly by society's standards – a garbage collector, an insect terminator, a maid? These are difficult questions, but the point is not what kind of job or life conception a person has, but what place he or she accords to sex and sexual activity. With the exception of a couple of possibilities that don't yet really exist, such as being a sex therapist or a sex trainer, the issue is whether one overvalues sex and sexual activity. In this respect, someone who decides to become a painter because painters are "chick magnets" and develops the stereotypical look of male painters – a brooding, melancholy, deep-looking individual – overvalues sex and even uses painting as a way to have sex, not as an activity worthwhile in itself. The issue, then, is how we value sexual activity: Do we enjoy it, seek it, and not be prudish about it without making it be the end-all, be-all of our lives, or do we elevate it to a place it does not deserve, even to the point where we pursue other things as a means to get to it?[5]

Note an interesting implication of this discussion, implicit in what I have said so far: we can no longer take for granted sexual practices traditionally considered wrong to be indeed wrong. Promiscuity and casual sex, for example, tend to receive social and moral disapproval. But on this view, whether they are wrong or right, temperate or intemperate, depends on two things. First, it depends on the kind of promiscuous or casual sex desired: Is it sex with children, animals, or cadavers? Does it involve general moral wrongdoing, such as deception and force? Second, it depends on how it fits the practitioner's life: Does it come at the expense of other important things? Thus, we cannot merely claim that promiscuity and casual sex are wrong, period. Whether they are depends on the above two factors. The same reasoning applies to other sexual practices, such as swingers' sex, non-deceptive adultery, open relationships, and so on.

Summary and Conclusion

Consequentialism, in relying on the results of sexual acts and practices, necessitates a careful examination of data so that we can have a well-founded idea of what these results are. Its evaluation of sex is likely to be messy and complicated (not necessarily a bad thing). Virtue ethics, with its emphasis not only on the virtues but also on the idea of a good life (as we have seen in the chapters on love), evaluates both sex acts and the role of sex in a good life. This role should not be overestimated, and sex, though good and pleasurable, may not be as important as other things and should therefore not come at their expense if our lives are to flourish.

Notes

1 The "East" is famous for such books on the subject. India gave us the *Kama Sutra* and Persia gave us *The Perfumed Garden*, for example.
2 There is a "natural law" variation on these arguments that attempts to infer what God wants us to do with our bodies and body parts by looking at nature. But the Christian philosopher Christine Gudorf says, the "majority [of women] require direct stimulation of the clitoris … If the placement of the clitoris in the female body reflects the divine will, then God wills that sex is not just oriented to procreation, but is at least as, if not more, oriented to pleasure as to procreation" (1994, 65).
3 Vannoy argues that sex without love is better than sex with love (1980, 23–28).
4 Some cases of deception are permissible, such as wearing loose clothing to conceal love handles, or make-up to conceal wrinkles (see Baumrin 1984, 301).
5 Here we should make room for age and other factors: teenagers and young people might be more obsessed with sex than others, and we cannot rashly judge their lives lacking in worth or unwise, period. They are still young and may grow out of it. There are also other people who have very little going for them except for their looks: they are not that smart, intelligent, or talented. So if they elevate sex and pursue it, this might be understandable in that it might be one of the few sources of fulfillment for them. However, unlike teenagers, we need not retract the judgment that their lives are going badly. They still are, though perhaps they are not responsible for this bad situation.

Further Reading

For more on pleasure and sex, see Singer (2001b, esp. ch. 4). On higher and lower pleasures, Plato is a good start, especially *Philebus*. Michael Levin is one philosopher who tries to argue that the pleasures of heterosexual sex are more intrinsically rewarding than homosexual sex; see Thomas and Levin (1999, pp. 112–132). On the evolutionary function of the clitoris, see Lloyd (2005). On consequentialism and virtue ethics, see the "Further Reading" section in Chapter 4. On consequentialism and sex, see Odell (2006). On virtue ethics and sex, see Putman (1991), Halwani (2003, ch. 3, 2006b), and the essays in Halwani (2007c). A good discussion of the moral status of offense is Feinberg (1985). Two crucial treatments of consent are Archard (1998) and Wertheimer (2003); see also West (2008). The literature on prostitution is vast. Some classics include Pateman (1983, 1988, esp. ch. 7), Ericsson (1980), and Shrage (1989). See also LeMoncheck (1997, ch. 4), Nussbaum (1999, ch. 11), Primoratz (1999, ch. 8, 2006), Stewart (2006), and Estes (2008). For a virtue ethics perspective on prostitution, see Halwani (2003, ch. 3, section 6). Bullough and Bullough (1987) provide a good history of prostitution, while Delacoste and Alexander (1987) and Nagle (1997) provide essays on sex work by both sex and non-sex workers. On action, see Bennett (1995) and Anscombe (2000). On temperance and intemperance, see Young (1988) and Halwani (2003, ch. 3, 2007a). On casual sex and promiscuity, see Ellis (1986), Elliston (1998), Kristjansson (1998), and Halwani (2006a, 2007b, 2008). On pornography and women, see Garry (1984), Dworkin (1974, Part II, 1989), Longino (1991), Lederer (1980), Hill (1991), MacKinnon (1987, Part III), McElroy (1995), LeMoncheck (1997, ch. 4), Cornell (2000), and Gruen (2006). See also Soble (2002) for criticisms of feminist positions on pornography.

7   Sexual Objectification

What Is Sexual Objectification?

At its core, objectification involves considering a person as only an object. *Sexual* objectification involves considering a person only as a sex object. Consider the following cases that allegedly involve objectification: (1) casual sexual activity (one-night stands, anonymous sex in sex clubs, bath houses and other sexual venues, sex with prostitutes, lap-dances, and rape); (2) watching pornography; (3) depictions of naked people or people having sex in pornographic material; (4) checking out someone or his or her "booty" as he or she walks by; (5) catcalling a woman (or a man) as she or he walks by; (6) sexually fantasizing about a particular person. Let us briefly look at each case.

(1) In casual sex, but not, say, sex between lovers, the parties hook up precisely because all they want from each other is sex, which makes them regard and treat each other as merely sexual objects. Thus casual sex is an obvious candidate for accusations of sexual objectification. Non-casual sexual activities, however, do not involve this treatment, so seem immune to the charge of objectification.

(2) We look at pictures of naked people (e.g., individual women in *Playboy*, individual men in *Playgirl*, or people having sex pictured in magazines or in movies), because we are interested in their sexual aspects, regarding them as mere sexual objects. But not just any type of looking is enough for objectification to occur. Someone (e.g., a philosopher of sex) may view such material for research purposes. Thus, what matters are the *reasons* someone looks at the pictures, not so much whether the pictured people are naked or clothed (in one *Seinfeld* episode, George Costanza is caught by his mother masturbating while looking at pictures in *Glamour*, a non-pornographic magazine). If the looker's reasons are prurient, he is likely to be alleged to objectify the pictured people.

(3) Although someone looking at pornography need not regard the depicted people as merely sexual objects (e.g., someone looking at the sexually explicit photographs of the artists Jeff Koons or Robert Mapplethorpe for artistic reasons), pornographic material already objectifies its actors and models. When *Playboy* depicts naked women or when the movie *Drill Bill* depicts men

having sex with each other, the magazine and the film objectify their models by presenting them to the viewers as nothing but sex objects, for the viewers' sexual pleasure.

(4), (5) When Jodi ogles a good-looking man, she is also said to objectify him in that she reduces him solely to his physical appearance. Similarly, when – to use a cliché – construction workers whistle at a beautiful woman or catcall her as she walks by, they, too, seem to reduce her solely to her physical appearance. There are two main differences between these two cases, both of which revolve around treatment. First, merely checking out someone might be less morally serious than also catcalling her. Second, if we define objectification as involving only treatment, then merely checking out someone would not be objectification (more on this shortly).

(6) Sexually fantasizing about a particular person, whether it is someone the fantasizer knows (e.g., a colleague) or someone famous (e.g., Brad Pitt or Sarah Palin), is also said to reduce the person merely to his or her sexual aspects, because the fantasizer is not interested in Sarah Palin's political acumen, but only in her physical attributes. It is difficult to decide whether concocting an *imaginary* person and fantasizing about him or her also involves sexual objectification. Not only is this type of fantasy rare, I am inclined to say that no objectification is involved because no real person is reduced to an object. One worry might be that in fantasizing about a made-up person – say, a woman – the fantasizer reduces all women to the status of objects since, somehow, the object of his fantasy symbolizes all women. However, first, whether this is true depends on what is going on in the person's mind and what he thinks about women in general. Second, the claim that the person reduces all women to the status of objects is itself unclear.

Whether the above cases count as objectification depends on how we define the concept. Consider the following definitions or characterizations of "objectification": "to objectify a person is to treat him or her only as an object" (Halwani 2008, 342); "a person is sexually objectified when her sexual parts or sexual functions are separated out from the rest of her personality and reduced to the status of mere instruments or else regarded as if they were capable of representing her" (Bartky 1990, 26).

My definition includes only *treatment* or behavior toward someone. If x only (mentally) regards y as merely an object, no objectification occurs. So cases (2), (4), and (6) would not be cases of objectification, but (1), (3), and (5) would be. In (1) the sexual partners treat each other as sexual objects, and in (5), whistling and catcalling are ways of treatment. Case (3) is more involved. The pornographer positions his models so that they are presented as sexual objects to the viewer, but it is unclear that in doing so the pornographer actually objectifies them. He may not view them sexually at all, but only "artistically" or with any eye toward selling the final product. But although this may preclude some types of objectifying treatment on the part of the pornographer, such as his own personal, sexual purposes, it does not preclude others, such as his financial purposes. Consider a pimp who does not sexually desire his prostitutes, but who nonetheless treats them in such a way to appear sexually enticing to others, thus inviting these others to view them as sexual objects. He treats the prostitutes as sexual objects; similar to the pornographer's case. The point is that in treating another as a sexual object, one need not always do so for one's *own* sexual purposes, but for others'.

On my definition, for x to sexually objectify y, x needs to treat y as a sexual object. If x merely eyes y sexually, or regards y in a sexual way, no objectification occurs. Not so for Bartky's definition: the second disjunct ("or else regarded as if they were capable of representing her") takes care of the regard business. As Bartky notes, the prostitute, the *Playboy* bunny, and the "bathing beauty" would be sexually objectified (1990, 26).[1]

Should we define "objectification" as involving only treatment or also regard? I have no decisive arguments for either option, but a definition that relies solely on the notion of treatment is less cluttered and more accurately reflects the problem with objectification: its impact on the objectified (often thought of as *victims*). Let us, then, rely on the following definition of sexual objectification: x sexually objectifies y if, and only if, x treats y *only* as a sexual object. Is "only" important? What does the definition mean with "only" in it? Here is one thing it does *not* mean. Sam and Ham have a good relationship; Sam treats Ham as fully human except when they have sex, during which Sam treats him as merely a sexual object. Sam's decent treatment of Ham outside sexual contexts should not matter, because during sex he still treats him merely as a sexual object, so during these times he still objectifies him. The issue is how we treat others during sexual *encounters* (including not only sexual activities, but sexual encounters in general, such as catcalling and ogling).

Perhaps "only" distinguishes between two types of *sexual* treatment. In the first, x treats y as merely a sexual object. In the second, x treats y as *both* a sexual object and something else. What "something else"? There are three possibilities: as fully human, as somewhat human, and as a non-sexual object. Being treated as fully human is incompatible with being treated as a sex object, because as soon as someone is treated as an object, he or she cannot, *at the same time*, be treated as *fully* human. Since "somewhat human" is either nonsensical or morally problematic, sexual objectification must then mean treating someone as a sexual object while also treating him or her as a non-sexual object. This must mean that x's treatment of y focuses on, or regards as primary, y's sexual aspects while at the same being mindful of or attentive to y's humanity: y's wishes, desires, needs, and so on. This may occur, for example, between two people in love while having sex. They have "hot" sex but are also attentive to each other's sexual needs, desires, and comfort in general. So to treat someone *only* as a sexual object means that x treats y in such a way as to focus on or regard as primary y's sexual aspects without being mindful of y's humanity, though x could still be *aware* of it.

The core moral problem with objectification is that if people are not only objects, treating them as such is not befitting; it dehumanizes or degrades them by lowering them to a level they should not occupy. In a famous essay

("Objectification"), Martha Nussbaum enumerates seven different ways in which a person can be objectified:

1 *Instrumentality*. The objectifier treats the object as a tool of his or her purposes.
2 *Denial of autonomy*. The objectifier treats the object as lacking in autonomy and self-determination.
3 *Inertness*. The objectifier treats the object as lacking in agency, and perhaps also in activity.
4 *Fungibility*. The objectifier treats the object as interchangeable (a) with other objects of the same type and/or (b) with objects of other types.
5 *Violability*. The objectifier treats the object as lacking in boundary integrity, as something that is permissible to break up, smash, break into.
6 *Ownership*. The objectifier treats the object as something that is owned by another, can be bought or sold, and so on.
7 *Denial of subjectivity*. The objectifier treats the object as something whose experience and feelings (if any) need not be taken into account (Nussbaum 1999, 218).

Two (or more) people can have sex yet not objectify each other in any of these ways. Two (or more) people can have sex yet objectify one another in one or more of these ways.

One other point is crucial before discussing the morality of objectification. If Nussbaum's seven ways are indeed ways of objectifying someone, and if *x*'s treating *y* only as a sex object means that *x* is heedless of *y*'s humanity, then instrumentality and fungibility should not be on Nussbaum's list of ways, because in either type of treatment *x* can be mindful of or attentive to *y*'s humanity. For example, as Matt has sex with Jen to satisfy his sexual desire (instrumentally), he is also attentive to her sexual desires and any other desires she might exhibit. And though he thinks of her as fungible, he is not heedless of her desires and needs during the sexual act. However, if we understand "humanity" to include not only Jen's feelings and experiences, but also her decisions and plans, then Matt cannot have sex with her by violating her, denying her autonomy, subjectivity, and agency, while at the same time being mindful of her humanity. Such denials are incompatible with being attentive to (though they are with being aware of) Jen's humanity. So if treating someone *only* as a sex object is a necessary component of any definition of "objectification," instrumentality and fungibility are not, as such, types of objectification, because they say nothing about disregarding another's humanity.

What Is Morally Wrong with Sexual Objectification?

The way many philosophers discuss objectification is problematic. They reason that unless sexual activity occurs in the context of love (or a similar emotion), it must involve objectification: if two people get together only for sexual purposes, they treat each other as sex objects because all they want is sex. On this argument, the sexual partners need not *intend* to objectify each other or to think this consciously (even unconsciously) for objectification to occur. The fact that they have sex for its own sake is enough.

This reasoning contains two mistakes. First, it is unclear how love removes the objectification: if two lovers have sex with each other like cats in heat, how can the love get rid of the objectification? I say more on this in section III. Second, the notion of "sex object" is a misleading phrase, making cases of sex for its own sake seem much worse than they are. Let's look at casual sex first and then see whether we can extend the argument to other types of cases involving alleged sexual objectification.

What typically happens during casual sex – I focus on one-night stands (heterosexual and homosexual) and anonymous sexual encounters occurring in especially gay sex establishments – the sexual partners do not usually treat each other as violable, as owned by each other, as lacking in agency, autonomy, or subjectivity. Not only are they aware of each other's humanity, they also *desire* it; they desire a sexual encounter with another human being, someone who can respond to their sexual desires and has sexual desires of his own. Had they wanted to have sex with something that they can violate or treat in any way they want, a dildo, an inflated doll, or any other suitable *object* to whose fate they are indifferent would have been sufficient. Instead, in typical sexual encounters a sexual partner stops doing what he's doing if his partner asks him to, and he is attentive to his partner's sexual desires. He does not treat him as something he can "break up, smash, break into." Indeed, the paradigm type of casual sex in which one partner is utterly heedless of his partner's humanity (though not unaware of it) is rape – not exactly the first example that comes to mind when thinking of casual sex. Indeed, rape fits to the hilt virtually all Nussbaum's ways of objectification. This sounds right, because many things are wrong with rape, including objectification.

That casual sex partners usually treat each other with a modicum of respect does not mean that they are always happy to stop doing what they're doing if asked or that they are always happy to have to do things they don't particularly want to do. And it doesn't mean that the sex is always enjoyable or satisfactory (recall Moulton's views). It also doesn't mean that all casual sexual encounters are devoid of objectification; some encounters have them. But the interesting question – one which I do not pursue – is that if in a casual sexual encounter one party turns nasty, proceeding to do what he wants regardless of the wishes of his partner, wouldn't this be rape? If yes, are there then *any* non-rape examples of casual sex in which one partner treats another merely as a sex object? Keep in mind that a case of casual sex in which one partner obliges the wishes of the other to be humiliated, flipped around, talked dirty to, slightly roughed up, and so on, is not a case of rape but one in which the obliging partner is *respecting* his partner's humanity by heeding his or her masochistic desires.

If "sexual objectification" means "treating another only as a sex object," and if this means "treating another only as a tool of one's sexual purposes while also being heedless of the other's sexual needs and desires," then in typical cases of casual sex, the sexual partners do not treat each other in five of Nussbaum's seven ways: as owned or violable objects, or as lacking agency, autonomy, or subjectivity. This leaves us with instrumentality and fungibility – an interesting conclusion since we're already clear that they don't fit the definition of "objectification" as using another *only* as a sex object.

Both instrumentality and fungibility are *pervasive* ways in which human beings treat each other. We constantly use each other as instruments, and it is hard to see how we can even survive if we don't do this. When I buy something from a shop, I use the seller as an instrument to satisfy my desire for the bought object. When I consult with a colleague about an issue, I use him or her for advice. When I go to the bank, I use the teller to fulfill my financial purposes. And so on. In short, not only is instrumentality morally permissible, it is necessary for life to go on. The problem is when we treat others *merely* as instruments (something which Nussbaum acknowledges; 1999, 223), when we are heedless or disrespectful of the other's needs, desires, and wishes – for example, stealing from a shop or paying the seller only what I wish to pay as opposed to the asking price. Because in casual sex partners do not usually treat each other this way, instrumentality is not a problem.

Fungibility is also a pervasive feature of our interactions with each other. The whole idea, for example, of *shopping* assumes fungibility as an underlying principle: shoppers are entitled to go from one shop to another until they buy what they like, thus treating different sellers and clerks as fungible. All sorts of people are fungible in this way: car mechanics, plumbers, computer geeks, flight attendants, teachers. But there are two types of roles in which people are not fungible. First, parents, children, lovers, siblings, friends, and others in similar intimate relationships are not fungible. It is at best a twisted joke and at worst a serious moral blunder to say to a parent whose child just died, "Why not adopt Jake? He looks just like your son, seems as talented, and is certainly much better behaved!" Second, there are people to whom we have obligations. If I promise the flower seller on my street to buy flowers from her, she is not fungible with other flower sellers; unless she releases me from the promise or an unusual circumstance arises, I am bound to *her*.

Because all people are fungible in some respect, so long as we treat them with respect, there is nothing wrong with treating them as fungible. So if objectification is wrong, fungibility cannot be objectification. Regarding sex, if I go out to a sex club, I do no wrong in regarding or treating each person as a potential sex partner, fungible with everyone else or with everyone in a similar category. First, I have no obligations to have sex with anyone in the club. Second, I have no special relationship with anyone that obliges me to treat them as non-fungible. If I have sex with someone, then, yes, I treat him fungibly, but this is not wrong (so long as I respect him).

Casual sex, as such, is not objectifying; whether it is depends on each case because we have to look at how the sexual partners actually treat each other. More strongly, we can claim that in *most* casual sexual encounters no objectification occurs because sex partners do not treat each other with disrespect or by neglecting each other's sexual desires and needs. Sex with prostitutes is similar: the client is interested in sex, the prostitute in money. Each treats the other as a tool for his or her purposes and as fungible (with other prostitutes of a similar type, with other clients of a similar type), but most clients do not treat prostitutes in any way they want; indeed, many prostitutes have rules: "I don't do this and I don't do that; you need to pay me up front," and so on, though data about how clients behave with prostitutes across the globe, especially women from third world countries and prostitutes at the lower end of the scale, are needed to settle such issues.

It may also be that the pornographer, in requiring his models to engage in particular sex scenes or in requiring them to pose in particular ways for the camera, and unless the models are thoroughly exploited, is also not heedless of their desires and needs. He does not act as if he owns them, does not require them to treat each other in violable ways, and does not treat them as lacking agency, subjectivity, and autonomy. Here we must not confuse two things. First, many models often work in pornography because it tends to pay well (and the industry has become glamorous in its own ways). They understand that they sometimes have to engage in sex scenes they may not otherwise desire or find comfortable. But this does not mean that they are treated as violable, as lacking in agency (many jobs involve difficult physical or mental acts). Second, there is the issue of how much agency, autonomy, and subjectivity the models are capable of exhibiting or are trodden upon by the pornographers (in the case of prostitutes, by the johns or the pimps). A woman actor might agree to perform a difficult sex scene or one she does not sexually desire, without this diminishing her agency or autonomy. The ability to make choices about what scenes to perform is a sign of autonomy on her part. Only when her choices are utterly or mostly eroded are her autonomy and agency trampled on, and only then the pornographer would objectify her.

Bizarrely enough, the case of a man catcalling a woman, it seems to me, exhibits more objectification than the above cases. First, saying sexual things to a woman as she walks by is a type of treatment, not only mere regard. Second, because she is most likely to have not consented to the act (if she welcomes the remarks or finds them flattering, this might be post-catcalling consent), the catcaller treats the woman as a mere instrument for the man's pleasure and also as merely fungible. The catcaller also seems indifferent to her autonomy, agency, and subjectivity; he says what he wants regardless of what she thinks, wants, or feels. Treating her as violable is tricky: he doesn't physically violate her, but psychologically he does by invading her space, her ability to walk freely without unwanted attention. And he does not treat her as owned, since she is a stranger who happens to walk by. He probably does not even think he owns her for similar reasons. Fantasizing about, ogling, and checking out someone cannot be objectification because they involve no treatment.

So whether someone is objectified in one or more of Nussbaum's seven ways is a matter *not* to be decided by the type of sexual encounter involved, but on a case-by-case basis. But might it be that we have fastened on to the wrong view of objectification? What if objectification is also a matter of regard, not just treatment? What if Matt has sex with Jen, takes heed of her sexual desires, wishes, and needs, but all the while he *regards* her as nothing but an object? This case might be incoherent, because if Matt heeds Jen's desires and needs, how can he regard her as only an object? It doesn't seem possible that he considers her as nothing but an object, but also treats her as if she is not only an object. However, it is possible that Matt either entertains nasty views of her (e.g., "What a bimbo! I'll just sexually please her so that she'll sexually please me"), or he holds no views about her but just wants her for sex; he regards her only as a "nice piece of ass" (both possibilities have in common Matt's not regarding Jen in any positive light). The second possibility is our old friend, instrumentality, and we've seen that there's nothing wrong with using others as tools as long as we don't use them only as tools. The first possibility might tell us something bad about Matt, but whether holding nasty views about someone is objectification is not obvious. What if Jen *is* a bimbo? Even if she's not, this might mean only that Matt has a bad character, not that he objectifies her. Moreover, we're not always required to have positive views of others in our interactions with them. We hold no views whatsoever about most people (because we don't know them), and those we do know are not always exactly perfect.

Sexual objectification needs to be handled very carefully for the following reason. The *idea* is sensible enough: it captures the phenomenon of reducing a person from a status he should occupy to one he should not. If human beings, regardless of individual merit, have elevated status in virtue of having a lofty property, such as rationality, humanity, dignity, autonomy, sophisticated mental structure, or even affinity with God, reducing someone to a lower level is a moral wrong. But the term "objectification" is dangerous, because it implies the reduction to the status of an object, even though this reduction rarely actually happens, especially in so-called sexual objectification. Outside rape, it is rare to treat our sexual partners as objects: not only are we aware of their humanity; we are also mindful of it. So we should be careful to not understand "objectification" in too literal a way. But if we were to understand it in a metaphorical way, what would it mean?

One obvious meaning is that we should not treat our sexual partners as less than human, as less than moral equals. The idea of treating someone as a moral equal, however, is not very clear (does it mean more than securing her consent and not violating her rights?). When it comes to sexual encounters, especially those alleged to be objectifying, if it means anything other than heeding the sexual wishes, desires, and comforts of one's sexual partner, we are in danger of turning all cases of casual sex – cases in which the *non*-sexual desires, wishes, etc. of the sexual partners are not heeded and which need not be heeded – into cases of objectification. So we have to be careful to not load the expression "treating someone as a moral equal" with so much moralism as to make most sexual activities objectifying (see LeMoncheck 1985).

In the vast literature on objectification, especially by feminist writers who focus on pornography, there is general disapproval of sex for sex's sake (see below). Add to this the usual suspects of sexual activities and encounters described as objectifying, such as casual sex, sex with prostitutes, depictions of nudity for the sake of sexual release, and any depiction of physical or sexual beauty, and you emerge with a common theme: a general discomfort with sex for its own sake. Somehow, love or other uplifting emotions or relationships must enter the picture to remove the objectification. This means that even in sexual activities and encounters in which the parties do not treat each other as violable and owned, as merely instrumental or fungible, and as lacking in agency, subjectivity, and autonomy, the objectification stems from the mere focus on what is sexual.

This is a problem. Although we are rational entities, we are also animals. Raw sexuality exhibits or, as the case may be, unleashes, the animal in us. Partners to casual sex often focus on these animal parts. Pornography depicts these animal tendencies. People go to prostitutes to have sex without the shackles of love and other complicated emotions. If objectification is a problem, it must be because it is never right to focus on the animal in us. But must we always conduct ourselves by discussing Proust and Michelangelo? May we not sometimes take time off to relish our animality? If it is not wrong to enjoy an afternoon shopping for shoes, why is it wrong to go to a sex club or a prostitute? It can't be because we're using our minds while shopping but not while having loveless sex. We never stop using our minds. It is not as if during casual sex we *literally* become animals. If in casual sex and other loveless but consensual sexual encounters we focus only on the sexual, there is no moral problem with this. And if to sexually objectify someone is to *focus* on his or her sexual aspects (not treat or regard him or her *only* as an object), objectification would not be morally problematic (thus, from the fact that *y* is sexually objectified we shouldn't infer that *y* is degraded or demeaned).

This conclusion is tentative. We still need to look at Kant's arguments and some feminist arguments that conclude otherwise. For now, let us consider Nussbaum's view that relationships make objectification not only permissible, but also a *good* thing.

Nussbaum on Objectification

In her essay, "Objectification," Nussbaum decides that, "In the matter of objectification, context is everything" (1999, 227) and that in some types of relationships, objectification is morally permissible: "We must point, above all, to the complete absence of instrumentalization [in D. H. Lawrence's description of the sexual relationship between the characters Mellors and Lady Chatterley, in *Lady Chatterley's Lover*], and to the closely connected fact that the objectification is symmetrical and mutual – and in both cases undertaken in a context of mutual respect and rough social equality" (1999, 230). Discussing *Playboy*, Nussbaum claims that it "depicts a thoroughgoing fungibility and commodification of sex partners and, in the process, *severs sex from any deep connection with self-expression or emotion*" (1999, 234, emphasis added). In the conclusion of her essay, she states, "Denial of autonomy and denial of subjectivity are objectionable if they persist throughout an adult relationship, but as phases in a relationship characterized by mutual regard they can be all right, or even quite wonderful in the way that Lawrence suggests" (1999, 238). So if two people sexually objectify each other but in the context of a mutually respectful relationship, the objectification is "all right," even "wonderful."

To Nussbaum, objectification does occur in such sexual encounters, but she believes it is either permissible or wonderful (it is unclear which view she holds; see Soble 2008b, 272–277).[2] She seems to offer three necessary conditions for objectification to be morally permissible or wonderful. First, the objectification has to be "symmetrical and mutual." Second, it has to occur within an otherwise mutually respectful relationship. Third, the parties to the relationship have to be (roughly) socially equal.[3] The objectification would be morally impermissible, then, if (1) two people have sex in a mutually objectifying way but don't have a respectful relationship; (2) if two people in an otherwise respectful relationship have objectifying sex but the objectification is not mutual; or (3) if two people have an otherwise mutually respectful relationship and mutually objectifying sex, but they are not of (rough) equal social status.

But Nussbaum does not stick to the three conditions. In criticizing the Andrea Dworkin–Catharine MacKinnon view of sex, which relies heavily on the idea of inequality between the two sexes, Nussbaum, endorsing D. H. Lawrence's "value of a certain type of resignation of control, and of both emotional and bodily receptivity," claims that our culture "is more heterogeneous and allows us more space for negotiation and *personal* construction than MacKinnon and Dworkin usually allow" (1999, 231, emphasis added). This means that even if two people are not approximate social equals, they can still negotiate a roughly equal relationship (which sounds right). But if *individuals* can negotiate their relationships, is (approximate) social equality a necessary condition for permissible objectification? If a Palestinian woman has a love relationship with an Israeli-Jewish man of European descent (she's at the bottom of the social and economic ladder given her ethnicity and gender and he's at the top of the ladder given his gender, religion, and ethnic origin), and if they have room to negotiate how respectful their relationship is, what roles exactly do gender, socioeconomic, and other types of status play? It's unclear.

Moreover, in discussing the example of Molly Bloom (one of the characters in James Joyce's *Ulysses*), Nussbaum is aware that the objectification is one-way: it is only Molly Bloom who sexually objectifies Blazes Boylan (another character). Yet Nussbaum has no problem with this, calling the objectification "a joyous part of sexual life" (1999, 232). If objectification can be unidirectional *and* "joyous," why insist that, for objectification to be morally acceptable, it has to be mutual?

So it seems that the only condition (perhaps both necessary and sufficient) for sexual objectification to be morally acceptable, if not also "wonderful," is for the two people to be in a mutually respectful relationship. The idea seems to be that if the problem with sexual objectification is that it involves the nasty treatment of someone during sex (e.g., as an instrument, fungible, lacking agency), then as long as the person is treated respectfully, as a person, outside the sexual act, we can celebrate the joys of sexual surrender and enjoy our animality, which, after all, is part of who we are.

This view implies that casual sex, including sex with prostitutes, involves morally problematic objectification. Nussbaum is explicit about this when discussing a passage from the English writer Alan Hollinghurst's *The Swimming-Pool Library*. The main character, William Beckwith, while taking a shower at a men's facility frequented for sexual purposes, mentally comments on the men under the showers around him. Nussbaum states that he focuses on the men's genitalia, associating them with racial stereotypes. She adds,

> there may ... be some connection between the spirit of fungibility and a focus on these superficial aspects of race and class and penis size, which do in a sense dehumanize and turn people into potential instruments. For in the absence of any narrative history with the person, how can desire attend to anything else but the incidental, and how can one do more than use the body of the other as a tool of one's own states?
>
> (Nussbaum 1999, 237)

Nussbaum's reasoning is sloppy. She wants to claim that in the absence of a narrative history (a relationship) between them, partners in casual sex use each other as tools for their "own states." But Nussbaum, who acknowledges that using someone as a tool is not a problem so long as one does not use someone *merely* as a tool, should have written, "For in the absence of any narrative history with the person, how can desire attend to anything else but the incidental, and how can one do more than use the body of the other *merely* as a tool of one's own states?" But had she written this, her conclusion would not be convincing, because it is not obvious how partners in casual sex would differ from parties to the many other types of encounters, in which people use each other as tools, but not merely as tools. And if, like other usual human encounters, partners to a casual sex act do not use each other only as tools, why is casual sex a problem? Why is narrative history necessary *here* but not in other relationships?

In addition, would a respectful relationship make objectification acceptable? Suppose that Belinda and Brian are in a mutually respectful relationship. Every now and then, however, Brian slaps Belinda around and orders her to clean his feet and then drink the water as a sign of respect for him. Obviously, slapping Belinda, making her wash his feet and drink the filthy water are wrong actions. Would the fact that they have an otherwise mutually respectful relationship make all this slapping, washing, and drinking morally acceptable, even "wonderful"? No, because if an action is wrong, it is wrong even if it is part of an otherwise morally good relationship. Therefore, if sexual objectification is wrong, it will remain wrong in such a relationship. As Soble puts the point, "But it is not, in general, right … that my treating you badly today is either *justified* or *excusable* if I treated you admirably the whole day yesterday and will treat you more superbly tomorrow and the next day" (2008b, 274). So Nussbaum's view is mistaken.

Another way to see why Nussbaum's view is mistaken is by answering the question, "What is it about a mutually respectful relationship that converts sexual objectification from being morally unacceptable to being morally acceptable?" In her essay, Nussbaum doesn't offer a clear argument for why or how this happens. In the quotation above about casual sex, she seems to imply, for example, that without narrative history, attending to the "incidental" (one's race or class or size of genitalia) means making the person a tool of one's purposes. But it is unclear why attending to the incidental (each partner's genitalia) in an otherwise mutually respectful relationship allows the partners to not use each other as tools (or mere tools).

My hunch is that Nussbaum's view seems convincing because the examples of sexual objectification she claims are rendered permissible or good by a respectful relationship are permissible or good *to begin with*. Nussbaum's resorting to respectful relationships does not play a role in reaching such a conclusion. If two people have sex with each other, whether in the context of a relationship or not, their sexual act is morally permissible so long as they have sex in morally acceptable ways, namely by consenting to what they do, by being attentive to each other's sexual needs and desires, and by respecting each other's limits and boundaries. In short, we are much better off arguing that in such cases there is no objectification to begin with, instead of engaging in mental gymnastics to try to show that there is objectification but that it is okay or good. Instead of objectification, what is present in such respectful sexual acts is a focus on the sexual and on each other as sexual beings. But this is not objectification, because there's no reduction here, literal or metaphorical, of a person to the status of an object.

Soble on Objectification

In his book, *Pornography, Sex, and Feminism*, Soble makes the following claim, no doubt shocking to many:

> To complain that pornography presents women as "fuck objects" is to presuppose that women, as humans or persons, are something substantially more than fuck objects. Whence this piece of illusory optimism? … Pornography gives to no one, male or female, the respect that no one, male or female, deserves anyway. It demolishes human pretensions. It objectifies that which does not deserve not to be objectified. It thereby repudiates norms that Christian, Western culture holds dear, that people are not to be used or treated as objects or objectified or dehumanized or degraded.
>
> (Soble 2002, 51–52)

Soble does not deny that pornography objectifies both men and women, but that in objectifying them pornography also dehumanizes them – does something morally wrong. The illusion to which Soble refers is "the belief that humans are more than their bodies, more than animals, that, therefore, there is something metaphysically special about humans, their essential dignity, their transcendental value, that makes using them, dehumanizing, objectifying them, morally wrong." If we don't have transcendental value, in depicting us as mere animals pornography does nothing wrong. Soble accuses Kantian ethics especially (see the following section) of peddling such illusions (2002, 67).

Soble's view is part of his criticism of a feminist–Kantian objection against pornography, which is that human beings have a property, such as humanity, personhood, and dignity, in accordance with which we should be treated, such that if we are not treated accordingly we are wronged. By presenting people as nothing (or little) more than sex objects, pornography does not treat them in accordance with this property, thus degrading and treating them wrongly.

There are three issues here. First, do we have such a (metaphysical) property? Second, if we do have it, is it compatible with it to treat each other – at least sometimes – as primarily sexual creatures, as pornography does? Third, even if we do not have this property, can we still be degraded and dehumanized, and thus be treated wrongly? And is treating each other as mere sexual beings such degrading treatment?

Soble denies the existence of a metaphysical property, calling the belief in it "a nice bit of illusory human chauvinism." Requiring us to respect the dignity in human beings assumes that we have such dignity, but "most people in the real world are dirty, fat, ugly, dumb, ignorant, selfish, thoughtless, unreliable, shifty, unrespectable mackerel" (2002, 53–54). Of course, neither Kant was nor are Kantians under the illusion that most people are dignified in the ways that Soble denies they are. Kantian respect is directed at a property that people have in virtue of being persons, even if in their actual lives they make a bad job of properly displaying it (see the following section). So Soble's criticisms in the above quotation are not directed at the proper Kantian view.

Soble has another argument against dignity as a metaphysical property that people have in virtue of being persons, namely that it is difficult, if not impossible, to argue for its existence (2002, 55–63). This powerful line of reasoning can be put as follows. The alleged metaphysical property is elusive. It is difficult to see how we can know it exists if we merely observe people, because most do not conduct themselves in a dignified way. Moreover, studying people and animals indicates that there is no sharp break between them, so we have less reason to believe that humans possess a property that elevates them above animals. If we cannot discover this special property empirically, we might offer philosophical arguments for its existence (I consider one in the following section), but without empirical support, believing in its existence would be not much more than philosophical faith. So whether we have such a transcendental property is undecided.

But suppose that we have it (this is the second crucial issue) – dignity, rationality, autonomy – in accordance with which we should be treated. Does this proper treatment rule out being treated as primarily sexual animals? In the following section, I argue that being such a provider *is* compatible with Kantian dignity. For now, we should keep in mind that any dignity worth its salt will have to contend with – better yet, encompass – the fact that we are not disembodied brains or minds. We have bodies and physical functions and desires that essentially make up who we are and that don't exist only to serve our mental faculties and intellectual abilities. There are many lifestyles essentially revolving around the use of the physical parts of our bodies, all of which are dignified. Why, then, single out those who are or wish to be primarily providers of sexual pleasure – to have lots of sex, with many people, to enjoy it, and to try to ensure that their partners also enjoy it – as undignified? Unless there is something especially problematic about sex (see the following section), there seems to be no good reason for this.

The third issue relies on the distinction between metaphysical dignity and non-metaphysical dignity. Metaphysical dignity is a property we have in virtue of our personhood, rationality, and so on. But someone can deny that such a dignity exists without denying that people can be treated in undignified ways or of leading undignified lives. A maid from Sri Lanka who is slapped in the face when she does not do her job "right," who is allowed to eat only leftovers and only after the family she serves has finished eating, and who has her passport confiscated by the household she serves (as often happens in some parts of the Arab world) is treated in an undignified way, whether we believe in a transcendental property of dignity or not, whether the maid is a bad person in general or not (or is labeling this treatment "undignified" a hang-up from our beliefs in this transcendental property?). If we can treat others in undignified ways and if people can lead undignified lives without having to believe in dignity as a metaphysical property, then some types of sexual behavior – casual sex, depictions of men and women in pornography – can be undignified, too. This does not tell us whether they are undignified, only that it is *possible* that they are. Soble does not think that the way women are depicted in mainstream pornography is demeaning to them (or, as some feminists add, to women at large). In the final section of this chapter, I treat this issue more fully. For now we have to make another distinction that I explain by an example.

People sometimes feel humiliation for doing things they should not feel humiliated about. For example, being found out that one is gay is often experienced as shameful and humiliating, even if one doesn't believe there is anything wrong or shameful about being gay; as the philosopher Claudia Card puts it, "Our liability to shame or other emotional pain in being defenselessly exposed to others as despicable, contemptible, or ridiculous does not presuppose that we find those attitudes (contempt, etc.) deserved" (1995, 159). Roughly speaking, this happens because of internalized social norms. When society deems something or a practice wrong, people imbibe this value. When they grow up to do or be the things that society says is wrong, they feel shame for doing or being these things, and they feel humiliated when caught doing them. Sometimes it is right to feel ashamed or humiliated, but sometimes it is not. This depends on whether society is right to condemn the things it condemns. One should feel shame for stealing, but one should not feel shame for loving someone from a different race.

The point is that when we judge treating someone as demeaning, degrading, or humiliating, we need to ensure that our accusation is based on the proper moral beliefs and values. If, upon finding out that her daughter is dating a black man, a white mother exclaims, "I have never raised you to lead an undignified life," her accusation is based on social, erroneous beliefs that there is something unseemly and degrading about inter-racial dating. Now suppose that while watching a pornographic movie in which a female character screams with pleasure and has sex in all sorts of positions and ways, we wince with shame or humiliation on her behalf, thinking that this is demeaning to her. Is this because the sex she has *is* demeaning or is it because we have imbibed social views that women should not be sexual in "wanton" ways? I address this issue in the final section.

Kant and Objectification

Why Kant Viewed Sex with Suspicion

There are three reasons for discussing Kant's views on objectification. First, objectification originates in Kant's ethics. Kant's idea that treating the humanity in people only as a means (and not also as end) is wrong is another way of speaking about objectification, because when we treat the humanity in someone as a mere tool or means, we treat the person as an object – as something to do with as we please to achieve our purposes. A discussion of objectification that does not include Kant's views is like a discussion of evolutionary biology without including the views of Darwin: possible and meaningful, but lacking a crucial historical dimension.

More important is the second reason. We normally talk of someone objectifying *another* person. But to Kant, equally problematic is the idea that in sexual encounters each person also objectifies *him or herself*. Thus, discussing Kant on objectification adds a new twist, objectifying ourselves during sex.

The third reason is the most important because it captures the core of Kant's difficulties with sex: Kant was especially suspicious of sexual desire and thought it objectifying by its nature, because when we sexually desire someone, we desire her body and body parts, especially the sexual ones, which makes it very hard, if not impossible, to treat the humanity in her as an end. As Kant states,

> Because sexuality is not an inclination which one human being has for another as such, but is an inclination for the sex of another, it is a principle of the degradation of human nature .... The desire which a man has for

a woman is not directed toward her because she is a human being, but because she's a woman; that she is a human being is of no concern to the man; only her sex is the object of his desires. Human nature is thus subordinated. ... Human nature is thereby sacrificed to sex. ... Sexuality, therefore, exposes mankind to the danger of equality with the beasts.

(Kant 1963, 164)

To Kant, only the sexual impulse among our inclinations is directed at human beings as such, not "their work and services." He adds,

Man can, of course, use another human being as an instrument for his services; he can use his hands, his feet, and even all his powers; he can use him for his own purposes with the other's consent. But there is no way in which a human being can be made an Object of indulgence for another except through sexual impulse.

(Kant 1963, 163)

It is morally permissible ("can") to use each other for all sorts of purposes so long as those purposes are morally permissible and consensual. By hiring a plumber, I use his hands and some of his abilities to fix my plumbing. So long as the plumber consents, and given that getting my plumbing fixed is morally permissible, the interaction is morally permissible. Sexual interactions are different. If two people consent to a casual sexual encounter, consent is not enough, because the very activity is not morally innocent, since sexual desire makes another an *object*. Kant says:

Human love is good-will, affection, promoting the happiness of others and finding joy in their happiness. But it is clear that, when a person loves another from a purely sexual desire, none of these factors enter into the love. Far from there being any concern for the happiness of the loved one, the lover, in order to satisfy his desire and still his appetite, may even plunge the loved one into the depths of misery. Sexual love makes of the loved person an Object of appetite; as soon as that appetite has been stilled, the person is cast aside as one casts away a lemon which has been sucked dry.... Taken by itself [sexual love] is a degradation of human nature; for as soon as a person becomes an Object of appetite for another, all motives of moral relationship cease to function, because as an Object of appetite for another a person becomes a thing and can be treated and used as such by everyone.

(Kant 1963, 163)

We need to explain Kant's argument, trace its implications, and briefly discuss Kant's solution. Only then can we figure out whether his views are convincing.

The primary reason why Kant indicts sexual desire is the idea that it is, "taken by itself," nothing but an appetite for a human being as such. Because this is the nature of sexual desire, when we sexually desire others we turn them into objects, thus inhibiting "all motives of moral relationship." What does this mean?

Suppose that Mark is sitting in a café, watching passersby. A good-looking woman walks by and he "checks her out": he looks at her breasts, her behind, her thighs, and so on. Mark is not interested in any other aspect of the woman. He cares about her only as a sexual being. Now suppose that the woman – Mandy – sits in the café. Mark strikes up a conversation with her and soon enough she invites him over to her hotel room (she's visiting town) for a bit of "fun." They go to the room and satisfy each other's sexual desires on and with each other. Once they are done, they say their goodbyes and that's it; they discard each other like lemons "sucked dry."

From sexual desire to sexual activity, the partners view each other merely as sex objects. But this cannot be all that Kant means. Suppose I hire Jamal the plumber. I don't care about any other aspect of him except for his plumbing abilities. He does not care about any other aspect of me except for my paying abilities. Once he's done fixing my sink I pay him and we say our goodbyes. We discard each other like lemons "sucked dry." Kant must be aware of situations like these. Why did he single out sexual desire?

The answer lies in Kant's remark that sexual desire targets people as sexual beings, not their "work and services." What he means, I think, is this: When I hire a plumber, I am interested in a particular ability of his, the ability to fix whatever plumbing problem I have. When I hire a math tutor, I am interested in his mathematical abilities. When I hire a masseuse, I am interested in his massaging abilities. In virtually every interaction we have with another person, we are interested in some ability or service he or she can perform, an aspect of people intimately connected – to Kant – to their humanity. In these cases, what I desire is not the people themselves, but their abilities, talents, or services. Only with sexual desire do I desire the person as such, as a body, as an object. I want to enjoy the person *himself*, not his beautiful voice, his company, or his massaging abilities. Thus, sexual desire renders people *objects*. Kant did not mean that the person who desires another views him or her as *inanimate*, like an inflated doll. Rather, we desire a living human being, but as an object, as something with which we can satisfy our sexual urges. We are not interested in what the person can do, say, or produce, but in the person as a tool for desire satisfaction. Sexual desire is thus *incompatible* with viewing people as beings with humanity and dignity. I cannot simultaneously adopt an attitude toward the same entity as an object and as something with dignity. Because we are always required to view other human beings as beings with dignity, Kant claims that human nature is "sacrificed to sex" when it comes to sexuality, and that sexuality endangers our dignity by putting us on a level with the beasts.

One immediate consequence of this view is that consent is not sufficient to render sex permissible (though it is necessary). Suppose that Mark and Mandy, instead of having sex, agree to rob a bank, go cow tipping, or burn down a forest. The fact that they consent to these activities does not make them morally permissible. Similarly, because to Kant sexual activity is morally problematic, consent to it does not make it permissible.

We need to underscore a crucial aspect of this discussion. When Mark and Mandy agree to have casual sex, each views the other as an object. But in agreeing to allow Mark to use her as an object, Mandy treats herself – or allows herself to be treated – as an object. Ditto for Mark. To Kant, the moral problem is not just x treating y as an object, but also with x treating x's self as an object (1963, 162–164).

Moreover, given the requirements of Kant's Formula of Humanity, it might be difficult for sexual activity to satisfy them. As we recall, Kant's Formula of Humanity states, "Act in such a way that you treat humanity in others and in yourself not only as a means but also as an end." It requires treating people in two ways. First, we must not use them as mere tools. Second, we must share or adopt their goals as if they were our own, which does *not* mean that we do so in order to attain our own, but *for their own sake*. Moreover, the goals have to be morally permissible (Soble 2008b, 262).

Mark and Mandy may consent to their casual sex, but if their goals are sexual satisfaction, and if sexual desire objectifies, their ends are not acceptable and should not be adopted. Furthermore, when Mark and Mandy agree to have sex, each desires the other, but here kicks in Kant's worry that when people sexually desire each other, they eye each other as objects with which to satisfy their desires. That is, when Mark desires Mandy he does not care about the satisfaction of *her* sexual desires but about the satisfaction of his own. If he does care about hers, chances are he does so only for the sake of his desires, because if Mandy is sexually satisfied, this enhances his sexual satisfaction (prostitutes usually resort to faking sexual pleasure to get the client "off" quicker). This makes it difficult indeed to see how sexual desire and activity can satisfy the Formula of Humanity.[4]

Let us take stock. Sexual desire and activity are to Kant especially problematic because they make us view people as objects, an attitude toward people incompatible with viewing them as rational human beings endowed with dignity. We view them as objects with which to satisfy our lust, making it difficult to take their goals and ends seriously. Even if two sexual partners are considerate of each other's sexual goals, chances are they do so only instrumentally, to satisfy their own sexual ends. Thus, it is difficult to see how two people who desire to have sex with each other can fulfill the requirements of the Formula for Humanity. The bottom line for Kant is that sexuality, sexual desire, and sexual activity are incompatible with viewing and treating others and ourselves as beings with dignity and rationality.

Evaluating Kant's Views

The evaluation of Kant's views targets three parts: Kant's views on the nature of sex, on the moral implications of the nature of sex, and on human dignity.

(1) Kant is right about a crucial aspect of sexual desire: it targets the human being as a body and some of its body parts. As Soble puts it, "The other's body, his or her lips, thighs, buttocks, and toes, are desired as the arousing parts they are, distinct from the person" (2008b, 260). In this respect, Kant is correct that sexual desire and activity are different – perhaps even unique – from the usual ways with which we view others and interact with them. However, Kant draws wrong conclusions from these observations.

(2) Kant thinks that a sexual view of human beings is incompatible with viewing them as endowed with dignity. The problem here, I think, is that whereas this is true in some instances of sexual desire and activity, it is not always true. Kant's mistake lies in thinking that this view *necessarily* character-izes sexual desire. Let us elaborate.

When sexually desiring another human being, there are at least three ways with which we can view him or her, and Kant short-changes the third. First, we can view the person literally as an object, as something lacking in subjectiv-ity, autonomy, desires. This view plays no part in Kant's argument and for good reason: it is rare that people adopt this view toward each other. The second view plays the major role in Kant's argument: viewing another person as a living human being but also as a mere tool for our sexual pleasure – as an object in the sense of lacking dignity, humanity, or rationality. The third view is close to the second but different: we view the person who is the target of sexual desire as an object of desire but also as a living human being with the ability to make decisions and set goals for himself, as one with rational capac-ities and dignity. It is this view that often compels people to back off in the face of sexual rejection and to behave themselves during sexual activity.

Kant may or may not have had this view in mind when discussing sexuality, but what he says makes me suspect that even if he did, he thought little of it. For instance, when he claims that in order to satisfy his sexual desire a man "may even plunge the loved one into the depths of misery" (1963, 163), he seems to have in mind a case in which a man, faced with initial rejection by the woman with whom he wants to satisfy his lust, is willing to go to great lengths to attain his purposes, even if this means making the woman miserable (e.g., by hounding her, pressuring her, and generally making her life difficult). But either this is an extreme example of what Kant has in mind – in which case it would not tell us much about the *nature* of sexual desire – or it is a common example, in which case it seems to not adequately characterize sexual desire for the simple reason that many people would not go to such great lengths to satisfy their desires. We are all familiar with examples of deep sexual longing for another but such that no action is taken to satisfy this longing for various reasons, many of which are moral.

Kant was right about the dangers of sexual desire and activity. For example, and borrowing a list of such dangers from Soble (who wrote it as a way of understanding what Kant might have had in mind), (1) we often wear certain clothes and use make-up to make ourselves look more sexually attractive than we actually are, thus engaging in deception; (2) we often lie to others about ourselves to make a good impression; (3) when in the grip of sexual desire, we are at the mercy of the person whom we desire, thus making idiots of ourselves by being willing to do and say things that demean us; (4) when in the grip of sexual desire, we are also willing to undertake risks and to do stupid things in order to satisfy it; we tell ourselves lies so as to make these undertakings much more rational and normal than they actually are; finally, (5), sexual desire is often experienced as coercive and as having power over us that we cannot shake off (Soble 2008b, 260–261). To say the least, none of these things (except perhaps for (1) which seems morally innocent) are uplifting when it comes to human beings endowed with Kantian dignity.

However, these actions and attitudes do not *necessarily* characterize sexual desire and activity. We may think someone highly desirable, but not engage in foolish, immoral, and demeaning things to have sex with that person. Moreover, one main reason why we sometimes do not act in these demeaning ways is that we view them as beneath or not befitting us, that we view ourselves as dignified, or that we exercise our rational powers in the proper ways, seeing things in their right perspective ("Yes, Brenda is gorgeous, but I'm not going to play silly games to get her, and I'm certainly not going to risk my marriage and career to do so"; or, "Yes, Brenda is gorgeous, but I respect her too much to lie to her just to get her into bed"). So although sexual desire can have subversive effects on our rationality and dignity, it need not. If Kant thought that sexual desire *necessarily* has these effects, he was wrong.

We must also ask another question: whether other desires, passions, and emotions can subvert our rationality and dignity. They surely can. Virtually every emotion and desire can be experienced as coercive, and can make us do stupid, immoral, or undignified things. Yet Kant never thought that these emotions are inherently incompatible with dignity. He warned against their dangers and in some cases (e.g., envy and malice) argued that we should get rid of them. But only in the case of sexual desire did he think that it is inherently incompatible with dignity. No doubt this is because he thought that it made us view other people as objects, but I have argued that it is one thing to claim that sexual desire and activity make us focus on human beings as human beings, not their abilities or services, and another to infer that this focus is necessarily incompatible with viewing them as creatures with dignity. As Allen Wood puts the point,

> Plainly there is far more to sex than the desire to use another's body in a degrading manner for your selfish pleasure. Even the elements in sexual desire closest to this are combined, at least in healthy people, with other elements of human emotion that radically transform their meaning. So it appears pointlessly reductive to dwell on only one aberrant aspect of sexual desire, as Kant does.
>
> (Wood 2008, 227)

What repercussions does this have for the Formula of Humanity? If sexual desire and activity are not inherently morally problematic, sexual activity is not always morally impermissible. Whether it is depends on the specific type of activity. Generally speaking, if two people (Mark and Mandy) consent to have sex with one another, this seems to satisfy the part of the Formula that enjoins us to not treat others as mere tools. As to the part that enjoins us to adopt another person's ends, there is no reason to believe that people cannot desire to please someone else sexually for the person's own sake, even in casual sex. Moreover, in cases in which someone pleases another in order to attain his own pleasure, this is not always wrong. Cases in which partners view each other as beings with dignity *are* cases in which consent is necessary *and* sufficient for permissible sex. Mark and Mandy can have sex with each other on condition that they both freely consent in an informed way, and can attend to each other's sexual desires, though they need not do so for their sake, much like I may attend to the plumber's desire to be paid without doing so for its own sake. Indeed, according to Wood's interpretation of Kant, this conclusion finds support from Kant himself in some of his other writings, where Kant claims that sexuality in human beings is drastically different from that of animals, making it difficult to separate sexuality from humanity, rationality, and dignity (Wood 2008, 231–237). Wood concludes, strongly, "Even casual sexual encounters for mutual pleasure might be regarded as permissible, as long as they involve no kind of coercion or exploitation or the betrayal or degradation of anyone. All these matters … should be left to autonomous individuals to decide freely for themselves" (2008, 237). He warns, however, that such interactions may be problematic in societies with power inequalities or in the grip of traditional sexual views, an issue I address in the following section.

Sexual encounters, then, can be compatible with Kantian dignity. But we should never lose sight of the fact that sexual desire is very powerful, more powerful perhaps than other desires. It might not *necessarily* have the effects that Kant worries it has, but the question remains to what extent people are generally able to successfully pull off a proper relationship between their rationality and their sexual desires. To put the point using the language of Aristotelian virtue: it is possible to be temperate regarding sexual desire, but the question remains as to how easy this is to accomplish if sexual desire is a powerful force. Just because sexual desire and dignity can coexist, it does not follow that they frequently do. There is a reason why Kant worries about their relationship so much. I return to this point in what follows.

(3) In his Formula of Humanity, Kant does not say – as I have sometimes sloppily put it – that we should treat ourselves and others as ends, not only as tools, but that we should treat the *humanity* in us as an end, not only as a tool. Humanity (or rational nature) to Kant is a property of rational creatures; it is our ability to set ends (goals), good and bad ones, and act on them, including the capacity to act on moral ends (Hill 1980). To Kant, humanity is not something we can bring into existence or increase in amount; it already exists and is not something, like pleasure, that can be added to or subtracted from. Moreover, it is an objective end in that it is true for and binding on everyone;

whether we should act for its sake does not depend on our individual goals or desires to do so. Most important, humanity to Kant is the most fundamental value and on which his Categorical Imperative is based. Because it is the most fundamental value, it commands our *respect*. The question is: What arguments can be offered for this fundamental value?

In his most famous and popular book on moral philosophy, *Grounding for the Metaphysics of Morals*, Kant gives a brief and dense argument as to why humanity as an end in itself exists, culminating in his statement of the Formula of Humanity:

> [R]ational nature exists as an end in itself. In this way man necessarily thinks of his own existence; thus far is it a subjective principle of human actions. But in this way also does every other rational being think of his existence on the same rational ground that holds also for me; hence it is at the same time an objective principle, from which, as a supreme practical ground, all laws of the will must be able to be derived. The practical imperative will therefore be the following: Act in such a way that you treat humanity, whether in your own person or in the person of another, always at the same time as an end and never simply as a means.
>
> (Kant 1981, 4: 429)

In what follows, I rely on Allen Wood's interpretation of this argument (2008, 90–93).

In claiming that each human being "necessarily" thinks of his own existence as an end in itself, Kant seems to say that given the way we act and the things we say, we can infer that individuals think of their existence as an end in itself (we don't necessarily *consciously* think this; many people don't think of themselves in these terms). When people set goals for themselves, they also set the means or the ways to attain them. Moreover, in setting these goals, people think of them as good (or else why set them?). If I set the goal of writing a book on sex and love, I also set the necessary and sufficient means to achieve the goal. To me, the goal is good, even if sometimes I don't feel like taking the needed steps to attain it (a common feature of human action and thought).

However, in order to be able to set ends or goals for ourselves, we need to believe that we have the capacity – the rational capacity – to set them. Stated differently, in believing that we are capable of determining which goals to set, and thinking of these goals as good, we must believe that our capacity to set them is also good. It follows, however, that I must also regard myself as the entity, the being, that has and is able to act on these rational capacities. Moreover, because I have this capacity, I must also respect (or esteem) it; it is *the* ability on my part to set goals and directions for my life and the means to achieve these goals. Note that because the object of this respect is the *capacity* to set ends, its being an object of respect does not vary from one individual to another; it does not depend, say, on whether the goals are intelligent, stupid, moral, or immoral.

Because every rational entity, not just me, represents its existence as an end in itself (an object of respect), the requirement that I treat humanity in myself not only as a means but also as an end is an objective principle, applying to me and every other rational creature. Moreover, because every rational being has this capacity, I ought to treat it with respect as it exists in me and in every rational being. Hence, we reach the Formula of Humanity. Humanity – the capacity to set ends and act on them – is an object of respect in every rational creature, even if some act foolishly, immorally, or by demeaning themselves. The idea that humanity exists in every rational creature, regardless of his or her actual behavior, makes rational creatures autonomous beings in that they have the ability to act autonomously, even if they don't always do so. Humanity itself has dignity simply in virtue of being the capacity to set ends and the means to act on them (Kant 1981, 4: 436–439). The fact that dignity is grounded in or attached to a capacity that all rational beings have, regardless of how they actually act, makes Kantian dignity metaphysical or transcendental; it is unlike the kind of dignity that we attach to human beings depending on how they actually act and lead their lives.

Although it has serious limitations, as Wood acknowledges (2008, 93), this argument is powerful. Having the capacity to set ends is a valuable capacity in general, one that is good to have in particular, and one that commands our respect. So let us suppose that it shows we have Kantian dignity. The question is whether it is compatible with being a primarily sexual being. First, let us clarify some expressions.

"Being a primarily sexual being" means someone whose life revolves around sex and sexual activity. In addition, it can roughly mean either someone who does this professionally (e.g., pornography actor, prostitute, stripper), or someone who has sex for the sake of his or her own pleasure (and, to some extent, the sexual pleasures of those with whom he or she has sex). We should also be clear on the notion of "life." Sexual activity is tied – at least in contemporary times (I doubt it has ever been very different) – to youth and beauty (standards of beauty are, however, culture- and age-sensitive). It is rare for someone to be able to have virtually most of his or her life revolve around sex, whether professionally or non-professionally. We all age and get wrinkles; when this happens the sexual demand for us decreases (cosmetics, clever and flashy clothing, and plastic surgery can only go so far). So "someone whose life revolves around sex and sexual activity" really means, "someone who devotes a period of his life – anywhere from youth to late middle age – to sex and sexual activity." This applies to professionals as much as it does to non-professionals.

Is such a life compatible with Kantian dignity? Unless we debase the sexual – consider it lowly, not part of who human beings are – it is. First, if one's life plan, including being primarily sexual, is freely set and acted upon, and its content does not defeat the very ability we have to set ends and act on them, it seems compatible with human dignity. After all, part of what it is to have dignity is to set goals and act on them.

This is *generally* true, but we have to be careful. In discussing Aristotle's virtue ethics, I noted that the sexually temperate person is someone who is able to bring his sexual desires within the control of his reason. Something similar must be true in Kantian ethics if we are to claim that a primarily sexual life is compatible with dignity. Here's what I mean. Because sexual desires can be experienced as coercive, can make us say and do foolish things, and can make us undertake serious and unnecessary risks, they can make us demean ourselves. Moreover, because of its power, sexual desire can make us exploit others, telling them lies and deceiving them just to get them to have sex with us (more astounding is that sometimes the liars believe their own lies when in the grip of sexual desire: "*Of course* I love your mind, too! You're as smart as you are beautiful"; the next day they may think, "God! What was I thinking?").

There are two connected points to make. The first is that if sexual activity is to be compatible with dignity, we must act in ways that do not demean ourselves and our sexual partners. Second, we need to ensure that our sexual desires do not set the agenda of our lives, which needs to be set by our rational powers. Consider three people, Chad, Gilad, and Iyyad. Gilad says to himself, "I am pretty much incapable of doing anything. All I have is a pretty face and a nice body, including a nice endowment 'down there.' So I will enter the porn business and make some decent money. Besides, I really like to have lots of sex." Iyyad says to himself, "I know I can be a brilliant biologist, and although I like biology, I do like to have sex, and I have the 'equipment' for it. So I'm going to enter the porn business, make a decent buck, enjoy myself, and then maybe later I can pursue a biology career." Chad wants to be a scientist but he is just over-sexed: he goes out all the time to pick up women, watches porn all the time, masturbates a few times a day, and whenever he sits down to study, he just cannot keep his mind off sex. The main difference between Gilad and Iyyad, on the one hand, and Chad, on the other, is that the sex lives of Gilad and Iyyad are ruled by their reason. It is their free and informed decision to devote a part of their lives to sex, and it is their reason that sets their life plans. Not so with Chad. He is not an unthinking person, blindly following his sexual lust wherever it leads him, but he does use his reason to satisfy his sexual desires. Sexual desire is powerful enough to make reason its own tool; it can subvert our rational capacity to set ends. People who are primarily sexual beings can then be divided into two types: those whose reason rules their lives and those whose reason is a tool for their desires. The first such types lead sexual lives compatible with dignity. The second do not, because their sexuality subverts their end-setting capacities. Note that professional sex workers (porn actors, prostitutes) are less likely to endanger their dignity by undermining their reason because their sex lives are driven by job-related considerations, not sexual desires.

Sexuality, however, is sometimes more than compatible with dignity; it can remind us of people's humanity. In 2006, the artist Barbara DeGenevieve created a series of photographs and videos (collectively entitled *The Panhandler Project*) that depict five African-American male homeless people in the nude.[5]

Homeless people and other groups of people who are severely disenfranchised (the extremely fat, the severely disabled) are often relegated to the margins of society. DeGenevieve's photographs of naked panhandlers are a powerful reminder of their humanity. One in particular – *Michael Stewart* – shows Michael with a fully erect penis, which reminds us of Michael's humanity because it symbolizes that he, too, like us, has desires. He, too, is human, and thus the bearer of Kantian dignity. In this sense, images of naked people and of people having sex are powerful, especially when it comes to those whom society forgets are human. Sexuality here is not only compatible with dignity; it is also an emblem of it.

There is one more point to be made about dignity. The notion of dignity has different meanings. One meaning is that of social or economic dignity, a type of dignity people have or are thought to have in virtue of their social or economic status. In most societies today, being a sex worker is considered demeaning. It can produce shame and embarrassment in most sex workers and is one reason why they often operate clandestinely. Now although in this sense sex workers do not have dignity or are not dignified, this is not the Kantian sense. Whether someone threatens his or her dignity or demeans him- or herself in the Kantian sense does not depend on social views and ideologies, but on whether what one does and thinks is objectively demeaning.

Social meanings figure prominently in discussions of pornography. Moreover, sexual interactions that are otherwise compatible with dignity might be problematic in societies with power inequalities or in the grip of traditional sexual views. Both these issues arise in pornography. To this we now turn.

Women and Pornography

Pornography may be read ("adult" books) or viewed (photographs, films). Not all pornography involves depictions of sexual activity between two or more people; it contains images of individually naked men or women. Some depict solitary masturbation, some men or women displaying their sexual parts to the viewer (some images are also cartoons, whether animated or still). There's heterosexual, gay male, and lesbian pornography (made by lesbians for lesbians, or lesbian scenes in heterosexual pornography). Some pornography crosses these boundaries, including bisexual and trans-sexual pornography. Some targets specific sexual tastes, be they straight, gay, bisexual, or intersexual, including S/M, foot fetishism, interracial sex, "water sports," and others. Pornography is a vast and varied terrain; to discuss it intelligently, we must be cognizant of this fact and familiar with its diversity.

While pornography is consumed in one form or another in all parts of the world, its defenders are few. Its critics, however, are numerous, with some bizarre, albeit unintentional, alliances forming, most notably between social and religious conservatives and anti-porn feminists. But while conservatives often accuse it of ruining the traditional family, leading to sexual addiction, and higher incidences of crime and rape, anti-porn feminists claim to not be anti-sex as such, and criticize pornography on grounds having to do with women's issues, implicated in abuse against women, higher incidents of rape, and even creating a climate in which women are silenced and their civil rights eroded. A common element to feminist and conservative criticisms is consequentialism: pornography has bad effects, for society in general or women in particular.

The criticism I address is different. It is a non-consequentialist, Kantian one: pornography degrades people, especially women. I explain and examine this criticism by referring to three of its advocates' views: Judith Hill, Helen Longino, and Ann Garry.

Judith Hill claims that to be degraded is to be lowered in moral status: "to give this account a Kantian interpretation: degradation involves being treated as though one were a means only, as though one were not an end in herself, as though one were something less than a person" (1991, 64). But she insists that, "it is a necessary condition of degradation that a person *be perceived* – by herself or by others – as being treated as something less than a person. Degradation occurs with the creation of a public impression that a person is being treated as something less than a person" (1991, 64). So if someone treats me as his personal mule by forcing me to carry on all fours his furniture, but such that no one, including myself, considers this degradation, I am, according to Hill, not degraded (an un-Kantian and implausible claim).

Unlike some other anti-porn feminists, Hill does not wish to condemn the entire pornography industry, but only what she calls "victim pornography," which is:

> the graphic depiction of situations in which women are degraded by sexual activity, *viz.*, (a) situations in which a woman is treated by a man (or by another woman) as a means of obtaining sexual pleasure, while he shows no consideration for her pleasure or desires or well-being, and (b) situations in which a woman is not only subjected to such treatment, but suggests it to the man in the first place. Furthermore, Victim Pornography presents such activity as entertaining. There is no suggestion that women should not be treated as less than persons; and often there's no hint that a woman might dislike such treatment.
>
> (Hill 1991, 67–68)

For a type of pornography to count as victim pornography, according to Hill, two conditions must be satisfied. First, women must be depicted as degraded, in the way explained above. Second, there must be no suggestion that the depiction is wrong (I take it that Hill equates "being entertaining" with "no suggestion that women should not be treated as less than persons," even though they need not be: a documentary can be entertaining as it cautions its viewers against treating women as less than persons; but I think by "entertaining" Hill means "aimed at sexual arousal").[6]

Hill's first condition is unclear. Although being sexually degraded by a man means that the woman's desires are not taken into account even if the woman requests such selfish sex, Hill also writes, "I am ... concerned here with ... Victim Pornography: depictions of women being bound, beaten, raped, mutilated, and, as often as not, begging for more" (1991, 68). But this characterization is different from the first. Binding, beating, raping, and mutilating are a far cry from sexual activity in which the man does not heed the woman's pleasure. One doesn't even include another: very few women, if any, would desire to be mutilated, beaten, and raped (though being bound and gagged might be more common). Thus not-selfish sex can include a man's catering to the desires of a woman precisely by binding her. Conversely, a man can have sex with a woman by thrusting his penis into her vagina, anus, or mouth despite the woman's lack of desire for this activity, selfish sex on the man's part that does not involve binding, mutilating, raping, and beating (that the woman does not desire the sex does not amount to rape: willing to do something undesired is not the same as being forced to).

Helen Longino's view is similar to Hill's. She defines "pornography" as "verbal or pictorial explicit representations of sexual behavior that, in the words of the Commission on Obscenity and Pornography, have as a distinguishing characteristic 'the degrading and demeaning portrayal of the role and status of the human female ... as a mere sexual object to be exploited and manipulated sexually'" (1991, 85). In pornography women are represented as slavish to men; they have no sexual desires of their own, except for those catering to the men's. If women's sexual pleasure is represented, it is represented only as a means to the pleasure of men, not as its own end (1991, 85–86). Moreover, according to Longino, sexually explicit material could depict what pornography depicts without being morally problematic, because such material could explore the consequences of such degrading treatment to its victim (e.g., documentaries). Pornography, however, *endorses* or recommends such degrading treatment of women, not just represents it (1991, 86–87). The endorsement claim is very similar, if not identical, to Hill's claim that pornography provides no suggestion that women should not be treated as less than equals. This lack of suggestion might precisely be what it means for a work of sexually explicit degradation to endorse or shun its representative content (Longino states something similar; 1991, 86).

Degrading treatment to Longino "includes physical harm or abuse, and physical or psychological coercion. In addition, behavior which ignores or devalues the real interests, desires and experiences of one or more participants in any way is degrading. Finally, that a person has chosen or consented to be harmed, abused, or subjected to coercion does not alter the degrading character of such behavior" (1991, 87). Again, this is similar to Hill's selfish sex and being beaten, mutilated, and so on.

Like Hill but unlike Longino, Ann Garry does not think that *all* pornography is degrading: "some pornographic films convey the message that all women really want to be raped, that their resisting struggle is not to be believed. By portraying women in this manner, the content of the movie degrades women" (1984, 314). It is not clear in this account what the degradation is (despite Garry's claim that "to degrade someone ... is to lower her/his rank or status in humanity"; note 5, p. 323) or how widespread it is in pornography. If a scene depicts a woman resisting rape but then agreeing to it and implying that her resistance has been a sham, we can see the degradation in that we are perhaps told that what women say they want (not to be raped) is not really what they want (to be raped). Thus, we are to sidestep a woman's explicit decisions in favor of what we think are her real desires. Doing so is a form of paternalism, in which we treat women, at best, as children, not taking seriously their explicit pronouncements or decisions. But it is unclear whether Garry believes degradation is confined to such rape scenes or whether it includes other scenes.

What is clear is her answer to the question about who is being degraded. Garry is not concerned only with the women on screen, but with *all* women. Her argument takes three steps. First, degrading pornography sends a message about all women: "If one sees these women as symbolic representatives of all women, then all women fall from grace with these women" (1984, 316). Why all women should suffer this fate is the second step in the argument. If we assume, along with traditional, sexist views about women and sex, that sex is dirty and that only bad women have sex and lots of it, then we will associate the women in pornography with bad women. If we see them as symbolic of all women, then we will associate all women with badness. But why should an enlightened feminist such as Garry accept traditional assumptions about sex and women? The answer – the third step in the argument – is that because "in our culture we connect sex with harm that men do to women, and because we think of the female role in sex as that of a harmed object, we can see that to treat a woman as a sex object is automatically to treat her as less than fully human" (1984, 318). To put the argument concisely: some works of pornography send the message that women want to be raped, humiliated, and exist just to sexually please men. Because sex is connected with "harm," pornography fosters a climate of disrespecting women by thinking of them as bad women. We will continue to look at women as fallen because we associate them with dirtiness, sex, and badness. This outlook is degrading to women. Thus, pornography degrades all women.

Hill's view is not far from Garry's:

> The pornography industry regularly publishes material which, speaking conservatively, tends to contribute to the perpetuation of derogatory beliefs about womankind ... we might say that it offers a perspective on the actual nature of womankind. The perspective offered by Victim Pornography is that, in general, women are narcissistic, masochistic, and not fully persons in the moral sense.
>
> (Hill 1991, 69)

Pornography does this by trafficking in sexually arousing stereotypes and shunning "character development"; victim pornography "defames" women, and in so doing it degrades them (1991, 70–71). Longino does not claim that in lying about the nature of women pornography degrades all women, but she comes close. She accuses pornography of supporting sexism, thus reinforcing "the oppression and exploitation of women" (1991, 89). If pornography plays a role in maintaining the oppression and exploitation of women, it must play a role in their degradation, since it is hard to see how an entire sex can be oppressed and exploited without also being degraded. Indeed, to exploit someone is to use her, among other things, as a mere means to one's goals, a definition of degradation that Hill uses.

Let us ask a crucial question: Other than scenes in which women are depicted as being raped, beaten, mutilated, "snuffed," which we can agree are degrading to women, which scenes depict degradation and which do not? Set aside sadomasochistic scenes in which women play the role of masochists and scenes of bondage and domination in which women are bound and domi-nated, because one can argue (I suppose) that women in bondage, who are whipped and stepped upon, are degraded. Focus instead on what goes on in mainstream pornography, and imagine a series of depictions: a man putting his penis into a woman's vagina, then into her mouth, then into her anus, then into her mouth; or a scene in which three women have sex with one guy, alter-nately having intercourse with him and in different orifices; or a scene in which two or more men have sex with one woman: as one puts his penis into her mouth, another puts his penis into her vagina, while a third puts his penis into her anus. In all these scenes, the men and the woman take up different posi-tions: sometimes the woman is on her back, sometimes on her stomach, and so on. Which, if any, of these scenes is degrading to the woman and why?

A social or religious conservative might claim that they are all degrading: no good, decent woman should have any of this sex, and if she does, she is degraded. But this is not an explanation feminists should accept, because they usually reject a view of women that considers them suitable only for certain kinds of sex (reproductive or "decent"). Or, we might argue, with Soble (1996, 215–216), that some sexual postures are degrading in themselves: performing oral sex on someone means putting your head in that person's crotch, a not-so-uplifting place, especially while on one's knees, a position we associate with subjugation or humiliation. But, again, that's not what anti-porn feminists have in mind, because they claim to not be anti-sex as such and because such positions demean both men and women, whereas their arguments are about *women*, not about men. So what could they have in mind?

One of two things (or both): either it is part of the meaning of the image or scene that the woman is degraded or this is how the scene will invariably be understood by the viewer. Hill, Longino, and Garry have both in mind. Let us start with the first possibility.

Consider Longino's claim that in pornography women are represented as slavish to men; they have no sexual desires of their own, except those that cater to the men's. If represented at all, women's sexual pleasure is represented only as a means to the pleasure of men, not as an end of its own (1991, 85–86).

Thus if a sexual scene represents a woman as not slavish to a man, as having sexual desires of her own, and ("or"?) which represents her sexual pleasure for its own sake, the scene would not depict the woman as degraded. But there are two problems. First, in the majority of heterosexual porn, the woman's pleasure and sexual desires *are* depicted. Women scream, demanding more and more intercourse. Men perform oral sex on women while they moan with pleasure. These seem to be scenes that do not depict women as slavish to men and that emphasize their pleasure. Indeed, this is how pornography succeeds in getting men to masturbate to orgasm, because it enables male viewers (or some of them) to derive sexual pleasure from witnessing another man, or imagining themselves to be that man, pleasuring a woman.[7] So the first problem is that much heterosexual pornography does provide a prominent place for the woman's pleasure and sexual desires.

The second problem is that it is hard to see how pornography could represent men and women as being morally equal in *ways other than* by showing them both frolicking in all sorts of sexual positions and enjoying everything they do. No doubt, some women (and men) would not want to have the kind of sex we see in films and magazines. But pornography presents a world of sexual fantasy, and fantasy, by its nature, shuns those details that ruin it. When animating and scripting *Snow White*, we are not going to describe all the insect bites that Ms. White gets from constantly venturing into the forest, unless we want to ruin the effect. Similarly, a pornography movie is not going to depict the characters arguing about Kant's views or even, more relevantly, arguing about which sexual positions they prefer to make it more realistic or to have it send the message that both the men and the women have equal voices. In the world of pornography, the sex is always good and there is always agreement on what positions to adopt. That's the whole point about pornography: it's about sex, sex, and nothing but sex. As Soble puts it,

> most heterosexual, orgiastic pornography, in creating a fantasy of an ideal sexual world, rarely shows men and women quibbling about positions and acts. In pornographic fantasy, because the parties spontaneously want the same thing, women's preferences and desires are automatically given their due.
>
> (Soble 1996, 232)

Thus, it is difficult to see how pornography can depict a woman's pleasure as an end on its own and not merely as a means for the man's pleasure. The depiction of a woman moaning with pleasure as a man performs cunnilingus on her doesn't tell us one way or another whether her pleasure is for its own sake or for the man's. Depending on our views, we can read it either way. I don't mean only that an anti-porn feminist would see it as slavish while a non-anti-porn feminist would see it as a woman asserting her right to pleasure. Even your average Joe six-pack can see it in different ways. If he "gets off" on seeing women being sexually demanding, he would view the scene as one in which the man attends to the woman's pleasure for its own sake. If he "gets off" on seeing women provide pleasure to men, he would see her pleasure as catering to the man's. If he is looking at the picture of a naked woman in *Playboy*, he may, if he is cocky, think she is displaying herself for his own pleasure, telling him that she is his to do with as he pleases; but if he has low self-esteem, he may think that she is telling him that that's all he's getting, that her beauty is out of his league because *she* would never have sex with *him*.

What complicates things is that even if a woman is depicted as demanding sexual intercourse or as desiring to perform oral sex on the man, some anti-porn feminists think this turns women into sluts, and so degraded (see Hill above). But then if scenes depicting women as demanding sexual pleasure and activity show that they are being degraded, we are in a pickle indeed because we are at a loss to *really* see how pornography can show women as equal to men – damned if you do, damned if you don't. The only option is to abandon the genre of pornography as it is done today and to place the sexual scenes amidst a longer narrative depicting women and men in respectful and respected positions. But this probably won't work, either because the audience would still see the women as "playthings or unusual prostitutes" (Garry 1984, 323), or because it would be boring: the male viewers will fast-forward or skip to the sex scenes, neglecting the respect-me-and-I-respect-you filler material. (Will it work in a society in which men's sexual desires are radically transformed? I mention this issue at the end.)

However, there are pornography scenes or whole movies that, even though not violent in the usual sense, make plausible the feminist idea that the women are degraded. They fall into two types. The first, somewhat common in hetero-sexual pornography, are scenes in which a man has anal intercourse with a woman, then the woman fellates him, then he has more anal sex with her, then she fellates him again, and so on. Because of associations between fecal matter and disgust, having to fellate a penis after it has been in someone's anus is a degrading action, even if we believe that the actors have "cleaned themselves on the inside" and even if the woman moans with pleasure and demands more. This is rare in mainstream gay pornography; when it happens, the man's penis is sheathed with a condom, which is removed for the fellatio (much hetero-sexual pornography still contains intercourse without the use of condoms). And although some might not find such fellatio degrading (say, people who are into sexual acts involving feces), the action does have this social meaning, a meaning, I should add, due not to social bias, but to human beings' general tendency to be repulsed by fecal matter.

The second type is when it is obvious that the female actor is having such a difficult time with the scene that she can barely bring herself to feign pleasure. There are quite a few heterosexual pornography movies (and a few gay ones) in which it is obvious that the female actors are just not into it. In this respect, such scenes are degrading to the actors. It is a type of degradation commonly attributed to people who have to do a lowly job and have a miserable time doing it. (I am tempted to claim, though I am not yet quite sure why, that scenes in mainstream pornography – not as common as they used to be – depicting beautiful and physically fit women having sex with men who are not physically desirable, and shown to be enjoying it and asking for more, are degrading to the women; the idea that most women, in real life, would not sexually give such men the time of day has something to do with it but cannot be the whole story.)

So within non-violent heterosexual pornography, some depictions do mean that the woman is degraded, even if she is screaming with pleasure, and some depictions do not. Much will depend on the details of the scenes and the movie. In other words, distinguishing between violent and non-violent pornography, or S/M and non-S/M pornography, might be irrelevant. Across all these distinctions, whether women are degraded depends on what the films portray.

We have not yet addressed Longino's claim that pornography *endorses* the degradation, or Hill's similar view that it "offers a perspective on the actual nature of womankind … that, in general, women are narcissistic, masochistic, and not fully persons in the moral sense" (1991, 69). This is crucial because someone might claim that even though individual scenes or photographs might not, in themselves, tell us one way or another whether the depicted women are degraded, taking in the larger context of the movie or magazine or other relevant aspects might make the degradation more evident.

The notion of endorsement is crucial in the philosophy of art. The theory of ethicism, for example, claims that a work of art's artistic goodness or badness depends partly on its ethical or moral content. "Moral content" means the point of view or perspective that the work adopts toward its representations, not the representations themselves. For example, Leni Riefenstahl's notorious film *Triumph of the Will* not only shows or describes Hitler's words and actions during the 1934 Nuremberg rally for the Nazi party, but also seems to view it with favor, as if saying, "What I show you is a good thing." John Milton's poem *Paradise Lost* depicts Satan as powerful and seductive. However, the poem does not endorse this view, but that Satan is especially evil, and we should always be on our guard because he is very seductive. In short, works of art sometimes adopt points of view that either approve or disapprove of their own content.

With pornography, especially the narrative sort – movies as opposed to still images – something similar might be true. While a movie might contain individual scenes that emphasize the sexual desires and pleasures of their female characters, the movie as a whole might adopt the point of view that such pleasures are subservient to the men's, that women always need men and their penises to sexually "get off," or that women are nymphomaniacs, masochists, or sluts. So it is not enough that a movie should represent women as treated with respect or their pleasures as central; it must also endorse this view if the depicted respect is not sarcastic, facetious, or for sexual titillation. Note that being fantasy does not preclude pornography from having a point of view regarding its content. Fairy tales, science fiction, and romance novels are all fantasy, but they can still endorse, reject, or have a point of view about their content.

The question, however, is what it means for pornography to have a point of view regarding its content. A. W. Eaton claims that "pornography endorses by representing women enjoying, benefiting from, and deserving acts that are objectifying, degrading, or even physically injurious and rendering these things libidinally appealing on a visceral level" (2007, 682). The issue is not just depicting men and women enjoying degrading and submissive sexual activity, but also that pornography *eroticizes* this behavior, making it sexually arousing to the audience (Eaton 2007, 682). Eaton claims this of inegalitarian pornography, pornography that eroticizes gender inequity (2007, 676).[8] In short, the way pornography endorses women's degradation is by (1) representing degrading sexual acts as pleasurable to the characters; (2) suggesting that such treatment is "acceptable and even merited"; and (3) eroticizing this behavior (2007, 682).

Pornography certainly represents sexual acts as pleasurable and acceptable to the characters (I'm not sure what "merited" means). It also eroticizes them in order to arouse the viewer (its point, after all). The issue is whether it represents *degradation and*, in doing all three, it *endorses* anything. Eaton does not defend or elaborate the view that certain types of pornography are degrading. But she needs to, because, as we have seen, the bulk of heterosexual pornography depicts men and women involved in all sorts of sexual acts that do not belong in special categories (e.g., masochism, sadism, bondage, urination, defecation) that one might think are degrading because of their very nature (e.g., defecating on someone's chest). Unless we regard sex itself or particular sexual positions and acts as themselves degrading, we have no reason to believe that the bulk of pornography is degrading. Whether it is depends on the individual viewer and his moral background.

This means that if pornography endorses anything, it is the unsurprising idea that "sex is pleasurable and we want the viewer to find it pleasurable, too." The typical heterosexual pornography film seems to endorse the following bland view (if, that is, it endorses any view at all): "The men and women depicted in this film enjoy having sex; sex is good, and we want you, the viewer, to enjoy it, too." This is a bland message, one that is almost universal in content, covering most heterosexual pornography (of course, some individual films, magazines, or internet sites might adopt more specific points of view toward their content). This is to be expected for two reasons.

First, unlike works of art, which seem to have no general purpose, pornography is a mass or popular medium whose function is to sexually arouse the viewer. Because individual works of art have some insight to offer, some message to convey, some point of view to share, it is important for critics to consider what each says, what worldview it has. One reason why works of art are valuable is that we understand them to offer new, unique, or special insights. We thus take seriously not only the works' representations, but also the points of view they adopt toward their content. Our interest, for example, in Rawi Hage's novel *De Niro's Game* is not simply its depiction of the Lebanese civil war, but also what the novel itself has to say about it. If we did not take an interest in the latter, we would not understand that many of the protagonist's actions, though brutal, are also sad, tragic, and the vehicle through which the novel indicts the war.

Not so with pornography. Its individual works have no special insights about their characters or actions, because providing insight is not the purpose of pornography and that is not why it is viewed. Pornography is just sex. This is why pornography's message or point of view, if it has one at all, is bland. Unless much of its content does indeed involve meanings about degradation, humiliation, and objectification – meanings that are "objective" to the film and not attributed to it by the viewer – there is not much substance in pornography's view of the world (if we can call it that).

The second reason why pornography's vacuous message is not surprising is that were pornography to have any more detailed, nuanced, or specific points of view toward its content, these viewpoints would have to be either obvious or hidden. If hidden, we need to interpret the films, magazines, or internet sites to figure them out. But pornography is not the type of medium that allows for deep interpretation. There's not much more to it than what meets the eye. If its point of view were obvious, pornography would shoot itself in the foot, because one of the main ways in which pornography works is by presenting its viewers with images and scenes in a way that leaves room for the audience's imagination to roam. Any obvious meanings or points of view about its content would direct the viewer in how to see the images and understand them, limiting his imagination and thus making it sexually less enjoyable. As Soble says, "the variety of [pornographic] images provides raw material from which individual consumers select their own point of focus or construct their own story" (1996, 233). For works of art that have a perspective on the world to succeed, the artist has to structure her work in a way to *guide* the viewer or reader to discern this point of view, a phenomenon not usually found in pornography. Guiding the viewer, even in subtle ways, to whatever point of view a work of pornography has (if it has any) undermines the viewer's ability to construct his own stories and fantasies. That is why camera work in pornography does not usually try to frame the scenes in particular ways, giving the viewer instead as many shots and angles as possible so that he can pick and choose the scenes that arouse him the most. Titles of pornography movies or photo essays in magazines – unlike those of artworks – also do not help; they can be witty, playing on titles of mainstream films or daily expressions (*Splendor in the Ass* plays on the film *Splendor in the Grass*; *Cumcoction* plays on the expression "concoction"), bland, or "absurd," and usually "ignored by the consumer or replaced mentally by his own caption" (Soble 1996, 219).

For these reasons, pornography does not endorse any deep meanings about the world or women. It does not offer the perspective that women are sluts or masochists. It just tells us that their characters like to have sex and that sex is good. That's about it.

I have mentioned already that the meaning that pornographic images have may depend on the viewer. Is this true? If the pornographic material itself does not guide the viewer into any meanings because it itself has none, does *anything* guide the viewer? Here, a powerful feminist contention comes into play: given that we all live in sexist societies, individuals' thoughts and desires are at least partly constructed by sexist views of women. Such views may play a crucial role in how viewers, especially men, look at and "understand" pornography; they help shape what meanings viewers attribute to pornographic imagery. To investigate this view, we should first consider Soble's "polysemicity" thesis.

Consider the following claims which Soble makes:

> [T]he meaning of the content of the various pornographies cannot be read straight off from the surface content of the images; the images are more complex … especially when we take into account what the images mean to those who consume them for purposes of sexual arousal and sexual pleasure. The intrusion of the wishes, fears, and values of the viewer into the viewing experience … colors or changes the surface content in idiosyncratic ways.
>
> (Soble 2002, 19–20)

Or:

> we cannot tell from the photograph [of a close-up of a woman's buttocks spread to show her anus and vagina] alone what the model meant to expose or what the photographer meant to capture or, especially, what the viewer focuses on when looking at the image.
>
> (Soble 2002, 28)

Or:

> Because pornographic images are polysemic, we can see the woman eagerly performing fellatio as submissively subservient solely to the man's desire, or as a sluttish glutton for her own pleasure, or as a woman enjoying sex without making excuses. Each of us should be able to imagine interpreting such a photograph in all three, if not more, ways. The fact that someone sees the active, promiscuous woman … predominantly as a slut tells us more about the viewer's values and sexual presuppositions … than about the photograph or the sexual act itself.
>
> (Soble 2002, 98)

Finally,

> Feminist and conservative critics of pornography read pornographic images literally, as if engaged in a fundamentalist reading of Genesis.

They lack the imagination or sympathy to read the images in multiple and flexible ways, to try to see them from the various perspectives of their viewers.

(Soble 2002, 196)

Soble's polysemicity thesis is that pornographic images do not have intrinsic, surface meanings; any meanings they have are attributed to them by the viewers, who decide on which aspect of an image or series of images to focus and how to read those images. Depending on the viewer's individual and social history, he will see the image in a particular way. As stated, however, Soble's claim is exaggerated. Clearly, pornographic images have some basic meanings that frame further, more sophisticated meanings attributed by the viewers. They limit any further attributed meanings. For example, an image of a woman fellating a man basically means what I just wrote. If one asks, "What is this an image of?" the answer is that it is an image of a woman fellating a man. This answer, which supplies the basic meaning of the image, places restrictions on further attributed meanings, ruling out many, such as that the woman is cooking the man breakfast or – more to home – that she is having sexual intercourse with him.

Moreover, some images of pornography may be described as degrading to the characters or actors, as discussed above. Beyond basic meanings and such degrading scenes, however, the viewer is free to construct further meanings. Here, two types of meaning emerge. The first involves the viewer in constructing a story surrounding the image (if no such story is supplied by the context of the image – the movie or the theme of a special issue of the magazine, say) or filling in the details of any story that is supplied. For example, the viewer could see the woman as the man's secretary, wife, student, or teacher. The viewer probably does this because such fantasies sexually arouse him (of course, the viewer need not construct any such stories, focusing solely on the sexual imagery). The second type of meaning is one where the viewer attributes particular views to the characters on the screen, views that might derive from more basic ones about the nature of men or women. For example, the viewer may not only see the woman fellating the man as his secretary, but he may also think of her as a "typical secretary, giving blow jobs to rise to the top." This may derive from views which he has about women in general, working women in particular, or just secretaries. But they might not; he might add this detail to the story because it sexually arouses him. The meanings which a viewer attributes to an image are a function of his social and individual history.

It is plausible that the cultural meanings that circulate in society have some influence on how a viewer looks at pornography. That women, in Western cultures at least, are pervasively portrayed as primarily objects of physical beauty might encourage some viewers to see women in pornography as basically fit only for sexual pleasure (their own or the men's). To the extent that we still live with the social division of women into "whores" and "Madonnas," some male viewers may see the women in pornography as "whores." The issue is the *extent* to which this happens (Soble does not deny that misogynist meanings can shape or supply the content of the meanings that some viewers attribute to pornographic images; 2002, 27–28).

Short of extensive empirical studies of individual societies, the answer to the above question is not forthcoming. Some anti-porn feminists often write as if the answer is clear. When Garry, for example, states, "If one sees these women as symbolic representatives of all women, then all women fall from grace with these women" (1984, 316), it is unclear why anyone should see the women in pornography as representative of all women. What male viewer, except for the deranged, would make such an association? It is even unclear why male viewers in general would see the women in pornography as representative of even a *class* or *type* of woman. Short of figuring out the extent to which sexism in society pervades the minds of men and determines their thoughts, we can confidently only say that some men might do so and some might not.

In making claims about how pornography affects men's attitudes, we must take into account not only how sexism influences men's understanding of pornography, but also three additional factors. First, men, like women, cover the spectrum as far as intelligence and ability for independent thinking are concerned. Much as we should not view women as sluts or fit only for bearing and raising children, we should not view men as incapable of disagreeing with or going against the views and ideology of sexism. Second, men, like women, cover the spectrum as far as individual agency is concerned. We should not view men as incapable of having sexual desires, fantasies, and so on that are not sexist in content. Even if many men's sexual desires are tainted with sexism, how they act on these desires is a different issue. Sexist desires tell against men's characters, but they need not tell against their behavior. Third, we need to factor in all the major influences on how men (and women) come to have the views they have. Men's overall views about women do not have pornography as their only source, but have multiple sources, some good (not sexist) and some bad (sexist). A crucial factor here, however, is how men retain the information: Do they passively accept it? Do some reject it while others accept it? The picture, then, is complex, and how we accurately *test* for men's attitudes about women is even more so.

Someone might object that because the heterosexual pornography industry today caters to heterosexual men, it is plausible that it would depict its female characters in slavish ways in order to make pornography arousing to these men, so anti-porn feminist objections are quite reasonable. However, this reasoning assumes what it sets out to show. While it is true that the pornography industry caters to men, we need to *assume* that men (or most of them) are indeed sexually aroused only by depictions of women as slavish to be convinced that the imagery of pornography intentionally depicts women in a sexist light – the very conclusion that the objection aims to reach. Moreover, pornographers need not make such assumptions. They need only assume that men are aroused by scenes depicting sexual activity, and make as varied images and films as possible in as diverse ways as possible to cater to men's sexual imaginations, leaving it up to the men to read the images in ways that arouse them. So the objection fails.

Who exactly is degraded in pornography? To claim that *all* women are degraded by pornography is implausible. First, why a viewer would think that the characters or models in pornography represent or symbolize all women is a mystery. Second, even if some viewers think this, it is does not mean that the women are in fact degraded. Thinking that they are says more about the viewer than about the women.

This means that we are left with two options. Pornography is degrading either to the (1) women models or to the (2) characters the models play. From a Kantian perspective, and if being a primarily sexual being is compatible with dignity, being a pornography model need not be incompatible with dignity so long as the model does this of her own free choice in a way that does not undermine her reason.

However, even if a pornography model chooses her line of work, she can still be degraded on the job. She may be asked to enact scenes that are physically demanding and socially distasteful, such as sexually taking on two men or more. But many lines of work are physically demanding, such as being an athlete, a maid, a parent, and a painter's model. The physical hardship is not at issue, rather the sexual positions and actions, viewed by many as degrading because "no decent woman would do such unspeakable things." But we should not buy into the sexist view that women who are in the sex industry are undignified. Just because a prudish society with deeply entrenched religious views about sex believes this does not make it true. So as long as the model is not forced into anything on the job, and so long as we set aside sexual actions that *might* be inherently degrading (e.g., whipping, bondage), there seems to be nothing undignified about sex work.

Are the characters, such as a French maid, a prostitute, and a nymphomaniac college sophomore, degraded? Even though fictional characters don't exist, we do attribute properties to them: Homer Simpson is stupid, Romeo is in love with Juliet, and The Bride (in Tarantino's *Kill Bill*) is vengeful. So we can attribute lack of dignity to fictional characters, and pornography is no exception. But unless the character played is itself one that is truly undignified, such as that of a slave or a rape victim, there is no reason to attribute to it lack of dignity simply because they are horny and sexually wild. Doing so again smacks of buying into the very social attitudes that sex is dignified only if done in a certain way, with a particular person, and so on.

This is actually what is troubling about some of the views of anti-porn feminists. When Ann Garry, for example, complains that pornography treats women as sex objects, she bypasses what goes on in pornography and relies on the fact that *society* connects sex with harm. What matters to her is how *viewers* of pornography see women: "I may not think that sex is dirty and that I would be a harmed object, I may not know what your view is, but what bothers me is that this is the view embodied in our language and culture" (1984, 318).

If this view is indeed embodied in our language and culture to the extent that Garry thinks it is, she is right to think it is bothersome. But this does not mean we should indict pornography. Being a janitor is viewed by society as lowly – a bothersome issue – but it is a mistake to infer that being a janitor is itself degrading. No wonder, then, that Soble levels the following accusation at anti-porn feminists:

> Feminist critics of pornography, in purporting to find degradation in its images, buy into – uncritically accept – traditional social standards of what is sexually degrading to the human person. How they read pornography is determined by dominant social meanings, which they in effect endorse (as do the conservative critics of pornography) instead of condemning or transcending.
>
> (Soble 2002, 195)

This point is worth emphasizing: If someone claims to not be against sexual activity in itself, why does he or she find the image of a woman simultaneously fellating two or three men degrading? If women, like men, are sexual beings, why are they, but not the men, described as degraded when they enjoy, or are depicted as enjoying, sex with abandon? It is because we subscribe to social views about women to the effect that good, proper women do not and should not have this kind of sex. This is a bad view, denying women their sexual agency and sexual equality with men.

If sex as such is not degrading or demeaning, we are more justified in criticizing archaic or unfounded social meanings instead of pornography (and prostitution). Sex work in general may be one of the few bastions of resistance to hegemonic, traditional, conservative views. And while the current sexual inequality between men and women, along with poverty and other factors, strongly influences how pornography is *made*,[9] what pornography *depicts* may be one of the areas in which men and women are shown as equal sexual beings. Feminists and their allies should fight traditional views of sex, along with the social inequality of men and women, instead of what pornography depicts.

Summary and Conclusion

Sexual objectification may not be as morally severe as it is often claimed to be. Moreover, Kant was right to detect something especially suspicious about sex, leading him to worry about objectification. But Kant exaggerated, and, though we should not underestimate the power of the sexual drive, it can be controlled by reason, allowing for a primarily sexual life to be compatible with both social and Kantian dignity. In addition, the claim that most pornography is degrading to women is false and ultimately relies on false, social views of women that treat them as men's sexual unequals. One further issue worth thinking about is this: if sexist views shape some men's desires for women, would men have such dark desires in a non-sexist society? The answer "no" is tempting but simplistic. If some people are aroused only by viewing the object of their desires as abject, degraded, and attendant to their sexual whims, then even in a non-sexist society some men would view the women whom they find attractive as debased in order to attain a heightened, sexually pleasurable experience. In a non-sexist society, however, such a view would not depend on social, cultural meanings of men's and women's social roles, and it would be held by men and women, heterosexual and homosexual. Sexism debases the object of desire. But the object of desire can also be debased without sexism.

Notes

1 Bartky also claims that the "female breeder" would be sexually objectified because in this case a woman's sexual functions (breeding) are "separated out" from the rest of her personality by using the woman merely for breeding purposes.
2 Other philosophers agree:

> If sexual relations involve some sexual objectification, then it becomes neces-sary to distinguish situations in which sexual objectification is oppressive from the sorts of situations in which it is not. The identification of a person with her sexuality becomes oppressive, one might venture, when such an identification becomes habitually extended into every area of her experience.
>
> (Bartky 1990, 26)

3 Nussbaum believes that the third condition holds when it comes to Lady Chatterley, an English aristocratic woman, and Mellors, the gamekeeper at her estate. Chatterley's low status as a woman is offset by her aristocratic high status, while Mellors' low status as a gamekeeper is offset by his high status as a man, thus making them roughly equals (1999, n39). But, as Soble has convincingly argued, this "is glaringly insensi-tive to the psychological dynamics between two particular persons, which cannot be read straight off from their socioeconomic status and gender" (2002, 118).
4 Kant's solution to the problem of objectification is that sex is permissible only in legal marriage (1963, 166–167; 1966, 6: 277–279). This solution is riddled with difficulties that I do not discuss here. See Denis (1999) and Soble (2003, 2008b, 278–282).
5 The photographs, videos, and DeGenevieve's statement are at www.degenevieve.com.
6 According to Hill's definition, no homosexual victim pornography can exist, even though some homosexual pornography might satisfy both conditions; perhaps Hill should have called the pornography she's interested in "Heterosexual Victim Pornography."
7 "[I]f women in reality always accommodated to the sexual desires of men, if women were in fact full sexual slaves, then the depiction of their accommodation in pornog-raphy might not arouse" (Soble 1991, 97–98).
8 Eaton is unclear on how gender inequity is represented in pornography. She also doesn't elaborate the idea of endorsement. In fairness, her essay is really about how to make sense of the idea that pornography causes harm to the viewers and to other parties.
9 The website, kink.com, is interesting in this respect: it contains videos of non-mainstream pornography often associated with degradation (e.g., sex in public, sex involving bondage and submission), and interviews with the women actors to allay worries about coercion, forced sex, and other concerns.

Further Reading

Most of the cited references and the references below contain further discussions of objectification. See also Eames (1976), Haslanger (1993), Moscovici (1996), Quinn (2006a), and Wertheimer (1996). On Kant and sex, see Belliotti (1993), ch. 4, Brake (2005) and (2006), Cooke (1991), Herman (1993), Morgan (2003b), and O'Neill (1989). On the desires involved in S/M, see Benjamin (1983), Califia (1988) and (1994, Part III), Grimshaw (1997), Quinn (2006b), and Weinberg (1995). On women and pornography, see, in addition to "Further Reading" at the end of Chapter 6 (this volume), Assiter and Avedon (1993), Copp and Wendell (1983), Kershnar (2007), Kimmel (1990), Langton (1993), Rubin (1993), Russell (1993), Segal and McIntosh (1993), Strossen (1995), and Zillman and Bryant (1989). For more on MacKinnon's views, see her (1993) and (1997), and MacKinnon and Dworkin (1997). For an elaborate defense of the views of MacKinnon and Dworkin, see Mason-Grant (2004). On ethicism, see Carroll (1996) and Gaut (1998). On endorsement in pornography and in art, see Brown (2002).

8 Sexual Perversion and Fantasy

Sexual Perversion

The conceptual and evaluative issues in sexual perversion are thorny. Before we start, some stage-setting is needed.

The expressions "good sex," "better sex," "bad sex," and "worse sex" are ambiguous. They refer to evaluative or normative aspects of sexual activity, but it is unclear what sort of goodness or badness is at issue. Three possibilities exist. First, "good sex" refers to *moral* goodness: a good sexual act is morally permissible or morally commended, whereas a bad sexual act is morally prohibited or discouraged. A sexual act that is *better* than another is morally more commendable than the other, and a sexual act that is worse than another is more morally discouraged or more stringently morally prohibited.

Second, "good sex" refers to pleasurable, exciting, or satisfying sex (among others). In this sense, a good sexual act is pleasurable, exciting, satisfying, rewarding, and so on. A sexual act that is better than another is more pleasurable, exciting, satisfying, or rewarding than the other. A bad sexual act is unpleasant (even painful), unexciting (even boring), unsatisfying (even frustrating), or unrewarding (even impoverishing). A sexual act that is worse than another fares worse than the other on one or more of these four criteria.

Third, "good sex" means "natural or normal sex," whereas "bad sex" means "unnatural, abnormal, or perverted sex." A bad sexual act is a perverted or unnatural one. A sexual act that is worse than another is more perverted or more unnatural than the other. Does goodness in this sense admit of degrees? Can we speak of a "better sexual act" to mean "more natural or more normal than another"? It is unclear what this would mean, and the answer might depend on unpacking what the "natural" and "normal" themselves mean.[1]

Sexual acts can be good in one sense but not in another. Consider the following examples. First, if Joe and Jane engage in consensual, pleasurable, non-kinky sexual intercourse, their sexual act is good in all three senses.

Second, suppose that licking feet is perverted. If both Joe and Jane consensually do it and find it pleasurable, the act is morally good, pleasurable, but perverted.

Third, suppose that Joe and Jane decide to try licking each other's feet, but find the act boring and unexciting. If this activity is perverted, their act is morally good, but unpleasurable and perverted.

Fourth, suppose that Jane agrees to have sexual intercourse with Joe believing he is single, whereas he has lied to her to get her into bed. They enjoy the act. It is then pleasurable and "natural" but immoral.

Fifth, suppose that Joe lies to Jane about his marital status and they have sexual intercourse that both find unpleasant. Their sex act is immoral, not pleasurable, but natural.

Sixth, suppose that Joe (again) lies to Jane about his marital status. They have sex by licking each other's feet, but find it boring. Their sexual act is bad in all three senses.

Thus sexual acts can occupy different combinations on the goodness–badness grid.

When philosophers attempt to give an account or a definition of sexual perversion, they could be giving one of two accounts (which they might confuse): either an account that attempts to faithfully reflect how the expression "sexual perversion" is actually used and what it usually means (a descriptive account), or an account of how the expression *should* be used (a prescriptive account that tells us what sexual perversion *really* is, even if the account does not conform to the way people usually understand sexual perversion). Each approach has its pitfalls. The first must face the might of counter-examples; if the account is to be successful, it must include sexual perversions and only sexual perversions. If, for example, it somehow entails that French kissing is perverted or that sex with animals is not perverted, something has gone wrong with it. Compounding the difficulty for this approach is that not many people, let alone everyone, agree on a list of sexual perversions. Perhaps coprophilia, necrophilia, water sports, bestiality, erotic asphyxiation, and other bizarre sexual phenomena are readily seen as perversions, but other practices are not. For example, pedophilia and rape, while morally wrong, are not clearly perversions. Some sadomasochism and some fetishes (shoe fetishism, foot fetishism, leather and rubber fetishism) may sound weird, but some might not call them perversions. More controversial are homosexual sex, anal sex, even oral sex or any other sexual position not to the taste of some; there is certainly no widespread agreement about *these* being perversions.

The second approach faces a different difficulty. While it need not worry about counter-examples (although if it diverges too much from the way we usually understand perversion, this would be a weakness), it should worry about providing convincing reasons as to why we should understand sexual perversion along the lines it prescribes. As we will see, both of these accounts and their difficulties are found in the literature.

Thomas Nagel's essay "Sexual Perversion" (2008) is the oldest in the contemporary discussion of perversion and has been very influential, so we start with it.

Thomas Nagel's Account

To his credit, Nagel offers a *psychological* account of sexual perversion, not a biological one: "if there are perversions, they will be unnatural sexual *inclinations* rather than just unnatural practices adopted not from inclination but for other reasons. … A sexual perversion must reveal itself in conduct that expresses an unnatural *sexual* preference" (2008, 32). If Nagel is correct, sexual perversion is not a matter of biology or departing from God's will, but of individuals' sexual, psychological desires and preferences.

To illustrate his view, Nagel gives the example of Romeo and Juliet, two strangers sitting in a bar full of mirrors. They can observe each other without, at first, knowing that each is observing the other. Romeo first notices Juliet and is sexually aroused by her. In Nagel's terminology, Romeo *senses* Juliet. According to Nagel, "X senses Y whenever X regards Y with sexual desire" (2008, 36). Then Juliet senses Romeo. At this point, neither Romeo nor Juliet is aware that each is the object of sexual arousal of the other. Here's what happens next:

> Romeo then begins to notice in Juliet the subtle signs of sexual arousal: heavy-lidded stare, dilating pupils, faint flush, etc. This of course intensifies her bodily presence, and he not only notices but senses this as well. His arousal is nevertheless still solitary. But now, cleverly calculating the line of her stare without actually looking her in the eyes, he realizes that it is directed at him through the mirror on the opposite wall. That is, he notices, and moreover senses, Juliet sensing him. This is definitely a new development, for it gives him a sense of embodiment not only through his own reactions but through the eyes and reactions of another. … But there is a further step. Let us suppose that Juliet … now senses that he senses her. This puts Romeo in a position to notice, and be aroused by, her arousal at being sensed by him. He senses that she senses that he senses her. This is still another level of arousal, for he becomes conscious of his sexuality through his awareness of its effects on her and of her awareness that this effect is due to him. Once she takes the same step and senses that he senses her sensing him, it becomes difficult to state, let alone imagine, further iterations. … Physical contact and intercourse are natural extensions of this complicated visual exchange, and mutual touch can involve all the complexities of awareness present in the visual case, but with a far greater range of subtlety and acuteness.
>
> (Nagel 2008, 37)

Thus, Nagel's account of natural sexual desire involves a multi-leveled mutual awareness by two people of each other. Unlike hunger, which is localized and which leads the person to interact with food, sexual desire pervades a person's whole body and leads to an interaction with another person. The body's saturation with sexual desire produces "involuntary reactions and spontaneous impulses" in the people with whom the person sexually interacts. The multi-levels of awareness occur when x perceives those reactions in y, when y perceives x's original perception, when x perceives y's perception of x's original perception, and so on (2008, 38–39). Sexual desire is not simply x's perceiving y's sexual arousal. It also enhances x's desire by x's sensing that y is aroused by x.

Nagel emphasizes that his account is general. In particular cases sexual acts

> will be psychologically far more specific and detailed, in ways that depend not only on the employed physical techniques and anatomical details, but also on countless features of the participants' conceptions of themselves and of each other, which become embodied in the act.
>
> (2008, 37)

Moreover, natural or unperverted sex need not be bad sex in the sense that it is not pleasurable; and even if perverted sex is bad sex in some sense, "bad sex is generally better than none at all" (2008, 42). Although Nagel acknowledges that to label a sexual act or person "perverted" is to evaluate the act or the person in some sense, the evaluation need not be moral, since such evaluations are not always moral ones: "We make judgments about people's beauty or health or intelligence which are evaluative without being moral. Assessments of their sexuality may be similar in that respect" (2008, 42). Thus, Nagel accepts the three different meanings of "good (and bad) sex."

Some philosophers have complained that Nagel does not describe what happens between Romeo and Juliet *after* their interaction at the bar, thus accusing him of giving a sexless account of natural sex (Solomon 2002). But this accusation is unconvincing if it is meant, on its own, to indict Nagel's view of natural sex. The whole point of Nagel's account is to locate perversion and naturalness in the very structure of sexual *desire*, and this need not occur only during sexual interaction. Presumably, if Romeo and Juliet, having reached at the bar the high levels of arousal that Nagel describes, go on to have sex without the complexity of multi-levels of awareness, they would not be perverts, because the complexity has already been reflected in their desires prior to their sexual act.

Does Nagel's view succeed in capturing what is usually considered sexual perversions? Since this is an account of natural sex, we expect Nagel to tell us that any sexual desire that deviates from it is, to some extent, perverted. Surprisingly, he doesn't. He hems and haws: "Even if this is a correct model of the adult sexual capacity, it is not plausible to describe as perverted every deviation from it," declaring that there is no simple dichotomy between perverted and unperverted sex. He gives, as an example of a non-perverted act that deviates from his account, two people having heterosexual sexual intercourse while fantasizing about other people and not recognizing each other as the real sexual partner (2008, 39). However, Nagel is silent on which deviations from his account constitute perversions and which do not.

Nagel claims that his view accounts for some phenomena considered perversions: "narcissistic practices and intercourse with animals, infants, and inanimate objects seem to be stuck at some primitive version of the first stage of sexual feeling" (2008, 40). Inanimate objects do not allow x to be aware of the object's embodiment of desire, because they have none. Animals and children do allow x to be aware of their embodiment, but they do not reciprocate: they do not perceive that x's arousal is due to their own "sexual awareness" (2008, 40). Exhibitionists do not want sexual attention from others, and voyeurs do not require recognition by their sexual objects. In all these cases, no higher levels of mutual awareness are reached. Although he also considers sadism and masochism to be perversions (but his remarks are terribly unclear), Nagel clears homosexuality (2008, 40–41). If common usage tells us that exhibitionism, voyeurism, narcissistic sex (whatever that is), sex with animals, infants, and inanimate objects, and S/M are perversions, Nagel's account coincides with it, so it is on the right track.

Nagel's treatment of these types of sexual practices is correct in that many people do consider them perversions, but his account does not end up giving the right results; it classifies many non-perverted sexual practices as perversions, and many perversions as non-perversions. The example he gives of the heterosexual couple fantasizing about other people during sex is an example of what most would consider a non-perverted sexual act but one that, on Nagel's view, should be perverted. Consider also the following examples: sex between a prostitute and her client, solitary masturbation, routine, unexciting sexual intercourse or oral sex between a heterosexual (or homosexual) couple. None exhibits the type of multi-leveled awareness that Nagel's view of natural sex requires, so they should be examples of perversions, but we would be hard-pressed to agree, though they may be bad in some other sense (e.g., immoral or boring).

One might argue that in the case of solitary masturbation, there is some sort of multi-level awareness that occurs if the masturbator masturbates while fantasizing about a person with whom he interacts in the ways Nagel requires (Soble 2008a, 84). However, Nagel insists on the perception of the actual embodiment of desire in another person; his claim that desire is "not merely the perception of a pre-existing embodiment of the other, but ideally a contribution to his further embodiment which in turn enhances the original subject's sense of himself" (2008, 39) implies that the interaction has to be real, not imagined. This also, by the way, addresses the interesting example that Soble (2008a, 84–85) gives of a prostitute who fakes arousal just to get her client "off" quickly. The client may believe the prostitute's arousal to be true and reciprocate, while she, in turn, reciprocates with more fake arousals. The man is not aroused by her desires, but by his belief that she desires him. If Nagel insists on the reality of the exchange of levels of desires, then this case, too, is one of perversion.

Nagel may have a good reply. We should not be blinded by examples focusing on *acts* and asking whether they are perverted. We must remember that

Nagel's view centers on sexual *desires* or *preferences*, not on acts (despite some of his own misleading wording). The example of the heterosexual couple fantasizing about others during sex would not be perverted on Nagel's view because in and of itself it says nothing about the structure of the couple's desires. Presumably, not only are they capable of multi-leveled awareness, they would also enjoy it were it not for the intervention of time and the withering of their lust for each other. Similar points can be made about the other examples: the solitary masturbator prefers sex involving multi-leveled mutual awareness; it's just that no other person is available. The same goes for the other examples. The point is that as long as the sexual preferences of the people *would* follow the path of multi-leveled mutual awareness under "ideal" conditions, neither the *people* nor their *desires* are perverted. And if someone can enjoy sex *only* by masturbating or only with prostitutes, it may be plausible to describe him as perverted. And so on. All this implies that a young, male shepherd in the hills of Greece who occasionally has sexual intercourse with his sheep out of boredom or sexual frustration is not perverted (though the acts he engages in might be), because his sexual preference is not for sheep; the sheep are a substitute, and, after all, "bad sex is generally better than none at all."

Although this reply on Nagel's behalf goes some way in responding to the counter-examples given against his view in the philosophical literature, his view still fails. Consider a commonly agreed-on perverted sexual preference: coprophilia, the use of or focus on feces in a sexual act. Coprophilia takes many forms, most of which are simply fondling or smelling feces while masturbating. One other form is defecating on a partner's chest; another is smearing feces under the nose of one's partner; another is masturbating while watching or listening to one's partner or a stranger defecate (knowingly or unknowingly on the defecator's part); another is removing one's penis from the unclean anus of one's partner and inserting it into her vagina or into her or his mouth. These details are crucial for the truth of accounts of perversion, because many of these sexual acts involve the knowing participation of another person, indicating that multi-leveled mutual awareness can occur, despite, even because of, the use of feces.

Consider: even though Nagel claims that "the object of sexual attraction is a particular individual, who transcends the properties that make him attractive" (2008, 34), during sexual acts partners often focus on particular body parts without necessarily losing sight of the whole person as being the object of their sexual desire. If Kim and Mary sexually desire each other, then, according to Nagel, each one as a whole is the object of the other's sexual desire. Nonetheless, during their sexual act Kim and Mary are probably going to focus every now and then on each other's particular body parts – the clitoris, the breasts and nipples, the ears, the neck. On Nagel's view, none of this is an obstacle to Kim and Mary attaining higher and higher levels of mutual awareness and arousal.

But now the same may be said about Tim and Gary who very much sexually desire each other but who are also both coprophiles. Smearing Gary's feces under Gary's nose before kissing him heightens their arousal of each other, spiraling them into higher and higher levels of arousal. When Sam goes into a frenzy as he sucks on Alicia's big toe, sending Alicia herself into a frenzy as she senses Sam's heightened arousal, he is sucking Alicia's toe because it is the toe of that individual whom he finds sexually attractive. Foot fetishists, coprophiles, and other people who are into what are considered sexual perversions do not usually and simply have intercourse with "inanimate objects" as Nagel seems to think (2008, 40). Male foot fetishists usually do not just want to insert their penises between the toes of a dismembered foot or the foot of just any person, but incorporate them into a complex sexual act with someone whom they find sexually attractive. If Kim's focus on Mary's clitoris during their sex is not enough to make Kim a pervert, why then should Tim's focus on Gary's feces do so? If it has something to do with feces and Tim's sexual proclivity for it, then it has nothing to do, as such, with levels of mutual arousal. Coprophilia may very well be a perversion, but not for the reasons that Nagel offers.

In short, two people can instantiate Nagel's multi-levels of arousal during sexual activities that most people consider perverted. A preference for the use of feces during sex is considered perverted, but it is also compatible with multiple levels of arousal. This means that Nagel's account may be interesting, but it is not going to tell us how to explain why one preference is perverted but another is not.

However, wouldn't Nagel's view correctly explain why bestiality, necrophilia, and pedophilia are perversions given that animals, children, and human corpses cannot reciprocate sexual desire? Isn't Nagel's view useful here? Not quite. To see this, we need to make a brief detour.

Consider Newt. Newt is your average guy but with a rare sexual proclivity: he can enjoy sex (intercourse and oral sex) only if it does *not* involve Nagel's multiple levels of awareness. He prefers to be turned on by a good-looking woman, for her to be turned on by him, and to then have sex as if judgment day is tomorrow, without the higher levels of arousal. Is Newt sexually *perverted*? We might agree that he's weird, even feel sad for him because he's missing out on pleasurable, multi-layered sex, but we would not call him sexually perverted. To consider someone sexually perverted is to issue a strong negative evaluation, and Newt does not deserve the label. At minimum, the answer is not at all clear. This indicates that Nagel's account has not hit upon the correct explanation for why some sexual preferences are perverted and others are not.

Nagel's view is not commonsensical; it is not the first thing that comes to mind when we think of perverted sexual desires. If perversion is opposed to naturalness, perhaps the first thing that does come to mind is a biological account – an idea that Nagel explicitly rejects (2008, 32). So we should ask: *Why* does Nagel hit upon this view to explain perversion and naturalness? I can find no argument in his essay, except an appeal to our intuitions about the subject. Although appeal to intuitions can be useful in philosophical arguments, the intuitions to which we appeal should be common and somewhat obvious. The intuitions to which Nagel appeals are found in the core idea that often in sexual activity the arousal of one sexual partner increases the other's arousal. If someone finds his partner's sexual arousal non-arousing or – even worse – dampening of his own arousal, we might think that there is something wrong with this person. So much is true, I think, with the intuitions on which Nagel relies.

But, first, the core idea in these intuitions is not the same as Nagel's account. It is one thing to claim that often in sexual activity each partner's arousal increases the other's, but it is a different claim that often (or ideally) in sexual activity the partners attain higher and higher levels of arousal. The second implies *multiple* levels of arousal, and – more important – is not intuitive at all. So while Nagel might be appealing to an intuition that forms the *basis* of or *motivating idea* for his account, the account itself is not very intuitive (though it's not downright unintuitive). Second, even if the account itself is intuitive, missing is an argument as to why deviations from it constitute sexual *perversions*. It is not obvious why people who do not have the kind of sexual preference or desire found in Nagel's account are sexually *perverted*, as opposed to sexually something else, such as impoverished, untalented, unsophisticated, and unwholesome (if, that is, their sexual preference is defective at all).

One final, somewhat minor, point before we leave Nagel's view: why does Nagel insist on *two* people? Why not three, four, or more? Suppose that Trinity enjoys sex only with two or more people, finding sex with only one person boring. When we ask her why, she says, "Oh, because I get very much aroused seeing the other two being aroused by each other, and then seeing them being aroused by my arousal of them being aroused by each other, and so on – hey, somebody's gotta be a Nagelian!" Is Trinity a sexual pervert on Nagel's view? In an earlier version of his essay, Nagel claims that "multiple combinations" are bound to raise "problems of multiple simultaneous interpersonal perception that can arise in even a small-scale orgy," and that it might be "inevitable that some of the component relations should degenerate into mutual epidermal simulation by participants otherwise isolated from each other. There may also be a tendency toward voyeurism and exhibitionism" (1984, 277).

Nagel may be correct that even in small orgies there is a tendency for some to couple, for others to not participate and just enjoy the spectacle, and for others to participate just so that they can derive pleasure from having others watch them perform. But these remarks are not necessary claims about orgies or orgy participants. Nagel must figure out what to do with orgies; to assert that they make the interpersonal awareness found in his account complicated may say nothing about orgies and those who like them, but everything about Nagel's account, namely that it itself may be too complicated to adequately explain "natural" sexual desire. What would he have to say to Trinity, whose sexual preference is a Nagelianism-gone-wild? Why insist on only two people in a non-biological theory of natural sexual desire? I am not sure how to answer this question, but it is worth thinking about.

Sara Ruddick, Robert Solomon, and Alan Goldman's Accounts

I remarked in connection with the intuitiveness of Nagel's account that perhaps the first thing that comes to mind when thinking about perversion is a biological view, if perverted sex is opposed to natural sex, and if natural sex has to do with nature. According to Sara Ruddick, "among the variety of objects and aims of sexual desire, I can see no other ground for selecting some as natural, except that they are of the type that can lead to reproduction" (1984, 287). By "objects" Ruddick means "living persons of the opposite sex, and in particular their postpubertal genitals." By "aims" she means those acts that complete it, namely genital intercourse.

We must not misunderstand Ruddick's account. If a sterile heterosexual couple engage in sexual intercourse, they are *not* having perverted sex, because they still have natural sexual desires that *"could* lead to reproduction in normal physiological circumstances" (Ruddick 1984, 288). If a non-sterile heterosexual couple have intercourse but intend to not procreate (they use contraception, say), they, too, are *not* engaging in perverted sex, because "natural sexual desire is for heterosexual genital activity, not for reproduction" (1984, 288). The reason is that a natural sexual desire is of the *kind* that, under "normal physiological circumstances," could lead to reproduction, *regardless* of the intentions of the couple that have sex. So if a heterosexual couple have sexual intercourse intending to not reproduce, they are nonetheless engaging in sexual activity that could lead to reproduction, which is enough to make their preference for it natural. Note that, like Nagel, Ruddick thinks that perverted sex is not necessarily immoral or unpleasurable (1984, 291–292).

Does this view succeed? Not according to Primoratz: "not only the main traditional perversions, but also such common practices as masturbation, petting to orgasm, or oral sex, will have to be characterized as unnatural and perverted. While the former (with the likely exception of homosexuality) might be thought appropriate, the latter implication is surely quite unattractive" (1999, 54). But this might be rash, because much depends on what Ruddick would say about people who have sexual preferences for genital intercourse but who also engage, on some occasions, in other sexual activities. Suppose that Brian and Janet enjoy sexual intercourse but they also sometimes have oral sex without intercourse. Suppose that John masturbates quite a lot but generally prefers sexual intercourse with the woman of his choice. Are these *acts* perverted even though Brian, Janet, and John are not? Or are they perverted for the duration of these acts (which sounds silly)? Her account is unclear on this partly because Ruddick shuttles back and forth between discussing natural sexual acts and natural sexual desires. If her view were about sexual desires, not acts, Primoratz's conclusions would be hasty, because someone masturbating says nothing, on its own, about her sexual preferences.

Nonetheless, the account fails because it gives the wrong results. If we focus on acts, Primoratz is right that masturbation, oral sex, and petting to orgasm would be perverted acts – an implausible implication. If we focus on preferences, anyone who finds heterosexual intercourse distasteful and prefers instead, say, heterosexual oral sex or mutual masturbation would be sexually perverted – which also sounds implausible. Moreover, any heterosexual couple that incorporate fetish objects, urine, feces, and so on, into their sexual *intercourse* would be sexually natural, a result that would be odd (to be fair to Ruddick, she states – without elaboration – that connecting sexual desire with reproduction is necessary but not sufficient for perversion (1984, 288); so desire for sexual intercourse may not be enough to make the desire natural, especially in cases where, say, urine is involved). If we focus on acts, people, or both, any type of homosexual sex is perverted, yet another result that many would find unacceptable.

If it is "natural" to offer an account of perversion in terms of biology and reproduction, what has gone wrong with Ruddick's view (and, I suspect, any similar view)? Two related reasons can sink such accounts. First, the concept of perversion is opposed not only to that of the natural, but also to that of the normal, and the natural and the normal do not overlap. When people think of normal sex, they need not be thinking of reproductive sex. Thus, oral sex may not be reproductive, but it is normal sex. Second, the concept of perversion is itself muddled and people mean different things by it (its being opposed to both the natural and the normal is evidence of this). People who think of perversion might think of the immoral, the disgusting, the bizarre, and the biologically unnatural, among others. Thus, any account that attempts to justify perversion only in terms of one of these factors may be doomed to fail. Incidentally, the muddle about perversions may also indicate that no neat or singular account of the concept is forthcoming. But this remains to be seen.

Robert Solomon's view considers sex to be a form of language. Arguing against a liberal "platitude" that sex has pleasure as its goal,[2] Solomon claims that the goal of sexual activity is "interpersonal communication" and that it uses body language to communicate attitudes and feelings: "shyness, domination, fear, submissiveness and dependence, love or hatred or indifference, lack of confidence and embarrassment, shame, jealousy, possessiveness" (2002, 28). He adds that some attitudes and feelings, such as "tenderness and trust, domination and passivity," are *best* expressed sexually (2002, 28).

As body language, "sex admits of at least two forms of perversion: one deviance of form, the other deviance in content" (Solomon 2002, 29). The second – which Solomon calls "semantic deviations" – is more important than the first in that it indicates the more problematic perversions, "of which the most serious are those involving insincerity, the bodily equivalent of the lie" (2002, 29). To pretend, during sex, to be tender and affectionate, only to say, "See ya" after attaining orgasm is, to Solomon, a "potentially serious perversion." He adds, "However ... I would argue that perverse sex is not necessarily bad or immoral sex" (2002, 29).

This account of perversion leaves much to be desired. First, modeling sexual activity on language is problematic. As Janice Moulton points out, language functions not only to express and communicate information, but to also "produce a shared experience, a feeling of togetherness or unity. Duets, greetings, and many religious services use language with little information content to establish or reaffirm a relation among the participants" (2008, 51). If Solomon thinks that the function of language is only communicative, and if he models sexual activity on that, we rightly wonder what a couple who have been together for a while have to communicate to each other sexually (Moulton 2008, 51). Moreover, as Moulton also points out, Solomon is wrong to say that the attitudes he lists are best expressed sexually. Trust is better expressed by opening a joint savings account and domination is better expressed by a beating (2008, 50). There is also always simple English: "Screw you, you lowly maggot" is a great way to express domination.

Distinguishing between intentional and unintentional communication has important implications for Solomon's view. For example, shyness, fear, lack of confidence, embarrassment, and shame (all on Solomon's list) are not usually intentionally communicated during a sexual act. One does not usually have sex with another with the intention to communicate that one is shy or embarrassed; the shyness or embarrassment comes out during the sex act almost inadvertently, as an overflow of one's character or mood at the time. If Solomon has in mind – and his view is unclear on this – intentional communication, this will be another difficulty it faces.

If the content of sex is communicating feelings and attitudes, and if perversion is a deviation in this content, Solomon would be right that the main (if not only) deviation will have to be some sort of pretense, sexually communicating something not true: pretending to be submissive (or dominant) because your partner will be more sexually excited or will fall in love with you, and so on. This has a strange consequence: if a heterosexual couple are engaging in what most people consider non-perverted sex – intercourse in the missionary position – but the woman, say, fakes an orgasm (a common occurrence), then the act is, on Solomon's view, perverted.

Masturbation – another activity not considered perverted – also raises problems for Solomon's view. Solomon says it's like talking to yourself (2002, 27). But, as Soble states, "some of the most fruitful discussions one can have are precisely with oneself, not as a substitute for dialogue with another person, and not as compensation for lacking conversation with another person, but exactly to explore one's mind, to get one's thoughts straight" (2008a, 86). Masturbation is not a perversion, yet Solomon's view implies that it is.

Solomon also claims that sadism and masochism are perversions because the first is an "excessive expression of a particular content, namely the attitude of domination, perhaps mixed with hatred, fear, and other negative attitudes," whereas masochism is the "excessive expression of an attitude of victimization, shame, or inferiority" (2002, 28). Suppose that Solomon gets sadism and masochism right (which he doesn't, as most practicing sadists and masochists don't express hatred and victimization). If the expression of hatred and victimization is truthful, sadism and masochism should not count as perversions on his view. Only some instances of sadism and masochism – those that express false attitudes – should count. Perhaps Solomon would say that pretense is not the only perversion, and that communicating some attitudes, such as hatred and domination, *especially* truthfully, is perverted. But then we run into the problem of having to decide which attitudes and feelings, when sexually communicated, count as perversions and which don't. I see no convincing way of doing this.

Fetishism and bestiality are also perversions, according to Solomon, because "the first is the same as, for example, talking to someone else's shoes, and the second like discussing Spinoza with a moderately intelligent sheep" (2002, 28; if the sheep were really stupid or really intelligent, would this make a difference?). Setting aside whether Solomon accurately depicts sexual activity involving a fetish, communicating a sincere attitude of love for the sheep or a sincere attitude of awe for the (Prada?) shoe should not count as a perversion on Solomon's view. At worst, it should be a deviation in technique, as he says, not content, because then the person would be talking to something that is not the right kind of thing to be talked to (sheep, shoes). This would make bestiality not a serious perversion, a result that many would reject.

Once again, we cannot appropriately account for perversion by thinking of it as opposed to communication or sincere communication, because both cut across natural and perverted sex. Moreover, what Solomon considers to be serious perversions – pretense and lying during sex – have less, if anything, to do with perversion, and more with morality, since deception and lying are two hallmarks of the immoral. This is ironic, since Solomon thinks that perversion has no necessary connections to morality. But if what he considers to be perverted is lying and pretense during sex, there is a *necessary* connection between the perverted and the immoral, because it turns out on Solomon's view that cases of pretense and lying are cases of both perverted and immoral sex.

Another account of perversion is by Alan Goldman, who thinks that there are two ways to evaluate sex: morally and by the degree of pleasure it yields (2008, 70). This means that perversion is not an evaluative concept but a statistical one: it's "a deviation from a norm, but the norm in question is merely statistical" (2008, 69). However, not every sexual act that deviates from the statistical majority is perverted (such as a three-hour-long sexual act, to use his example); instead, and keeping in mind Goldman's definition of sexual desire as desire for "contact with another person's body and for the pleasure which such contact produces" (2008, 56), the "abnormality in question must relate to the *form of the desire* itself in order to constitute sexual perversion; for example, desire, not for contact with another, but for merely looking, for harming or being harmed, for contact with items of clothing" (2008, 69). Moreover, like Nagel and Ruddick, Goldman sees no necessary connections between perverted sex, on the one hand, and immoral or unpleasurable sex, on the other (2008, 70–71).

For a desire to be perverted, according to Goldman, it must satisfy *two* conditions. It must statistically be in the minority and must be a desire not for contact with another person's body. But these two conditions are in tension with each other. The first is statistical, which means that relativism holds sway in sexual perversion: if in culture C1 the majority of people sexually prefer S but in culture C2 sexual preference for S is in a minority, the preference would be a perversion in C2 but not in C1. This does not sit well with the second condition, which is universal and non-relative: sexual desires not for contact with another person's body are perverted, period, regardless of culture. To see the tension in a different way, suppose that one day we wake up to find that the overwhelming majority of people's sexual desires are voyeuristic and exhibitionistic. Would voyeurism and exhibitionism no longer be perversions because they are now statistically normal? Or would they still be perversions because they deviate from the "normal" type of sexual desire for contact with another body? It is not clear what Goldman's view would claim.

The tension between the two conditions is fatal to Goldman's view. He needs to either reconcile them or to drop one. It is unclear how they can be reconciled, because there are no obvious or necessary connections between a sexual desire's being not for contact with another person's body and its being in the statistical minority (indeed, it is not clear why Goldman insists on the statistical condition). If Goldman drops the abnormality-in-form condition, non-perverted sexual preferences statistically in the minority (such as a three-hour-long heterosexual intercourse) become perverted, which is an implausible result. If he drops the statistical-abnormality condition, many instances of solitary masturbation would be perverted, which is also an unacceptable result.

We are still left with a severe question for Goldman (raised in the discussion of sexual desire): given his definition of "sexual desire," is a sexual desire not for contact with another person's body an *abnormal sexual* desire or is it not a sexual desire *at all*? Until this issue is resolved, it is difficult to evaluate his view of sexual perversion.

Before concluding this section, consider incest, a sexual practice widely considered a perversion. On all the accounts we have considered, incest need not be a perversion. If a brother and sister have sex with multi-leveled arousal, they pass Nagel's test for natural sex. If they have intercourse, they pass Ruddick's test (unless her claim that intercourse is necessary but not sufficient for perversion plays a role). If they truthfully communicate to each other what Solomon would consider to be the right attitudes, they pass his test. Since they desire contact with each other's body and the pleasure this brings, they satisfy a crucial condition of Goldman's view for non-perverted sex. Only incestuous sex that has either no multi-leveled arousal, that is non-heterosexual, that is non-communicative or falsely communicative, or that is exhibitionist or voyeuristic fails one or more of these tests and so is perverted. This is not right.

The icing on the cake comes in the following example. Suppose that a brother and a sister are in love with each other. He is a coprophile and his sister likes to indulge him by smearing her feces under his nose, during and after which they have intercourse with rising levels of arousal. This is a sexual act that passes all the above four accounts as natural sex. Again, this is not right.

Roger Scruton's Account

To Roger Scruton, because human beings are social and political animals, "we must count among [the human person's] most important motives the interpersonal attitudes which express his recognition of his social nature ... these attitudes are elements of normal human nature, and to lack them is to be a deviant" (1986, 289). This idea is a central pillar in Scruton's account of perversion. It also implies another central pillar having to do with sexual desire. If being a normal human being means having these interpersonal attitudes, sexual desire must have a proper direction; it must involve the "marshalling and directing of animal urges toward an interpersonal aim, and an interpersonal fulfillment" (1986, 289). Because we have both an animal and a rational nature, these two aspects of our being must be united in sexual desire. If the unity is not attained, sexual desire is deviant or perverted (1986, 289). This view necessarily connects perversion with morality: what is perverted is also immoral. If sexual desire does not achieve this unity,

> we remove from the sphere of personal relations the major force which compels us to unite with others, to accept them and to compromise our lives on their account ... we remove what is deepest in our selves – our life – from our moral commerce, and set it apart, in a realm that is free from the sovereignty of a moral law, a realm of curious pleasure, in which the body is both sovereign and obscene.
>
> (Scruton 1986, 289)

There is another sense in which perversion is immoral. To Scruton, erotic (romantic) love is a virtue, and virtues are necessary for a well-lived life. It is then necessary that we acquire and maintain love in our lives. Sexual desire should be directed to love, which, to Scruton, is the ultimate goal of sexual desire (1986, 339). But it can be hindered in this process by "sexual habits which are vicious, precisely in neutralizing the capacity for love" (1986, 338). Perversion has many incarnations, all of which are vicious habits; it is "the habit of finding a sexual release that avoids or abolishes the *other*, obliterating his embodiment ... Perversion is narcissistic, often solipsistic, involving strategies of replacement which are intrinsically destructive of personal feeling. Perversion therefore prepares us for a life without personal fulfillment" (1986, 343).

To summarize: sexual perversion is any way of sexually relating to another person such that the person is not recognized as a person but is reduced to his animal components (that is why Scruton says that the person's body is viewed as obscene). Once this happens, it is not possible for sexual desire to come to its natural conclusion – love – with that person. Thus perversion is sufficient to impede erotic love (but not necessary because love can be impeded in other ways). If sexual perversion is sufficient to impede love, if love is a virtue, and if virtues are necessary for a flourishing life, sexual perversion is an impediment to this life. Because of reliance on notions such as virtue and flourishing,

Scruton's account of sex and perversion is Aristotelian in these respects. Let us see how it applies to some sexual preferences.

"The bestial person sees himself as he sees the object of desire: a 'mere' animal, acting in a realm where no moral idea troubles the senses, a realm from which the crippling awareness of the other's perspective has been removed" (1986, 292). There are two problems with bestiality that make it the paradigm of perversion to Scruton (1986, 292–293). First, it avoids the inter-personal element of sexual desire. Second, in seeing himself as a mere animal, the bestial person reduces himself to such a status; his body becomes a mere body, not the body of a person. Thus, bestiality makes the body obscene. The same reasoning applies to necrophilia (1986, 294–295) and to fetishism (the fetishist focuses on "the shoe 'for its own sake,' with just the same kind of indi-vidualizing intentionality, and perhaps even a parody of the tenderness, that normal people direct towards their lovers" (1986, 317), though fetishism is "the most harmless and amusing of all perversions" (1986, 315).

Unlike necrophilia, the pedophile does want another person but in a "diminished form" (1986, 295). The pedophile desires to "relive the child's experience of forbidden things, so as to recreate the excitement of uncovering them" (1986, 297). The problem is that adult–child sex cannot experience the full range of interpersonal interaction proper to sexual desire: "A child can be sexually excited by an adult, and can obtain sexual pleasure. But the result will not be desire for the adult, nor will it express knowledge of, and consent towards, the adult's own desire" (1986, 297–298).

One form of sadomasochism, according to Scruton, is a perversion: the sadist "fails to acknowledge" the other as a person (1986, 298). A non-perverted sadist inflicts pain, and the non-perverted masochist receives pain, but the pain is part of their "love-play, and is thereby transcended. … Both can take pleasure in the other's desire, without reducing the other to a mere instrument of desire. In this 'normal' course, the sado-masochistic impulse is incorporated into an interpersonal relation, and so transcended in the affirmation of mutual respect" (1986, 301–302). Sadism is perverted when it includes an element of slavery, the desire to reduce the object of desire to a mere "dummy": "The victim is erased from the sadist's intentionality and replaced by a fantasy of the sadist's own devising. The sadist, like the necrophiliac, the paedophile, and the rapist, can accept the other only on terms that are dictated by himself" (1986, 302). The perverted masochist matches the desire of the sadist by wanting to be reduced to a "dummy."

Scruton is undecided about whether homosexuality is a perversion. He is sympathetic to the idea that, like heterosexuality, only some forms of it are perverted (1986, 305). However, because he claims that it might be morally inferior to heterosexuality, homosexuality might be, as such, a perversion. It is inferior to heterosexuality because each gender has its own "mysterious quality … a sphere of actions, emotions and responses which is peculiar to it, and which defines it as a moral kind. … Precisely when [in the sexual act you are] most compelled to see yourself *as* a woman or *as* a man, you are confronted with the mystery of the other, who faces you from across an impassable moral divide" (1986, 306). So when one opens one's self to the other gender, one takes a risk – a risk that can be overcome by a vow to trust each other. This is sexual maturity: "Without the fundamental experience of the otherness of the sexual partner, an important component in erotic love is therefore put in jeopardy" (1986, 307). This risk and its overcoming are missing in homosexuality because the homosexual "knows intimately in himself the generality that he finds in the other," so sexual maturity may be hindered, which, in turn, implies that homosexuality is a perversion. Heterosexual "arousal is arousal by something through and through other than oneself, and other as *flesh*. In the heterosexual act ... I move out *from* my body *toward* the other, whose flesh is unknown to me; while in the homosexual act I remain locked within my body, narcissistically contemplating the other in an excitement that is the mirror of my own" (1986; 310; Scruton emphasizes that this is only a suggestion, not a proof). Locking into one's own body makes the body obscene, which brings homosexuality dangerously close to being a perversion (Scruton makes similar remarks about incest, calling it a perversion but "only in an attenuated sense"; 1986, 313–314).

Finally, Scruton distinguishes between two forms of masturbation. The first "relieves a period of sexual isolation, and is guided by a fantasy of copulation." The second *replaces* sexual human encounters; it is thus perverted because it is a "bending of the sexual impulse away from interpersonal union – a bending, however, that occurs under the pressure of fantasies of sexual union" (1986, 317). Although a "normal" masturbator uses sexual fantasy to masturbate, the fantasy is not a substitute for the real sexual act, to which the masturbator's "body tends." The perverted masturbator, however, does use fantasy as a substitute to avoid "all the dangers and difficulties that surround the sexual encounter" (1986, 319). Thus, this type of masturbation avoids interpersonal encounters, which is the hallmark of perversion. Scruton, however, also claims that "normal" masturbation is obscene in its focus "on the body and its curious pleasures." In an infamous passage, he claims that a woman who massages her clitoris during sexual intercourse "affronts her lover with the obscene display of her body, and, in perceiving her thus, the lover perceives his own irrelevance. She becomes disgusting to him, and his desire may be extinguished. The woman's desire is satisfied at the expense of her lover's, and no real union can be achieved between them" (1986, 319).

What are we to make of these views? Even if Scruton is wrong that erotic love is a virtue, as I argued in previous chapters, he may be right that it is the goal of sexual desire. So we need to address this claim.

Scruton's view that sexual desire is inherently "nuptial" indicates that he is giving a descriptive claim, describing the normal course of sexual desire. But as a descriptive claim it is not true. The reason is that sexual desire and love differ in crucial respects, so any view that links them in a descriptive way has its work cut out. First, as Goldman points out, we usually love very few individuals during a lifetime, whereas we can sexually desire thousands of people during a lifetime; "it may even be … that sexual desire in humans naturally seeks variety, while this is obviously false of love," and that's why, according to Goldman, monogamous sex almost always requires a sacrifice on the part of the lovers whereas monogamous love does not (2008, 60–61).

Second, sexual desire and love feel differently. Sexual desire often revolves around one's or another's flesh, and it seeks bodily pleasure. Love is more encompassing, revolving around being with another, having shared experiences with him or her, and being concerned for his or her welfare. Indeed, during sex even lovers often reach a point when the love is set aside, so to speak, and they surrender to lust. As Vannoy delicately puts it, "For who thinks of love when one surrenders himself fully to lust and willingly becomes a sex object of another?" (1980, 10). Biologically speaking, sexual desire is "based" in our sexual organs, connected with our ability to reproduce, whereas love as such seems divorced from this. Culturally speaking, members of all cultures experience sexual desire, and all cultures build different moral and social guidelines surrounding sex and sexual activity, whereas erotic love has not been a prominent phenomenon in all cultures and at all times. Because of these differences between them, any descriptive claim that love is the goal of sexual desire is likely false.

This means that Scruton might be offering the prescriptive claim that sexual desire *should* culminate in love. It would be a conservative and traditional view of sex and love: that sexual desire and activity should be exercised either in the context of love or to lead to love – a debatable and controversial claim.

This does not mean that the rest of Scruton's view is also implausible, because the idea that sexual desire is normally exhibited between two persons and exhibiting interpersonal attitudes is reasonable. Scruton's mistake lies in perhaps restricting sexual interpersonal interaction to love. If we set love aside – obviously, love is not the only type of interpersonal interaction – Scruton is right that we are social beings and, to that extent at least, expect our sexual desires to exhibit themselves in interpersonal ways. Unlike hunger, sexual desire is typically directed at other people. When it deviates from manifesting itself in interpersonal ways, we suspect that it is a deviation – a perversion, as Scruton claims. Thus, there is something right in Scruton's claims about bestiality, necrophilia, pedophilia, and certain types of sadomasochism, *when* they describe a person's standing desires and preferences (as opposed to describing encounters with animals, corpses, and children as ways of experimenting or to alleviate sexual frustration or boredom). For then the sexual desires and preferences are for animals, human corpses, or children, or human beings. (Even here we should be cautious in accepting what Scruton says about the psychology of the necrophile or pedophile; it does not seem to be a necessary explanation of, for example, pedophilia that the pedophile wishes to relive childhood experiences, though it might be true of some.)

If interpersonal attitudes were all that it takes to avoid perversion, then casual sex, promiscuity, one-night stands, sex with prostitutes, and so on would not be perverted on Scruton's view (though not to Scruton's liking), because they all involve interpersonal attitudes. But obscenity also plays a role in Scruton's account. If in such sexual encounters we see ourselves only as mere animals, as Scruton would claim, then they, too, would border on perversions. "Seeing ourselves as mere animals," however, is a problematic idea and its meaning is by no means clear. Taken literally, it is false, because few humans (if any) are able to achieve this. The very act of seeing ourselves as mere animals (or anything else) is a particularly human act (animals cannot see themselves as mere anything, because they don't have the complex mental repertoire that humans have). Even if we can pull off "seeing ourselves as mere animals," we must still continue to think about the actions we take, why we take them, and so on. Our actions, sexual and non-sexual, are intentional. We cannot see ourselves as mere animals in any literal sense.

The only other sense is that we see ourselves as sexual beings, focusing on our sexual pleasures and acts, and this is surely what happens in casual sex and similar sexual encounters. But, of course, we *are* sexual beings, and seeing ourselves as such on occasion does not mean that we shed our humanity, so it is not a deviation from our normal being or a perversion, even for people who prefer this kind of sexual activity to ones involving love. This is why Scruton's claim that all masturbation, including the "normal" type, is obscene sounds silly and reveals, perhaps, his own personal revulsion with the human body. His claim about the woman who plays with her clitoris during sex also reveals more his personal tastes in sex instead of a truth about sex, as some philosophers have noted (e.g., Baltzly 2003, 17). Perhaps Scruton is disgusted with such a sight, but many men (and women) find it sexually exciting, making the sexual bond between the man and the woman even stronger (Soble 2008a, 93).

Even with perverted masturbation we have to be careful. Scruton may be correct if we are talking about someone who can only, or mostly, enjoy sexual pleasure if it is through solitary masturbation, because then he would be someone whose very sexual preference avoids the type of interpersonal interaction found in sexual desire. But not all masturbation that replaces a human sexual encounter is done because the person prefers it to human encounters. Someone may rightly prefer masturbation to a human encounter because he knows that having this encounter would be a mistake (morally or otherwise). So Scruton is wrong to claim that only masturbation that relieves "sexual isolation" is normal; some types of replacement masturbation are also normal.

This leaves us with fetishism, homosexuality, and incest. Insofar as the fetishist incorporates his fetish in a sexual act, even one with an erotic lover, he escapes Scruton's worry about avoiding interpersonal interactions. Indeed, Scruton seems to mistakenly believe that a fetishist somehow focuses solely on the fetish at hand (e.g., a shoe), which leads him to claim that fetishism is a perversion. This may describe some fetishists, but not all; many enjoy their fetish because it is part of a sexual act with another person.

Scruton's argument regarding homosexuality is bewildering.[3] Although I suspect that Scruton exaggerates the gulf between the genders, I set this issue aside, focusing instead on why knowledge of the opposite gender must be sexual. Sexual knowledge of the opposite sex can best inform us about the biological sexual aspects of it and of what makes members of that sex sexually tick (assuming, somewhat plausibly, that we can make meaningful generalizations about the sexual properties of each gender through sexual activity with and knowledge of one individual). Beyond this, however, I see no important knowledge of the opposite sex to be gained through sexual interaction. Even sexual activity as part of a love relationship has little to tell us about all sorts of aspects of the opposite sex because the one individual with whom another is in love is hardly a representative of his or her gender, even in one single society, let alone a representative of his or her gender, period, across cultures. Moreover, there is no reason why sexual knowledge of the opposite sex has to be gained through sexual activity. A few good biology, sociology, and history books can adequately do the job. The only type of sexual knowledge attained through sexual activity and not through textbooks is *experiential* knowledge, knowledge gained through actual experience, whereby one knows, through first-hand encounters, what the opposite gender is sexually all about.

But here an interesting issue arises. It might be important for a heterosexual man or woman to have this experiential knowledge of the opposite sex, because, after all, as heterosexuals they have a sexual investment, so to speak, in the opposite sex. However, why a homosexual should have this experiential knowledge of the opposite sex when she has no sexual investment in it, and why the failure to take risks and acquire this knowledge is important is unclear, unless we are supposed to take risks just for the sheer hell of it. In other words, we can see the point in the failure of a heterosexual to take risks in experientially knowing the opposite sex, but I see no point in the failure of a homosexual to do so.

Moreover, as Martha Nussbaum points out (1999, 208), Scruton's argument has strange implications. Does it mean that people from different races, cultures, or age groups show a serious failure if they do not know each other sexually (and, more along Scruton's preferences, love each other)? Men and women intermingle with each other in all cultures, so they tend to know *something* about each other as genders. But there are lots of cultures and races that have no knowledge of each other, so it would seem that intercultural and inter-racial sexual knowledge is more imperative than gender knowledge. The point is not that there should be no intergenerational, interracial, or intercultural sexual activity – that would be absurd and bigoted – but that people who do not engage in such activities are not to be blamed along Scrutonian lines. So Scruton's argument against homosexuality as possibly obscene and so perverted is unconvincing.

Depending on how much we pack into the notion of "interpersonal attitudes" (does it include erotically loving another or merely having sex with another *person*, as opposed to a sheep or a shoe?), and depending on the role of obscenity and regarding one's body or another's as a "mere" body, Scruton's argument may or may not be successful. If, plausibly but un-Scrutonianly, we leave love out of this discussion, Scruton's idea that perversion is a deviation of sexual desire from interpersonal interaction is plausible, and accounts for bestiality, necrophilia, pedophilia, and some forms of fetishism and sadomasochism. But even with this charitable reading, Scruton's view still has one serious, counter-intuitive result, namely that incest is not a perversion (unless it involves adult–child sex).

Dirk Baltzly's Account

Dirk Baltzly offers an Aristotelian view of perversions, which he identifies with dispositions. He defines "sexual dispositions" as "standing dispositions to derive sexual gratification in the prospect of a kind of sexual behavior because one correctly believes that one would take pleasure in performing that kind of activity" (2003, 11). Although perversions are dispositions, they are not, as such, vices (which, according to Aristotle, are also dispositions), because vices preclude having a flourishing life, whereas not all perversions do this. If homosexuality and masturbation were perversions, they would be compatible with a flourishing life (2003, 13–14).

However, perversions are "inextricably" connected to vices in two ways. First, some sexual dispositions are perversions "because they are manifestations in the sphere of the sexual of other more far-reaching moral vices." Second, others are perversions because their possession is "psychologically incompatible with the possession of some recognized moral virtue" (2003, 18). So a sexual disposition is a perversion if, and only if, it *either* implies the existence of a vice *or* it implies the non-existence of a virtue. For example, if bestiality involves cruelty to animals, a zoophile would then have the vice of cruelty or, at least, lack the virtue of kindness. So zoophilia would be a perversion.

Note that if a sexual disposition implies the existence of a vice, it automatically implies the non-existence of the virtue opposed to that vice. But the reverse is not true, because one can lack a virtue but not have the opposed vice. Someone can be a zoophile but agonize over being cruel to animals; he would lack the virtue of kindness (if he had it he would not be cruel to animals in the first place), but he need not have the vice of cruelty. Why does he have sex with animals if he agonizes about hurting them? Because his sexual desires overpower his reason: he cannot help but hump that sheep even if he'll cause it pain.

Note also that on this analysis, a person is sexually perverted if he has the above types of sexual disposition, even if he never *acts* on them. But things are more complex. Recall Huck from Chapter 6, the voyeur who never entertains or even fantasizes about peeping at people. Voyeurism plays no role in his life, even though he has it as a disposition. Is he, according to Baltzly, sexually perverted? No, because Baltzly claims that for someone to have a sexual perversion that person must take sexual gratification in a kind of activity either by engaging in it or *at the prospect* (idea) of the activity (2003, 18). Huck neither engages in voyeurism nor obtains sexual gratification from its prospect (if anything, he is horrified by it).

Before we test Baltzly's view against counter-examples, a difficulty arises owing to something that Baltzly says:

> I want to make it perfectly clear that I do not think that all the things that have been thought traditionally to be perversions ... meet these conditions. Rather, I want to claim that this is the framework within which people argue about whether something really is a perversion. ... Our (relatively) enlightened attitudes toward many sexual practices have come about as a result of the realization that these practices do not actually meet these conditions, though they were once widely thought to meet them.
>
> (Baltzly 2003, 19)

Because Baltzly declares that he does not think all the traditional perversions meet his conditions, it is unclear which perversion would count as a proper counter-example to his conditions and which would not. For example (and to illustrate the rest of Baltzly's quotation), according to Baltzly male homosexuality was thought to be a perversion because it lacks male courage (virtue), and lesbianism was thought to be a perversion because it also lacks feminine virtue (2003, 19–23). However, now that we no longer buy into distinct male and female virtues, we have one less reason for thinking homosexuality perverted. So using Baltzly's framework, we can see how a sexual disposition traditionally thought to be a perversion does not meet his conditions. Furthermore, if to test Baltzly's conditions we offer homosexuality as a counter-example, the test fails because homosexuality is precisely one of those sexual dispositions traditionally thought to be a perversion no longer (widely, at least) thought to be one.

However, if it turns out that Baltzly's view implies that *most*, or even many, of what are usually considered perversions to be non-perversions, or that most (or even many) of what are usually not considered perversions to be perversions, the view fails. The view is safe as far as the second possibility is concerned, but it faces severe difficulties with the first. Let us see, first, what Baltzly says about some sexual dispositions that many would agree are perversions (his remarks are brief).

Baltzly claims that pedophiles probably do not "hold autonomy as an important value," and that necrophiles, especially when it comes to having sex with a corpse of someone who would not have consented to the act, "will be disinclined to respect the autonomy of others" (2003, 23–24). Bestiality, since it involves cruelty to animals, is incompatible with the virtue of kindness (2003, 24), while sadists, voyeurs, and exhibitionists may very well lack the virtue of sensitivity to the feelings and desires of others (2003, 24). Masochism, fetishism, and coprophilia are incompatible with self-regarding virtues – of the very people who have these sexual dispositions. First, Baltzly thinks that they involve bizarre and odd objects of desire (e.g., leather, shoes). Second, attaining these objects and the resulting sexual gratification often involves serious risks (think of stealing your neighbor's dirty underwear, or meeting another foot-fetishist, who is a total stranger, online, or trusting someone whom you barely know to administer the doses of pain you want so much, or lurking in a public bathroom stall smelling and listening to a person defecate). Both the oddness of the objects and the risks involved in attaining them indicate that the masochist, the fetishist, and the coprophile might have the wrong conception of what is worthy about life and how to go about securing these worthy things. That is, they shed doubt on their practical wisdom.

These remarks are brief. Baltzly advances them tentatively without endorsing them (2003, 25). Nonetheless, they can tell us whether such an approach to sexual perversion is promising. Alas, it has three problems. First, it implies that some *forms* of these perversions are not perversions at all. For example, a fetishist, a coprophile, and a masochist who act on their sexual desires safely (within a circle of trusted sexually like-minded people or with their spouses) not only avoid the charge of taking unnecessary risks, but might avoid these risks precisely because they believe that taking risks is unwise. As to oddness, this is a tricky concept in need of fleshing out, which Baltzly does not do: Is it statistical? If yes, why would it be relevant to issues of virtue and vice? Is it psychological oddness? If yes, what would this mean? And can we give it content while not assuming the concept of perversion, the very concept we want to explain by using that of oddness? Even if we set these questions aside, it is unclear what oddness as such has to do with being wise. Many people pursue and collect lots of odd objects, often going to great pains to acquire them. In sex, many people have odd desires, be they for objects, sexual positions, fantasies, and so on. They, too, often go to great pains to attain them. This means that we need to decide which odd objects are rightly connected to perversion, to inhibiting a flourishing life, and to taking silly risks, and which are not. I can see no clear and convincing way of doing this.

Baltzly may be right that the necrophile, the pedophile, the voyeur, the exhibitionist, and the sadist lack the virtue of respect for the autonomy of others, and that the zoophile lacks the virtue of kindness, but he uses a blunt instrument. How does a woman having sexual intercourse with a male horse or a dog – with the animals clearly excited by the act – exhibit "cruelty" toward the animal? Whatever is wrong with these acts might not be cruelty but something else (and if the animal enjoys the act even though it is put in a physically uncomfortable – so somewhat painful – position, is this cruelty?). So perhaps only that type of zoophilia that involves genuine cruelty to animals is incompatible with kindness. Moreover, much sadism is consensual, so it is only some forms of it – those involving ignoring the consent of the other party – that involve lack of respect for the autonomy of others. Similar remarks apply to exhibitionism and voyeurism, since they can be practiced with a consenting party. So for Baltzly's conditions to be successful, we should say, "*This* type of coprophilia is not a perversion but *that* type is." However, this means that we cannot claim categorically that coprophilia and bestiality are perversions, a result that many would not accept. Indeed, when it comes to such sexual practices, there is no *traditional* way of thinking about them from which Baltzly's framework liberates us. They are perversions, period, whether compatible or incompatible with virtues or vices.

Second, the account is not sufficiently fine-tuned. Consider rape. Rape is a horrible sexual wrong, but it is not obviously a perversion. It usually involves heterosexual intercourse, a sexual act that is itself not perverted, and if it turns out that males are somehow by nature disposed to rape, there would be nothing unnatural about it (in one sense of "unnatural"). Yet on Baltzly's view, if someone were sexually disposed to force himself on women, he would be sexually perverted, since he likely lacks the virtue of respecting others' autonomy. Thus, Baltzly's view does not capture *only* those sexual dispositions that are perversions. The point is that there could be sexual dispositions that imply either vice or lack of virtue but which are not perversions.

This leads to the third objection, that Baltzly's view does not explain *why* a sexual disposition is a perversion instead of being morally wrong. Virtues and vices are *moral* dispositions; they dispose their agent to do what is morally right or wrong. This means that, on the face of it at least, if a trait of character (whether sexual or non-sexual) implies vice or lack of virtue, the trait is *morally* defective in some way. So it is not obvious why it is a *perversion* (sexual or non-sexual), especially since Baltzly does not clarify the connection between a disposition's implying vice or lack of virtue and its being a perversion as opposed to something else that is wrong with it. Given that virtues and vices are moral traits, the explanation needs to tell us why sexual dispositions that are contrary to virtues are *perversions*. The example of rape I gave above does not afford me much hope that this can be done.

Concluding Remarks

Let us conclude with some remarks about the prospect of defining "sexual perversion." There is some truth to the idea that sexual perversion is better understood in psychological rather than biological terms. But I doubt that such an account will succeed if it is descriptive, because our thoughts and intuitions about sexual perversion are a mess. An Aristotelian approach might not be fruitful, because its distinctive emphasis on the virtues and vices and their connection to a flourishing life would not capture what is *perverted* about some sexual inclinations. It would also not capture the possibility that some sexual perversions are morally innocent or not an obstacle to a flourishing life.

Any account of perversion might then have to be prescriptive, capturing a crucial core of what perversion is but not necessarily accounting for all our beliefs about it and would have to explain why our beliefs are mistaken in those cases where they are. Furthermore, it will likely have to be a psychological account, something along the lines that a sexual perversion is a disposition to have sex involving this or that type of object. The "objects" would have to be connected to what is natural to us, specifically in terms of our human tendencies to distance ourselves from what is anti-life (which could also be disgusting, revolting, and so on), such as bodily waste and trafficking with the dead in generally improper ways (having sex with or eating corpses), and distancing ourselves from what is biologically odd, such as inter-species sexual intercourse.

The idea is that we start with a list of things or activities that are usually taboo. This is where the naturalness part comes in. We then claim that some people are disposed to sexually engage with these objects. This would be the psychological part. The final step is prescriptive: we argue that such people are sexually perverted. In so doing, many of what are thought to be sexual perversions would have to be excluded. If, for example, consensual sadomasochism does not involve objects or activities associated with taboos, sadomasochists would not be perverted; if people believe otherwise, they would be wrong.

It is at this point that an Aristotelian view can be useful. It can tell us which of the sexual perversions are contrary to virtue, so immoral, and which impede a flourishing life, even if not contrary to virtue. For example, having sex using feces might be compatible with virtue and a flourishing life, but having sex with animals is not.

This approach may or may not succeed. The concept of perversion refers to a large variety, possibly contradictory, of intuitions, whereby even a prescriptive account might not succeed. This need not mean, as some philosophers desperately think, that the concept should be gotten rid of (after all, how many other concepts did we successfully define in this book?). It may mean, instead, that it should be used with caution.

Fantasy

Sexual fantasies, like perversion, might indicate something about a person's character. The objects of sexual fantasy – what the sexual fantasy is *about* – are not always morally innocent: fantasizing about performing oral sex is, but fantasizing about rape is not. Following John Corvino (2002), let us call fantasies whose object is immoral "naughty fantasies." Are people who have naughty fantasies bad? This is our central question.

Patrick Hopkins, in a discussion of S/M activities involving naughty fantasies – such as playing the roles of rapist and raped, slave owner and slave, and Nazi and Jew – attempts to salvage the moral innocence of the participants by arguing that they do not desire real rape or slavery; they do not *settle* for a copy or simulation of the real thing because they cannot experience the real thing. Instead, they desire the simulation itself, "the context of a negotiated and consensual 'submission' or 'domination.'" The sadomasochist "can *desire the simulation itself*, not as inferior copy of the real thing, not as copy of anything at all, but as simulation qua simulation" (Hopkins 1997, 198). Hopkins gives the analogy with roller-coaster riders: they don't desire to plummet to their deaths, and they are not after a weak imitation of such feelings of fear; instead, they desire the simulation of "these lethal experiences" (1997, 198–199). If Hopkins is right, the fantasies would not reflect badly on the participants' characters, because the object of the fantasy is not an attenuated version of an immoral activity, but the simulation, the context in which the fantasies are played out.

Although Hopkins is right that roller-coaster riders don't desire death, this does not mean that they don't desire real feelings of fear (I'm not sure, actually, what the simulation Hopkins claims they desire is; the thrills and fears felt on a roller-coaster ride are real enough). Moreover, as Corvino argues (2002, 215), S/M participants do *not* desire the context in which such roles are enacted; such a desire would be unusual. They desire the sexual roles and activities themselves, but played out in a safe context. So Hopkins's defense of such fantasies and their enactment is unconvincing. The issue of whether such fantasies reflect badly on the person who has them is still unsettled.

We need to distinguish between four different types of cases before we can make any further headway in this discussion. (1) Someone might have naughty fantasies, desire the activities the fantasies involve, want to act on them, and want to act on them in real, not simulated, ways. For example, someone might fantasize about rape, desire to rape, desire to act on his desire, and to do so by actually raping someone. (2) Someone might have naughty fantasies, desire the activities the fantasies involve, want to act on them, but want to act on them only in simulated, consensual ways (as in some S/M role-play). (3) Someone might have naughty fantasies, desire the activities the fantasies involve, but *not* want to act on them in any way. (4) Someone might have naughty fantasies but not desire the activities the fantasies involve.

(1), (2), and (3) involve a desire to act on the object of the fantasy. But the presence of sexual desire assimilates the discussion of naughty fantasies to that of sexual desires, because it is *not* possible to have a fantasy and not desire its activity (see next paragraph). So any discussion of sexual fantasies is a discussion of the involved sexual desires. Since we already know that immoral sexual desires reflect bad character, we know that (1), (2), and (3) are about people whose characters are morally defective in some way or other. So to find out whether naughty *fantasies*, not desires, say something about a person's character, we need to discuss sexual fantasy in isolation from desire.

Is it true that it is impossible to fantasize about an activity without sexually desiring it? One can *imagine* an activity without desiring it. I can, for example, imagine (or try to imagine) what it is like to have sex with sheep without desiring to have sex with sheep. But if I *fantasize* about having sex with a sheep, I do desire it (not all imaginings are fantasies, though all fantasies are forms of imaginings). For "fantasizing" is, almost by definition, a form of yearning for, of desiring the object of the fantasy. Not all desire is fantasy – I can desire the person sitting across from me on the train without fantasizing about him or her – but all fantasy is a form of desire (though the desire to *act* on the fantasy need not be involved). So it is impossible to fantasize about an activity without also desiring the activity. Desiring activity *A* is an essential aspect of fantasizing about *A*. Fantasy, we can roughly claim, is a combination of imagining an activity and desiring it. Indeed, because imagining something is in itself morally neutral (one can imagine something for many purposes: writing a novel, trying to see what it's like to do something or be someone, or even just whittling away the lonely hours by daydreaming), what is relevant as far as moral issues and fantasy are concerned is the desire; it is the notion that plays the role in our moral judgments about the fantasy.

It seems, then, that whether fantasizing about an activity is a moral defect is settled by addressing the issue of whether having certain sexual desires indicates a moral defect in someone's character. As discussed in previous chapters, having sexual desires for immoral things such as rape and pedophilia is a moral defect in a person's character. However, some people do not invest their desires with any value: they do not dwell on them, let alone act on them (recall Huck). These would be virtuous people. Those who do dwell on them but do not act on them are continent people. If fantasizing is a form of dwelling, then, interestingly, to fantasize about a sexual activity is to dwell on the activity. If the fantasies are naughty, the person dwells on immoral sexual activities, which would make him, at best, a continent person. This indicates that there is something morally defective about his character, though it need not be full-blown vice.

If the above-mentioned S/M practitioners desire dominant and submissive role-play *not* as a substitute for the real thing, their fantasies and role-play are entirely acceptable, because harm and lack of consent – the two main things that make real dominance and submission morally abhorrent – are missing. When two people desire sexual role-play involving such roles but *not* as a substitute for the real thing, they are not merely being *content* with consensual sex because that is the best they can get in the circumstances; they are not refraining from inflicting serious harm on each other because otherwise they would get into trouble or feel morally dirty; they *desire consensual, harmless* sex. This does not reflect badly on their characters.

But the details can matter. Do they play the roles of Nazi and Jew, of white slave owner and black slave, of Israeli Jew and Palestinian, or just generic roles of dominance and submission? The first types of roles go beyond the general desires for domination and submission into specific types. Even if the consent is genuinely desired and no serious harm inflicted, for the participants to sexually "get off" they adopt deeply problematic historic identities. Unless they pick the roles at random, as mere symbols of power, desiring to assume the role of a Nazi to feel sexual pleasure might say quite a bit about them, indicating a moral defect in their characters. To enjoy playing the role of a Nazi might be to enjoy the psychology of being a Nazi, and this is not a good sign. Similar things may be said for other such roles.

So whether fantasies reflect badly on a person's character depends on a few factors. If the content of the fantasy is an immoral activity, this reflects badly on the person. However, often the content of the fantasy resembles an immoral activity but includes the crucial elements of consent and lack of desire to inflict harm on the other party. If the person desires such a sexual activity merely as a *substitute* for one that lacks consent and does contain desires for harm, this also reflects badly on the person, because his or her desires are not in tune with what is minimally morally required. If the person desires such a sexual activity for itself – if, that is, he or she does not desire the activity as a substitute for the real thing – this tells us that his or her desires are in tune with what is morally required. But even here the desires might be to assume the mantle of a highly problematic figure, such as a Nazi or a white slave owner, in which case the desires might speak against the person's character.

Here's another question to do with fantasy: Is there something morally wrong with *x* fantasizing about *z* while *x* is having sex with *y*?

The main problem with fantasizing about someone other than the person with whom you're having sex is possible deception. Suppose that Kevin and Katie are having sex but Kevin is thinking about Angelina Jolie. Katie thinks that he is sexually focused on her, but he is not. The problem is that Kevin is, in some sense to be investigated, deceiving or lying to Katie. Let us assume in the following discussion, to keep things manageable, that the fantasies are not naughty.

Not all cases of fantasizing about someone while having sex with another involve deception. A couple may be honest with each other about this and may even make it part of their sexual thrill. The woman asks the man, "Are you thinking of Angelina Jolie as you do me?" and the man says breathlessly, "Yes!" to which she replies, "Yes! Yes! Yes! Do me like you'd do Angelina!" And then the sex gets much better. There are also cases involving role-play, in which the fantasy is part of the sex act: the woman knocks on the door of her house pretending to be a lost tourist and is then seduced by the husband pretending to be a lonely stud; or she dresses up in a French maid's costume; or he dresses up as a police officer who comes to check on a disturbance; and so on. These cases do not involve deception, and the fantasies make the sex more pleasurable.

There are also cases involving deception but the deceived party is not entitled to the truth. Suppose that Karl has just crushed Kim, who is madly in love with him. He told her to quit following him around, and that the sex they had that night was a one-timer. Feeling horrible, Kim goes to a bar intent on picking up a guy to make herself feel good and to make Karl feel bad (not that he really cares). She picks up Klimt, a wandering German tourist, and they have sex in his hotel room. During the sex Kim fantasizes about Karl, even though Klimt thinks she is with him body and soul. Although Kim deceives Klimt in some sense, the deception is not wrong. Being strangers, Klimt knows little about her and she does not owe him anything except for minimum decent treatment. Moreover, it is a one-night stand, and the ethics of one-stand stands are simple: unless the parties agree on certain things beforehand, neither can expect the other to have more than protected plain sex. Neither has a right to the other's thoughts and mind.

The moral problems, if any, with fantasizing about someone other than the person you're having sex with occur between two people who love or are in a relationship with each other. In such cases, there is an expectation that each be with the other in body and soul. So is it morally wrong when they are not? Much depends on the case. If it happens but only rarely, there is deception, but it is morally innocuous. It becomes serious when partners more or less regularly fantasize about others during sex, which usually happens when they have grown sexually accustomed to one another and are no longer thrilled by each other's bodies and sexual acts.

Couples do get sexually accustomed, even bored with each other. Sometimes having an open relationship allows them to keep some spice, but if they are monogamous it may not be reasonable for them to expect the sex to be unaided by fantasy. If this expectation were indeed unreasonable, fantasizing during sex would either be non-deceptive or deceptive but morally permissible. It might be non-deceptive not because couples are honest about it (though this might be true, too), but because they know that the sexual activity requires some support to make it exciting. Even if one partner is genuinely taken aback that her partner is fantasizing about others, she should have known better (x cannot deceive y about something if y refuses to see the facts as they are or make the obvious inferences from them). If we do want to claim that there is deception, it is not morally permissible for the same reason: the partner should have known better. (One complicating factor here is whom x fantasizes about: it is one thing for x to fantasize about Zack Efron, but another for x to fantasize about y's brother, father, or best friend.)

Why not argue that the partners should just be honest with each other? Because, first, such honesty may do more harm than good. If the partners know the facts and remain silent, this might be the wise course of action because it is a situation involving the "I know you know, and I know that you know that I know" kind of case, and the motives behind further verbal communication are questionable on grounds of cruelty: if you have good reason to believe that your spouse knows that you fantasize about someone else, and if you have good reason to believe that he is okay with it, to say more smacks of wanting to hurt your partner, to rub it in his face. Second, if you have good reason to believe that your partner is clueless, then whether you should be honest depends on the kind of relationship you have. If you believe that your partner won't mind hearing the truth, saying it (in the right way, at the right time) would be the right thing to do. But if you have reason to believe that your partner would be deeply hurt by it, keeping silent is the right thing to do. Although it is deceptive, we should keep five points in mind. First, your partner really should know better. Second, sexual fantasy during sex does not mean that you no longer love your partner, and if telling him is going to create a mess, it is wiser to keep silent and maintain the relationship. Third, if telling your partner means that your sex life will be ruined or badly damaged (either because he refuses to have sex with you anymore or because he is constantly worried about whether you are fantasizing, making the sexual activity an ordeal), you are morally justified to say nothing to keep the sexual activity on track. Fourth, fantasizing about z during sex with y does not usually mean that y is nothing but a bodily receptacle for x's fantasies or that x's mind is fully and entirely elsewhere. It is usually a mixture of both, whereby x is aware of the presence of y, is pleased by y's presence, desires to sexually please y, and so on. Cases involving the total use of y as physical means for x's imagination are rare and raise the specter of objectification. Fifth and most important, sexual activity, especially between two people who have been together for a while, does not have sexual pleasure as its only purpose. It also aims to reinforce the love by regularly bringing the couple physically together; it aims, in its almost ritualistic pattern, to reinforce the idea that all is well between them. If fantasizing helps the couple attain these goals by assisting them in making the sexual activity successful, there is nothing wrong with it. These five factors are important to whether fantasizing during sex is overall moral; dishonesty is not the only factor.

Fantasy is a difficult topic. Ultimately, two crucial factors need to be addressed when deciding whether fantasizing is morally wrong: the content of the fantasy (Who is the object of the fantasy? What activities are fantasized about?), and its purpose (Why is the person fantasizing? Does fantasizing result in any good or bad purposes?). We discussed the content of fantasies briefly, especially naughty fantasies, and we discussed a main purpose of fantasy: helping couples continue their relationship. If one fantasizes for this reason and if the content of one's fantasies is not "naughty," the fantasizing would not reflect badly on his or her character. Others might not be so lucky.

Notes

1 Soble adds two ways of evaluating sex acts, the legal – whether a sexual act is legally permitted or prohibited – and the pragmatic – whether a sexual act has generally good or bad consequences (1998, 42–43). Sara Ruddick (1984), inspired by Thomas Nagel's discussion (see below), introduces yet another way: completeness. It is an uncommon and a peculiarly philosophical way to discuss sexual goodness, so I don't discuss it here.
2 Janice Moulton rightly accuses Solomon of identifying pleasure simply with orgasm when he claims that the goal of sex is pleasure (2008, 49).
3 Jerrold Levinson (2003) accepts Scruton's argument, but qualifies it by confining it to the context of chosen homosexuality (whatever this means). My criticisms of Scruton's argument apply also to Levinson's.

Further Reading

For further discussion of perversion, see Gray (1978), Hoffman (2006), Levy (1980), Primoratz (1999, ch. 6), Ruse (1988, 197–201), Soble (1998, ch. 2), and Vannoy (1980, ch. 2). For a non-religious argument that homosexuality is abnormal, see Levin's contribution in Thomas and Levin (1999). Another view of perversion similar to Scruton's and Aristotelianism is Levinson (2003). For some views that the concept of perversion should be gotten rid of, see Humber (1997), Priest (1997), and Slote (1975). A good sourcebook on bizarre sexual practices is Love (1992). On fantasy, see Grimshaw (1997) and Kershnar (2005, 2006, 2007). Weinberg (1995) is a good anthology on S/M.

Part III
Marriage

9   What Is Marriage?

As I write this book, there's a raging debate about gay marriage in the United States. The debate raises two important factors that have been, are, and will continue to be, part of the debate about both gay marriage and marriage in general (this is why gay marriage is the focus of Chapter 10): the sex or gender and the number of the participants in marriage.

Defining Marriage

Definitions usually track how the concept being defined is used. This is especially true of dictionary definitions, which tell us how a word is currently used, often also giving a word's obsolete meanings. Philosophical definitions are different; they aim to give necessary and sufficient conditions of the applicability of a concept. If "table" is defined as "an object with a smooth surface and four legs," then only those objects with smooth surfaces and four legs are tables (this definition is of course false, because there are tables with rough surfaces, with three legs, with six legs, and so on). But philosophical definitions must also conform to common usage. When they don't, they should be revised for accuracy. During Plato's time, defining "art" as imitation was correct because most of the art then could plausibly be thought of as imitation. But as art changed (from imitation, to representation, to expression), the definition became inaccurate. This happened several times to the concept of art, and philosophers had to revise its definition to keep up. Today, when anything can be art ("can," not "is"), it is challenging indeed to correctly define it.

Some of those who define marriage as between one man and one woman seem to do so based simply on how it is used: they look around and see that marriages occur between only one man and one woman, and conclude that that's what marriage is. This seems to make sense, but it ignores the fact that a few countries (Canada, Spain, and South Africa, for example) have legalized gay marriage, so the current usage of the concept is not applicable to only "one man and one woman." Moreover, historically and culturally speaking, marriage has been a very diverse institution, in terms of both the gender and the number of participants. If we keep in mind that the current debate about defining marriage is about legal, policy, and moral issues, the definition we seek is a philosophical, not a dictionary, one. We want necessary and sufficient conditions that capture the essence of marriage. But then how marriage was practiced in the past and in other cultures becomes an important source of information, because we have no reason to believe that how some people think about marriage today captures the essence of the institution. Indeed, many supporters of gay marriage, in their own way, make this point when they wonder why our understanding of marriage should be confined to the formula of "one man, one woman" (and, as we will see, the debate about defining marriage is ultimately a normative one, about how we *should* understand marriage).

In many countries today, especially in Western cultures, most people believe that love and marriage go together; that we should marry the person we love. But in the past and in many cultures today, this idea is not prevalent, and is even strange or dangerous. As one scholar on marriage and the family, Stephanie Coontz, puts it,

> Until the late eighteenth century, most societies around the world saw marriage as far too vital an economic and political institution to be left entirely to the free choice of the two individuals involved, especially if they were going to base their decision on something as unreasoning and transitory as love.
>
> (Coontz 2005, 5)

According to Coontz, there are two commonalities to marriage found across cultures. First, and with the exception of one culture (the Na people in China), marriage is a universal social institution: every society had, and still has, one form of it or another. Second, marriage was always subject to some set or other of rules, though the rules were not always enshrined in law (Coontz 2005, 24–26). Within these two commonalities, marriage had many meanings and varieties. Consider the following list of examples of variety.

(1) Marriage does not always involve the cohabitation of the spouses:

> Among the Ashanti of Ghana and the Minangkabau of Indonesia, men traditionally live with their mothers and sisters even after marriage. Men of the Gururumba people in New Guinea sleep in separate houses and work separate plots of land from their wives. The only time husbands and wives get together on a daily basis is when the main meal is being cooked and eaten.
>
> (Coontz 2005, 26)

(2) Marriage does not always involve the economic cooperation of the spouses:

> Among the Yoruba and many other African societies, husbands and wives do not pool resources in a common household fund. Sometimes a couple

doesn't even share responsibility for their children's economic welfare. The child is supported by one parent's lineage rather than by the married couple. If the couple divorces, the child may not even be viewed as biologically related to the parent whose lineage isn't economically responsible for him.

(Coontz 2005, 26–27)

(3) Marriage does not always involve a man and a woman:

There are West African societies in which a woman may be married to another woman as a "female husband." In these cultures, if the wife brings children with her to the marriage or subsequently bears children by a lover, those children are counted as the descendants and heirs of the "female husband" and her extended family. Numerous African and Native American societies recognize male–male marriages.

(Coontz 2005, 27)

John Boswell (1995) has also documented same-sex marriages in early Christianity in Europe.

(4) More astoundingly, marriage does not always involve another human being as a spouse. There are, for example, "ghost" marriages: "What about traditional Chinese and Sudanese ghost or spirit marriages, in which one of the partners is actually dead? In these societies, a youth might be given in marriage to the dead son or daughter of another family, in order to forge closer ties between the two sets of relatives" (Coontz 2005, 27). Moreover, among the societies of the Bella Coola and the Kwakiutl (Pacific Northwest), "if two families wished to trade with each other but no suitable matches were available, a marriage contract might be drawn up between one individual and another's foot or even with a dog belonging to the family of the desired in-laws!" (Coontz 2005, 31).

(5) Marriage does not involve being married to only one spouse at a time. Until recently, Mormons in the United States were polygamous. Muslim men are allowed to marry up to four wives (on the condition that they treat them equally, as the Qur'an stipulates). Moreover,

among the Toda of southern India, a girl was married off at a young age, sometimes as early as two or three. From then on she was considered the wife not only of the boy to whom she was married but of all his brothers as well. When the girl was old enough to have sex, she usually had sexual relations with all her husbands.

(Coontz 2005, 27)

And until the Catholic Church cracked down on the practice, many kings of medieval Europe married more than one woman at a time (Coontz 2005, 92).

(6) Marriage does not always involve the regulation of property and inheritance rights:

> A child born out of wedlock among the Kachin of northern Burma was counted as legitimate if the father paid a fine to the girl and her family. Among the Kandyan of Sri Lanka, by contrast, a child's legitimacy derived from the mother. As long as the presumed father was not from a caste lower than the mother's, his actions, intentions, and marital status had no impact on the child's status.
>
> (Coontz 2005, 29)

(7) Marriage does not always involve the reproduction and rearing of children. In pre-Islamic Arabia, one customary practice (until Islam put a stop to it) was the wa'd – the burial of female daughters shortly after their birth. Shi'a Muslims (today and in the past) also practice mut'a (pleasure) marriages, the sole purpose of which is sex and sexual pleasure, enjoyed under the protection of the law, thus avoiding fornication (which is religiously proscribed). According to Coontz, ancient Babylonian Jews accepted a similar type of marriage (2005, 29). And, of course, all over the world, many couples marry without, for various reasons, intending to have or actually having children.

(8) Marriage does not always involve a non-related spouse. It is customary in many parts of the world for people to marry their first cousins (considered incestuous in the Western world). More shockingly perhaps is that in the ancient world, rulers sometimes married their own siblings:

> To rule out conflicts of interest between in-laws, an Egyptian pharaoh sometimes married a sister or, more frequently, a half-sister – a woman born by a different wife to the same father. This bolstered the claim to dynastic continuity both for the rulers and for any children they produced and eliminated the risk that husband and wife would be torn in different directions by the machinations of their respective kin.
>
> (Coontz 2005, 59)

(9) Marriage is not always regulated by the state. In both ancient Egypt and Rome, and unless high stakes were involved, marriage was a private contract drawn up by the involved families. For the poorer classes, private contracts were not even involved at all, and a man and woman were considered married when they established a household together (Coontz 2005, 66). In medieval Europe, among the common people (non-royalty), for two people to marry they needed only their consent and occasionally the blessing of parents. "It wasn't until the sixteenth century on the continent – and not until 1753 in England – that governments and churches could enforce a rule requiring specific legal and public formalities to validate a marriage" (Coontz 2005, 106). Read, for example, Daniel Defoe's 1722 novel *Moll Flanders* and note the ease with which the main character Moll Flanders dissolves one marriage

after another. The reason? She is a commoner, and marriage among commoners was a private contract.

Obviously then, marriage was, and is, not always for love. Indeed, it was rare that people married for love. If there were common reasons for marriage, they were for pooling economic resources, rearing children to increase a family's labor force, for obtaining in-laws to forge economic and, especially in the case of the ruling classes, political alliances, and for producing legitimate heirs to the throne (in the case of royalty).

We can draw two lessons from this brief historical and cultural foray into marriage. First, because of the lack of common elements to marriage (other than the uninformative ones of being universal and governed by culturally variable rules), no plausible definition of "marriage" can be based simply on how marriage is practiced today or in the past. Such a definition would be open to counter-examples (e.g., "Why not define marriage to allow for near relatives? Many marry their cousins and some used to marry their siblings!"). Not even listing every existing type of marriage will do, because the definition would be too long to be useful and could become false once a new marriage practice came along (similar to what happened to defining "art"). Perhaps, then, the more plausible way to define "marriage" is normatively: what marriage *should* be. For example, someone might claim, "I know marriage as an institution has had, and continues to have, many variations and to reflect the cultural practices of which it is a part. But marriage is *really* (or *should* be) about love" (or: "Marriage should really be between one man and one woman").

Second, the above list shows – and reason on its own could, too – that there are no conceptual or necessary connections between love, sex, and marriage, three things that many today consider to "naturally" come together. People marry for many reasons, not only for love, and people can love each other without marrying (as is common among many heterosexuals and among gay people where they cannot marry). So marriage and love conceptually come apart. People can certainly have sex with others whom they do not love, and people can love others without having sex with them. So love and sex also come apart. People can have sex with each other without being married to each other, and there are many marriages that are sexless (because the spouses are sexually bored with each other, because they married only for companionship, or because they married a ghost or someone else's foot). So sex and marriage also come apart. Having children is also not conceptually connected to any of the above three reasons: people have sex without intending to have or actually having children, and women can now get pregnant without having sex (not to mention cloning). So procreation and sex come apart. There are childless marriages (for all sorts of reasons) and there are children born out of wedlock. So procreation and marriage also come apart. Finally, two people can love each other without intending to have or actually have children, and people can have children even when they don't love each other – for example, accidental pregnancies due to casual sex or loveless marriages that produce children (cf. Soble 1998, 178–181).

Monogamy

"Monogamy" is an ambiguous expression. It could mean "marital sexual faithfulness," according to which two (or more) people are monogamous if they are sexually faithful to each other. This meaning is opposed to that of adultery. It also more often than not functions as an ideal, whereby spouses take vows or desire to be monogamous, but in fact depart from the ideal by one or both of them committing adultery. "Monogamy" could also mean "a two-, and only two-, person marital relationship." This notion of monogamy is opposed to that of polygamy.[1] Under this meaning, monogamy need not be restricted to heterosexual couples, and it need not be restricted to legal marriages: a same-sex couple who are not legally married would be monogamous in this respect. Let us address the morality of each.

Monogamy as Sexual Fidelity

Monogamy as sexual faithfulness means that spouses in a marital relationship (legal or substantive) are committed to not having sex with others outside the relationship. Although such relationships usually have two spouses, monogamy makes sense in a polygamous relationship: a man married to three wives, for example, can be sexually faithful by not having sex with any woman other than his wives, and each of his three wives can be monogamous by not having sex with anyone other than her husband. Moreover, if, say, three (or more people) are in a love triangle, they can be monogamous in that none of them has sex with anyone else other than the other two: x has sex with only y and z, not w, who is not a member of the triad; y has sex with only x and z, not w; and z has sex with only x and y, not w.

A crucial point to keep in mind is that breaking the vows of monogamy and committing adultery can take many forms. Mike need not cheat on Mira only by having an *affair* with another woman, but by having casual sex with another woman, either a prostitute or a non-prostitute. Moreover, although most people would agree that were Mike to only lust (in his heart) after another woman, engage in solitary masturbation, or read or watch pornography, Mike would not have cheated on Mira, other cases are not so clear: What if he has phone sex with another woman? What if he has cyber-sex with another person? What if he was raped? Would these instances count as adultery? Moreover, even if Mike were a heterosexual, he commits adultery if he sleeps with a man; that is, to commit adultery, Mike doesn't have to have sex only with another woman; it could be with a man (but what about a sheep, an inflated doll, or a human corpse?).

Traditional morality tells us that adultery is morally wrong, but many philosophers question this view (and the view itself has not had many philosophical defenders) and attempt to uncover the sources of the wrongness of adultery: If adultery is wrong, *why* is it wrong? One philosopher, Richard Wasserstrom, uncovers two sources: promise-breaking and deception. Adultery is wrong, one might argue, because spouses make promises to each other to be sexually faithful; committing adultery by spouse x means that x has broken his promise to y, his spouse. Because breaking a promise is morally wrong, adultery is morally wrong. Moreover, as Wasserstrom rightly observes, to many couples promises of sexual fidelity are very important, so breaking them is not just any moral wrong, but a *serious* moral wrong, which implies that adultery is a serious moral wrong (1998, 141).

The second reason why adultery is wrong has to do with deception. Adulterous spouses almost always have recourse to lies and deceptions in order to commit their deeds: John spends the afternoon with two prostitutes; on his way home he calls Sarah his wife. Consider the following dialogue:

"Sorry I couldn't call you earlier, honey, or return your text messages, but I was in an important meeting all afternoon."

"Oh," says Sarah, "You didn't tell me you had an important meeting today."

"It was last-minute."

"Couldn't you have called me quickly on your way in to the meeting to let me know you won't be calling me in the afternoon?"

"Yeah, I know, I'm sorry. But my boss popped into my office and practically took me by the hand to the boardroom."

John commits three major whoppers in order to conceal his sexual infidelity. Of course, he could have told Sarah in advance that he had a meeting, since he probably planned ahead his romp with the two prostitutes. But if Sarah has any reason to suspect John, he may have worried that telling her in advance would prompt her to call the office asking for him (she can still call after the fact and check whether there was a meeting, but such questioning is awkward and embarrassing for her). Not only is John lying and deceiving Sarah, he also has to go through his own mental gymnastics to cover his ground. If he frequently commits adultery, such mental gymnastics, lies, and deceptions are likely to take their moral toll on *him*.

There are three points to keep in mind. First, insofar as promise-breaking, lying, and deception are wrong in themselves, regardless of their consequences, and insofar as adultery involves one or more of them, adultery would be wrong in itself, regardless of the consequences of lying, deceiving, or promise-breaking. Second, promise-breaking, lying, and deception, especially when serious, often lead to harmful results to the person to whom the broken promise has been made, being lied to, or deceived. Moreover, if sex symbolizes emotional involvement, affection, or love, the harm to the cheated-on-spouse might even be deeper, since then the infidelity would not be only sexual, but also emotional. Harm also afflicts the person with whom the spouse is committing adultery, by perhaps being misled into thinking that the adulterous spouse has feelings for him or her. Third, continuous or persistent promise-breaking, lying, or deception often has harmful consequences for the adulterous spouse: his or her moral character starts eroding (or erodes even further if it is bad to start with). On all these points, adultery turns out to be a serious moral wrong.

What, however, if the spouses never made promises to each other to be sexually faithful? What if they did make such promises but later agreed to absolve each other of them? And what if they have an open relationship and have no need to be deceptive? If these conditions hold, the two sources for the wrongness of adultery would have to be restricted. We would have to claim that adultery is wrong only when it involves promise-breaking, lying, or deception.

Moreover, not all cases of promise-breaking, lying, and deception are wrong; some are permissible, because more important considerations come into play. Suppose that I promised my neighbor to help him move, but on that day a good friend of mine is involved in a car accident and I need to be by her side. In this case, even if my neighbor does not release me from my promise ("I don't care! The sky could be falling on our heads and you will still help me move!"), it is morally permissible for me to break it to be with my friend. Or suppose that someone asks me about something to which she has no right to know. Lying to her would be morally justified. In other words, promise-breaking, lying, and deception are wrong when we assume that there are no other considerations that outweigh them. But when there are such considerations they become permissible. (This does not mean that any consideration will do; indeed, many people frequently engage in the morally abhorrent practices of lying and breaking their promises, often using the flimsiest excuses for doing so.) It is possible, then, to have morally permissible cases of adultery that involve promise-breaking, lying, or deception. Thus, knowing *only* that a case of adultery involves lying (or deception, or promise-breaking) is not enough to know that the adultery is morally wrong, though it offers a strong presumption that it is.

At this point, those who wish to defend the view that adultery is wrong have at least two options: they can either raise doubts about open marriages or they can find sources for the wrongness of adultery other than lying and promise-breaking.

The first option might start with the following ideas and facts. First, in most societies today, sexual activity is connected with love; it is usually taken to express, symbolize, or indicate love or at least affection. Second, in most societies today, monogamy is the ideal; people strive for it (couples who are in open relationships or marriages often do not divulge this fact about their relationship to others, which indicates that the ideal of monogamy runs deep). Third, the ideal of monogamy and the connections between sex and love are not merely cultural views with no influence on the individuals who live in these cultures, but often profoundly affect individuals, shaping their psychologies and desires in deep ways. Fourth, sexual desire is powerful, with highly subversive abilities; even if open relationships are conducted according to rules (they would have to, or things would likely go out of hand), things will probably degenerate quickly, with spouses demanding more and more sexual access to other partners.

The upshot is that it is easier said than done to be in an open relationship. For one thing, couples need to be certain that being in such a relationship is something that they whole-heartedly believe in and accept, not something they do out of an ideological or theoretical commitment to some liberal view such as "free love," "sexual freedom," and "flower power." Nor should it be a relationship that one spouse agrees to because she (or he) wants to be nice or accommodating to her (or his) spouse. This is important, because if the commitment to open relationships is not whole-hearted, problems likely arise: jealousy, possessiveness, an increasing lack of attention to each other owing to the power of sexual desire, and so on. As these problems set in, spouses may or may not have the wisdom to deal with them. If they don't, they are likely to resort to deception, lies, and other immoral practices to cover more and more sexual activities that occur outside what is allowed by the rules of the open marriage. For another thing, if society does encourage us to see sex as connected with love, spouses may have little or no control over whether their sexual activities lead them to develop feelings of love for those with whom they have sex. This depends on the type of sexual activity allowed: if casual sex, chances that love develops diminish greatly; if affairs, the chances go up. For yet another thing, spouses who have children will have a hard time pulling off such open relationships. Young children require constant care and attention, and spouses have to develop rules for their open relationship, allowing them to conduct such a relationship while also giving their children the attention they need and ensuring that such rules are fair to both spouses. It takes some powerful spouses, indeed, to develop such rules and to properly adhere to them (as the children grow older, different sets of rules might be needed).[2]

This objection raises profound moral issues, having to do with how spouses relate to each other (jealousy, possessiveness), whether their adulterous behavior might evolve into a deeper type (emotional involvement with others), and how they are to properly raise children. Nonetheless, the objection is limited in scope in regard to both people and time. First, though some couples may not be able to really pull off an open marriage, others can and have. There are many heterosexual swinging couples, and it is presumptuous to claim that all are having a hard time being successful in their relationships. Many gay male couples have open relationships, and younger generations of lesbian couples are catching up. Second, the objection is limited in time. The facts on which it relies to make its points are culture-bound, so that changing cultural norms would greatly diminish the objection's power. If society came to accept open relationships, not view sex as connected with love (and to what extent does society – Western societies anyway – make this connection still?), and provide institutions that support couples' open relationships, the argument would not be as convincing, because there would be less reason to believe that couples will fail in their open relationships, that children would be adversely affected by it, and that sexual entanglements would evolve into emotional, affectionate ones (is it because gay male culture is more sexually oriented and accepting of open relationships that gay men have an easier time with them?).

The second option for the defender of the view that adultery is wrong is to find other sources for its wrongness. One such source is that it is important to prohibit adultery because sexual faithfulness strengthens the marriage of a couple: (1) by limiting the source of sexual pleasure to only one person – the spouse – thus putting the couple "in a position to provide an important source of pleasure for each other that is unavailable to them elsewhere in the society," and (2) by limiting a crucial source of intimacy – the intimacy of sexual activity – to only one person – the spouse (Wasserstrom 1998, 149). Although perhaps true for some couples, the limitation might frustrate the marriages of others, because there is no reason to think that having your spouse as the only source of your sexual pleasure would make the relationship stronger. Indeed, if the spouses experience the death of desire – if they get sexually bored with each other – a prohibition on outside sexual activity might get them to stealthily seek it, which means we are back to lying and deception. Moreover, spouses are allowed to have more than one source of intimacy: with their friends, relatives, and even co-workers. Why, then, sexual intimacy should be limited to only one person is not clear. We need a reason why it is important that sexual intimacy be confined to only one person. Thus this argument is inconclusive.

The philosopher Bonnie Steinbock provides another source for the wrongness of adultery. She stresses the connections between sex and emotion, arguing that sexual activity tends to result in love. First, it provides sexual partners with pleasure, and people tend to develop feelings of affection for those who make them happy or who give them pleasure. Second, because sexual activity is intimate, "involving both physical and psychological exposure," it requires and leads to feelings of trust, which are "closely allied to feelings of affection and love" (1991, 190). Thus, to Steinbock, claiming that sex and love *can* be divorced from one another is simplistic. We should instead acknowledge the *usual* connections between them, which means that having sex with someone other than your spouse cannot be brushed aside as only sex ("It didn't mean anything! Honest!"). Thus, adultery is a serious moral issue, and it is an ideal for which couples should strive, though not the only ideal (1991, 191).

Steinbock is right that sex and love are usually connected in the ways she mentions. However, her argument is still limited in scope. First, and as she acknowledges, it shows only that sexual fidelity is an ideal, not that it is the only ideal, so couples who have an open marriage are not thereby leading an immoral life. Second, her argument is seriously handicapped by the assumption that adultery takes the form of *affairs*. If we consider other forms of adultery – one-night stands, sex with prostitutes, anonymous sex in bath houses and other sexual venues – the argument weakens, because these forms of sexual activity involve little or no feelings of affection, and they do not usually lead to a prolonged sexual affair within which such feelings develop. Of course, they do involve trust (one has to trust one's casual sexual partner not to hurt or harm one before, during, and after the sexual activity), and they often involve a peculiar form of affection (e.g., tenderness during the sexual act, "thank you" after the act is over), but these are not the types of feelings of affection and trust that lead to romantic love (though if the casual sexual partners decide to meet up again, the feelings might transform into the type that does lead to love). Third, even in cases of adulterous affairs, not all develop into deep emotional commitments, let alone love. Whether they do depends on the case. So Steinbock's argument has serious limitations: it applies only to those adulterous affairs that result in deep emotional ties. Moreover, some of these cases may still be morally acceptable: if Gina is trapped in a marriage with Giovanni, an abusive husband who treats her as his own personal doormat, it would be at best a bad joke and at worst sheer cruelty to tell her that the loving, sexual affair she is having with Leonardo is immoral.

Consider one final source for the wrongness of adultery. Sex is not a game; it has consequences. It can lead to serious sexually transmitted diseases, the simplest of which require serious treatment, and the hardest of which require even more serious, expensive treatment, sometimes proving fatal if the infected person cannot afford the needed medication (as in the case of medication for HIV infections, of which the non-generic brands are prohibitively expensive, and of which the generic brands can still be prohibitively expensive to the poor). Sex also leads to pregnancies. In the case of adultery, such pregnancies are almost always unwanted, leading the pregnant woman to either have an abortion – which involves the loss of a human life, that of the fetus – or to be saddled with a child she does not want: carrying it to term changes her life in drastic ways; if she gives it up, this is likely to be emotionally quite taxing, and if she keeps it, well, then her life has pretty much changed forever. Some philosophers brush these concerns aside as non-moral.[3] But this is false, as anyone who has lived with, for example, a terminally ill person can attest. Adultery, then, can lead to these consequences; therefore it is wrong.

Still, the argument does not show that adultery is wrong in itself. After all, contraception and methods of protection against sexually transmitted diseases are widely available. What it does show, instead, is that adultery is wrong *in those cases* when it has these consequences or when it carries their high risk. A married man who has unprotected sex with a prostitute (especially in places where prostitution is unregulated, as occurs in many poor neighborhoods in third world countries, where most prostitutes have myriad sexual diseases) commits a serious wrong, because he incurs a high risk of being infected himself and of infecting his wife (and, if she is pregnant or becomes pregnant, his future child). If he has sex again with another prostitute, he puts her at risk for being infected. Indeed, this is how many women contract HIV in some countries in Africa and Asia.

So the conclusion that adultery is immoral is by no means obvious; we may conclude that in those cases in which adultery involves breaking promises, lying, deception, emotional betrayal, harm to the children of the spouses and of the person with whom the spouse commits adultery, and harm to the involved parties, there's a presumption that it is wrong. But even then, some of these cases might be justified, depending on the particular circumstances of each case. Moreover, in those cases in which the spouses agree to have extramarital sex, adultery seems morally permissible, since it involves the free choices of the involved parties. Indeed, if the spouses freely undertake adulterous behavior, and if no serious harm attends to any party, adultery seems to be morally in the clear.

Polygamy and Polyamory

In assessing the goodness and badness of non-monogamous marriages – of polygamy and polyamory – we need to face up to the sheer difficulty of doing so. The difficulty has three main sources. First, polygamy and polyamory can come in a bewildering variety of different types. There's polygyny, polyandry, and group marriages, each of which can be heterosexual, homosexual, or both. They have legal and non-legal aspects. They are formed for a variety of purposes, which means that a moral discussion of polygamous marriages undertaken for purposes of, say, love is different from a discussion of it when undertaken for, say, political or economic reasons (cf. Casler 1974).

Second, a discussion of polygamous and polyamorous marriages in their legal forms is bound to be extremely difficult because in Western societies no polygamous or polyamorous marriages exist (and I know of no society in which the latter exists). Because marriage involves a host of legal rights, both as duties and privileges, trying to imagine how polygamous and polyamorous marriages would be legally organized were they to exist is, to use an understatement, daunting. We also cannot dismiss the legal aspects of marriage as morally irrelevant, because they are far-reaching and deeply affect people's lives. A further, related complication is that marriage, especially polygamous marriage in which one man has more than two wives, has been accused of sexism. As society heads toward being less and less sexist, one can claim that in a non-sexist, "utopian" society polygynous marriages would not be sexist. Although this sounds plausible, imagining what such marriages would "look" like is extremely difficult, one reason (among others) being the sheer difficulty of knowing what such a utopian society would itself look like.

Third, philosophers have written very little on this topic. Famously enough, Plato advocates group marriages in the *Republic* (1997f, Book V), but his discussion is brief and his advocacy confined to the guardians (philosopher-kings) of his ideal city. Another philosopher who advocates non-monogamous marriages is Arthur Schopenhauer, who is very much in favor of polygamy (1956). But his views are troubling given that they are mostly motivated by his view of women as inferior (e.g., "women exist in the main solely for the propagation of the species"). Most of the philosophers, moreover, who do discuss the issue of monogamy either don't question its goodness or, if they do, fall squarely on its side. Kant, for example, argues that because marriage involves each partner having complete rights over the person of the other, a man who marries two wives does something immoral because while he has rights over the whole person of each woman, each wife "would have but half the man" (1963, 167).

A few contemporary philosophers, however, do question monogamy's goodness. The title of John McMurty's famous essay on the issue says it all: "Monogamy: A Critique" (1984). Although McMurty's conclusion that marriage is a form of private property is implausible, although his essay often runs together marriage as a legal institution with monogamy as the practice of sexual exclusivity, and although his criticisms confusingly sometimes target marriage as a universal institution and sometimes marriage as it exists in specific periods or places (see Palmer 1984), his essay raises crucial issues. One crucial point to which I return in Chapter 10 in connection with Claudia Card's arguments against marriage is the restrictive role of the state in monogamous marriage. For now, three other points are worth addressing.

(1) Responding to the justification that monogamy fosters intimacy between the two spouses, McMurty claims that there are reasons to believe that it actually does the opposite: "Formal exclusion of all others from erotic contact with the marriage partner systematically promotes conjugal insecurity, jealousy, and alienation." It does so because it makes each partner the sole sexual outlet for the other, so that if the sex is disappointing or is not good, the partners feel insecure about themselves. Moreover, because our sexual needs are not naturally confined to one person, in monogamy each spouse might feel insecure and jealous that his or her spouse will seek sex with others. Such insecurities and jealousies are bound to make the spouses more and more alienated from each other (1984, 111–112; see also Gregory 1984).

There is something in what McMurty is saying. The attractive idea is that with more than two spouses in the mix, each spouse has sexual and emotional access to more than one person, thus eliminating the need to go outside the marriage for sexual and emotional outlets.[4] McMurty is right that monogamous marriage has had its share in promoting insecurities and jealousies among spouses, though, surely, the larger culture in which monogamous marriage exists plays a role in this, too. I would also add that emotional security is much more crucial than sexual security: if the spouses love each other, yet one spouse, x, proves to be abusive, to be undergoing difficulties that affect the marriage, then y often feels lonely, or at a loss. Y can turn to friends, of course, but in a culture that places much more importance on love than on friendship, spouses like y often feel on their own. Perhaps having other spouses who are in love with each other and with x might lessen the alienation and the loneliness, much as siblings grieving together for the loss of a parent have an easier time than a child grieving on his or her own.

But the proof is in the pudding: whether such non-monogamous arrangements work depends on how they are structured. There is no reason to believe that polygamous or polyamorous marriages will tend to contain any less jealousy or insecurity than monogamous marriages. They might even have their own problems. For example, Paul, one of the spouses in a group marriage, might ask himself, "Layla has had sex four times this week with John, and only once with me. She also did that last week and the week before. Is there something wrong with me? Why does she prefer John to me?" Moreover, we really know very little about how such arrangements might look like, how the spouses will relate to each other, how their individual privacy in such marriages will be structured, what legal mechanisms would have to be put in place, and so on. These obscurities prevent us from knowing whether polygamy and polyamory will fare better than monogamy in these areas.

Finally, we should remember that marriage has many purposes. If people marry for love, and if love, by its nature or for other reasons, tends to be exclusive, it is hard to see how polygamous and polyamorous marriages will work, because people simply tend to not romantically love more than one person at a time. Marriage will then have to be monogamous, and the spouses will simply have to deal with the jealousy, insecurity, and so on (make the marriage sexually open, for example). If marriage is instead about friendship or companionship, polygamous and polyamorous marriages may prove to be a better model than monogamous marriages, since people do not usually confine themselves to having one friend at a time. Thus, much depends on the purposes of marriage or at least on the reasons why individuals seek to marry.

(2) A more convincing point that McMurty brings up has to do with children: "Limitation of the marriage bond to two people necessarily restricts, in perhaps the most unilateral way possible consistent with offspring survival, the number of adult sources of affection, interest, and material support and instruction of the young." Monogamous marriage provides "the structural conditions for such notorious and far-reaching problems as sibling rivalry for scarce adult attention and parental oppression through exclusive monopoly of the child's means of life" (1984, 111). The idea is that with only two parents, children have to compete for their attention, instruction, and support. Having two parents also means fewer avenues for those children whose parents abuse their power over them. However, having more than two parents provides more sources of education, emotional and other kinds of support, and allows the children to get out of the grip of an abusive parent by going to the others for support.

One might object that the above problems need not only be alleviated by polygamous or polyamorous marriages; they can be alleviated by extended families, in which children live not only with their parents, but also with their aunts, uncles, cousins, and grandparents (if not in the same house, at least in the same building or neighborhood). I suspect, however, that extended families won't do the trick for the kind of issues McMurty raises. For one thing, children still understand who their parents are and they understand that an uncle is an uncle, not a parent. Given that parents tend to have stronger relationships with their own children, an uncle's support or attention might not be deep or strong enough to meet the children's needs. Moreover, uncles and other family relatives have more or less limited social, legal, and emotional access to their nephews, nieces, or grandchildren. This is not because of physical or emotional distance, but because of social and legal understandings that limit the roles that extended family members can play when it comes to the children of their siblings or their grandchildren. Finally, uncles, aunts, and grandparents often have their own children to deal with and their own set of problems to attend to. Extended families, then, might help lessen the problems that McMurty mentions, but they won't be enough.

However, and while McMurty's point regarding expanding the parental pool is well-taken, we, again, know very little about how such arrangements will actually look like to make us confident that they will work. So although his point is convincing in the abstract, the proof is again going to have to be in the pudding.

(3) McMurty also claims that "larger groupings" have resources and advantages that monogamous marriage lacks: "(a) the security, range, and power of larger socioeconomic units; (b) the epistemological and emotional substance, variety, and scope of more pluralist interactions; (c) the possibility of extra-domestic freedom founded on more adult providers and upbringers as well as more broadly based circles of intimacy" (1984, 112). The point is that groups larger than two tend to be stronger, more resourceful, more stable, and to contain more diverse avenues of emotional, educational, material, and other kinds of support.

This also sounds plausible. But, again, how it will actually work remains to be seen. We have to also keep in mind that although with larger groups comes larger variety, resources, etc., more conflict is also inevitable, because the more people are involved with each other, the more tastes, individual preferences, egos, etc., come into play. The more of them come into play, the higher is the probability of conflict. It is much easier for two people to agree on something than it is for three, four, or more people to. Of course, polygamous and polyamorous marriages will have to have some rules agreed to by the spouses to be workable. But what these rules are and whether they will work remains to be seen – a point part of the larger one that whether such marriages are successful is an issue on which we have little to go on to decide it. Moreover, we cannot discuss these marriages simply by imagining our culture and society as they are and on to which we graft the marriages; they cannot simply be part of current society. For them to exist, society will have to accept them, which means that it will have to undergo major changes, because as it exists today, society is hostile to them. So simply seeing how polygamous and polyamorous marriages would fit in today's society is a futile exercise.

Nonetheless, philosophically speaking there's one important point to be made in favor of polygamous and polyamorous marriages. If we (a) set aside the practical and legal difficulties certain to occur were society to allow them; (b) set aside any worries about the treatment of women in such marriages, especially in polygynous ones; (c) set aside immoral arrangements (incestuous marriages, e.g.); and (d) do *not prohibit monogamous* marriages, allowing *only* polygamous and polyamorous ones, there is no good, principled reason why polygamous and polyamorous marriages should not be an *option* for those who want them. Indeed, if we suspect that monogamous marriages raise some moral problems for the spouses and the children (á la McMurty), then, even if our suspicions are not strong enough to prohibit monogamous marriage, they might be strong enough to give other forms of marriage a chance. And even if monogamous marriage raises no problems, giving people the options of polygamy and polyamory is a good idea, provided, again, that the above, and other, caveats are in place.

Notes

1 "Polygamy" is the marriage of x to y, w, and z, but y, w, and z are not married to each other. "Polyandry" is the marriage of one woman to more than one man; "polygyny" is the marriage of one man to more than one woman; and "polyamory" is the marriage of a number of individuals to each other – hence the name "group marriage."
2 Though it is obvious to me that open marriages are real marriages, Wasserstrom discusses the issue whether they are (1998, 146–148).
3 For example, Anthony Ellis claims that such concerns are not morally relevant because they are "medical problems" (1986, 166). Although some medical problems are morally irrelevant (e.g., a huge pimple on one's thigh) or not morally serious (e.g., a serious flu that leaves a person bedridden for five days), others surely are (e.g., HIV infection, having one or more of one's limbs amputated).
4 McMurty, I believe, confuses "monogamy" meaning "marriage to one person only at a time" with "sexual exclusivity," but let's allow this one to slide.

Further Reading

Books on the history and institution of marriage are many. But in addition to Coontz's book, two others make for good reading: Cott (2000) and Graff (1999); Graff's is especially good on the purposes of marriage. A brief but good introduction to the history of the gay movement's advocacy of marriage is Chauncey (2004). A good essay on the legal and material rights and obligations of marriage is Chambers (1996). A good philosophical overview of the philosophical issues is Graybosch (2006). For other views on why adultery is wrong, see Wreen (1991), Martin (1998), and Marquis (2005). See also Cicovacki (1993), Halwani (1998), and Martin (2006). On the ethics of open relationships, see Halwani (2003, ch. 3). Taylor's (1982) book on love affairs is also crucial. Bertrand Russell also advocated open marriages (1970, ch. 10). On polygamous and polyamorous marriages, see Bayles (1984), Clark (1998), and Constantine and Constantine (1973).

10 Controversies over Same-Sex Marriage

Preliminaries

(1) Gay marriage is a contentious issue. Currently, the countries that grant same-sex marriages are Belgium, Canada, Holland (the first country to do so), Norway, South Africa, Spain, and Sweden. In the United States, Connecticut, Iowa, Maine, Massachusetts, New Hampshire, and Vermont are the states that grant same-sex marriages (New York and the District of Columbia recognize same-sex marriages performed in other states), but because of the Defense of Marriage Act (DOMA) passed by both houses of Congress in 1996, no state is required to recognize (to give "full faith and credit" to) same-sex marriages performed in another state.

(2) There are three dominant views regarding same-sex marriage. The first is in favor of it, and the people who advocate this position are sympathetic to gay people and their rights (many of them gay themselves). The second position is against same-sex marriage, and those who advocate this position are generally unsympathetic to gay people or, at least, to the gay "lifestyle," especially gay sex. The third position is also against same-sex marriage, but those who advocate it are sympathetic to gay people and their rights (most of them are gay themselves). Logically speaking, there could be a fourth position, one that is for same-sex marriage but such that those who advocate it are against gay people or the gay "lifestyle." I know of no one who actually subscribes to such a view, but it is rather humorous, since it is basically saying, "Why should only straight people suffer through marriage? Let gays suffer, too!" I have nothing to say about this position and set it aside.

(3) Marriage, at least in the United States, confers a number of legal benefits on married couples. John and Aida, unless related by blood, are prior to marriage considered strangers to each other from the legal point of view. Once married, they are legally considered next-of-kin, which entitles them to all sorts of rights. They have, for example, rights to hospital visitation (including the right to make medical decisions on each other's behalf were one of them to be incapable of doing so); to jail visitation; to inhabit places restricted to immediate family; to health insurance (by enrolling in each other's family insurance plans); to live in neighborhoods zoned only for "families"; to income tax

advantages (from deductions, to credits, to improved rates, to exemptions); to inherit the other's property upon death in the absence of a will; and to receive survivor's benefits. If John were a United States citizen and Aida a citizen of Egypt, she attains the right to receive U.S. permanent residency and eventually citizenship upon marrying John, in a process that is much faster than acquiring citizenship through, say, legal employment. In addition, neither John nor Aida can be compelled by a court of law to testify against the other (unless child abuse is involved). Each also acquires the decision of how the other is to be buried (in the absence of a will). Most crucially, and perhaps troublingly as we will see, although marriage creates the obligation for each spouse to support the other, it also gives each the right of access to the other person's home, person, and property. These are some of the main rights that spouses acquire once married.

So marriage is important for individuals given the benefits and rights it grants the spouses automatically upon marrying, and that prove crucial in assessing arguments for and against same-sex marriages from those who are sympathetic to gay people. But marriage is also an important *social* institution: it signals to the rest of society that two people have vowed to commit themselves to each other, allowing the couple to openly and publicly celebrate this commitment. Its legal backing is a way for the state to bless it.

(4) Many people consider homosexuality and homosexual sex immoral. *If* homosexuality is indeed immoral, it is very hard, if not impossible, to see why same-sex marriage should be legal, since then the state would in effect be blessing an immoral arrangement. Moreover, the views of the defenders of DOMA and of those who reject same-sex marriage would become more convincing. Domestic partnerships become a tricky thing, their status hostage to the issue of whether states can or should allow immoral contracts. As one philosopher puts it,

> While a society may for constitutional or prudential reasons have to tolerate conduct considered by many to be immoral (especially when it takes place in private), it does not follow that it has an obligation to accept or endorse that conduct, for example by making available an institutional resource such as marriage.
>
> (Freeman 1999, 9)

That is why we need to begin with the anti-same-sex position advocated by those who are not sympathetic to gay people, focusing on the arguments against homosexual sex given by the so-called new natural lawyers.

The Natural Law Tradition

The new natural lawyers are not lawyers in the usual sense of the term, who practice law in a law firm. They are "natural lawyers" – those who follow in the footsteps of the natural law theories, especially of the medieval philosopher

St. Thomas Aquinas. Aquinas does not use the term "natural laws" in the way scientists use it, to refer to the laws of physics and chemistry, for example. These laws *describe* the way physical objects behave under certain conditions. They are also inviolable – they cannot be broken by anyone (except by God, in which case He performs a miracle). To Aquinas, "natural law" refers to the laws given to us by God, which we discern by reason, and to which our actions should conform. Natural laws are, in short, principles of reason and morality that should guide our actions. So they are not descriptive, but normative (or prescriptive), and they are violable, meaning that human beings can choose to not act according to their dictates (Thomas Aquinas, 1964–1976, IaIIae 91, 2).

The basic moral principle to Aquinas is to do good and avoid evil. Since we cannot pursue the good, period, because it is an abstract concept, we are to pursue particular goods, such as life, knowledge, procreation, and society, goods that we should preserve, promote, honor, and so on, as the case may be. Although to Aquinas some actions are always prohibited, such as intentionally killing innocent people, whether an action is right or wrong often depends on the particular situation and aspects of the act; some acts, for example, are wrong because of the intentions behind them, others because they employ defective reasoning, even if the intentions are good (Thomas Aquinas, 1964–1976, IaIIae 94, 2; 92, 3).

Sexual acts are wrong if they are either non-procreative, such as homosexual sex, masturbation, or sex with animals; and non-procreative heterosexual sexual acts (oral and anal sex), or if they are procreative in kind but with the wrong party, such as heterosexual incest, rape, and adultery (Thomas Aquinas, 1964–1976, IIaIIae, 154, 1; 154, 11). The sexual acts in the first set are worse than those in the second, because they are against the natural laws that God laid down for us. The acts in the second set are wrong, but only because they are against how human beings are to relate to each other.[1] To Aquinas, the only morally acceptable sexual acts are between a husband and his wife that can result in procreation. It is crucial that the sex should occur between a married couple, because procreation means more than just bringing children into the world; it also means nurturing and educating them. That is why, according to Aquinas, marriage should endure for as long as the husband or wife is alive (1956, Book 3).

Aquinas's views form the theological and philosophical basis for the doctrines of the Catholic Church. For example, in his encyclical work, *Humanae Vitae*, Pope Paul VI accepts Aquinas's role of procreation in evaluating marital sexual acts, but he also fuses it with love: the idea that sex must be open to procreation

> is founded upon the inseparable connection, willed by God and unable to be broken by man on his own initiative, between the two meanings of the conjugal act: the unitive meaning and the procreative meaning. … By safeguarding both these essential aspects, unitive and procreative, the

conjugal act preserves in its fullness the sense of true mutual love and its ordination towards man's highest calling to parenthood.

(Paul VI 1984, 172)

In *Love and Responsibility*, Karol Wojtyla (Pope John Paul II) argues that sexual intercourse should occur only between a husband and his wife, and that they should only have sex when they accept the possibility of procreation. They should refrain from sexual intercourse when they do not accept this possibility or when they intentionally try to prevent it (by, say, using contraceptives). Wojtyla states the following claim, reminiscent of Kant and one we will see with the new natural lawyers:

> When the idea that "I may become a father"/"I may become a mother" is totally rejected in the mind and will of husband and wife nothing is left of the marital relationship, objectively speaking, except mere sexual enjoyment. One person becomes an object of use for another person, which is incompatible with the personalistic norm.
>
> (Wojtyla 1981, 237)

He allows married couples, in line with previous Catholic views, to use the "rhythm method" – to time their sexual intercourse during those periods when the woman is usually infertile.

Obviously, on these views gay marriage is unacceptable. If sexual intercourse should be confined to married heterosexual couples (even then only under certain conditions), and if homosexual sex is immoral, the state is under no obligation to recognize it. Moreover, since marriage today is not simply a private contract between two people, but a public recognition of their commitment, it has a celebratory dimension to it, in which the state plays a part. This is why the state is not required to recognize gay marriages if they involve immoral sex.[2]

Arguments of the New Natural Lawyers

The new natural lawyers are "new" because they amend and somewhat depart from previous natural law theories. They include John Finnis, Germain Grisez, and Robert George. They also, as the philosopher and legal scholar Andrew Koppleman puts it, offer perhaps the strongest argument against the morality of homosexuality, from a firm commitment to their own views, without "invoking false factual claims about gay people" (2008, 151), such as that gay people are child molesters.

Robert George claims that any non-penile–vaginal sexual act occurring outside marriage is both non-marital and immoral. George and other new natural lawyers understand marriage to be "a two-in-one-flesh communion of persons … consummated and actualized by sexual acts of the reproductive type" and to be a basic human good, providing the spouses with a reason to perform marital sexual acts (George and Bradley 1995, 301–302), much as knowledge – another basic good – gives us reason to seek it for its own sake. Marriage itself, not having children, sexual pleasure, recreation, and other reasons, is both a necessary and sufficient reason for the spouses to engage in sex: "It is our position … that [pleasure or the expression of love] are *not adequate reasons* for spouses – fertile or infertile – to engage in sexual relations" (1995, 305). Only sexual acts whose point is the good of marriage itself can be "truly unitive, and thus marital" (1995, 305). Any other type of sexual act is non-unitive and disintegrates the self. George and Bradley give the example of an elderly married couple who, while physiologically capable of having sexual intercourse, "no longer experience pleasure in their acts of genital discourse." Nonetheless, there is still a point for the couple to have genital sex "as a way of actualizing and experiencing their marriage as a one-flesh union" (1995, 310).

So what count as sexual but non-marital acts? The list includes sexual acts between (1) more than two people (e.g., threesomes), (2) members of the same sex, (3) non-married heterosexual people, (4) a married couple but such that the acts are only anal, oral, or, generally, non-penile–vaginal sex, and (5) a married couple but who engage in sex for reasons other than the good of marriage itself. Important for George is the *type* of sex: a married couple who are no longer capable of having children can still satisfy George's criterion for marital sex acts.

The sexual acts on the above list, whether between non-married or married couples, are non-marital sexual acts. So they are, according to George and Bradley, also *immoral*, because non-marital sex has the "grave defect" of damaging "personal (and interpersonal integrity) by reducing persons' bodies to the status of means to extrinsic ends" (1995, 313–314). The Kantian idea here is that people should not treat their bodies as mere instruments, because this damages "the integrity of the acting person as a dynamic unity of body, mind, and spirit" (1995, 314). How so? In a co-authored article with Patrick Lee, George and Lee distinguish – as do many other new natural lawyers – a person's consciously experiencing and desiring self from a person's bodily self. Claiming that these are "metaphysically inseparable," when a person "existentially" separates them for the sake of "extrinsic goals, such as producing experiences desired purely for the satisfaction of the conscious self," he or she disintegrates him or herself as an "acting person," and "one treats the body as a mere extrinsic means: one regards the body as something outside or apart from the subject, and so as mere object. A certain contempt for the body inheres in such choices" (Lee and George 1997, 139). In short, one uses one's body simply to get a particular feeling or sensation (1997, 139, note 13).

Biological unity plays a crucial role in the arguments of the new natural lawyers. On a number of occasions, George states that when engaged in a reproductive act type, the male and the female "form a single reproductive principle; they become 'one flesh.'" This is a matter of simple biology (George 2003, 125) and the "two-in-one-flesh" expression is to be understood literally, not figuratively (George and Bradley 1995, 301, note 1). Because George views marriage as an intrinsic good and understands it as "the community formed by a man and a woman who publicly consent to share their whole lives, in a *type of relationship* oriented toward the begetting, nurturing, and education of children together" (Lee and George 1997, 143), not only is sexual intercourse appropriate and expected in marriage, but a particular one at that – penile–vaginal intercourse. Marriage can properly be realized sexually as a good only through penile–vaginal intercourse, because it is reproductive and allows the couple to form a biological unit.

John Finnis's view is similar to George's. Following Aquinas's lead, Finnis claims that homosexual sex fails to realize the crucial good of marriage: "Marriage, with its double blessing – procreation and friendship – is a real common good. Moreover, it is a common good that can be both actualized and experienced in the orgasmic union of the reproductive organs of a man and a woman united in commitment to that good" (2008, 136). Two men or two women who think they are actualizing marriage or even expressing their mutual affection when having sex traffic in illusions, because their reproductive organs cannot make them a single unit and they cannot have children (2008, 136). Finnis puts the point in strong terms: "In reality, whatever the generous hopes and dreams with which the loving partners surround their use of their genitals, *that use* cannot express more than is expressed if two strangers engage in genital activity to give each other orgasm, or a prostitute pleasures a client, or a man pleasures himself" (2008, 137).

Moreover, to Finnis, that homosexual sex brings pleasure to its participants does not make it morally acceptable, because whether pleasurable activity is morally good depends on the type of activity in question, not on its being pleasurable (see Aristotle 1999, 1175a22–1176a30). If one derives pleasure from committing murder, the pleasure does not make the activity acceptable. Similarly for homosexual sex, whereby the body "now is functioning not in the way one, as a bodily person, acts to instantiate some other intelligible good, but precisely as providing a service to one's consciousness, to satisfy one's desire for satisfaction" (2008, 137). In other words, because homosexual sex is itself immoral (it does not realize or promote an intrinsic good), being pleasurable is not going to make it moral.

Let us put the new natural lawyers' argument more succinctly. First, marriage (not pleasure) and the integrity of the self are basic, intrinsic human goods (marriage is understood as a community by a man and a woman in a form of relationship open to begetting and raising children). Second, sexual acts are moral only when they involve interpersonal unity (not the disintegration of the self), thus realizing the good of marriage. Third, only marital sex allows the couple to participate in non-disintegrating sexual activity and to realize the good of marriage. Therefore, fourth, to be moral, sexual acts must be marital; any other sexual activity involves using the body, whether one's own or another's, as a means to pleasure. It disintegrates the self and is therefore immoral.

Because all non-marital sexual acts are immoral and homosexual sex is non-marital, it is also immoral. It is therefore unclear why the state should recognize same-sex marriages when they revolve around homosexual sex (the possibility of some sexless gay marriages notwithstanding). Those who think that homosexual sex is not as such immoral, and who want to make a strong case for same-sex marriages, need to clear this hurdle. I do so by criticizing the view of the new natural lawyers.

Evaluating the Arguments of the New Natural Lawyers

There are numerous problems with this view. I focus on four.

(1) It is entirely unclear why we, the general public, should accept George and others' definition of marriage. It rests on a particular view of marriage, one not consonant with how we generally understand it. George admits that society has recognized, and continues to recognize, marriages whose spouses intend them for procreation, companionship, or other purposes, but he claims that they are "specifically distinct from the intrinsic good of marriage" (Lee and George 1997, 145). This is true only in that such marriages depart from what *George* thinks are real marriages, but he gives no *argument* to support his own definition, and few people today accept his definition. Because the new natural lawyers offer a normative definition of "marriage," they need to argue for it, not merely assert it.

(2) We should reject George's definition of marriage on grounds other than that he has not supported it. Even though it is a matter of simple biology that neither males nor females can reproduce on their own, it is unclear what it means that they become one union "literally." It seems to me that they do not, and that all that happens is that their bodies are incredibly close to each other in the sexual act of intercourse. Even if we accept the biological unity point, no moral conclusions follow, because biology by itself tells us little, if anything, about how we should act. We are biologically equipped and even "designed" to eat meat, but this tells us nothing about whether meat-eating is moral. Had George understood "union" in a metaphorical or moral way, whereby the spouses desire to become one in their act of intercourse, his view would have been different, but it could not rule out other sexual acts that unite two lovers, such as sex between gay couples and non-penile–vaginal sex between heterosexual couples. Indeed, this is why the new natural lawyers insist on biological unity, because only it gives them the union they seek while also ruling out non-penile–vaginal sex.

(3) To the new natural lawyers, non-marital sex is immoral. It involves the use of one's body in a merely instrumental way, leading to the disintegration of the self. But when a married couple intend to have sex for the "sake of bodily marital unity," their action as intentional agents is the same as their action as bodily agents, so there is no disintegration. George and Lee give the example of John and Susan who have non-marital sex: John "uses Susan's body to obtain sexual pleasure … her personal presence is irrelevant; that it is Susan and not some other woman, is irrelevant, is not essential, to the intentional action he is performing, which is getting gratification or pleasure"

(Lee and George 1997, 141). This example is strange. It may illustrate *some* forms of sexual encounters, say, between people who seek casual sex *and* who have few, if any, requirements regarding their partner's personal qualifications. But if John and Susan love each other, like each other very much, or are just attracted to each other for what they are physically, it would greatly matter to John that he has sex with *Susan*. As Thomas Nagel claims (2008, 35), we don't usually care which omelet we eat as long as it satisfies certain requirements (e.g., fluffy, made only of egg whites), but when it comes to people, we do care: John wants to have sex with Susan, not someone else; it is Susan's body, her laugh, her mannerisms that attract John. John does not want just pleasure, as George and Lee put it, but pleasure-with-Susan or pleasure-from-Susan. Contrary to George, non-marital sexual acts are not all of one type. Sometimes x does use y simply for x's pleasure and does not really care that y is y, but sometimes x desires sex specifically with y. In such cases, it is not clear at all that x is merely using y's body. George must clarify his conceptual terrain when it comes to sexual pleasure because there are different types of cases lurking here.

Interestingly, George, along with Finnis, also claims – again in a Kantian way – that in non-marital sex x not only uses y's body for mere pleasure, but also x's own body. X wants only to produce in himself pleasurable sensations, and uses his body to this effect. But this is contrary to how many couples experience their sexual experiences. Many have sex to express affection, love, tenderness, trust, and so on, and they experience pleasure *as* they do so. George insists that the good of marriage is the only good that can make sex non-instrumental, and Finnis that such pleasures are not good because they are not part of a good activity, such as realizing the good of marriage. But this flies in the face of the experiences of such couples, and it begs the question, because we must *first* establish that such sexual activity is not an intrinsic good *before* declaring its pleasures unacceptable. That is, if love and pleasure are intrinsic goods, couples could have sex intending to promote them. Thus, George and Finnis's claims are unconvincing.

So far, I have argued that George is mistaken about a whole class of non-marital sexual acts, in which couples have sex because they love each other or because they want to please each other. There remains the class of casual sex, and many people, not just the new natural lawyers, consider it wrong because it involves objectification – the use of another's and one's own body for sexual purposes. But George's arguments for this view are unclear regarding what treating one's body as "if it were outside oneself, a sub-personal project" means. To George (and Finnis), "since we are our bodies (and do not merely inhabit them), it is treating a person (ourselves) as a sub-personal project" (Lee and George 1997, 155). So it violates one's self-integration. But it is difficult to understand how this disintegration can happen. Unlike my house, which I inhabit and which is not me, I cannot use my body separately from my conscious self. Indeed, if x masturbates, x experiences the pleasures of orgasm in x's body, not merely in x's conscious self (whatever this means).

So the disintegration that George speaks of is non-physical and moral. George often makes the analogy with using heroin, whereby one's body is merely treated as a vehicle for bringing about a drug-induced mental state. But the analogy is problematic: the drug user not only uses his body to produce certain experiences, he *abuses* it, thus getting himself into all sorts of problems, moral and non-moral. Non-marital sexual activity, however, does not, as such, lead to the practitioners' moral demise, even if done frequently. People who masturbate, have casual sex, and so on are not dying in droves or begging for change in street gutters. Their careers, friendships, hobbies, family relationships, and other goods are not usually jeopardized because of their sexual activities. There are cases of sex addiction, and sometimes sexual activity has pernicious effects, but they are usually incidental to the case and do not stem from the fact that, as George wants to claim, the sex is non-marital. Thus, George's idea of disintegration is unclear.

(4) Infertile or sterile heterosexual couples raise hurdles for the new natural lawyers. Such couples can have sex and be biologically "united" in that the man can have penile–vaginal intercourse with the woman, but it is unclear why this morally differentiates them from a loving homosexual couple. Germain Grisez, another new natural lawyer, claims that if a "couple know or come to learn that they will never be able to have children, their marital communion is no less real and no less fulfilling as a communion of complementary persons, even though it always will lack the fulfillment of parenthood" (1993, 572). But, again, it is unclear why a homosexual couple cannot have the same fulfillment. Finnis adopts a different strategy, claiming that a sterile heterosexual couple is still engaged in the *kind of sexual act* that is marital:

> a husband and a wife who unite their reproductive organs in an act of sexual intercourse which, so far as they then can make it, is of a kind suitable for generation, do function as a biological (and thus personal) unit and thus can be actualizing and experiencing the two-in-one-flesh common good and reality of marriage, even when some biological condition happens to prevent that unity resulting in generation of a child. Their conduct thus differs radically from the acts of a husband and a wife whose intercourse is masturbatory, for example sodomitic or by fellatio or coitus interruptus.
>
> (Finnis 1997, 35–36)

It also "radically" differs, of course, from homosexual sex. Yet why should this kind of act make a moral difference? Like homosexual couples, infertile heterosexual couples cannot have children by having sex with each other. Like homosexual couples, they can be loving and affectionate. Why a biological process or difference in organs should spill into a moral difference remains a mystery.

So the new natural lawyers have not made a good case that non-marital sex, including homosexual sex, is immoral.

There are other arguments having nothing to do with new natural law that gay sex is wrong, but none is successful (see Corvino 1997, Jaeger 2008, Mohr 1988, ch. 1, Ruse 1988, ch. 8). Moreover, no moral theory entails the immorality of homosexual sex. Of the three moral theories we considered in this book, consequentialism clearly does not. Virtue ethics' stress on the virtues says nothing about the morality of homosexuality, because knowing only that someone is gay (or straight, for that matter) says nothing about whether she is courageous, wise, just, temperate, and honest – whether she is virtuous or vicious (Hooker 2002, Hursthouse 2002). And although Kant himself (mistakenly; see Soble 2003) thought that homosexual sex is wrong, Kantian ethics does not (see Denis 1999, 2007). The road is clear, then, for the state to accept same-sex marriages as far as the morality of their sexual activities are concerned.

The Slippery-Slope Argument

The Causal Version

The essence of the slippery-slope argument is that accepting same-sex marriages opens the door to accepting other forms of marriage that are immoral, such as group marriages and marriages between siblings, parents and children, and people and animals. The argument has two forms. The first is causal: accepting same-sex marriage will actually lead (or will probably lead) to these unacceptable marriages. The second is the "lack of principles" form: accepting same-sex marriages removes any principles on which basis we could prevent these unacceptable marriages, even if they do not actually occur.

Stanley Kurtz, a conservative writer, gives the causal version of the slippery-slope argument:

> Among the likeliest effects of gay marriage is to take us down a slippery slope to legalized polygamy and "polyamory" (group marriage). Marriage will be transformed into a variety of relationship contracts, linking two, three, or more individuals (however weakly and temporarily) in every conceivable combination of male and female.
>
> (Kurtz 2008, 180)

The evidence Kurtz gives for these likely effects of accepting same-sex marriage is that a growing number of academics, lawyers, and organizations have already begun agitating for polygamy and polyamory (2008, 180–182, 185–189). But his reasoning is weak. Just because some people advocate for these types of marriages does not mean that they will, or will likely, come about. After all, there are also people like Kurtz who advocate against such marriages.

More interesting is why Kurtz finds polygamy and polyamory problematic. Note that the slippery-slope argument against same-sex marriage might or might not work depending on what it claims same-sex marriage leads to. If it claims to lead to any type of marriage whatsoever, then accepting same-sex marriage might be troubling because we wouldn't want to accept marriages between, say, siblings or between parents and children. But if, as in Kurtz's version of the argument, same-sex marriage leads to only polygamy and polyamory, the argument is not obviously troubling, because we need a good reason to think that polygamy and polyamory are unacceptable.

Unlike the reasons usually offered against polygamy – that it usually takes the form of one man married to more than one woman, which usually means that men treat their wives unfairly and that in patriarchal societies polygamy is a deeply sexist form of marriage – Kurtz's reason is different:

> it erodes the ethos of monogamous marriage. Despite the divorce revolution, Americans still take it for granted that marriage means monogamy. The ideal of fidelity may be breached in practice, yet adultery is clearly understood as a transgression against marriage. Legal polygamy would jeopardize that understanding.
>
> (Kurtz 2008, 182)

However, Kurtz never tells us how and why polygamy would endanger the ethos of monogamy. He needs to, because if most Americans were *committed* to the ideal of monogamy, polygamy would not threaten it. Perhaps the idea is that if it is sanctioned by the state, the state sends the message that it is okay, even good, to be in a polygamous marriage, and this gets Americans thinking of switching over from monogamous to polygamous marriages. But it is hard to predict how things will be if polygamy became enshrined in law – maybe people just won't be attracted to it, even if the state sends the message that it is "good." Moreover, Kurtz states that "in our world of freely choosing individuals, extended families fall away, and love and companionship are the only surviving principles on which families can be built" (2008, 182). If monogamous marriage is the time-tested form of marriage for Westerners, and if love and companionship were its only, or prevalent, surviving bases, one would think that polygamy will have a hard time destabilizing monogamy.

But suppose that state-sanctioned polygamy affects Americans' thinking on this issue to the point where many start switching over to polygamous forms of marriage. Would this be a problem? Not obviously. First, it would have been "freely choosing individuals" who decide to make the switch. Second, it is unclear why monogamy is so morally absolute. Why can people not have the choice between monogamy and non-monogamy (see Chapter 9)? Moreover, Kurtz shouldn't take the claim that polygamy is opposed to monogamy for granted. If "monogamous marriage" means "marriage between two and only two people," then polygamy would be opposed to it. But if "monogamous marriage" means "marriage in which the parties are faithful to each other," polygamy would not be opposed to monogamous marriage, but could be one form of such marriage if the spouses are faithful to each other. So if "monogamy" means "marital faithfulness," as Kurtz seems to think, polygamy need not threaten its ethos.

Moreover, many people distinguish between loveless sexual activity and sex with love. Married couples can agree, and many have, to have open relationships and understand marital fidelity in emotional, not sexual, terms. Because such arrangements are not necessarily immoral, it is not obvious that monogamy is such a sacred cow after all, and Kurtz needs to convince us why it is.[3]

But suppose that polygamy and polyamory threaten monogamy. What has accepting same-sex marriage got to do with them? According to Kurtz, once

> we say that gay couples have a right to have their commitments recognized by the state, it becomes next to impossible to deny that same right to polygamists, polyamorists, or even cohabitating relatives and friends. … The only way to stop gay marriage from launching a slide down this slope is if there is a compelling state interest in blocking polygamy or polyamory that does not also apply to gay marriage.
>
> (Kurtz 2008, 190)

Kurtz claims that although the state does have a compelling interest, which is that polygamy and polyamory threaten the ethos of monogamy, he claims that this interest applies also to gay marriage on the same grounds: gay marriage threatens the ethos of monogamy.

The idea that same-sex marriage threatens the ethos of monogamy is conceptually distinct from that which leads society down the slippery slope to polygamy and polyamory. Kurtz could have directly argued against same-sex marriage on the ground that it endangers monogamous marriage, without having to go through the slippery-slope argument. This is a different argument against same-sex marriage that I put below, where I discuss the view that same-sex marriage directly threatens "traditional" marriage.

So far, then, Kurtz's reasons that same-sex marriage will actually lead to polygamy and polyamory, let alone to other clearly unacceptable forms of marriage, are unimpressive. Note that if the ethos of society were generally hostile to such arrangements, but not to same-sex marriages, accepting the second would not lead to the first. If the ethos is generally indifferent or even accepting of different types of marriage – a "marry, and let marry" type of attitude – then which forms of marriage should be accepted by society would have to be discussed on a case-by-case basis. There may be no good reasons (except, perhaps, practical ones) to reject group marriages, but there may be good reasons to reject incestuous marriages. There may be good reasons to accept same-sex marriages, and good reasons to reject other types of marriages. This denial of different good reasons for different types of marriages is the essence of the "lack of principles" version of the slippery-slope argument.

The Lack of Principles Version

A number of conservative commentators have voiced this version of the argument. Replying to the views of the gay conservative writer Andrew Sullivan, William Bennett states,

> Broadening the definition of marriage to include same-sex unions would stretch it almost beyond recognition – and new attempts to expand the definition still further would surely follow. On what principled ground can Andrew Sullivan exclude others who most desperately want what he wants, legal recognition and social acceptance? Why on earth would Sullivan exclude from marriage a bisexual who wants to marry two other people? After all, exclusion would be a denial of that person's sexuality. The same holds true of a father and daughter who want to marry. Or two sisters. Or men who want (consensual) polygamous arrangements.
>
> (Bennett 1997, 275)

Hadley Arkes, another conservative thinker and new natural lawyer, states,

> I want to make clear that I am not offering a prediction. I am not saying that if we accept gay marriage we will be engulfed by polygamy and incest and other exotic arrangements. I am raising a question of principle about the ground on which the law says no [to these other arrangements].
>
> (Arkes 1997, 277)

Finally, the conservative commentator Charles Krauthammer states,

> The problem here is not the slippery slope. It is not that if society allows gay marriage, society will then allow polygamy or incest. It won't. … The point is why they won't allow it. They won't allow it because they think polygamy and incest wrong or unnatural or perhaps harmful. At bottom, because they find these practices psychologically or morally abhorrent, certainly undeserving of society's blessing. Well, that is how most Americans feel about homosexual marriage.
>
> (Krauthammer 1997, 284)

Common to these three views is the idea that once we accept same-sex marriages, we lose the ability to reason cogently against other forms of marriage. There is a deep flaw in this argument that I explain below. For now, consider two replies to it. First, Andrew Sullivan argues that homosexuality and heterosexuality are "states," whereas polygamy is an activity. As states, sexual orientations are deep human traits and on whose basis people partly organize their lives, including choosing their companions and lovers (1997). Think of it this way: there are both heterosexual and homosexual polygamists, heterosexual and homosexual incestuous relationships. If we decide, on rational grounds, that polygamy, incest, and sex with animals are bad things, this will be so for both heterosexuals and homosexuals. Same-sex marriages, as such, have no necessary connections with polygamy, incest, and other "exotic" forms of relationships.

Offering a reply similar to Sullivan's, Jonathan Rauch states, "no serious person claims there are people constitutively attracted only to relatives, or only to groups rather than individuals" (1997a, 286). This is a good reply (but is anybody attracted to a "group," as Rauch says, or to the individual members of that group?) and goes some way toward addressing the objection, because insofar as homosexuality (and heterosexuality) is a deep trait on which basis we decide whom we want to be with, love, or spend the rest of our lives with, they make for a compelling case for marriage. Not so for polygamy and incest: there are no sexual orientations for these (but are we sure? and what about zoophilia and necrophilia?). The reply, however, doesn't go far enough, because the issue is ultimately not sexual orientation, but happiness and people's ability to lead their lives as they choose. The reason why Sullivan and Rauch emphasize that homosexuality and heterosexuality are deep character traits is because to most people these traits are the basis on which they choose their romantic mates (or life partners), and people choose their particular mates in order to lead happy, fulfilled lives. If someone were not interested in having a mate, marrying, or being in love, his or her sexual orientation would (or should) not play a role in Sullivan and Rauch's arguments.

But then what about someone who cannot be happy unless he marries his sister, his brother, his pet iguana, or his three roommates? He might say, "Look. It doesn't matter whether I'm gay, straight, or bi. What matters is that I want to spend the rest of my life with Tom, Dick, and Harry, and they want to spend theirs with me and with each other. We also want everybody to recognize it. So we want to marry each other." At this point, we can either argue that the relationship into which he wishes to enter is immoral and so the state is under no obligation to sanctify it through marriage, or we can argue that because the type of relationship into which he wishes to enter does not serve the purpose or purposes of marriage, the state is also under no obligation to sanctify it.

If the relationship is immoral, we have a principled reason against it, contrary to what Arkes, Bennett, Krauthammer, and others think. If the relationship is moral, then we have no principled reason to reject blessing it with marriage unless it does not serve marriage's purpose or purposes, which brings us to the second point: the purpose of marriage. To Rauch, the purpose of marriage is not love, but to (1) bind pairs with each other so that they can take care of each other, thus relieving society and the state from having to, (2) provide a good environment for raising children, and (3) domesticate men: the power of marriage is "to settle men, to keep them at home and out of trouble" (1997b, 312). To Rauch, polygamy, incest, and other aberrant forms of marriage go against these purposes, and this is what, according to him, supplies us with a reason for rejecting them (1997a, 287). Polygamy goes against the purposes of marriage because "if one man has two wives, it follows that some other man has no wife," with the result that "many low-status males end up unable to wed and dangerously restless" (1997a, 287), which goes against two of the above purposes of marriage, namely that many men would be unsettled and would have no one, in their old age, to take care of them. Incest undermines marriage's purposes because a society which allows incest would "devastate family life by, effectively, legitimizing sexual predation within it" (1997a, 288).

Same-sex marriages would not undermine marriage's purposes. One might think they do because if lesbians marry other lesbians, this would result in leaving many men unsettled. This is not true, because even if lesbians do *not* marry other lesbians, they would not marry men anyway. However many men are unsettled, lesbian marriages would not be the cause. Lesbian marriages do, as far as we can tell, provide good homes for raising children, and they would allow lesbian couples to take care of each other, thus fulfilling two purposes of marriage. Gay men marrying each other, in addition to fulfilling these two purposes, also fulfill the purpose of settling men, since two gay men would domesticate each other (perhaps not as effectively as one woman domesticating another man, but some domestication is better than none). If gay men don't marry each other they wouldn't marry women, and so would be undomesticated.

There are two problems with this argument, one of which Rauch himself is aware. Gay group marriages fulfill Rauch's purposes of marriage: spouses would take care of each other, provide an environment for raising children (some would say a more stable one than two-parent households), and settle men (in gay male group marriages). So we would still have polygamy, albeit of the same-sex sort. Rauch's reply that "no homosexuals that I know of want the right to marry two or more same-sex partners, and society has no earthly reason to sanction such a frivolous right anyway" (1997a, 288) is weak, because the point is whether there are reasons, period, to demand this right, not whether Rauch knows of anyone who wants group marriage. Moreover, society could have good reasons to sanction such rights (polygyny might be justified if society's male population is being depleted due to war). So there are "earthly" reasons. And they don't have to be dramatic, like wars: if some individuals make a good case that they should be allowed a group marriage, or if a woman offers religious reasons why she should marry three men, society could sanction such marriages, on a case-by-case basis, thus side-stepping the problems, according to Rauch, of *widespread* polygamy or polyandry and undermining the proper functioning of society.

The second problem with Rauch's view is that it is not obvious that marriage domesticates men, whether they are straight or gay. Part of the issue here is that "domesticate" means different things, with one meaning (emphasized in gay marriage debates) being "dampening male promiscuity." If by "promiscuity" we mean lots of casual sexual encounters with many different people, marriage probably helps to stop this, because from a practical point of view it is hard to maintain a home or domicile while one (or both) of the spouses is continuously bed-hopping. But if "promiscuity" means "the opposite of monogamy," marriage does not seem to work as well. Many gay male couples have open relationships, and some straight couples, too. Many spouses cheat on each other. For sexual hunger for variety, marriage can only do so much.

There is, however, a better reply to the slippery-slope argument than Rauch's or Sullivan's: unless we can convincingly argue that "traditional" marriage has one or a few specific and primary purposes, defenders of the traditional one-man, one-woman marriage face the same slippery-slope objection (cf. Corvino 2005). Here's how. Suppose that someone says, "Well, once you say that marriage is between one man and one woman, you have no principled reason why it cannot be between two men, or between two women, or between one man and two or more women, or between one woman and two or more men, or between two siblings, or between a parent and his or her child, or between .... The only reason you might have is tradition – that's-how-marriage-has-always-been. But even if marriage has always been this way – and it has not – this is not a good, principled reason." Think of it this way: polygamy as such has nothing to do with being heterosexual or homosexual (historically speaking, virtually all forms of polygamous marriages have been between either one man and more than one woman, or, more rarely, one woman and more than one man). If marriage is between one man and one woman, what principled reason can be given for why a man (or a woman) should not marry more than one woman (or man)? Incest, as such, has nothing to do with heterosexuality or homosexuality (indeed, most cases of incest take the form of a father or stepfather sexually molesting his daughter). If marriage is between one man and one woman, what principled reason can be given why the two should not be closely related to each other? The same reasoning can be raised about other, more "exotic" forms of marriage.

Does marriage have one, two, or a few purposes that can stop the slippery-slope argument facing the traditional view of marriage? We can rely on either historical, actual, or normative purposes. Historical, actual purposes won't help the defender of traditional marriage for two reasons. First, people have married, and continue to marry, for various purposes, as stated in the previous chapter. If, for example, people have married in the past for economic reasons, these same reasons can rule in favor of polygamous marriages (e.g., group marriages are stronger economic units than two-partner marriages). This is also true of marriage as an *institution* (as opposed to the individual couples), which has had many purposes throughout history and across cultures. Second, historical, actual reasons by themselves carry no principled weight; the fact that people have married for such-and-such reasons says nothing, in itself, about whether these reasons are principled. We would still have to argue why such-and-such reasons, not others, should be *the* purposes of marriage.

We are left with normative reasons. I am not sure how one goes about arguing that some purposes, and not others, are normative when it comes to marriage. But from a list of plausible purposes, none preserves the traditional view of marriage. One such purpose is romantic love. Love rules out marriage between a person and an animal (even if the person claims to *romantically* love the animal, we are hard-pressed to believe that the animal, even if from a higher species, reciprocates). But it would not rule out incestuous relationships in a principled way, because, even though siblings do not usually romantically fall in love with each other, it is possible that they do (similarly for parents and children). Nor would romantic love rule out polygamous relationships: it is possible, and has happened, that one man loves more than one spouse, say. It certainly doesn't rule out same-sex marriages. So if love is a normative purpose of marriage, it won't exclude same-sex marriages, and may even allow some polygamous and incestuous marriages.

Companionship, another plausible normative purpose for marriage, fares worse: it does not in principle rule out *any* form of marriage. People may want to marry their pets; they, after all, make excellent companions (they may not want to or actually have sex with their pets, by the way, for them to marry each other; lots of marriages are sexless). People may want to marry their book collections; books also make for good companions. The same reasoning applies to polygamous, incestuous, and other forms of marriage. It certainly applies to same-sex marriages.

Procreation, another plausible purpose, rules out *too* many forms of marriage while not ruling out others: it rules out marriages between people and animals, same-sex marriages, marriages between heterosexual couples past the ability to procreate, and heterosexual couples one or both of whom is sterile, but it does *not* rule out heterosexual incestuous or polygamous relationships! Moreover, more sophisticated versions of the procreation purpose – such as the new natural lawyers' – while formulated so as to rule in the right and rule out the wrong ones, are implausible.[4]

I am not hopeful that one, two, or a few normative purposes of marriage exist such that only traditional marriage ends up being *the* right or proper form of marriage. First, speaking of the purpose of marriage could mean "whatever reasons the married partners have for getting married" or "the social function that marriage as an institution serves, regardless of the specific reasons that the married partners have." If the first, people marry for many reasons, and we are hard-pressed to know which one is the normative purpose of marriage. The second meaning is more plausible because it makes more sense to speak of the function of marriage as a whole, but what criteria should we use to decide the purposes of marriage as an institution? And how can we differentiate between *purposes* of marriage and its *byproducts*? To see the difficulty here, consider again Rauch's views. Rauch argues for marriage's purposes, specifically "settling males and providing reliable caregivers" (1997b, 312), by reminding us that whenever packs of young males get together we can expect trouble, and that when a single person gets sick it is his friends, his family, or even social institutions who will have to take care of him. Thus he infers that the purposes of marriage are to domesticate men and to provide caretakers. Fair enough, and the purposes he gives sound plausible.

But, first, the purposes Rauch gives are plausible only in our time or in particular societies. In the past, marriage functioned as cementing political alliances, with husbands often taking on numerous mistresses (no domestication here). For individuals to be able to strike out on their own away from their parents, they married and had children, because wives and children were a form of labor without which individuals could not live independently from their parents. Thus marriage also provided labor in the form of a wife and children. But this is not caretaking as Rauch understands it. In some societies, it is the family of the spouse that takes care of him or her when he or she grows old, not the other spouse.

Second, Rauch's views equally support the idea that male domestication and caretaking are good *byproducts* of marriage (not its purposes). Looking only at how marriage functions in society rather than the married couples' reasons for marriage, we cannot tell that these are marriage's *purposes* instead of its byproducts. We know that holding pens is a good byproduct of a mug, not its purpose, only because we already know that the purpose of mugs is for drinking. Not so with marriage. We have no universal blueprint for its purposes, so differentiating its purposes from its byproducts is difficult, if not impossible.

The point is that even if Rauch's purposes for the institution of marriage sound plausible, we cannot be confident that they are culturally and temporally universal, or that they are purposes rather than byproducts. From what history tells us, chances are that the purposes of marriage depend on time and place. Of course, we can agree with this point and discuss marriage and its purposes contextually. In the case of contemporary Western societies, we can say, marriage provides caretakers and domesticates men, in addition to providing companionship, providing a stable context for raising children, and allowing couples to have their love legally and socially recognized. But a contextual understanding of marriage's purposes won't rule out same-sex marriage for Western societies: gay men need as much domestication as straight men do (if not more, given the highly sexualized gay urban culture); both gay men and lesbians could use caretakers in their old age; they both need life companions; many want children; and both want their loves celebrated by society and recognized by law.

Without a proper set of normative purposes for marriage, we can launch the slippery-slope argument in the face of any form of marriage. We are better off throwing this argument in the philosophical trash bin. Whether a form of marriage is acceptable depends not on what other forms of marriage it can lead to, but on other considerations: if we think that marriage between a man and a dog is unacceptable, this is not because it will lead to marriage between men and crickets or between women and trees, but because marriage between humans and animals is not a good idea. So whether same-sex marriage should be legalized ought to be considered on its own merits.

The "Undermining Marriage" Argument

The main idea behind this argument is that same-sex marriage weakens the idea of "traditional" marriage. There are many possible ways in which it can do this. One way is by leading to other types of marriage (as the slippery-slope argument claims), in which case traditional marriage would become one among many, thus weakening its social status. Another way, however, is more direct. Let us see how this might work.

Stanley Kurtz argues that the "conservative" case for same-sex marriage (by people like Sullivan) "holds that the state-sanctioned marriage will reduce gay male promiscuity. But what if the effect works in reverse? What if, instead of marriage reducing gay promiscuity, sexually open gay couples help redefine marriage as a non-monogamous institution?" (2008, 190) Citing a few studies showing that substantial percentages of gay male couples have open relationships and would continue to have them were they to be legally married (2008, 190–192), Kurtz worries that gay male couples might influence straight people to become less and less monogamous. As to lesbian couples who tend to be more monogamous than gay men, Kurtz says:

> Lesbians who bear children with sperm donors sometimes set up de facto three-parent families. Typically, these families include a sexually bound lesbian couple, and a male biological father who is close to the couple but not sexually involved. Once lesbian couples can marry, there will be a powerful legal case for extending parental recognition to triumvirates … [which] will eventually usher in state-sanctioned triple (and therefore group) marriage.
>
> (Kurtz 2008, 192)

However, many lesbian couples use sperm banks, and so have no intimate knowledge of the biological father of the child; nor do they wish to. And lesbian couples that do involve the biological father in some way in their lives tend not to want to do so deeply – certainly not by having a three-parent family (this is not to mention childless lesbian couples). So Kurtz's "lesbian marriage" reasons against same-sex marriage are weak. Even if Kurtz is correct that gay marriages would tend to be non-traditional either because they are open or because they involve more than one party, this still does not explain how – let alone show why – such non-traditional marriages weaken monogamy. What exactly is the line of reasoning? Perhaps some straight couples would find such arrangements more suitable for them and would start abandoning the ship of monogamy. Although this might happen, it is a far cry from undermining monogamous marriage as such. Even if some (or many) straight couples found such arrangements suitable, this is not an obviously morally perturbing result, because, again, we shouldn't assume monogamy and traditional marriage to be absolute, untouchable goods.

In the end, whether same-sex marriage affects straight, traditional marriage and in what ways remain to be seen. We should keep two points in mind. First, how same-sex marriage will affect traditional marriage is not settled by mere speculation; relevant data need to be considered, especially data from countries that grant same-sex marriages. Even though it is still too early to tell, in those countries that have same-sex marriages, straight marriages don't seem to be affected (see Eskridge and Spedale (2007) for some data from Scandinavian countries).

Second, marriage has itself changed over the years for reasons having nothing to do with same-sex marriage or gay people. Laws regulating spousal relationships and divorce, and a host of other changes have happened to marriage due to a large number of historical, social, and political changes. Heterosexual marriage itself exhibits variety from country to country, culture to culture, and time to time. It is itself a changing institution, sensitive to changes in its social landscape (nothing surprising here; all social institutions change over time). Indeed, according to Stephanie Coontz,

> the demand for gay and lesbian marriage was an inevitable *result* of the previous revolution in heterosexual marriage. It was heterosexuals who had already created many alternative structures for organizing sexual relationships or raising children and broken down the primacy of two-parent families based on a strict division of labor between men and women.
>
> (Coontz 2005, 274, emphasis added)

It is not as if heterosexual marriage has remained the same for years, waiting to change for gay marriage to happen. Women's equality in marriage did not come about because gay marriage came into existence: women did not first see how gay couples didn't conform to gender roles and then decide to demand fewer gender roles in their own marriages. Instead, changes in the gender roles in heterosexual marriages came about as a result of economic, historical, and political factors, none of which had much to do with the gay rights movement. Of course, same-sex marriage can change heterosexual marriage further. But these changes are still unclear, so whether they are desirable is also unclear and depends on the nature of the change, not on the fact that it is change, period.

Richard Mohr's Argument for Same-Sex Marriage

Perhaps the most prominent philosopher to argue for same-sex marriage is Richard Mohr, who begins by relying on a non-legal, substantive definition of marriage: "the development and maintenance of intimacy through the medium of everyday life, the day-to-day." He puts it poetically as "the fused intersection of love's sanctity and necessity's demand" (2005, 61). On this view, x is married to y when x and y's love for each other is "grounded in and grows from the very means by which [x and y] jointly meet [their] basic needs – maintain a household and fulfill other everyday necessities" (2005, 61). Note immediately one interesting, and possibly unacceptable, consequence of Mohr's poetic version of the definition: it rules out any marriages in which the spouses do not love each other (e.g., some arranged marriages and those marriages that begin with love but eventually lose it). But if we accept the non-poetic version (which we should), such marriages would not be ruled out, because even loveless marriages contain a fair amount of intimacy. The non-poetic version of the definition also rules in all past marriages undertaken for political and economic reasons, because, they, too, contain much intimacy. The definition does rule out – a good thing, too – roommate relationships (which are not usually intimate) and friendships involving the cohabitation of the friends, which do not maintain themselves through life's daily necessities (2005, 61–62).

Mohr's argument for same-sex marriage takes seven steps. (1) If the above definition is correct, marriage clearly does not *require* its participants to be of the same sex or gender (2005, 65). Although doubts about whether the definition accurately covers all marriages, past, present, and future, no definition of "marriage" could withstand them, and Mohr's definition seems to accurately reflect our current idea of marriage. Since we have seen in this chapter that no good reasons exist (except for tradition – not a good reason) for why marriage has to be between one man and one woman, we should accept the first step of Mohr's argument.

(2) The available accounts on how committed gay couples conduct their lives fit the definition (2005, 66). That is, they cohabit, share finances, are privy to the details of each other's lives, take on each other's burdens and joys, and so on. Thus, as a first conclusion, and the third step in Mohr's argument, (3) these gay couples are married already, though, of course, in a substantive, non-legal sense. It is the next steps in the argument that are crucial, for they provide the bridge to Mohr's desired conclusions and the very issue at hand, namely that the state should legally recognize these substantive marriages. To cross this bridge, Mohr relies on the concepts of equality and dignity.

(4) To Mohr, moral equality is "at heart a principle that asserts individuals as having equal dignity or personhood … [it] is the authoritative claim that a person will not be held in lesser regard – as having less worth – unless that lesser regard is warranted by something the person has (or has not) done" (2005, 74). If x lies, cheats, murders, or does not support x's children, x may be held in lesser regard. But x should not be held in lesser regard simply because of who x is, because x is, say, African-American, a woman, an Arab, or gay. So equality in this sense is individual dignity, and to assault it is to presume that x is to be "held in morally lesser regard independent of what [x] has done. It is to suffer degradation and humiliation" (2005, 76). Note that if x is only *regarded* in inequitable ways, x need not thereby be *harmed* (although if x is *treated* inequitably, chances are that x will be harmed), because merely to regard x with inequity is to think of x as not being a full moral agent or person. It is to disrespect x in basic ways. Disrespect might not harm x, but it assaults x's dignity. This view of equality is plausible, insofar as we agree that we should regard or

treat people unequally only on the basis of what they do, not on the basis of who they are.

(5) Gay oppression is primarily a denial of moral equality. Using examples of popular, derogatory terms for and cultural stereotypes of gay people, Mohr argues convincingly that society's negative view of gays is one of fundamental disrespect. For example, the negative view of gay men as effeminate derives from society's view of what gay men *are*, not do, namely as lowly as women, perhaps even worse, because they are men and not women (2005, 77–81). In addition, three of society's crucial institutions reflect society's view of the low status of gay people. The military, after first banning them, now admits them so long as they do not declare their gayness; the Catholic Church and many Protestant churches generally view gay people as morally disordered; and the medical establishment has been motivated to combat AIDS largely due to worries about it spreading to heterosexuals (2005, 81–83). These three institutions have not necessarily treated gay people in bad ways, but their *attitude* reflects their disrespect, perhaps even contempt, for gay people. The military, for example, tells gay people in its "don't ask, don't tell" policy, "We'll admit you into the military so long as you hide who you are; try to be open and we will either not admit or discharge you" (cf. Card 1995, ch. 9).

(6) The *law* treats gay people inequitably if it draws on or enhances the view that gay people are held in lesser respect regardless of what gay people do or how they act (Mohr 2005, 87). (7) Denying gay people marriage is precisely such an inequitable treatment, because it considers gay people as not good enough to participate in one of the most sacred institutions in this country: marriage. How so? Although most states are willing to give gay couples domestic partnerships that typically mimic the rights and privileges of marriage, they do not allow them to marry. This explains, to Mohr, the indignity that gay people suffer: there is simply no obvious reason to deny gay people marriage given that the state is willing to allow them domestic partnerships, except for the insulting one that gay people are somehow not good enough for marriage, not because of anything that they do or do not do, but because they are lesser moral beings. Therefore, (8), for America to treat gays as equals, it must give them the option to marry (Mohr 2005, 89), a necessary, but not sufficient, condition for America to treat gay people with equality and dignity.[5]

Note that the Massachusetts Supreme Judicial Court, ruling in 2003 in favor of same-sex marriage (more accurately, ruling against prohibiting same-sex marriages), gave reasons virtually identical to Mohr's:

> The Massachusetts Constitution affirms the dignity and equality of all individuals. It forbids the creation of second-class citizens. In reaching our conclusion we have given full deference to the arguments made by the Commonwealth [of Massachusetts]. But it has failed to identify any constitutionally adequate reason for denying civil marriage to same-sex couples.
>
> (quoted in Chauncey 2004, 134–135)

The Supreme Court of Massachusetts declared that no good reason has been offered why gay couples should not have the right to marry. Without good reasons, denying them this right is tantamount to regarding them as second-class citizens.

Mohr's argument is powerful: why, indeed, is the state willing to allow same-sex couples to form legally recognized domestic partnerships, with all (or almost all) the practical and legal benefits that married people have, but won't allow same-sex couples to marry? It won't do to argue that marriage is by definition between a man and a woman, because this definition has no good philosophical backing, and because Mohr's substantive definition of marriage is plausible, at least in contemporary societies. Moreover, some of those who push us to accept marriage as by definition between a man and a woman seem to do so merely as a rationalization, because they are perhaps embarrassed to admit that they consider gay people less worthy than straight people and marriage as too good an institution for gay people (is this the reason why some find gay marriage to demean the institution of marriage?).

One possible response is that the state denies same-sex marriage not because of who gay people are, but because of what they do, namely engage in gay sex. This reply, if successful, goes against step (5) in Mohr's argument, thus blocking its conclusion. But the reply has two defects. First, there are no good reasons to believe that gay sex is immoral and so deserving of sanction. The views of the new natural lawyers are implausible, and no other moral theory seems to entail that gay sex is immoral. Second, if gay sex is bad enough to provide a good reason to bar gays from marrying each other, it should be bad enough to provide a good reason to bar gays from domestic partnerships, which, as mentioned, contain almost identical rights and privileges to those of marriage. So this reply won't do. The state has no good reason to prohibit same-sex marriages. It thus treats gay people inequitably and disrespectfully.

Cheshire Calhoun's Argument for Same-Sex Marriage

Cheshire Calhoun, in *Feminism, the Family, and the Politics of the Closet* (2000), analyzes the arguments used by members of Congress to defend DOMA, who viewed marriage as a pre-political institution, having a foundational status in society.[6] That is, "although states may create the legal package of rights and benefits that attach to marriage and may set age, sex, biological relationship and other restrictions on who may marry, the state does not create the institution of marriage itself" and the state "does not *choose* to recognize marriages" precisely because civil society's very existence depends on people getting married and forming families. In short, the state has no option but to recognize marriage. So, at least in the eyes of DOMA's defenders in Congress, those who are somehow fit to enter marriage have a distinctive political status. Therefore, "conversely, if a particular social group is deemed *un*fit to enter marriage and found a family, that group can then be denied this distinctive political status"

(Calhoun 2000, 124). Because the defenders of DOMA consider homosexuality immoral, to "recognize same-sex marriages legally would place the sacred institution of marriage in the disreputable company of immoral, unnatural unions, thus cheapening its status" (2000, 125).

However, Calhoun argues that immorality cannot fully explain the attitudes of those who were against same-sex marriage during the DOMA debates, because they were not generally against domestic partnerships. She concludes that the real reason against same-sex marriages was that they would demote heterosexual marriage from its special status as a pre-political institution. The defenders of DOMA seem to think that if the state recognizes same-sex marriage, marriage would become a contract between two individuals, on a par with other such contracts, implying that marriage is no longer a sacred institution. Since marriage is not your everyday, personal contract, same-sex marriages could not be allowed (2000, 126).

Thus, to Calhoun, it is crucial to fight for the right to same-sex marriages. Prohibiting same-sex marriage does not

> represent merely one among many ways that the state may discriminate against gays and lesbians by enacting laws based on stereotypes of lesbians' and gay men's gender deviance, undisciplined sexual desire, and unfitness for family life ... marriage bars enact the view that heterosexual love, marriage, and family have a uniquely prepolitical, foundational status in civil society.
>
> (Calhoun 2000, 127)

Because only heterosexuals' moral superiority to gay people makes them fit for marriage, only they can lay claim to the unique status of somehow being proper citizens. So prohibitions on same-sex marriage send the message that homosexuals are not fit to be citizens, according to Calhoun; they, in effect, displace gay people from civil society (2000, 127). In a way, Calhoun exposes marriage rights as special rights – special for straight people, which is ironic because many who are against gay marriage argue that granting it means granting gay people a special right.[7]

In light of this, gay people have two options as far as political strategy is concerned. They can either accept – or rather buy into – the idea that marriage is a pre-political institution and fight for inclusion, or they can reject such a purported status for marriage and, while fighting to make marriage available to all, fight also to disillusion the public from its enchantment with marriage, relegating it to the status of one type of contract among many. Calhoun opts for the first strategy, arguing that state neutrality – required by the second option – is effective only in societies that *already* treat all their citizens equally. Because American society treats gay people as second-class citizens, they need to fight for inclusion so that they can *come* to be full and equal citizens. It matters to Calhoun not only *that* gay people attain the right to marry, but also *how* they attain it. That is, which arguments are culturally circulated to attain this right is important, and only arguments for inclusion are able to move gay people from displaced to full citizenry (2000, 130–131). Think of it this way: if gay people fought for gay marriage on the basis that it is just one type of contract among many (the second strategy), then, if they win, this will likely not change their lowly status in the eyes of (American) society. However, if they fight for the right to marry by arguing that they, too, deserve to be part of that pre-political institution that is marriage, then, if they win, they raise their cultural, social, and political status to that of equality with straight people.

Mohr's and Calhoun's arguments are similar because they share a crucial concern with social and political attitudes. To both Mohr and Calhoun, society treats gay people as lesser beings, by, to Mohr, regarding them as morally less worthy, and by, to Calhoun, regarding them as non-citizens. Both also believe that arguing for the right to same-sex marriage is important for the very social and moral status of gay people. To Mohr, attaining the right to same-sex marriage allows them to assert their dignity by getting the state to treat them as full equals to heterosexuals, while to Calhoun it forces the state, and, in the process or eventually, the entire culture, to see gay people as full citizens.

However, Mohr is not as concerned as Calhoun is with which arguments gay people and their allies make to attain marriage rights. Moreover, although Calhoun is right to be so concerned, her position is morally dangerous. First, knowing what we know about the history of marriage, it is simply false that marriage actually has a sacrosanct position in social formations and that it predates political institutions. This is bad history (see Coontz 2005, Cott 2000), and insofar as the defenders of DOMA peddled this view of marriage, they were peddling lies (culpably, though perhaps unintentionally). While it may be true that marriage as an institution is, and has been, foundational and crucial in many respects, this is not the same claim as that it is pre-political. Such an important but non-pre-political status of marriage would not have given the defenders of DOMA what they wanted, namely to deny rights to gay marriage, because merely arguing that marriage is a crucial social institution is not enough to bar gay people from it (and the defenders of DOMA probably knew this, which is why they went for the stronger idea that marriage is a pre-political institution).

If gay people and their allies were to choose Calhoun's first option, they would adopt a strategy that relies on a falsehood, engaging in bold-faced lying. Sometimes lying is justified if there are good reasons for it. But in this case there are none. Calhoun's reason that "only the first option permits us to put into cultural circulation legal arguments that directly challenge the ideology sustaining gays' and lesbians' social equality" (2000, 131) is true but only because it is narrowly construed: of course only the first option allows gay people to pursue such *direct legal* arguments. But if, as Calhoun rightly observes (2000, 130–131), the ultimate goal is society's acceptance of gay people as equals, not mere tolerance of their existence, there are many ways that gay people can attain society's acceptance without having to engage in outright falshoods about the nature of marriage.

Note that there is another class of people as deserving as gays and lesbians are of attaining equality through marriage: trans-sexual and trans-gender people. The first are those who desire to change, or have changed, their sex, from male to female or female to male. The second are those men and women who adopt the identity of the opposite gender, even though they do not desire a sex change. It is unclear how the current law would treat marriages involving these two groups. It should not be an obstacle to trans-gender people if it treats their marriages as heterosexual, but it would be an obstacle if it treats them as same-sex marriages. Things are different with trans-sexual people. In each of the four court cases that have occurred so far, the courts annulled heterosexual marriages because one of the partners was a post-operative trans-sexual. The courts believe that what matters is the person's sex at birth, so if a male-to-female trans-sexual marries a man, the courts consider this a same-sex marriage, thus prohibiting it (see Nunan 2008, 448–449). One would have thought that so long as the part-ners to a marriage are of different sexes at the time of marriage, the law would not have a problem. In any case, trans-gender and (especially) trans-sexual people are likely to present challenges to current law. If same-sex marriages were allowed, these challenges might be easily met, and trans-gender and trans-sexual people would attain their equality through marriage as would gay people.

Claudia Card's Argument against Same-Sex Marriage

Although both Mohr and Calhoun are correct in analyzing the nature of soci-ety's insult to gay people in denying them marriage, both of their arguments must face an important argument by Claudia Card, a lesbian philosopher who is against marriage.[8]

Card begins by drawing attention to the fact that issues surrounding gay marriage admit of two questions. The first is whether the state treats gay people inequitably in not extending to them the right to marry. The second is whether gay people should pursue the right to marry (1997, 320). She answers the first question affirmatively, the second negatively. She gives the example of a mythical society in which men but not women have the right to own slaves. In this society, the law surely treats women inequitably in not giving them the same right, but the right in question is not one that women should pursue. The reason is obvious: the right is immoral. Card makes a similar point about the right to marriage (she does not claim that the institution of marriage is similar to that of slavery): just because gay people are denied a legal right, it does not mean that they should pursue the right, because it might be immoral (and just because a right is legal does not mean it is moral; legal rights allowing owning slaves or husbands to have sex with their wives whenever the husbands wanted are, and were, immoral rights – they should have never been enshrined in law). Indeed, to Card the right to marry *is* immoral.

Card lists four problems with marriage, the last being the most powerful because, unlike the first three, fixing it would pretty much do away with the institution of marriage. The first problem is that "employers and others (such as units of government) often make available only to legally married couples benefits that anyone could be presumed to want, married or not, such as affordable health and dental insurance, the right to live in attractive residential areas, visitation rights in relation to significant others and so forth" (1997, 322). This problem will not be fixed if the state and other institutions decide to provide such benefits to same-sex couples by allowing them to marry, because the problem is state discrimination between married couples, same or opposite sex couples, and non-married couples. As Card puts the point in another essay, "Thus legal regulation of same-sex marriage in the U.S. at present supports a profoundly unjust distribution of benefits" (2007, 25). Unsolved, this problem leads to another: because these benefits are usually vital and basic, they often provide an "ulterior motive for turning a lover relationship into a marriage – even for pretending to care for someone, deceiving oneself as well as others" (1997, 324). The idea is that as marriages are currently structured, they provide many spouses with the wrong reasons to marry (e.g., economic and healthcare benefits), and not always the right reasons (e.g., love or commitment).

However, and as Card recognizes (1997, 322), this problem with marriage can in principle be solved by eliminating the discrimination between married and non-married people. If this happens, all people would have access to these vital benefits, thereby eliminating both the unjust distribution of benefits and some wrong reasons for marrying. This solution, moreover, would not diminish the cultural and social viability and importance of the institution of marriage.

The second problem with marriage is divorce. Even though divorce procedures and regulations have been greatly reformed recently, "the consequences of divorce can be so difficult that many who should divorce do not," and if one spouse can sue the other for money and post-divorce payments, then spouses are sometimes motivated not to divorce, thus remaining in "emotionally disastrous unions" (1997, 322–323). Furthermore, "No-fault divorce in many states means only that spouses who *mutually agree* are no longer guilty of the crime of collusion," a relief not sufficient "to allow a spouse to terminate a marriage unilaterally without showing grounds acceptable to the state." She adds, "As long as the state retains a divorce-granting power that prevents unilateral dissolution at will … marriage is a trap for abused partners and their children" (2007, 25). This is a problem because such marriages take their emotional and sometimes physical toll on the spouses, and because they prohibit the spouses from developing other satisfying love relationships (1997, 324). Again, however, this is not a decisive objection to marriage because divorce laws can be reformed even further (I return to this issue below).

The third problem is that marriage is monogamous, *not* in the sense that adultery (or open relationships) is illegal (in many places it is not and in many others the laws are not enforced), but in the sense that it is *one spouse at a time*.

If *x* is married to *y*, *x* (or *y*) cannot also be married at the same time to *z*, and *x*, *y*, and *z* cannot all be married to each other. Card states that this issue should be "seriously troublesome to many lesbians" because many "have more than one long-term intimate relationship during the same time period" (1997, 323). Furthermore, even though this reason against marriage can be remedied in principle by allowing multiple, simultaneous marriages, it is easier said than done because the remedy "would have economic implications that I have yet to see anyone explore" (1997, 323).

I find this reason vague. First, it is unclear how many lesbians are in such intimate relationships; if their number is not large enough, then a small number of non-monogamous lesbian relationships may not be a strong enough reason against monogamous marriage. Second, it is unclear why Card mentions only lesbian non-monogamous relationships, since monogamy is supposed to be a problem with marriage in general, in which case other segments of the population need to be considered. But if so, we also need to consider how many such non-monogamous relationships currently exist, because, again, a small number would not constitute a strong reason against monogamous marriage (unless we can show that couples who are not in non-monogamous relationships would want them were they to be legally available). Third, it is unclear what Card means by "intimate relationships" and what type(s) of intimacy she has in mind. Is it the type we associate with current marriages (love and companionship)? Or is it broader, including friendships and other similar relationships? This is important because, depending on the type of intimacy, it may or may not be the type to which society should grant marriage rights. Card merely says, "The same reasons that lead one to want those benefits for a spouse can lead one to want them for additional significant others" (1997, 325). This does not clarify things.

The fourth and decisive problem with marriage is "that the legal rights of access that married partners have to each other's persons, property, and lives make it all but impossible for a spouse to defend herself (or himself), or to be protected against torture, rape, battery, stalking, mayhem, or murder by the other spouse. ... Legal marriage thus enlists state support for conditions conducive to murder and mayhem" (1997, 323). The issue is not that most or even many marriages are violent, but that when they are, the law makes it very difficult for abused spouses to protect themselves. It even abets the abusive spouses. Marriage, in short, makes spouses give up their individual privacy in a problematic way: should something go wrong, each spouse can rely on the law to access information, property, and so on belonging to the other spouse. Card is not against intimacy or intimate relationships in which partners do give up much of their privacy, but against the state's sanction of rights of access. As she puts it, non-married couples who cohabit "may seem to give up similar privacy. Yet, without marriage, it is possible to take one's life back without encountering the law as an obstacle" (1997, 328–329).

Card mentions, but does not elaborate, that such legal rights of access to each other's person and property are essential to marriage, such that without them it is doubtful whether what remains would be marriage (1997, 329). She is certainly right about the following point: we should not rashly claim that the institution of marriage would still exist if such rights of access and cohabitation were no longer part of it. For if we are concerned with the state's role in legalizing marriage, what role would be left for the state to play in marriage if it is not the provision and enforcement of rights of access and cohabitation? That is, if the state is to play any role in marriage, it would be this one.

We might argue that the state's role can be merely symbolic: through state officiation of marriage, a married couple declare to the world their love and eternal commitment to each other. That may be, but note three things. First, if the state were to play a merely symbolic role, what would this role be exactly? Would any substantive laws be involved? If yes, what laws? Would the state, for example, still issue marriage licenses? This is crucial: if the state's role is merely symbolic, there is no obvious reason why it should also legally regulate marriage. Second, there are many milestones in our lives that we celebrate without state involvement, such as graduations, baptisms, bar and bar mitzvahs, and birthdays. Why should marriage be any different? Third, many marriages have nothing to do with love and commitment, but are about green cards, status, and so on; therefore the state's role of officiating them might not make sense *if* confined to mere symbolism. Given these three points, do we really wish to retain the state's role as symbolic?

Let us recast Card's argument in a more compact and powerful form. First, there are serious problems with marriage stemming from the state's role in it; we can fix or change this role in the morally desired ways, but this may leave us with very little to recognize in marriage as a *state-officiated* institution. Second, there is little else for the state to be involved in if we get rid of its current role. Third, couples can easily form their own intimate relationships and celebrate them with others, perhaps even draw their own legal contracts. So, fourth, either we fix or reform the state's role in marriage in a satisfactory way, with the result that the state ends up with no real role to play, thus eroding the very institution of marriage, or we do not reform the laws of marriage (or not in a fully satisfactory way), in which case marriage is still a problem because the state would still play an invasive role in the spouses' lives. Either way, marriage is in trouble. Therefore, fifth, gay people and their allies should not be agitating for the right to marry, not even for reforming it, since a satisfactory reform is tantamount to abolishing marriage.

While Mohr and Calhoun are right to claim that marriage in our society has a high status and that in not allowing gay people to marry, the state treats them as if they have inferior status, this does not mean it is morally proper to pursue marriage if it is a bad institution. After all, historically speaking the state's role in it has been recent, and perhaps marriage is nothing but a tradition that is "glorified and romanticized" (Card 1997, 323). So although Card would agree that society treats marriage as sacrosanct and that in not extending marriage rights to same-sex couples it regards and treats gay people inequitably, this would still not settle the issue of whether gay couples should want or pursue the right to marry. Recall her mythical society: by not extending to women the right to own slaves, the men reveal perhaps their lesser regard toward them ("women are not fit to own slaves"). Still, women should not agitate for the right to own slaves because this right is immoral.

What are we to make of Card's argument? It hangs on the point of the badness of marriage and its possible reform, because if marriage is not as bad (indeed, evil, as we will see shortly) as Card alleges, or can be reformed in a satisfactory way without eroding the institution of marriage, we would have no good reason to claim that gay people should not pursue the right to marriage.

Card's point about battery and abuse in marriage is that when they occur, it is difficult for spouses to easily opt out of their bad marriages owing to the state's role. Given that the state's role is obstructive, she states, "My ideal is that the law not define or in any way regulate durable intimate unions between freely consenting adults" (2007, 27). To Card, while denying benefits to same-sex partners is an injustice, marriage as an institution is an *evil*. Evils are "culpable wrongs that foreseeably produce intolerable harms" (2007, 30). Legal marriage is

> an evil, to the extent that it facilitates the infliction and cover-up of reasonably foreseeable intolerable harm to those unlucky enough to find themselves trapped with violently abusive spouses. What makes marriage an evil when it is not merely an injustice is that it hinders an abused spouse from exiting an abusive relationship before intolerable harm is done.
>
> (Card 2007, 31)

But Card's claim may be overblown. *If* marriage is a wrong and *if* it leads to intolerable harm, then it would be a culpable wrong, because we know about its harms and we (or some people, anyway) are in a position to abolish it. But the intolerable harm of which Card speaks can be avoided by reforming divorce laws. As Card recognizes, some states have adopted unilateral divorce, divorce that may be attained once one of the spouses desires to dissolve the marriage. The divorcing spouse does not have to *prove*, in the face of the other spouse's unwillingness to dissolve it, that the marriage needs to or should be dissolved. If divorce laws can be thus reformed, marriage would no longer be an evil. It might still be problematic for the state to have such an intimate involvement in a couple's life, but it would be a far cry from being an evil.

To Card, however, even though unilateral divorce goes a long way in allowing abused spouses to more easily exit bad marriages, it may not do much to help the children of those marriages: "The marriage may be over, but there may still be a relationship giving an abuser a dangerous legal right of access that would never have existed without a history of marriage." Even if unilateral divorce removes the obstacle of having to prove that abuse exists for one spouse to be able to divorce another (often a difficult and emotionally taxing task), "it may still be necessary to establish abuse to prevent an abuser who is a legal guardian from retaining a legal right of access to the children," and through them to the abused, now-divorced spouse, who wanted to get away from the abuser in the first place (2007, 32).

Card's point about the limited benefits of unilateral divorce is crucial but defective. Even if the state does not regulate intimate relationships, it is hard to see how the state cannot *but* interfere in those relationships that involve children, because it has a justified interest in the well-being of children and *some* laws will have to exist to ensure their well-being. In the event of a couple's breakup, these laws, or a subset of them, will have to apply to how the children will relate to their parents after their parents' breakup. If there was spousal abuse, the abused spouse will still have to prove it if the state is not to allow (or not to allow unsupervised) the abusive parent's legal access to the children. The point is that the abolition of marriage would in all likelihood *not* get around the state's role in monitoring the lives and future of the children of broken-up intimate unions. This is not just a factual point or a prediction of the future course of the law. It is also a normative point: the state has good reasons to ensure that children are well brought up and looked after decently. Thus, even if the state should not act paternalistically and enact laws regarding the intimate relationship of the parents, it should do so regarding the welfare of children. So even though unilateral divorce does not help when it comes to the children of abusive relationships, abolishing marriage is not going to either, and it is questionable whether it should.

In addition, if the state provides benefits for all its citizens, regardless of their marital status, marriage as an institution would not be complicit in an overall unjust distribution of benefits, and individuals would not need to marry just to attain those benefits. Thus, making unilateral divorce legal and ensuring a just distribution of benefits would, I contend, disarm much of the power of Card's criticisms against marriage. Intimate state involvement may still be a problem, but it would not be an evil, as Card contends.

So marriage as an institution might be a good thing if it is reformed to allow for unilateral divorce and if healthcare is reformed so that all people are able to receive health benefits, regardless of their marital status, thus eliminating the need for some couples to marry just so that they can attain these health benefits. If this happens, marriage would not be a trap for unlucky couples and would retain its social symbolic role. However, reforming marriage laws and providing universal healthcare are long-term goals – *very* long-term goals, given the political landscape of the United States. So even if we agree that in principle marriage can be reformed, the *political* question of whether we should seek same-sex marriages is left unanswered. I address this issue in the final section. For now, I turn to two other arguments against marriage.

The Assimilation and Cultural Injustice Arguments against Same-Sex Marriage

Like Card, the lawyer Paula Ettelbrick states, "gay marriage will not topple the system that allows only the privileged few to obtain decent health care.

Nor will it close the privilege gap between those who are married and those who are not" (1997, 122–123). But she gives another reason against marriage: marriage "will not liberate us as lesbians and gay men. In fact, it will constrain us, make us more invisible, force our assimilation into the mainstream, and undermine the goals of gay liberation" (1997, 119). This is because:

> being queer is more than setting up house, sleeping with a person of the same gender, and seeking state approval for doing so. It is an identity, a culture with many variations .... Being queer means pushing the parameters of sex, sexuality, and family, and in the process transforming the very fabric of society.
>
> (Ettelbrick 1997, 120)

This argument against same-sex marriage relies on the idea that such marriages would assimilate gay people into mainstream society (Kurtz's opposite worry), thus eroding their unique identities and unwittingly undermining any goals to transform society.[9] But there are two reasons why this is not a serious worry. First, legalizing same-sex marriages does not mean that gay and lesbian couples *have* to marry each other; it merely gives them the option, much as straight couples have the option of marrying, though some choose to not exercise it. Thus many gay people may choose not to marry, in which case they won't be assimilated into mainstream society (whatever that means). Second, it is unclear that those gay and lesbian couples who marry will assimilate, because they might conduct their marriage in new and interesting ways, thus changing marriage and our understanding of it, which in turn might change the fabric of society. Indeed, heterosexual couples have themselves not assimilated into marriage in fixed, unchanging ways. As Calhoun puts it,

> evolution in both marriage law and marital and parenting practices has been a result of heterosexuals' *resistance* to the legal and social conception of traditional marriage .... If having the right to marry has not prevented heterosexuals from challenging legal and social conceptions of marriage, there is no reason to suppose that gays and lesbians will cease thinking critically about marital norms once granted a right to marry.
>
> (Calhoun 2000, 113)

This sounds reasonable, but we have to be cautious, because changes in marriage over time have not come about owing to one cause or to simple causes, but owing to myriad social, political, religious, and economic factors. The idea that same-sex marriages would change marriage for the better, make it more open, and so on is simplistic. Thus although the assimilationist argument is unconvincing, we should also not be too confident that same-sex marriage would usher in any radical or deep changes in marriage. Whether and how marriage changes remains to be seen.

The queer theorist Michael Warner offers the second argument (1999), which I call the "Cultural Injustice Argument."[10] Warner correctly notes that the right to marry is not a private choice, with no consequences for others (1999, 95–96). Marriage is a powerful cultural, social, and legal institution, with normative consequences for the non-married. People who are married have a privileged status in society, and marriage itself is a normative institution, a standard by which other people's sexual lives are negatively compared (1999, 82). Warner states,

> The impoverished vocabulary of straight culture tells us that people should be either husbands and wives or (nonsexual) friends. Marriage marks that line. It is not the way most queers live. If there is such a thing as a gay way of life, it consists in these relations, a welter of intimacies outside the framework of professions and institutions and ordinary social obligations. Straight culture has much to learn from it, and in many ways has already begun to learn from it. Queers should be insisting on teaching these lessons. Instead, the marriage issue, as currently framed, seems to be a way of denying recognition to these relations, of streamlining queer relations into the much less troubling division of couples from friends.
>
> (Warner 1999, 116)

What are these relations that Warner speaks of?

> Between tricks and lovers and exes and friends and fuckbuddies and bar friends and bar friends' tricks and tricks' bar friends and gal pals and companions 'in the life,' queers have an astonishing range of intimacies. Most have no labels. Most receive no public recognition. Many of these relations are difficult because the rules have to be invented as we go along. … Who among us would give them up?
>
> (Warner 1999, 116)

The argument seems to be that because marriage is a normative institution, demarcating the line between good and bad sexual relationships, initiating same-sex marriage would have the result of only recognizing a segment of the myriad types of gay relationships. The rest would still be confined to the "bad" or "not-so-good" type of relationship (hence my calling the argument the "cultural injustice" argument).

Note three crucial things about this argument's logic. First, even if marriage is legally reformed and even if universal healthcare extends to everyone, it still remains a powerful symbolic and normative institution. Its existence would continue to imply that non-marital relationships are second-tier at best. Second, even though society recognizes (non-sexual) friendships, it does not accord them the same elevated status as marriage, so even if all the non-marital gay relationships Warner mentions were to be considered forms of friendship, they would still be second-tier. Third, the "cultural injustice" argument applies to both gay relationships and straight relationships that do not conform to society's requirements of desiring people to be either married or non-sexual friends.

If convincing, Warner's argument offers a strong reason to not only give up the pursuit of the right for same-sex couples to marry, but to also abolish marriage altogether. For even if marriage is legally reformed and its benefits extended to single people and non-married couples, in its elevated social status it would continue to relegate to second-best status all those other non-marital relationships.[11] If these other non-marital relationships should not be considered second-best, marriage would play a culturally unjust and invidious role. Given all the other problems that go with it, we might as well just abolish it. I am, however, a little dubious about the idea that marriage relegates other relationships to a lower status, not because marriage does not have a superior status in most societies or because some relationships are not seen by society as not good enough or beyond the pale, but mainly because the claim is unclear. First, from the mere fact that marriage occupies an elevated status in society, it does not follow that "it is designed both to reward those inside it and to discipline those outside it" (Warner 1999, 89). The elevated status of marriage says nothing about whether it is *designed* to "discipline" other relationships, whether this is its purpose, or whether it actually achieves its purpose. The language of "disciplining" and similar concepts (e.g., "regulating") is also unclear: How exactly does marriage discipline these other relationships? Second, as a claim about how particular people view particular relationships it is false. Some parents, for example, fully realize that the heterosexual marriage of one of their sons is an utter disaster, while the gay, non-legal marital relationship of their other son is wonderful. To these parents, the gay relationship may be more valuable than the heterosexual marriage of their other son.

Third, though Warner is correct that many gay people (and, we may add, straight people) have non-traditional relationships, it is an open question as to what extent they have the depth and commitment that substantive relationships – whether marital or non-marital – have. Why my relationship with my bar friends should have an elevated status in the eyes of society, should be deemed worthy of recognition of sorts, or should be on the same level as marriage, remains a mystery. The fact, in short, that gay people have multiple and diverse forms of relationships says nothing, in and of itself, about the desirability of these relationships and what status they should occupy in society.

Nonetheless, the "cultural injustice" argument points to a crucial idea that, to my mind, puts the final nail in the coffin of marriage: in the end, the elevation of marriage to the status it currently occupies seems to be entirely arbitrary, the product of a long historical process that has no proper moral justification. In other words, (1) given that marriage is not necessarily about love, commitment, or companionship, but may be about money, political status, or procreation, (2) given that other relationships can as profoundly express love and commitment and be for the same reasons as any marriage, and (3) given that marriage is not the only environment in which children can be raised (there is no reason to believe that single parents, friends, extended households, or gay couples cannot raise children as adequately as any married couple can), there is no good, principled reason why marriage should have the kind of status and glory it currently has.

One might object that because society considers marriage a serious matter, this provides married couples with the incentive to stay together and to take their relationships seriously, thus also allowing for a more stable environment for raising children. Society does not take other relationships as seriously, allowing their easy dissolution and an unstable environment for raising children – not good things.

This objection is unconvincing. First, while society currently does provide incentives for married couples to "stick with their marriages," this is not always a good thing. It is when the marriage is either functioning well or has a chance to do so, because it ensures that the married couple work hard to make their relationship succeed. But when the marriage is hopeless, it provides one of the worst reasons for two people to stay together, thus also making for a bad environment in which to raise children. More important, the objection misses the mark. We already know that society takes marriage seriously; the point is that it has no good reason to do so, and that it should also take many other relationships as, if not more, seriously. To claim that society's serious treatment of marriage has such-and-such consequences, as the objection does, is to neglect that the reason why other relationships do not have the social incentives marriage has is not their fault, but society's fault for not taking these relationships seriously to begin with.

One might also object that it is the very legal entanglements of marriage that indicate why it should occupy an elevated status in society. For when couples willingly get married, enter the legal web, and accept the state's role in regulating their lives, they indicate the strength and depth of their commitment to each other. And such strong and deep commitments ought to be recognized and given an elevated status.

This objection is also not convincing. First, it is debatable to what extent couples are aware and knowledgeable of the legal web that is marriage; it seems that many are actually ignorant of the legal machinations they allow into their lives when they marry. Without proper knowledge of the legal aspects of marriage, it is impossible to make a convincing case that married couples *willingly* accept them. Second, and more important, there is no reason to believe that a couple's knowing and willing acceptance of the legal aspects of marriage shows that they have a stronger and deeper commitment to each other than a couple who refuse to get married. Why not say instead that the second couple have as deep and strong a commitment but that they insist on keeping their options open *precisely* because, were things to go wrong, they want to be able to let go of each other with the least amount of pain and emotional stress possible? In other words, sparing each other the potential pain of divorce might signal this couple's deeper love and commitment for each other than the other couple.

Given the dubious role of the state in marriage, given that marriage discriminates against non-married people by giving the first, but not the second, a package of benefits, and given that there is absolutely no good reason why marriage should have the glorified status in society that it has, its current social, institutional existence is utterly unjustified. Neither the state nor society has any good reasons to treat marriage in a special way. We are better off leaving it up to individuals to form their own commitments and relationships, and to celebrate them in the way they see fit. Of course, the state will still have to play some role in ensuring the welfare of any children involved in these relationships, and we need moral limits on the types of relationships allowed (no incestuous, bestial, or pedophiliac relationships, for example). But other than that, the way is clear for individuals to be free to lead their lives as they see fit, to pursue their happiness, without having to lead a second-tier way of life in society's eyes.

The Political Question

The following facts, however, remain unquestionable (at least in the United States). First, marriage is a glorified, crucial institution, and its being socially equated with other, similarly deep relationships seems remote. Second, marriage has been much reformed, with many states allowing unilateral divorce. Third, universal healthcare seems not to be in the horizon, let alone available in the near future. Fourth, many same-sex couples are in dire need of the benefits that marriage confers. Fifth, if same-sex couples do attain the right to marry, this will elevate gay people almost automatically in the general eyes of society. These facts lead to the following crucial question: Granted that the institution of marriage is in many ways unjust and that we are better off abolishing it in the future, but seeing that this is not going to happen any time soon, should the gay movement and its allies advocate for same-sex marriage, at least as a short-term strategy to attain an even better future later? In other words, it might be that the moral, theoretical arguments we have engaged about the status of marriage do not settle the *political* question about what to do with same-sex marriage.

There are at least three political options. The first is to agitate for the right to same-sex marriage, while hoping that after the right is attained, things might change on their own for the better (people might start thinking, for example, that if gay couples can get married, why not friends? And if friends and other parties in similar types of relationships can get married, marriage might with time lose its cultural and social importance). Or, instead of hoping for such changes, gay people and their allies can agitate for the expansion of marriage after the right to same-sex marriage is attained. Under this option, one might argue that if same-sex couples attain the benefits that come with marriage, this does not mean that single people or unmarried couples are worse off. It just means that more people (gay couples) are now enjoying the benefits of marriage.[12]

The second option is to not agitate for the right to marry, but for the reform of marriage, even its abolition, and campaign to educate the public about the arbitrariness of marriage as an elevated social institution and about the importance of other significant relationships. The third option is to combine both the first and second options, arguing for the right to same-sex marriage and for the eventual abolition of marriage. Despite its seeming incoherence, the third strategy is coherent, because it adopts two goals, one short-term – rights to same-sex marriage – and one long-term – the abolition of marriage.

Which of these strategies should right-thinking people adopt? The third strategy seems to be a non-starter. No politician, let alone the public at large, in the current climate would take it seriously, even as a long-term goal. At this point, very few Americans want to do away with marriage, though they are willing to tolerate and even accept other relationships. Moreover, even if marriage has a unique, albeit unjustified, status in society, this does not make abolishing it a high priority, so long as marriage is reformed in desirable ways (e.g., unilateral divorce). The second option also suffers the same fate for the same reasons.

The first option has the highest chance of success, and has good supporting reasons. In addition to the arguments for gay marriage that we have addressed, the horror stories of gay people, mostly men, who were not able to tend to their partners when the latter got sick with AIDS, who were not able to arrange their funerals and their burials, and who were unable to have access to their joint possessions after their partners died, simply because they were not married, are enough to convince many of the need for marriage rights for gay people. It is not only gay couples stricken with AIDS who could use the benefits of marriage. Any same-sex couple could stand to see their relationship go down the drain in the event of an emergency simply because the state does not recognize them as married. Without such an institution, many such couples may very well be deprived of even the minimal access that one should have to one's partner. This is intolerable, both morally and psychologically. Powers of attorney do not guarantee these rights, because some states refuse to recognize them if drawn in other states. In a society that tends to be homophobic, gay partners will need those rights of access to ensure that they are able to be with their partners when they need to be (Chauncey 2004, 96–119).

So the best strategy is for gay people and their allies to agitate for marriage rights, while also agitating for the reform of marriage (by at least allowing unilateral divorce) and for universal healthcare. Unilateral divorce allows a spouse to dissolve the marriage at will, but it will not deny spouses access to each other while the marriage is intact, thus also securing the above-mentioned crucial rights of access. Universal healthcare allows same-sex couples the benefits of marriage without others (e.g., single people and unmarried couples) being deprived of them (although universal healthcare is not in the offing, it is on the table and its language is not as alien or as frightening to American ears as "let's abolish marriage!"). Attaining the right to marriage would still be attaining the right to an arbitrarily glorified institution, but if reformed in the right ways, it won't be obviously bad or evil, and a benign, arbitrarily glorified institution is better than an evil, arbitrarily glorified one. And if, down the line, marriage somehow disappears, then so be it. We may all be better off.[13]

Conclusion

Sexual desire, though layered with cultural meaning, is ultimately natural. Romantic love, one may argue, is similar. But there is nothing natural about marriage. It is a socially constructed institution through and through. It has no essence or purpose etched into an eternal rock somewhere, and changes as societies and times change, adapting itself to people's needs. To deny adult human beings the right to marry just because they are of the same sex on the ground that marriage is somehow pre-political or is "in essence" between one man and one woman is both unjust and disingenuous. But marriage's social nature also indicates that its elevated social status may be unjustified. People who clamor to marry and who think that life without marriage is impoverished may very well fail to exhibit a proper attitude toward life. And a society that acculturates its members (especially women) to chase after marriage and that relegates them to its margins when they do not marry is both unjust and has the wrong set of priorities.

Notes

1 Compare what Kant says about wrong sexual acts (1963, 169–171).
2 I do not discuss the issue of whether the state should maintain neutrality regarding its citizens' moral views or support particular ones (e.g., homosexual sex is immoral), and assume that a state should not support immoral activities. Jordan (1998) argues – mistakenly – that if the state allows same-sex marriages, it abandons its neutral position.
3 Kurtz's explanation for how polyamory threatens monogamy is similar: "Once the principles of monogamous companionate marriage are breached, even for suppos- edly stable and committed sexual groups, the slide toward full-fledged promiscuity is difficult to halt" (2008, 184). My criticisms apply here, too.
4 According to John Corvino (2005, 523–525), it is debatable whether the new natural lawyers can rule out heterosexual polygamy and incest.
5 Mohr's argument applies to those countries that deny gay people marriage rights because of attitudes and laws similar to the ones found in the United States. I know of no country that denies these rights for reasons different from the United States'.
6 Many DOMA debaters also argued that homosexual sex is immoral (Congressman Henry Hyde of Illinois, for example, claimed that those who are against same-sex marriages are invoking a moral issue). To this extent, they would not be, *á la* Mohr, attacking gay people because of who gay people are, but because of what they do.
7 Thanks to Steve Jones for pointing this out.
8 Both Mohr (2005, 67) and Calhoun (2000, 109) are aware of this objection, but their treatment of it seems to indicate their failure to appreciate its weight.
9 Some gay writers think this is a *good* thing. We have seen this with Rauch, and Andrew Sullivan agrees (1995, esp. ch. 5). The subtitle of William Eskridge's (1996) book says it all: *The Case for Same-Sex Marriage: From Sexual Liberty to Civilized Commitment.*

10 Warner's argument draws on many issues already discussed in this chapter (e.g., marriages' legal benefits denied to the non-married). In presenting it, I focus on those strands of the argument that are conceptually distinct from these other points.

11 That's why Warner fails to take his argument to its logical end. He accepts a political agenda that includes the reform of marriage, abolishing anti-adultery laws and other laws that regulate sexuality, allowing domestic partnership and similar laws to both gay and straight people, and "be responsive to the lived arrangements of queer life" (1999, 146). But if marriage has the status Warner claims it has, initiating these reforms may not prevent relegating non-marital relationships to a second-tier status.

12 Christine Pierce puts this point differently: "The fact that achieving the right to marry will not benefit everyone or everyone equally or solve all the world's problems is not an argument against it" (1997, 172).

13 There are other options: We could spend political energy on issues other than marriage, such as the United States' lousy and unjust foreign policies, poverty (local and global), and the environment (see Card 2007, 32–37).

Further Reading

A good overview of the philosophical issues in the debate over same-sex marriage is Calhoun (2006). In addition to the ones cited, some crucial works by the new natural lawyers are Finnis (1980), (1991), and (1998), Finnis and Nussbaum (1993), George (1999), and George and Elshtain (2006). For some replies to the new natural lawyers, see Biggar and Black (2000), Koppelman (2002), and Macedo (1995, including his "Reply to Critics"). See also Wardle, Strasser, Duncan, and Coolidge (2003). For an interesting reply to the slippery-slope argument, see Donovan (2002). Rogers (2002) is a good source book on religion and sex. Two authors who offer liberal Christian views on sex are Gudorf (1994) and Jordan (2002). For more on Mohr's views, see especially (1988) and (1994). Other crucial arguments for gay marriage are Wedgwood (1999), Kaplan (1997, ch. 7), and Elliston (1984). Many of the philosophical debates are found in Baird and Rosenbaum (1997). Two influential non-philosophers who argue for same-sex marriage are Eskridge (1996) and Sullivan (1995). A recent book about the law and its extension to non-traditional families is Polikoff (2008). On marriage and trans-sexual and trans-gender people, see Robson (2007). For another argument against same-sex marriage (but one that is sympathetic to gay people) see Vanderheiden (1999). Both Thomas and Levin argue against same-sex marriage (Thomas and Levin 1999, 54–58, and 133–137, respectively), but Thomas is more sympathetic, and advocates for legal recognition of non-heterosexual unions and childless heterosexual ones.

Concluding Remarks

I have discussed both conceptual and evaluative issues found in the philosophy of love, sex, and marriage, thereby offering a somewhat detailed introduction to students and the general reader. To my mind, the evaluative issues are in a sense more important than the conceptual ones because they have a more direct connection to people's lives. Specifically, the issue of what importance we should give to romantic love, sex, and marriage in our lives is paramount. How people think of love, sex, and marriage and what weight they give them tells us quite a lot about their characters and their ability to reflect wisely and maturely on them. I take morality and moral requirements to be pervasive features of life, found in every nook and cranny of daily living. I also take them to be overriding: when morality says "no" to something, no other value can trump it. So I disagree with those who justify actions in the name of love, sex, and marriage. Lying isn't okay or excusable simply because it is done out of love, sexual desire, or the desire (or pressure) to marry. Both romantic love and sex are wonderful things, but that should not make them immune to moral requirements. There are other wonderful things in life with no such immunity, and love and sex should not be treated differently. Indeed, they are very powerful drives that often make people weak when in their grip. This makes them in especial need of moral control and scrutiny.

As important is the idea that, each in their own ways, love, sex, and marriage are not basic, crucial values that people need to lead happy, flourishing lives. Although they need love and intimacy in general, people do not need romantic love, and those who go without it are not to be pitied. Many people have led wonderful lives without it. Sexual desire, while persistent and forceful, is not as basic as hunger and thirst. We cannot survive without eating and drinking, but we can survive – even be happy – without satisfying sexual desire. No doubt, having sex in our lives makes us happier, even relaxed and more at ease, but no person should give it more worth than it deserves. Those who relentlessly pursue it, using their reason to attain more and more sexual satisfaction, have a wrong conception of what is important about life. And those who pursue it at the expense of their talents are downright wasting their lives.

Don't get me wrong: I'm not arguing that we should do away with romantic love and sex. We can't, and they are important, in many ways giving life meaning.

But they should be put in their proper places, under the watchful, stern gaze of morality.

Marriage is a different story. It is a thoroughly socially constructed institution that in the past has served many nefarious political goals. In many countries it gives benefits to couples that everyone should have, and discriminates against same-sex couples and those who want polygamous marriages. More important, it has an elevated status in society that is hard to justify. The ways in which weddings are celebrated and the amount of money spent on them are mind-boggling, especially when so many marriages end in divorce and when marriage has no purpose that cannot be attained by non-married couples. At least celebrating other events is justified in the sense that the achievements are irrevocable: once you graduate, you graduate, and no one can take that away from you (perhaps at weddings we should say to the spouses "Make it stick!" instead of "Congratulations!"). At the very least, marriage should in the short run be reformed to make divorce easier and its benefits universal. In the long run, if it goes away, so much the better.

Bibliography

Anscombe, G. E. M. 2000. *Intention.* Cambridge, Mass.: Harvard University Press.

Archard, David. 1998. *Sexual Consent.* Boulder, Colo.: Westview Press.

Aristotle. 1999. *Nicomachean Ethics,* 2nd edn. Trans. T. Irwin. Indianapolis, Ind.: Hackett.

Arkes, Hadley. 1997. "The Role of Nature." In SSM.

Armstrong, John. 2003. *Conditions of Love: The Philosophy of Intimacy.* New York: W. W. Norton.

Assiter, Alison, and Carol Avedon, eds. 1993. *Bad Girls and Dirty Pictures.* London: Pluto Press.

Badhwar, Neera Kapur, ed. 1993. *Friendship: A Philosophical Reader.* Ithaca, N.Y.: Cornell University Press.

Baier, Annette. 1991. "Unsafe Loves." In PEL.

Baird, Robert, and Stuart Rosenbaum, eds. 1997. *Same-Sex Marriage: The Moral and Legal Debate.* Amherst, N.Y.: Prometheus Books.

Baltzly, Dirk. 2003. "Peripatetic Perversions: A Neo-Aristotelian Account of the Nature of Sexual Perversion." *The Monist* 86: 3–29.

Baron, Marcia. 1995. *Kantian Ethics (Almost) without Apology.* Ithaca, N.Y.: Cornell University Press.

Baron, Marcia, Philip Pettit, and Michael Slote. 1997. *Three Methods of Ethics.* Malden, Mass.: Blackwell.

Bartky, Sandra. 1990. *Femininity and Domination: Studies in the Phenomenology of Oppression.* New York: Routledge.

Baumrin, Bernard. 1984. "Sexual Immorality Delineated." In PS2.

Bayles, Michael. 1984. "Marriage, Love, and Procreation." In PS2.

Belliotti, Raymond. 1993. *Good Sex: Perspectives on Sexual Ethics.* Lawrence, Kans.: University Press of Kansas.

Benatar, David. 1997. "Why It Is Better Never to Come into Existence." *American Philosophical Quarterly* 34: 345–355.

Benjamin, Jessica. 1983. "Master and Slave: The Fantasy of Erotic Domination." In *Powers of Desire: The Politics of Sexuality,* eds. A. Snitow, C. Stansell, and S. Thompson. New York: Monthly Review Press.

Bennett, Jonathan. 1995. *The Act Itself.* Oxford: Clarendon Press.

Bennett, William. 1997. "Leave Marriage Alone." In SSM.

Bentham, Jeremy. 1984. "An Essay on 'Paederasty.'" In PS2.

Berkowitz, Leonard. 1997. "Sex: Plain and Symbol." In *Sex, Love, and Friendship: Studies of the Society for the Philosophy of Sex and Love, 1977–1992.* Amsterdam: Rodopi.

Biggar, Nigel, and Rufus Black, eds. 2000. *The Revival of Natural Law: Philosophical, Theological, and Ethical Responses to the Finnis-Grisez School.* Aldershot, U.K.: Ashgate Press.

Bloomfield, Paul, ed. 2008. *Morality and Self-Interest.* New York: Oxford University Press.

Blum, Lawrence. 1980. *Friendship, Altruism, and Morality.* London: Routledge & Kegan Paul.

Boswell, John. 1995. *Same-Sex Unions in Pre-Modern Europe.* New York: Vintage Books.

Brake, Elizabeth. 2005. "Justice and Virtue in Kant's Account of Marriage." *Kantian Review* 9: 58–94.

Brake, Elizabeth. 2006. "Kant, Immanuel." In SPP1.

Brentlinger, John. 1989. "The Nature of Love." In EAP.

Brown, Curtis. 2002. "Art, Oppression, and the Autonomy of Aesthetics." In *Arguing about Art*, 2nd edn, eds. A. Neill and A. Ridley. London: Routledge.

Bullough, Vern, and Bonnie Bullough. 1987. *Women and Prostitution: A Social History.* Buffalo, N.Y.: Prometheus Books.

Calhoun, Cheshire. 2000. *Feminism, the Family, and the Politics of the Closet: Lesbian and Gay Displacement.* New York: Oxford University Press.

Calhoun, Cheshire. 2006. "Marriage, Same-Sex." In SPP2.

Califia, Pat. 1988. *Macho Sluts.* Los Angeles, Calif.: Alyson Books.

Califia, Pat. 1994. *Public Sex: The Culture of Radical Sex.* Pittsburgh, Penn.: Cleis Press.

Campbell, Tom. 2006. *Rights: A Critical Introduction.* New York: Routledge.

Card, Claudia. 1995. *Lesbian Choices.* New York: Columbia University Press.

Card, Claudia. 1997. "Against Marriage." In SS.

Card, Claudia. 2007. "Gay Divorce: Thoughts on the Legal Regulation of Marriage." *Hypatia* 22: 24–38.

Carroll, Noel. 1990. *The Philosophy of Horror, or Paradoxes of the Heart.* New York: Routledge.

Carroll, Noel. 1996. "Moderate Moralism." *British Journal of Aesthetics* 36: 223–238.

Carver, Raymond. 1989. *What We Talk About When We Talk About Love: Stories.* New York: Vintage.

Casler, Lawrence. 1974. "Permissive Matrimony: Proposals for the Future." *The Humanist* 34 (March/April): 4–8.

Chambers, David. 1996. "What If? The Legal Consequences of Marriage and the Legal Needs of Lesbian and Gay Male Couples." *Michigan Law Review* 95: 447–491.

Chauncey, George. 2004. *Why Marriage? The History Shaping Today's Debate Over Gay Equality.* New York: Basic Books.

Christina, Greta. 2008. "Are We Having Sex Now or What?" In POS5.

Cicovacki, Predrag. 1993. "On Love and Fidelity in Marriage." *Journal of Social Philosophy* 24: 92–104.

Clark, Stephen. 1998. "Sexual Ontology and Group Marriage." In PS3.

Conlon, James. 1995. "Why Lovers Can't Be Friends." In *Philosophical Perspectives on Sex and Love*, ed. R. M. Stewart. New York and Oxford: Oxford University Press.

Constantine, Larry, and Joan Constantine. 1973. *Group Marriage: A Study of Contemporary Multilateral Marriage.* New York: Macmillan.

Cooke, Vincent. 1991. "Kant, Teleology, and Sexual Ethics." *International Philosophical Quarterly* 31: 3–13.

Coontz, Stephanie. 2005. *Marriage, a History.* New York: Penguin.

Copp, David, and Susan Wendell, eds. 1983. *Pornography and Censorship*. Buffalo, N.Y.: Prometheus Books.

Cornell, Drucilla, ed. 2000. *Feminism and Pornography*. Oxford: Oxford University Press.

Corvino, John. 1997. "Why Shouldn't Tommy and Jim Have Sex? A Defense of Homosexuality." In SS.

Corvino, John. 2002. "Naughty Fantasies." *Southwest Philosophy Review* 18: 213–220.

Corvino, John. 2005. "Homosexuality and the PIB Argument." *Ethics* 115: 501–534.

Cott, Nancy. 2000. *Public Vows: A History of Marriage and the Nation*. Cambridge, Mass.: Harvard University Press.

Darwall, Stephen. 1998. *Philosophical Ethics*. Boulder, Colo.: Westview Press.

Darwall, Stephen, ed. 2003. *Consequentialism*. Malden, Mass.: Blackwell.

de Beauvoir, Simone. 1952. *The Second Sex*, trans. H. M. Parshley. New York: Vintage Books.

Delacoste, Frederique, and Priscilla Alexander, eds. 1987. *Sex Work: Writings by Women in the Sex Industry*. Pittsburgh, Penn.: Cleis Press.

de Montaigne, Michel. 1987. *The Complete Essays*, trans. M. A. Screech. London: Penguin.

Denis, Lara. 1999. "Kant on the Wrongness of 'Unnatural' Sex." *History of Philosophy Quarterly* 16: 225–248.

Denis, Lara. 2001. "From Friendship to Marriage: Revising Kant." *Philosophy and Phenomenological Research* 58: 1–28.

Denis, Lara. 2007. "Sex and the Virtuous Kantian Agent." In SE.

Dilman, Ilham. 1998. *Love: Its Forms, Dimensions, and Paradoxes*. New York: St. Martin's Press.

Donovan, James. 2002. "Rock-Salting the Slippery Slope: Why Same-Sex Marriage is Not a Commitment to Polygamous Marriage." *Northern Kentucky Law Review* 29: 521–590.

Dover, K. J. 1989. *Greek Homosexuality* (updated edn). Cambridge, Mass.: Harvard University Press.

Dworkin, Andrea. 1974. *Woman Hating*. New York: Plume.

Dworkin, Andrea. 1987. *Intercourse*. New York: Free Press.

Dworkin, Andrea. 1989. *Pornography: Men Possessing Women*. New York: Dutton.

Eames, Elizabeth. 1976. "Sexism and Woman as Sex Object." *Journal of Thought* 11: 140–143.

Eaton, A. W. 2007. "A Sensible Antiporn Feminism." *Ethics* 117: 674–715.

Ehman, Robert. 1989. "Personal Love." In EAP.

Ellis, Anthony. 1986. "Casual Sex." *International Journal of Moral and Social Studies* 1: 157–168.

Elliston, Frederick. 1984. "Gay Marriage." In PS2.

Elliston, Frederick. 1998. "In Defense of Promiscuity." In PS3.

Ericsson, Lars. 1980. "Charges against Prostitution: An Attempt at a Philosophical Assessment." *Ethics* 90: 335–366.

Eskridge, William, Jr. 1996. *The Case for Same-Sex Marriage: From Sexual Liberty to Civilized Commitment*. New York: Free Press.

Eskridge, William, Jr., and Darren Spedale. 2007. *Gay Marriage: For Better or for Worse? What We've Learned from the Evidence*. New York: Oxford University Press.

Estes, Yolanda. 2008. "Prostitution: A Subjective Position." In POS5.

Ettelbrick, Paula. 1997. "Since When Is Marriage a Path to Liberation?" In SSM.

Farrell, Daniel. 1989. "Of Jealousy and Envy." In *Person to Person*, eds. G. Graham and H. LaFollette. Philadelphia, Penn.: Temple University Press.

Feinberg, Joel. 1984. *Harm to Others: The Moral Limits of the Criminal Law.* New York: Oxford University Press.

Feinberg, Joel. 1985. *Offense to Others: The Moral Limits of the Criminal Law*, vol. 2. Oxford: Oxford University Press.

Finnis, John. 1980. *Natural Law and Natural Rights.* Oxford: Clarendon Press.

Finnis, John. 1991. *Moral Absolutes: Tradition, Revision, and Truth.* Washington, D.C.: Catholic University of America Press.

Finnis, John. 1997. "Law, Morality, and 'Sexual Orientation.'" In SS.

Finnis, John. 1998. *Aquinas: Moral, Political, and Legal Theory.* Oxford: Oxford University Press.

Finnis, John. 2008. "The Wrong of Homosexuality." In POS5.

Finnis, John, and Martha Nussbaum. 1993. "Is Homosexual Conduct Wrong? A Philosophical Exchange." *The New Republic* (November 15).

Firestone, Shulamith. 1970. *The Dialectic of Sex.* New York: William Morrow.

Fisher, Mark. 1990. *Personal Love.* London: Duckworth.

Foot, Philippa. 1995. "Does Moral Subjectivism Rest on a Mistake?" *Oxford Journal of Legal Studies* 15: 1–14.

Frankfurt, Harry. 1971. "Freedom of the Will and the Concept of a Person." *Journal of Philosophy* 68: 5–20.

Freeman, M. D. A. 1999. "Not Such a Queer Idea: Is There a Case for Same Sex Marriages?" *Journal of Applied Philosophy* 16: 1–17.

Freud, Sigmund. 1912. "On the Universal Tendency to Debasement in the Sphere of Love." In *The Standard Edition of the Complete Psychological Works of Sigmund Freud*, ed. and trans. J. Strachey. London: Hogarth Press, 1953–1974.

Garry, Ann. 1984. "Pornography and Respect for Women." In PS2.

Gaut, Berys. 1998. "The Ethical Criticism of Art." In *Aesthetics and Ethics: Essays at the Intersection*, ed. J. Levinson. Cambridge: Cambridge University Press.

Gensler, Harry. 1998. *Ethics: A Contemporary Introduction.* New York: Routledge.

George, Robert P. 1999. *In Defense of Natural Law.* Oxford: Oxford University Press.

George, Robert P. 2003. "Neutrality, Equality, and 'Same-Sex Marriage.'" In *Marriage and Same-Sex Unions: A Debate*, eds. L. D. Wardle, M. Strasser, W. C. Duncan, and D. O. Coolidge. Westport, Conn.: Praeger

George, Robert P., and Gerard V. Bradley. 1995. "Marriage and the Liberal Imagination." *The Georgetown Law Journal* 84: 301–320.

George, Robert P., and Jean Bethke Elshtain, eds. 2006. *The Meaning of Marriage: Family, State, Market, and Morals.* Dallas, TX: Spence Publishing.

Goldman, Alan. 2006. "There Are No Aesthetic Principles." In *Contemporary Debates in Aesthetics and the Philosophy of Art*, ed. Matthew Kieran. Malden, Mass.: Blackwell.

Goldman, Alan. 2008. "Plain Sex." In POS5.

Gordon, Chris. 2004. *The Book of Weird Sex.* London: Allison & Busby.

Gosling, J. C. B. 1983. *Plato.* London: Routledge & Kegan Paul.

Graff, E. J. 1999. *What Is Marriage For?* Boston, Mass.: Beacon Press.

Graham, George, and Hugh LaFollette. 1989. *Person to Person.* Philadelphia, Penn.: Temple University Press.

Gray, Robert. 1978. "Sex and Sexual Perversion." *Journal of Philosophy* 75: 189–199.

Graybosch, Anthony. 2006. "Marriage." In SPP2.

Green, O. H. 1997. "Is Love an Emotion?" In *Love Analyzed*, ed. R. E. Lamb. Boulder, Colo.: Westview Press.

Gregory, Paul. 1984. "Against Couples." *Journal of Applied Philosophy* 1: 263–268.

Grimshaw, Jean. 1997. "Ethics, Fantasy, and Self-Transformation." In POS3.

Grisez, Germain. 1993. *The Way of the Lord Jesus,Volume 2: Living a Christian Life*. Quincy, Ill.: Franciscan Press.

Gruen, Lori. 2006. "Pornography." In SPP2.

Gudorf, Christine. 1994. *Body, Sex, and Pleasure: Reconstructing Christian Sexual Ethics*. Cleveland, Ohio: The Pilgrim Press.

Halperin, David. 1990. *One Hundred Years of Homosexuality*. New York: Routledge.

Halwani, Raja. 1998. "Virtue Ethics and Adultery." *Journal of Social Philosophy* 29: 5–18.

Halwani, Raja. 2003. *Virtuous Liaisons: Care, Love, Sex, and Virtue Ethics*. Chicago, Ill.: Open Court.

Halwani, Raja. 2006a. "Casual Sex." In SPP1.

Halwani, Raja. 2006b. "Ethics, Virtue." In SPP1.

Halwani, Raja. 2007a. "Sexual Temperance and Intemperance." In SE.

Halwani, Raja. 2007b. "Casual Sex, Promiscuity, and Temperance." In SE.

Halwani, Raja, ed. 2007c. *Sex and Ethics: Essays on Sexuality, Virtue, and the Good Life*. Basingstoke: Palgrave Macmillan.

Halwani, Raja. 2008. "Virtue Ethics, Casual Sex, and Objectification." In POS5.

Halwani, Raja, and Steven Jones. 2007. "*The Birds*: Plato and Romantic Love." In *Hitchcock and Philosophy: Dial M for Metaphysics*, eds. D. Baggett and W. Drumin. Chicago, Ill.: Open Court.

Hamilton, Christopher. 2008. "Sex." In POS5.

Hannay, Alastair. 1991. *Kierkegaard*. London: Routledge.

Harding, Jennifer. 1998. *Sex Acts: Practices of Femininity and Masculinity*. London: Sage.

Haslanger, Sally. 1993. "On Being Objective and Being Objectified." In *A Mind of One's Own: Feminist Essays on Reason and Objectivity*, eds. L. Antony and C. Witt. Boulder, Colo.: Westview Press.

Herman, Barbara. 1993. "Could It Be Worth Thinking About Kant on Sex and Marriage?" In *A Mind of One's Own: Feminist Essays on Reason and Objectivity*, eds. L. Antony and C. Witt. Boulder, Colo.: Westview Press.

Hill, Judith. 1991. "Pornography and Degradation." In *Pornography: Private Right or Public Menace?*, eds. R. M. Baird and S. E. Rosenbaum. Buffalo, N.Y.: Prometheus Books.

Hill, Thomas. 1980. "Humanity as an End in Itself." *Ethics* 91: 84–90.

Hoffman, Sarah. 2006. "Perversion, Sexual." In SPP2.

Hooker, Brad. 2000. "Moral Particularism: Wrong and Bad." In *Moral Particularism*, eds. B. Hooker and M. Little. Oxford: Oxford University Press.

Hooker, Brad. 2002. "The Collapse of Virtue Ethics." *Utilitas* 14: 22–40.

Hooker, Brad, and Margaret Little, eds. 2000. *Moral Particularism*. Oxford: Oxford University Press.

Hopkins, Patrick. 1997. "Rethinking Sadomasochism: Feminism, Interpretation, and Simulation." In POS3.

Humber, James. 1997. "Sexual Perversion and Human Nature." In *Human Sexuality*, ed. I. Primoratz. Aldershot, Hants: Ashgate.

Hunter, J. F. M. 1980. *Thinking About Sex and Love*. New York: St. Martin's Press.

Hursthouse, Rosalind. 1986. "Aristotle, *Nicomachean Ethics*." In *Philosophers Ancient and Modern*, ed. G. Vesey. London: Cambridge University Press.

Hursthouse, Rosalind. 1999. *On Virtue Ethics*. Oxford: Oxford University Press.

Hursthouse, Rosalind. 2002. "Virtue Ethics vs. Rule-Consequentialism: A Reply to Brad Hooker." *Utilitas* 14: 41–53.

Jaeger, Gary. 2008. "Homosexuality and Morality." *Metaphilosophy* 39: 434–438.

Jeske, Diane. 1998. "Families, Friends, and Special Obligations." *Canadian Journal of Philosophy* 28: 527–556.

Jordan, Jeff. 1998. "Is It Wrong to Discriminate on the Basis of Homosexuality?" In PS3.

Jordan, Mark D. 2002. *The Ethics of Sex*. Malden, Mass.: Blackwell.

Kagan, Shelly. 1998. *Normative Ethics*. Boulder, Colo.: Westview Press.

Kant, Immanuel. 1963. *Lectures on Ethics*, trans. L. Infield. Indianapolis, Ind.: Hackett.

Kant, Immanuel. 1981. *Grounding for the Metaphysics of Morals*, trans. J. W. Ellington. Indianapolis, Ind.: Hackett.

Kant, Immanuel. 1996. "Metaphysics of Morals." In *Practical Philosophy*, trans. M. Gregor. Cambridge: Cambridge University Press.

Kaplan, Morris. 1997. *Sexual Justice: Democratic Citizenship and the Politics of Desire*. New York: Routledge.

Kershnar, Stephen. 2005. "The Moral Status of Sexual Fantasies." *Public Affairs Quarterly* 19: 301–315.

Kershnar, Stephen. 2006. "Fantasy." In SPP1.

Kershnar, Stephen. 2007. "Pornography, Health, and Virtue." In SE.

Kierkegaard, Søren, 1962. *Works of Love*, trans. H. and E. Hong. New York: Harper & Row.

Kimmel, Michael, ed. 1990. *Men Confront Pornography*. New York: Meridian.

Koppelman, Andrew. 2002. *The Gay Rights Question in Contemporary American Law*. Chicago, Ill.: University of Chicago Press.

Koppelman, Andrew. 2008. "Homosexuality and Infertility." In POS5.

Kosman, L. A. 1989. "Platonic Love." In EAP.

Krauthammer, Charles. 1997. "When John and Jim Say 'I Do.'" In SSM.

Kripke, Saul. 1972. *Naming and Necessity*. Cambridge, Mass.: Harvard University Press.

Kristjansson, Kristjan. 1998. "Casual Sex Revisited." *Journal of Social Philosophy* 29: 97–108.

Kurtz, Stanley. 2008. "Beyond Gay Marriage: The Road to Polyamory." In POS5.

Langton, Rae. 1993. "Speech Acts and Unspeakable Acts." *Philosophy and Public Affairs* 22: 293–330.

Lederer, Laura, ed. 1980. *Take Back the Night: Women on Pornography*. New York: William Morrow.

Lee, Patrick, and Robert P. George. 1997. "What Sex Can Be: Self-Alienation, Illusion, or One-Flesh Union." *The American Journal of Jurisprudence* 42: 135–157.

Lehrer, Keith. 1997. "Love and Autonomy." In *Love Analyzed*, ed. R. Lamb. Boulder, Colo.: Westview Press.

LeMoncheck, Linda. 1985. *Dehumanizing Women: Treating Persons as Sex Objects*. Totowa, N.J.: Rowman & Allanheld.

LeMoncheck, Linda. 1997. *Loose Women, Lecherous Men: A Feminist Philosophy of Sex*. New York: Oxford University Press.

Levinson, Jerrold. 2003. "Sexual Perversity." *The Monist* 86: 30–54.

Levy, Donald. 1980. "Perversion and the Unnatural as Moral Categories." *Ethics* 90: 191–202.

Lewis, C. S. 1960. *The Four Loves*. San Diego and New York: Harcourt, Brace, Jovannovich.

Lloyd, Elisabeth. 2005. *The Case of the Female Orgasm: Bias in the Science of Evolution*. Cambridge, Mass.: Harvard University Press.

Longino, Helen. 1991. "Pornography, Oppression, and Freedom: A Closer Look." In *Pornography: Private Right or Public Menace?*, eds. R. M. Baird and S. E. Rosenbaum. Buffalo, N.Y.: Prometheus Books.

Love, Brenda. 1992. *Encyclopedia of Unusual Sex Practices*. New York: Barricade Books.

Macedo, Stephen. 1995. "Homosexuality and the Conservative Mind." *Georgetown Law Journal* 84: 261–300.

MacKinnon, Catharine. 1987. *Feminism Unmodified: Discourses on Life and Law*. Cambridge, Mass.: Harvard University Press.

MacKinnon, Catharine. 1993. *Only Words*. Cambridge, Mass.: Harvard University Press.

MacKinnon, Catharine. 1997. "Pornography Left and Right." In *Sex, Preference, and Family*, eds. D. Estlund and M. Nussbaum. New York: Oxford University Press.

MacKinnon, Catharine, and Andrea Dworkin, eds. 1997. *In Harm's Way: The Pornography Civil Rights Hearings*. Cambridge, Mass.: Harvard University Press.

Marquis, Don. 2005. "What's Wrong with Adultery?" In *What's Wrong? Applied Ethicists and Their Critics*, eds. D. Boonin and G. Oddie. New York: Oxford University Press.

Martin, Mike. 1996. *Love's Virtues*. Lawrence, Kans.: University Press of Kansas.

Martin, Mike. 1998. "Adultery and Fidelity." In PS3.

Martin, Mike. 2006. "Adultery." In SPP1.

Mason-Grant, Joan. 2004. *Pornography Embodied: From Speech to Personal Practice*. Lanham, Md.: Rowman & Littlefield.

McElroy, Wendy. 1995. *A Woman's Right to Pornography*. New York: St. Martin's Press.

McMurty, John. 1984. "Monogamy: A Critique." In PS2.

McNaughton, David. 1988. *Moral Vision*. Malden, Mass.: Blackwell.

Mendus, Susan. 1989. "Marital Faithfulness." In EAP.

Mill, John Stuart. 1987. *Utilitarianism*. Buffalo, N. Y.: Prometheus Books.

Mohr, Richard. 1988. *Gays/Justice: A Study of Ethics, Society, and Law*. New York: Columbia University Press.

Mohr, Richard. 1994. *A More Perfect Union: Why Straight America Must Stand Up for Gay Rights*. Boston, Mass.: Beacon Press.

Mohr, Richard. 2005. *The Long Arc of Justice: Lesbian and Gay Marriage, Equality, and Rights*. New York: Columbia University Press.

Morgan, Kathryn Pauly. 1991. "Romantic Love, Altruism, and Self-Respect: An Analysis of Beauvoir." In PEL.

Morgan, Seiriol. 2003a. "Sex in the Head." *Journal of Applied Philosophy* 20: 1–16.

Morgan, Seiriol. 2003b. "Dark Desires." *Ethical Theory and Moral Practice* 6: 377–410.

Moscovici, Claudia. 1996. *From Sex Objects to Sexual Subjects*. New York: Routledge.

Moulton, Janice. 2008. "Sexual Behavior: Another Position." In POS5.

Nagel, Thomas, 1984. "Sexual Perversion." In PS2.

Nagel, Thomas. 2008. "Sexual Perversion." In POS5.

Nagle, Jill, ed. 1997. *Whores and Other Feminists*. New York: Routledge.

Newton-Smith, W. 1989. "A Conceptual Investigation of Love." In EAP.

Nozick, Robert. 1991. "Love's Bond." In PEL.

Nunan, Richard. 2008. "Homosexuality and the Law." *Metaphilosophy* 39: 442–449.

Nussbaum, Martha. 1986. *The Fragility of Goodness*. Cambridge: Cambridge University Press.

Nussbaum, Martha. 1997. "Love and the Individual: Romantic Rightness and Platonic Aspiration." In *Love Analyzed*, ed. R. Lamb. Boulder, Colo.: Westview Press.

Nussbaum, Martha. 1999. *Sex and Social Justice*. New York: Oxford University Press.

Nygren, Anders. 1953. *Agape and Eros*, trans. Philip S. Watson. Philadelphia, Penn.: The Westminster Press.

Odell, S. Jack. 2006. "Consequentialism." In SPP1.

O'Neill, Onora. 1989. "Between Consenting Adults." In *Constructions of Reason: Explorations of Kant's Practical Philosophy*. Cambridge: Cambridge University Press.

O'Neill, Onora, and William Ruddick, eds. 1979. *Having Children: Philosophical* and *Legal Reflections on Parenthood*. New York: Oxford University Press.

Pakaluk, Michael, ed. 1991. *Other Selves: Philosophers on Friendship*. Indianapolis, Ind.: Hackett.

Palmer, David. 1984. "The Consolation of the Wedded." In PS2.

Pateman, Carole. 1983. "Defending Prostitution: Charges against Ericsson." *Ethics* 93: 561–565.

Pateman, Carole. 1988. *The Sexual Contract*. Stanford, Calif.: Stanford University Press.

Paul VI (Pope). 1984. *Humanae Vitae*. In PS2.

Paul, Ellen Frankel, Fred Miller, and Jeffrey Paul, eds. 1997. *Self-Interest*. Cambridge: Cambridge University Press.

Pierce, Christine. 1997. "Gay Marriage." In *Same-Sex Marriage: The Moral and Legal Debate*, eds. R. M. Baird and S. E. Rosenbaum. Amherst, N.Y.: Prometheus Books.

Plato. 1997a. *Euthyphro*, trans. G. M. A. Grube. In *Plato: Complete Works*, ed. J. Cooper. Indianapolis, Ind.: Hackett.

Plato. 1997b. *Lysis*, trans. S. Lombardo. In *Plato: Complete Works*, ed. J. Cooper. Indianapolis, Ind.: Hackett.

Plato. 1997c. *Parmenides*, trans. M. L. Gill and P. Ryan. In *Plato: Complete Works*, ed. J. Cooper. Indianapolis, Ind.: Hackett.

Plato. 1997d. *Phaedo*. trans. G. M. A. Grube. In *Plato: Complete Works*, ed. J. Cooper. Indianapolis, Ind.: Hackett.

Plato. 1997e. *Phaedrus*, trans. A. Nehemas and P. Woodruff. In *Plato: Complete Works*, ed. J. Cooper. Indianapolis, Ind.: Hackett.

Plato. 1997f. *Republic*, trans. G. M. A. Grube and C. D. C. Reeve. In *Plato: Complete Works*, ed. J. Cooper. Indianapolis, Ind.: Hackett.

Plato. 1997g. *Symposium*, trans. A. Nehemas and P. Woodruff. In *Plato: Complete Works*, ed. J. Cooper. Indianapolis, Ind.: Hackett

Plato. 1997h. *Timaeus*, trans. D. J. Zeyl. In *Plato: Complete Works*, ed. J. Cooper. Indianapolis, Ind.: Hackett.

Polikoff, Nancy. 2008. *Beyond (Straight and Gay) Marriage: Valuing All Families under the Law*. Boston, Mass.: Beacon Press.

Price, A. W. 1997. *Love and Friendship in Plato and Aristotle*. Oxford: Oxford University Press.

Priest, Graham. 1997. "Sexual Perversion." *Australasian Journal of Philosophy* 75: 360–371.

Primoratz, Igor. 1999. *Ethics and Sex*. London: Routledge.

Primoratz, Igor. 2006. "Prostitution." In SPP2.

Putman, Daniel. 1991. "Sex and Virtue." *International Journal of Moral and Social Studies* 6: 47–56.

Quinn, Carol. 2006a. "Objectification, Sexual." In SPP2.

Quinn, Carol. 2006b. "Sadomasochism." In SPP2.

Rachels, James. 1986. *The Elements of Moral Philosophy*. New York: Random House.

Rauch, Jonathan. 1997a. "Marrying Somebody." In SSM.

Rauch, Jonathan. 1997b. "Who Needs Marriage?" In SS.

Riley, Jonathan. 1998. *Mill on Liberty*. New York: Routledge.

Robson, Ruthann. 2007. "A Mere Switch or a Fundamental Change? Theorizing Transgender Marriage." *Hypatia* 22: 58–71.

Rogers, Jr., Eugene, ed. 2002. *Theology and Sexuality: Classic and Contemporary Readings*. Malden, Mass.: Blackwell.

Rubin, Gayle. 1993. "Thinking Sex: Notes for a Radical Theory of the Politics of Sexuality." In *The Lesbian and Gay Studies Reader*, eds. H. Abelove, M. A. Barale, and D. Halperin. New York: Routledge.

Ruddick, Sara. 1984. "Better Sex." In PS2.

Ruse, Michael. 1988. *Homosexuality*. Cambridge, Mass.: Blackwell.

Russell, Bertrand. 1970. *Marriage and Morals*. New York: Liveright.

Russell, Diana, ed. 1993. *Making Violence Sexy: Feminist Views on Pornography*. New York: Teachers College Press.

Sartre, Jean-Paul. 1956. *Being and Nothingness*, trans. H. E. Barnes. New York: Washington Square Press.

Schopenhauer, Arthur. 1956. "On Women." In *Schopenhauer Selections*, ed. D. H. Parker. New York: Charles Scribner's.

Schopenhauer, Arthur. 1958. *The World as Will and Representation*, vol. II, trans. E. F. J. Payne. New York: Dover Publications.

Scruton, Roger. 1986. *Sexual Desire: A Moral Philosophy of the Erotic*. New York: Free Press.

Segal, Lynne, and Mary McIntosh, eds. 1993. *Sex Exposed: Sexuality and the Pornography Debate*. New Brunswick, N.J.: Rutgers University Press.

Shaffer, Jerome. 1978. "Sexual Desire." *Journal of Philosophy* 75: 175–189.

Shoemaker, David. 2006. "Egoisms." In *Conduct and Character: Readings in Moral Theory*, 5th edn, ed. M. Timmons. Belmont, Calif.: Wadsworth.

Shrage, Laurie. 1989. "Should Feminists Oppose Prostitution?," *Ethics* 99: 347–361.

Shrage, Laurie. 1994. *Moral Dilemmas of Feminism: Prostitution, Adultery, and Abortion*. New York: Routledge.

Sibley, Frank. 2004a. "Aesthetic Concepts." In *Aesthetics and the Philosophy of Art: The Analytic Tradition*, eds. P. Lamarque and S. H. Olsen. Malden, Mass.: Blackwell.

Sibley, Frank. 2004b. "Particularity, Art, and Evaluation." In *Aesthetics and the Philosophy of Art: The Analytic Tradition*, eds. P. Lamarque and S. H. Olsen. Malden, Mass.: Blackwell.

Sihvola, Juha. 2002. "Aristotle on Sex and Love." In *The Sleep of Reason: Erotic Experience and Sexual Ethics in Ancient Greece and Rome*, eds. M. Nussbaum and J. Sihvola. Chicago, Ill.: University of Chicago Press.

Singer, Irving. 1984. *The Nature of Love, Volume 1: Plato to Luther*. 2nd edn. Chicago, Ill.: University of Chicago Press.

Singer, Irving. 2001a. *Explorations in Love and Sex*. Lanham, Md.: Rowman & Littlefield.

Singer, Irving. 2001b. *Sex: A Philosophical Primer*. Lanham, Md.: Rowman & Littlefield.

Slote, Michael. 1975. "Inapplicable Concepts and Sexual Perversion." In *Philosophy and Sex*, ed. R. Baker and F. Elliston. Buffalo, N.Y.: Prometheus Books.

Slote, Michael. 1992. *From Morality to Virtue*. New York: Oxford University Press.

Soble, Alan. 1989a. "Section IV: Contemporary Analysis." In EAP.

Soble, Alan, ed. 1989b. *Eros, Agape, and Philia: Readings in the Philosophy of Love*. New York: Paragon House.

Soble, Alan. 1990. *The Structure of Love*. New Haven, Conn.: Yale University Press.

Soble, Alan. 1991. "Defamation and the Endorsement of Defamation." In *Pornography: Private Right or Public Menace?* eds. R. M. Baird and S. E. Rosenbaum. Buffalo, N.Y.: Prometheus Books.

Soble, Alan. 1996. *Sexual Investigations*. New York: New York University Press.

Soble, Alan. 1997. "Union, Autonomy, and Concern." In *Love Analyzed*, ed. R. Lamb. Boulder, Colo.: Westview Press.

Soble, Alan, 1998. *The Philosophy of Sex and Love*. St. Paul, Minn.: Paragon House.

Soble, Alan. 2002. *Pornography, Sex, and Feminism*. Amherst, N.Y.: Prometheus Books.

Soble, Alan. 2003. "Kant and Sexual Perversion." *The Monist* 86: 55–89.

Soble, Alan. 2006a. "Activity, Sexual." In SPP1.

Soble, Alan, ed. 2006b. *Sex from Plato to Paglia: A Philosophical Encyclopedia* (2 vols). Westport, Conn.: Greenwood Press.

Soble, Alan. 2008a. "Masturbation, Again." In POS5.

Soble, Alan. 2008b. "Sexual Use." In POS5.

Solomon, Robert. 1990. *Love: Emotion, Myth, and Metaphor*. Buffalo, N.Y.: Prometheus Books.

Solomon, Robert. 1991. "The Virtue of (Erotic) Love." In PEL.

Solomon, Robert. 2002. "Sexual Paradigms." In POS4.

Solomon, Robert. 2006. *About Love: Reinventing Romance for Our Times*. Indianapolis, Ind.: Hackett.

Steinbock, Bonnie. 1991. "Adultery." In POS2.

Stendhal (Marie Henri Beyle). 1975. *Love*, trans. G. and S. Sale. London: Penguin.

Stewart, Robert M. 2006. "Sex Work." In SPP2.

Strossen, Nadine. 1995. *Defending Pornography: Free Speech, Sex, and the Fight for Women's Rights*. New York: Scribner's.

Sullivan, Andrew. 1995. *Virtually Normal: An Argument about Homosexuality*. New York: Vintage Books.

Sullivan, Andrew. 1997. "Three's a Crowd." In SSM.

Swanton, Christine. 2003. *Virtue Ethics: A Pluralistic View*. Oxford: Oxford University Press.

Taylor, Gabriele. 1979. "Love." In *Philosophy As It Is*, eds. T. Honderich and M. Burnyeat. London: Penguin Books.

Taylor, Richard. 1982. *Having Love Affairs*. Buffalo, N.Y.: Prometheus Books.

Thomas Aquinas. 1956. *Summa contra Gentiles*. New York; Doubleday.

Thomas Aquinas. 1964–1976. *Summa Theologiae*, 60 vols. Cambridge: Blackfriars.

Thomas, Laurence, and Michael Levin. 1999. *Sexual Orientation and Human Rights*. Lanham, Md.: Rowman & Littlefield.

Thomson, Judith Jarvis. 1990. *The Realm of Rights*. Cambridge, Mass.: Harvard University Press.

Vanderheiden, Steve. 1999. "Why the State Should Stay Out of the Wedding Chapel." *Public Affairs Quarterly* 13: 175–190.

van Inwagen, Peter. 1993. *Metaphysics*. Boulder, Colo.: Westview Press.

Vannoy, Russell. 1980. *Sex without Love: A Philosophical Exploration*. Buffalo, N.Y.: Prometheus Books.

Vannoy, Russell. 1997. "Can Sex Express Love?" In *Sex, Love, and Friendship: Studies for the Society of Sex and Love, 1977–1992*, ed. A. Soble. Amsterdam: Rodopi.

Vernon, Mark. 2005. *The Philosophy of Friendship*. Basingstoke, UK: Palgrave Macmillan.

Vlastos, Gregory, ed. 1978. *Plato I: Metaphysics and Epistemology*. Notre Dame, Ind.: University of Notre Dame Press.

Vlastos, Gregory. 1989. "The Individual as the Object of Love in Plato." In EAP.

Wardle, Lynn, Mark Strasser, William Duncan, and David Orgon Coolidge, eds. 2003. *Marriage and Same-Sex Unions: A Debate*. Westport, Conn.: Praeger.

Warner, Michael. 1999. *The Trouble with Normal: Sex, Politics, and the Ethics of Queer Life*. New York: Free Press.

Wasserstrom, Richard. 1998. "Is Adultery Immoral?" In PS3.

Wedgwood, Ralph. 1999. "The Fundamental Argument for Same-Sex Marriage." *The Journal of Political Philosophy* 7: 225–242.

Weinberg, Thomas. 1995. *S&M: Studies in Dominance and Submission*. Amherst, N.Y.: Prometheus Books.

Wertheimer, Alan. 1996. *Exploitation*. Princeton, N.J.: Princeton University Press.

Wertheimer, Alan. 2003. *Consent to Sexual Relations*. Cambridge: Cambridge University Press.

West, Robin. 2008. "The Harms of Consensual Sex." In POS5.

White, Richard. 2001. *Love's Philosophy*. Lanham, Md.: Rowman & Littlefield.

Williams, Clifford, ed. 1995. *On Love and Friendship: Philosophical Readings*. Boston, Mass., and London: Jones and Bartlett.

Wojtyla, Karol (Pope John Paul II). 1981. *Love and Responsibility*. New York: Farrar, Straus, and Giroux.

Wolf, Susan. 1982. "Moral Saints." *Journal of Philosophy* 79: 419–439.

Wood, Allen. 2008. *Kantian Ethics*. New York: Cambridge University Press.

Wreen, Michael. 1991. "What's Really Wrong with Adultery." In POS2.

Young, Charles. 1988. "Aristotle on Temperance." *The Philosophical Review* 97: 521–542.

Zagzebski, Linda Trinkaus. 1996. *Virtues of the Mind*. New York: Cambridge University Press.

Zillman, Dolf, and Jennings Bryant, eds. 1989. *Pornography: Research Advances and Policy Considerations*. Hillsdale, N.J.: Erlbaum.

Index

Other titles from Routledge

On Criticism
Noël Carroll

"This book is badly needed, as much by critics as those who read them, as much by teachers of criticism as those who would like to write criticism."

– Arthur C. Danto

"This little book runs directly counter to the modern orthodoxy that proper art criticism is all about interpretation and contextualizing. With admirable clarity and disarming candor, it defends the unfashionable view that the heart of art criticism is giving reasoned evaluations of artistic achievement. Everything else passing under this label – from gender theory to Derridean deconstruction – is secondary. What makes the book specially persuasive is Noël Carroll's unrivalled expertise in all things aesthetic."

– Gordon Graham, Princeton University

In a recent poll of practicing art critics, 75 percent reported that rendering judgments on artworks was the least significant aspect of their job. This is a troubling statistic for philosopher and critic Noël Carroll, who argues that the proper task of the critic is not simply to describe, or to uncover hidden meanings or agendas, but ultimately to determine what is of value in art.

Carroll argues for a humanistic conception of criticism which focuses on what the artist has achieved by creating or performing the work. Whilst a good critic should not neglect to contextualize and offer interpretations of a work of art, he argues that too much recent criticism has ignored the fundamental role of the artist's intentions.

Including examples from visual, performance and literary arts, and the work of contemporary critics, Carroll provides a charming, erudite and persuasive argument that appraisal and evaluation of art are an indispensable part of the conversation of life.

Noël Carroll is the Andrew W. Mellon Professor of the Humanities at Temple University, USA.

Hbk ISBN 13: 978-0-415-39620-2
Pbk ISBN 13: 978-0-415-39621-9

Available at all good bookstores
For ordering and further information please visit:
www.routledge.com

Other titles from Routledge

On Architecture
Fred Rush

Architecture is a philosophical puzzle. Although we spend most of our time in buildings, we rarely reflect on what they mean or how we experience them. With some notable exceptions, they have generally struggled to be taken seriously as works of art compared to painting or music and have been rather overlooked by philosophers.

In *On Architecture*, Fred Rush argues this is a consequence of neglecting the role of the body in architecture. Our encounter with a building is first and foremost a bodily one; buildings are lived-in, communal spaces and their construction reveals a lot about our relation to the environment as a whole.

Drawing on examples from architects classic and contemporary such as Le Corbusier and Frank Lloyd Wright, and exploring the significance of buildings in relation to film and music and philosophers such as Heidegger and Merleau-Ponty, Fred Rush argues that philosophical reflection on building can tell us something important about the human condition.

Contents: 1. Bodies and Architectural Space
2. Architecture and Other Arts
3. Buildings, Buildings, and More Buildings

Fred Rush is Associate Professor of Philosophy at the University of Notre Dame, Indiana, USA. He is the editor of the *Cambridge Companion to Critical Theory*.

Hbk ISBN 13: 978-0-415-39618-9
Pbk ISBN 13: 978-0-415-39619-6

Available at all good bookstores
For ordering and further information please visit:
www.routledge.com